MW00575733

## PRAISE FOR
## *WHAT IS ORTHODOXY?*

"Antoine Arjakovsky is interdisciplinary and authentically ecumenical in his intellectual method. His theological, geographic, and diachronic breadth is matched by largeness of heart and deep reflection guided by lived experience and eschatological hope. Though intricate conceptually, this book is not dry academic theology, for the author is penetrating and passionate in his writing as well as in his personal witness."

—BISHOP BORYS GUDZIAK, Ukrainian Greek Catholic Church

"If you are looking for another introduction to the Orthodox Church, this is not it. Rather, Antoine Arjakovsky has written a sweeping scholarly account of how the very concept of 'orthodoxy' has been approached historically, philosophically, and theologically over the last two millennia. He shows convincingly that the concept of truth as conformity to reality has 'traveled side by side' with the Christian vision of truth as 'participation in the life of a divine-human person.' In this rich exploration beyond the closed spheres of confessionalism, heterodoxy versus orthodoxy, and our 'epistemic ghettos,' Arjakovsky sees the possibility of 'a common shared consciousness' that could open 'a new ecumenical history of the Church and a new history of philosophy.' This kind of rethinking is always risky. But in our polarized world of ecclesial and political stalemates, isn't that a risk worth considering?"

—FR. JOHN A. JILLIONS, Chancellor, Orthodox Church in America

"In this remarkable book, Antoine Arjakovsky shows why a theological Church History is crucial for theological understanding. Orthodoxy is not such, if it is only about right belief. It is, rather, about the participation of human existence and history in the divine and angelic wisdom which is itself a metahistorical drama, at once personal and substantive. Orthodoxy is a 'true understanding' which strives partially to assess and to live out this reality."

—CATHERINE PICKSTOCK, University of Cambridge

"Antoine Arjakovsky's historical scholarship opens onto an astonishing array of sources, ancient and modern, offering us a vitally important exploration of Orthodoxy that is both theologically faithful and historiographically self-critical. Here is wisdom for a brighter Christian future: Let us be attentive!"

—A.A.J. DEVILLE, University of Saint Francis

"This volume is no mere historical overview of Orthodox Christianity, but an extraordinary multidimensional exploration of what Orthodoxy has tried to confess and enact of Christ's Gospel. The author draws us into this witness of the past and what it offers to the world today from the inside out — something no other scholar has done! An exciting, provocative, and most important contribution to theology and church history."

— THE V. REV. MICHAEL PLEKON, Professor Emeritus, City University of New York

"Antoine Arjakovsky offers a provocation to orthodoxy that is rooted in genuine *metanoia*, and thus irreducible to the triumphalism of ecclesial bureaucracy and confessional boundaries. An important and highly-recommended work."

— AARON RICHES, Seminario Mayor San Cecilio, Granada, Spain

What is Orthodoxy?

# WHAT IS
# Orthodoxy?

## A GENEALOGY OF CHRISTIAN UNDERSTANDING

BY ANTOINE ARJAKOVSKY

*Translated by* Jerry Ryan and Penelope Cavill

*Foreword by* John Milbank

Angelico Press

Originally published in France as
*Qu'est-ce que l'orthodoxie?*


First published in the USA
by Angelico Press 2018


For information, address:
Angelico Press, Ltd.
169 Monitor St.
Brooklyn, NY 11222
www.angelicopress.com

pb 978-1-62138-420-5
cloth 978-1-62138-421-2
ebook 978-1-62138-422-9

Book and cover design
by Michael Schrauzer

# CONTENTS

# FOREWORD

*John Milbank*

ALTHOUGH "ORTHODOXY" HAS COME TO BE THE defining term of the Eastern branch of the Christian Church, it is also taken to be a crucial mark of all the other branches which adhere to Biblical and Patristic tradition. So in the following book Antoine Arjakovsky rightly but uniquely treats the question of the identity of "the Orthodox Churches" and of Christian orthodoxy in general as inseparable. He also extends his inquiry to include the metaphorically extended sense of any "orthodox" belief.

Detached, scientific inquiries into the constitution of the latter tend, via a usurpation of the originally literal sense of the word, to treat Christian orthodoxy as but one instance of a wider sociological *genus*. This concerns the prevailing and most fundamental beliefs of any culture or period. Such beliefs are then often seen by detached, objectivizing historians as brought about by various social mechanisms of domination and successful manipulations of public rhetoric. However, Arjakovsky suggests that, ironically, the initial secular understanding of orthodoxy as "correct belief" borrows this restriction from a Christian theology that has too narrow an understanding of what "orthodoxy" has historically meant within Christian tradition. The social and practical dimension of the constitution of orthodoxy is wrongly seen as extrinsic to its innermost character in such a way that this dimension can then be appealed to in order questionably to "explain" widespread orthodox adherence.

Despite this critique of critical approaches themselves, Arjakovsky is nonetheless receptive to them insofar as they do place emphasis upon the changing cultural and intellectual settings for the formation of Christian orthodoxy. For if the latter is a more dynamic matter of seeking to find the "right direction" through life in all its aspects and in a deepening participation in God, then to be orthodox is itself to enter into a historical process, and the "historicizing" of what it has meant to be an orthodox Christian is not, after all, alien to the inner consistency of this notion. Once this has been understood, it becomes possible to tell a complex story in which it is not so much that "right belief" was imposed by independently constituted social forces, as that the notion of "right belief" itself as for a time defining of "orthodoxy" only emerged in a particular set of historical circumstances which were shaped from within the Christian community as much as by external factors to which it had to respond.

This emergence in the post-Constantinian era was, in Arjakovsky's view, a partial development, rather than one wholly to be celebrated or wholly to be deplored. Just because "orthodoxy" is a matter of integral participation in the true life of God, different eras are likely to exhibit different facets of orthodoxy and to neglect others. From this perspective one could even say no historical orthodoxy altogether escapes the "heretical," if by that we mean the partial—just as, inversely, heresies often contain excessively strong emphases, as in the case of Gnosticism, whose positive import an adequate orthodoxy must nonetheless strive to include. Orthodoxy remains a horizon, and just for this reason a space of the "heterodox" between orthodoxy and heresy has always been recognized. It might even seem that, within time, none of us can entirely escape what is "otherwise" to a true direction and adequate sharing in the divine.

Arjakovsky therefore concludes that it is harder to react angrily towards Christian orthodoxy from without than the critical perspective might conclude and for metacritical reasons. Of itself, orthodoxy already aims to be a right liturgical and social practice, a true historical memory, and a mode of just knowing that attends to right participation and economic distribution of resources (in every sense) in a particular time and place. It is, from the outset, constitutively self-critical in a way that can welcome and not dismiss an external scientific critique, in the sure knowledge that its own sense of the critical pressure of the divine will outrun any such critique—though it may well be, in part, mediated by it. Additionally, any detached historical approach, while it can partially account, synchronically, for the dominance of a reigning orthodoxy in any given slice of time, ultimately faces the problem of the continuity of a tradition—for example, Christian tradition—over a long temporal tract, despite the ruptures and the discontinuities. Is the sense of "one thing"—in this case, Christianity—remaining the same through a long process of non-identical repetition a simple internal illusion? But in that case the question of the constitution of the identity of the cultural phenomenon is as much a problem for science as for inward belief, since this belief only exists *from the outset* as a certain unprescribable sense of valid continuity, of what belongs and what does not, of a true development and a false. To deny altogether this specifically analogical consistency would invite a degree of skepticism so problematically dissolving of its very object of study that, in reality, few even objective students of "orthodoxy" would ever care to venture there. For this reason, Arjakovsky boldly and rightly claims that the inner Christian sense of what is validly orthodox has of itself a critical and historical purchase.

In order to develop this sense, he distinguishes between an original and pre-Constantinian sense of literal "right glory"—right prayer, right praise, right offering, including the offering of ethical practice—and a later post-Constantinian epoch of "right belief" that he plausibly sees as correlated with an era of problematic blending between ecclesial and political order. This is exceeded in turn by an early modern epoch of "right memory," in which the rise of the nation state on pessimistic foundations as to its understanding of human nature, together with the rise of a more limited and positivist conception of valid knowledge, is both challenged and mirrored by an ecclesial authentication of orthodoxy in terms of strict allegiance to historical foundation and precedent whether Biblical or apostolic or traditional. Finally, an era of "just understanding" equally suspicious of the bounds of nationalism, verifiable science and exclusive confessional claims.

But in a complex fashion, these four accounts of orthodoxy are for Arjakovsky all permanently necessary facets of Christian sensibility, besides being successive biases and excessive concentrations. "Right glory" remains for him in one sense the most normative and the most fundamental: the creedal bounds of true belief were at first referred to this doxological context and not to a political one. Yet the problems of politics that inevitably emerged once Christianity became hegemonic are not seen by Arjakovsky as merely alien to the substance of orthodoxy, nor the modern issues related to "true memory" which in part witness to a heightened historical sense. Just for this reason it would seem that, for him, it is "just understanding" that is yet more comprehensive than "right glory," since it possesses both a more reflexive and critical sense of historical emergence and a stronger sense of the need to reflect adequately the divine order in specific circumstances of the here and now, including its social and political—and today, ecological—dimensions.

The limitation that Arjakovsky sees even in Patristic "right glory"—for all that it remains fundamental and potentially all-embracing—is specifically linked by him to what he regards as the finally inadequate Patristic treatment of the Biblical theme of *Sophia*. The personal wisdom of God is, for Arjakovsky, following Sergius Bulgakov, at one with the divine essence that is common to all three Trinitarian persons. Thus the sophianic is imparted to the Creation, not just in terms of the *Logos* and Christ, or of the Spirit and the Church, but in terms of its immanent and self-creative sharing in the whole dynamic exchange of the Trinitarian life, which surfaces most to view in human existence. Here it should be said that the way in which Arjakovsky, adverting to the work of Jean-Luc Marion, manages to link Augustine's understanding of the image of the Trinity in Man to this wider sophiological context is ecumenically admirable.

It is this participation in the Trinitarian exchange of glory and of gift which Arjakovsky sees as restored by the double descent of the *Logos* and the Spirit in the Incarnation and the ecclesial Bride of Christ. History is here for him fundamental, not just because of this reinauguration, but because it reveals apocalyptically a "metahistory," a process of cosmic rupture and renewal that is a supratemporal event affecting the angelic realm as well as the eternal human essence as created in Adam. This process is also mysteriously an eternal event, since it concerns the loss and recovery of the divine glory, an event which somehow (even though God is immune to all events) belongs to God, since He does not exist apart from His glory. It is just this "gnostic thematic" which Arjakovsky deliberately associates with orthodoxy as "just understanding," along with the need to recover "the symbolic realism of letters and ciphers," or a stronger sense that the whole temporal world is an allegory of this eternal drama.

On this enriched understanding of orthodoxy, therefore, the circumstances of historical arrival are in no conceivable sense secondary to propositional content or even "true prayer," which should not be conceived as removed to an impregnable citadel, away from all contingency and conflict. To the contrary, it is orthodoxy's very concrete specificity which most of all apocalyptically discloses eternal events which even involve (and with a hypertrophy of paradox that need not lead us into Hegelian error) a self-constitution of the Godhead itself. In the act of creation, the divine essence, the personating power of Sophia, is handed over to the risk of the finite spiritual response of both angels and humans—a risk whose resultant tragedy can only be resolved through divine descent into the material order, where there exists greater possibility of change and the redemptive rereading of signs than among the stabler, purely spiritual entities. Yet even the final redemption of the created order and the rescuing of the divine glory in Christ can only be achieved as a synergic work—as a theo-anthropomorphic labor of collaboration in which the created will is healed because it is now able, through fusion with the divine, to heal itself—no extrinsic healing being, tragically, in any way possible.

For this reason, in Arjakovsky's thought the sophiological perspective, as a more adequate reading of the Bible, implies a much stronger sense of the part played by creative human cultural action than has ever been attained within the Patristic vision. The right giving of glory now much more involves a right reading of natural and historical signs, just as its theurgic action now much more also includes a just repair of the social realm. Given this perspective, Arjakovsky remains somewhat ambivalent about the modern international order of nation-states and human rights. He rightly allows that it has been to a significant degree infused since World War II (after Maritain and Berdyaev, etc.) by a personalism lying close to his sense of the sophianic; but he also considers that, in its otherwise correct rejection of the theocratic (associated by Arjakovsky with "right order") it has too much inverted this as the sheerly anthropomorphic, often linked with a gloomy and limited view of human capacity. By contrast, a theo-anthropomorphic order remains yet to come, and is necessarily linked to that God-Manhood which is in turn inseparable from the descent of human active participation in the sophianic life of the Trinity. Beyond the humanistic community of liberty and happiness which ignores truth, and therefore all grounds for just mediation, lies the real community of *sobornost* which proclaims the real human relating as a reflection of the divine glory, just as, inversely, *pravda* does not separate truth from its participation in just human association. At this point Arjakovsky's invocations of the most ancient Czars' concern with *pravda* would suggest that there are still things to be learned from the Constantinian epoch, for all the admitted dangers of the sacralization of the state and the inverse (and more Latin) danger of the secularization of the Church. For today, indeed, Christians are confronted with the rapid breakdown of a supposedly neutral anthropomorphic political order which they may once have been overtempted to see as a work of providence, as witnessed by its increasing religious intolerance and the abandonment of Christian attitudes towards life, nature, death, sex, gender, money, justice and the purposes of social existence.

It is clear then that Arjakovsky thinks that only a historicization of the question of Christian orthodoxy can do it any intrinsic justice. But one could say that he also inverts this emphasis to give us not just a sophiological history of orthodoxy, but also an orthodox and so (in accordance with the primacy of "just understanding") a sophiological account of history.

For one of the most remarkable things achieved by this diffuse and endlessly informative and rewarding volume is a new insistence upon the theological character of Church history. On the one hand, as we have seen, Arjakovsky renders this subdiscipline a *necessary* part of any systematic theology (for how, otherwise, can we consider "orthodoxy" in its four unfolding facets, linked to the event of the Church as intrinsic to revelation); on the other hand he also thinks that it must ultimately be conducted in a theological and not merely "detached" fashion if it is to meet the demands of a comprehensive science. We have already seen this argument with respect to the problem of defining orthodoxy as a consistent development. Therefore the most exemplary Church historian remains for Arjakovsky St. Luke, precisely because he rethinks the entire genre of historiography by recording the events of Christ's life (and supremely the institution of the Eucharist) in such a way that this recording becomes in itself a mode of historical action. In this way, not a sub- but a supra-critical insight is gained, since in the end there can be no specific historical action that is not comprised of both memory and historical recording, while equally there can be no historical recording that does not involve interpretation and an implicit demand for a revised attitude and mode of action in the future. Luke's Gospel and his account of apostolic actions seize cognizance of this circumstance in the face of events that uniquely require repeating and are inseparable from this repeating.

Thus, for Arjakovsky the four historical idioms of orthodoxy are exactly matched by four ways of writing history in general. There is, crucially, the evangelical mode which records not just events but inner spiritual attitudes, which can scarcely be mentioned without interpretation and assessment, else they would remain (in seeming contrast to objective facts) "unplaced." There is the register of correct and false beliefs, closely allied to the imposition of political order. There is the empirical archive of the past which can serve to ensure continuity. And finally, there is the linking of internal, evangelical history to human actions and external events in an attempt to unite the subjective and the objective. This attempt at a more total historical interpretation, linked to the pragmatic goal of a more just understanding and performance, is what Arjakovsky himself in this book most successfully and admirably undertakes.

In doing so he explains to the reader how Christianity has not offered to the world a fixed dogmatism as to the certain truth. This has rather been the boast of philosophy, and the riposte has often been various degrees of skepticism as to the existence of truth at all. But instead of "mere opinion" either philosophically despised or arbitrarily asserted, Christianity has suggested the radical modesty of a "right opinion" that, without being able to seize hold of the infinite truth, still claims to lie upon the many-stranded track towards it. This track is simply the way of mysterious revealed coincidence between God who is the goal and humanity who is the quester. What they now, after the Incarnation, are revealed as holding in common is the life of *sobornost*, or of sophianic exchange between persons in the definite but personalizing power of things, or "essence." Philosophy, according to both Bulgakov and Arjakovsky, in its claim to absolute truth, can tragically only exhibit Trinitarian heresy or "partiality." In consequence, modern philosophy either derives all from a solipsistic and finite mind, or else abases this mind before an impersonal and objective essence. It fails to arrive at the truth which could only arrive (at one time and in one place) towards us: namely that the encounter with the objective other is also an encounter with a personal other with which we must paradoxically be at one if we are to be ourselves. This is the absolute truth of God in which we can but partially share. Arjakovsky persuades us that history is the tragic and salvific record of this attempted sharing, and that human orthodoxy is the lived opinion that this is indeed the case, now and into whatever future can possibly remain a human one.

# ACKNOWLEDGEMENTS

I WARMLY THANK ALL THOSE WHO ENCOURAGED me to undertake and then redact this study.

First of all, I want to thank the French language publication initiator Eric Vigne of Gallimard, who stimulated my research by proposing that I write this text and inspired me to reflect on a synthesis of contemporary *doxa* and traditional Christian thought. I am deeply grateful for the confidence, exaggerated in great part, which he showed in me.

My work would not have been possible without the friendship and support of Professor Peter de Mey and his colleagues at the Catholic University of Leuven who granted me a research scholarship for 2010–2011. I had the pleasure of working in the library of the Faculty of Theology of the Catholic University of Leuven, and writing in the Beguine convent of that beautiful city, close to the statue of Erasmus.

I also thank Bishop Borys Gudziak, the rector of the Catholic University of Ukraine, and my friends at the Institute for Ecumenical Studies of Lviv who accepted my leave for this sabbatical year. Equally, I am grateful to Father Antoine Guggenheim, director of the Research Center of the College of the Bernardins, my new home base since the beginning of the 2011 academic year, for his seminar on "Theology and History" which enlightened the research that has been my passion for so many years.

I wish to thank Alexander Eltchaninoff and Didier Rance who, as far back as 2003, had faith in my project of a history of orthodox thought. I have a debt of gratitude towards my students, especially Father Laurent Cleenewerck and Ron Harrison who followed my course on the history of Christianity by correspondence as part of the Master's program in ecumenical studies at the Ecumenical Institute of Lviv. They stimulated my research through the quality and openness of their own works. Among my colleagues, I would like to especially thank Lea Oksman who helped me with the English translation of my course.

Obviously, throughout this research I thought affectionately of all my former teachers and colleagues whom I had the joy of knowing personally. I would like to mention in particular Olivier Clément, Jean Delumeau, Georges Nivat, Pierre Nora, René Rémond, François Furet, Nicole Lemaître, Gerard Cholvy, Yves-Marie Hilaire, Msgr. Yves Marchasson, Christian Buchet and René Pillorget. All gave me a taste for history through their teaching, research, consideration and sometimes friendship.

A heartfelt thanks to those who, like Guy Bédouelle and Philippe de Manet, agreed to review my text and to pass on their suggestions.

I would also like to express my gratitude to Jerry Ryan for his English translation of my text. The text was reviewed and revised with great skill by Penny and Jenny Cavill. This was the opportunity for me to experience, with a renewed intensity, the link between friendship and the quest for truth. It is what the Russians mean by *sobornost'*, a word translated approximately by "catholicity." As Barbara Cassin remarked, there are many words which cannot be translated. But if we situate ourselves in the metarational level of knowledge-friendship, we can rediscover access to the universals.

Angelico Press, for its part, agreed to publish my book in the United States. It is a great honor for me and my gratitude to John Riess is profound, especially since I know that this kind of historical, theological and philosophical text receives fewer and fewer readers. John Milbank agreed to take this work seriously and to write the foreword. His fine understanding of my purpose encourages me. His thought is for me one of the main reasons for hope in the coming century.

Finally, I tenderly thank my wife, Laura, and my children Mathilde and Etienne, without whose love not a line of this research would ever have been written.

# PREFACE

IN THE YEAR 2000, THE ECOLE FRANÇAISE OF ROME published a collection which tried to explain orthodoxy in a "scientific" way.[1] Researchers from the Villa Medici, from the University of California (Berkeley) and from the Ecole des Hautes Etudes en Sciences Sociales of Paris had been working resolutely and in a non-confessional manner on this concept of orthodoxy since 1995. By extracting orthodoxy from the exclusive domain of theology to which it was normally confined, these intellectuals tried to shed light upon the processes by which the truth and identity of a group are constantly being reformulated. Rather than define orthodoxy, they chose to observe how it is defined, maintained and questioned over time and throughout different regions. In so doing, they were in the line of the analyses of the mechanisms of the social construction of "normalization"[2] presented by Michel Foucault in his book *Discipline and Punish*. In this manner, the concept of orthodoxy emerged from the epistemic ghetto to which it had been confined for so long a time.

The rapport between truth and orthodoxy cannot be circumscribed simply by the understanding of religious revelation. The comprehension of orthodoxy, understood in a dynamic and postmodern context, has recourse to philosophy, sociology, and history, and more generally to all the sciences. The researchers at Rome, Berkeley and Paris do not give priority to the study of the content of a truth defined by a church, but rather to the conflicting processes and the negotiations within communities in a state of permanent redefinition which permit or prohibit the adhesion and internalization of a given belief, and so in turn determine its rejection or innovation. As

1 *Orthodoxie, Christianisme, Histoire*, ed. Susanna Elm, Eric Rebillard, and Antonella Romano, Rome, Ecole Française de Rome, 2000.

2 Stéphane Legrand, *Les Normes chez Foucault*, Paris, PUF, 2007. After an analysis of the way actions act on other actions in a disciplinary network, Stéphane Legrand shows how the subjects themselves are implicated in these networks and how the heterogenic normative codes can articulate themselves with respect to one another.

Pierre-Antoine Fabre has written, orthodoxy has a particular status: "It does not define itself by itself, but appears as always defined and is, by that very fact, indefinable."

This poses several questions: how can orthodoxy be the foundation of a power when this power itself is constitutive of orthodoxy? How is the rapport of mutual legitimation between orthodoxy and tradition established? Finally, how is it that the same expression may or may not be considered correct and therefore able or not able to justify its orthodox character? In contrast with the preceding historiographical period which focused on the study of heresies, today the attention of historians is centered on the question of assent. According to Dominique Julia, "our colloquium is taking place within the context of a historiographical moment where the historian is more interested in the means by which a society succeeds in establishing devices which simultaneously regulate public professions, the circulation of opinions and practices."[3]

This new method is important for the measure in which it manifests the practical truth and the social, linguistic and institutional dimension of orthodoxy. We will give a brief presentation of some of the conclusions of these authors, first with regard to Christian antiquity. Daniel Caner explains the philosophical and social dimensions of the words *districtio* or *akribeia,* terms used by writers of the late fourth and early fifth centuries. These words refer to rigorous discipline and are used to describe correct monastic practices, i.e., orthodox practices, but they also indicate the continuity between the apostolic and monastic traditions as well as the degree of possible conformity with the social codes of a given epoch. The truth of this configuration of orthodoxy as represented by John Cassian or Gregory of Nyssa is still not yet either conceptual or detached from personal virtue. In the Gospel of Matthew (6:25–33) earthly cares are only overcome by the quest for the Kingdom of God, and this implies the risk of social poverty. Within this perspective there cannot be a precise definition of orthodoxy. Such a definition supposes a permanent effort to construct meaning on the basis of the words used in Scripture and on the interpretive examples drawn from tradition. Father Robert Dodaro points out the importance of rhetoric and, especially, of the notion of "propriety," which designates the necessary harmony between the idea and its verbal expression, according to the definition of orthodoxy in the works of St. Augustine.

3 Ibid., 392.

Susanna Elm analyzes the works of Gregory of Nazianzus. She discovers a change in his conception of orthodoxy around the year 364, when, according to one of the Fathers of Christian orthodox thought, he began to think that it was no longer enough to be a free man of noble birth to be a good pastor, as was the case with Gregory's own father, whose piety was irreproachable. Due to "our present theological maladies . . . [of] atheism, Judaism and polytheism,"[4] Gregory considers that henceforth it is necessary to insist upon orthodoxy as essentially a continual effort to imitate, intellectually and ascetically, the prototypes of the pastor as found in the Scriptures. But the intellectual effort required by Gregory also has juridical, and hence political, consequences. This is a point emphasized by Caroline Humfress, who insists that the idea of "erroneous belief" did not exist in Roman law prior to the fourth century AD, insofar as no interior conviction was required in the ritual practices of the Empire. The "superstitions" which could eventually be found among the followers of Mani were simply considered civil crimes or public disturbances. With Christianity, however, worthy glorification had to go hand in hand with correct doctrine. The doctrines themselves were to be determined by catholicity, by the degree of communion among the disciples of Christ. From the very beginning, as witnessed by the episode of Simon the Magician (Acts 8:4–25)—a Samaritan baptized by Philip but rejected by Peter because he offered money to the apostle in return for the gift of the imposition of hands—the Church repudiated innovations not recognized by the apostles. It was for this reason that Constantine viewed doctrinal heresy as a *crimen publicum*. This concept was embraced by the church of Antioch in 341. Forty years later, in 381, the Emperor Theodosius, by the Edict of Thessalonica, reserved to himself the right of deciding the correct interpretation of the Nicene Creed by relying on the communion existing among certain bishops. Thus, because of this innovative link between knowledge and ritual practice there emerged a juridical categorization of the various religious beliefs and heresies, a categorization which itself came to influence the definition of Christian doctrine. But only the collaboration between the bishop and the civil magistrate allows judgment to be passed on the accused. Such a mentality paved the way for the medieval tendency to attempt "to index juridical truth on the last judgment."[5]

4 S. Elm, "Gregory of Nazianzus' Theory of Orthodox Priesthood," in *Orthodoxie,* 95.
5 *Orthodoxie*, 356.

The European and American scholars also analyzed the medieval period. This study is presented by one of the most eminent scholars in this field, André Vauchez, director of the Ecole Française in Rome from 1995 to 2003. In his contribution entitled "Orthodoxie et hérésie dans l'Occident médiéval," looking at the 10th to 13th centuries, Vauchez finds that, on the one hand, the study of heresies is inseparable from the study of orthodoxy and, on the other, that knowledge of the context of the formation of orthodox institutions is meaningless unless it is absorbed into the context of general religious history. Vauchez makes special mention of the work of Janet Nelson, who affirms that "there was a crisis of theodicy around the year 1000 which would explain the birth — or rebirth — of heresy in the West from that time on."[6] For Vauchez, this mutation of representations is synchronic with the changes in ecclesiastical power which, by becoming progressively more vertical during the Gregorian reforms and accentuating more and more the distinction between the clerical as sacred and the laity as profane, continuously provoked protest movements right up to final rupture with the Reformation and the dawn of the Enlightenment. A new configuration of orthodoxy came to exclude the possibility of error as to what constitutes Christian identity, first on an intellectual and then on a social level. Vauchez concludes that "heresy does not exist in itself; it is, in some way, created or invented by orthodoxy."[7] The French historian suggests that the Church, in its effort to combat simony, eventually attempted to do away with the old anthropological model of the gift as part of an ensemble of exchanges among partners situated on the same level. In the same way, in its crusade against disordered sexual practices, the Church came to assimilate its clerics to monks and thus upset not only political and social relations but also "the economy of salvation."[8]

Nina Caputo shows in her study of the definition of orthodoxy within medieval Judaism how certain eminent figures, such as Nachmanides de Gerone (Moses ben Nahman [1195–1270]), succeeded — in spite of the opposition of a group of rabbis from Montpellier who wanted to exclude the writings of Maimonides from the canonical commentaries — in maintaining the biblical understanding of the possibility of unity amidst a diversity of

6 J. Nelson, "Society, Theodicy and the Origins of Heresy: Toward a Reassessment of the Medieval Evidence," in D. Baker, ed., *Schism, Heresy and Religious Protest,* Cambridge, Cambridge University Press, 1972, 61–67.

7 A. Vauchez, "Orthodoxie et hérésie dans l'Occident médieval," in *Orthodoxie,* 329.

8 A. Vauchez, *Les laïcs au Moyen Age. Pratiques et expériences religieuses,* Paris, Cerf, 1987.

traditions and doctrinal coherence on the basis of a semantic approach to Scripture. Victoria M. Morse studies the works of Opicinus de Canistris (1296–1354) in order to show the consciousness which existed in the 14th century of the limits of institutional orthodoxy and of the need to work on the imagination of the people through an individual analysis of one's own conscience. Two centuries later, Ignatius of Loyola took up this same need in his *Spiritual Exercises*, which aimed precisely at establishing the modalities of an "orthodox" imagination. Lastly, Dominique Julia, in his conclusion to the collection, insists on the significance of the emergence of the medieval universities in the 12th century—new institutions for the definition of orthodoxy—at the very moment of a realization that the Patristic rule of consensus in the definition of truth was inadequate. For the Catholic theologian and nominalist philosopher William of Ockham, not all truths are necessarily "catholic" nor necessary for salvation: "There are thus types (*genera*) of error as of truth and, within these types, degrees (*gradus*). A heresy which is opposed to a truth *fide divina credenda* is different from an error contrary to a truth *fide tantum ecclesiastica credenda*."[9]

The Modern period is introduced by Jacques Le Brun, whose contribution demonstrates the very limited attention shown to the concept of orthodoxy in theology subsequent to the Reformation. The French dictionaries of the 17th century bear witness to the evolution of this concept. The 1690 dictionary of Furetière presents *orthodoxy* as an adjective related to the noun *catholic*: "Orthodox, adj. a Catholic who believes in the truths revealed in the Scriptures. This prelate is *orthodox*, believes in the Roman Church. The word is also applied to holy doctrine. All the propositions contained in this book are *orthodox*." Orthodoxy becomes more and more synonymous with membership in the Church, so much so that eventually Pascal wrote that its doctrinal meaning had been lost.[10] For his part, Bossuet defines the "true orthodox" as someone who knows how to take a clear and wholehearted stand against quasi-heresy—that is, in contemporary terms, ideology. Personal opinion and desire for confrontation become suspicious. From such a perspective, orthodoxy becomes the consequence of a truth more than a criterion of discernment. This definition of orthodoxy has been accepted

9 Dominique Julia, "La production de l'orthodoxie," *Orthodoxie*, 397.

10 "What is catholic in the Fathers becomes heretical in M. Arnauld . . . what was heretical in the semi-Pelagians is found to be orthodox in the writings of the Jesuits": *Dictionnaire* de Richelet, Paris, 1679, in Pascal's *Provinciales*, Paris, Cognet, 1965, 9–10.

up to the present day. Jacques Le Brun sees in the absence of a definition of orthodoxy in the *Dictionnaire critique de théologie*, published in 1998 under the direction of Jean-Yves Lacoste, a sign that we are still living in an era where there is a confessional understanding of orthodoxy. Pierre-Antoine Fabre, in his article "Ignace de Loyola en procès d'orthodoxie (1525–1622)," demonstrates how, during the Counter-Reformation, the canonization process was used by the Roman Church to reinforce its own institutional orthodoxy. At a moment of crisis in the rapport between faith and reason and, hence, in the absence of complete certainty concerning the holy election of the person in question, the authority of judgment takes precedence over its evidence. In Fabre's opinion, henceforth the historian should not define the functions of orthodoxy. To do so would reflect a confessional approach to orthodoxy. From now on it is a question of examining "the relationships or rapports which authorize the definition of orthodoxy." The three couplets of authority and power, tradition and origin, and enunciation and what is enunciated should mark out a triple difference "in relation to an institutional, dogmatic and discursive approach to orthodoxy."[11] This approach has the merit of drawing attention to the limits of orthodoxy within each confession.[12] This question of the canonization of saints as a source of self-legitimation for the glorifying authority is also treated by Laurence Moulinier in his essay entitled "Réflexions sur l'orthodoxie des écrits de Hildegarde de Bingen."

For the academic historian Bruno Neveu (1936–2004), the modern epoch has radicalized the distance separating fluctuating dogma from unchangeable dogma. However, if orthodoxy were once again understood as a concept both metatheological and metahistorical, it could be rediscovered in its role as the thread that joins the pearls on a necklace, "invisible but indispensable."[13] According to Neveu, orthodoxy is not only "the operation through which a community of believers gives itself a form and establishes links of membership." It is also "an act of definition which confers a dogmatic authenticity." Orthodoxy appears as a "normative operation of experimental character which proceeds by successive approximations and includes a

11 P. A. Fabre, "Ignace de Loyola en procès d'orthodoxie," *Orthodoxie*, 120.

12 It enables us to relate to what has elsewhere been defined as the different levels of the consciousness of orthodoxy: the zealot, the proselyte or missionary and the spiritual type. A. Arjakovsky, "Les Eglises orthodoxes et l'œcuménisme," in *En attendant le concile de l'Eglise Orthodoxe,* Paris, Cerf, 2011.

13 *Orthodoxie*, 379.

certain number of collective processes which are simultaneously genetic and dialectic."[14] Neveu recognizes that the Church has historically affirmed itself as an epistemic and a deontic authority, but he recommends distinguishing the exercise of these two powers.[15] The recent evolution of the magisterium leads us to think that "ipso facto, it is in the process of making known the nature and extent of the required assent." It is only such an introspective reflection of the magisterium that will enable it to reintegrate heterodoxy (not to be identified with heresy) into the domain of ecclesial truth and thus emerge from an epistemic, rationalist and institutional vision of the truth. He concludes by defining what is perhaps his own personal and institutional position: "The heterodox does not occupy an assignable position; he evolves outside of orthodoxy and incarnates an alterity which exposes him to suspicion and inclines him to disagree with what the ecclesial institution defines as *doxa*." For Neveu, orthodoxy "assures a dogmatism which is indissociable from ecclesial identity." He thus concurs with the theologian who identifies tradition with the workings of the Holy Spirit: "It is invisible because it is omnipresent." In this sense, Neveu sees orthodoxy as "consciousness and therapy."[16]

## THE LIMITS OF THE POSTMODERN UNDERSTANDING OF ORTHODOXY

These "scientific" approaches to the concept of orthodoxy have their limits. Insofar as they refuse to define orthodoxy historically (and consequently conceptually) they in fact render impossible any synthetic understanding of the rapport between truth and orthodoxy. Even if one recognizes (as does Eric Rebillard) that the historical formation of orthodoxy is a relationship of permanent reinterpretation of the Scriptures—"of the production of norms on the basis of values"—there is, nonetheless, the fact that for the majority of Christian theologians, orthodoxy implies a doctrinal unity which is an integral part of its very concept. According to the Patristic adage, the rule of faith is to believe what has always been believed, everywhere and by all. This adage, which has now become incomprehensible, essentially signifies that all the epochs of the Church are in conformity with the Gospel

14 Bruno Neveu, "Orthodoxie et innovation," *Orthodoxie*, 382.
15 Sacramental authority should be added to doctrinal and royal authority.
16 Ibid., 386–87.

revelation. It is for this reason that Claire Sotinel prefers to say that "implicit consensus is the foundation of orthodoxy."[17]

Moreover, by limiting themselves to an essentially semantic and sociological approach to orthodoxy, the researchers assembled by the Ecole Française de Rome deprive themselves of a historical and dynamic understanding of the totality of Western civilization. It is only fair to point out that during the 1996 colloquium at Rome, Alain Le Boulluec moderated his former enthusiasm for Walter Bauer (a matter to which we will return in our final section) in the latter's refusal to recognize the reality of a doctrinal orthodoxy during the first three centuries of the Church. Le Boulluec acknowledges that the *lex credendi* is inseparable from the *lex orandi* which is itself the source and boundary of the orthodoxy of primitive Christianity. Nonetheless, he seeks (at least in an interrogatory form) to "disregard the content of orthodoxy and to focus on its basic efficiency... and the history of its formation." William North claims that during the epoch of the bishops Bruno de Segni (1078–1123) and Yves de Chartres (1040–1116), institutional orthodoxy was continually remodeled because of the need to respond to the tensions between the permanence of the institution and its orthodoxy, on the one hand, and the constant changing of its representatives, each with their own private orthodoxy, on the other. De Chartres manages to resolve the problem of investitures through a fundamental juridical intuition.[18] Lay investiture became a sin of the hands and not of the spirit, but this distinction between the truths of the faith and the laws of the Church only became paradigmatic in modern times. It is therefore incorrect to draw general conclusions on the makeup of orthodoxy for an epoch when the laws of the State were designed to correspond to the laws of the Church. A similar observation can be made regarding the contribution of Claire Sotinel. She rightly points out that the Roman Pontiff was not the exclusive guarantor of orthodoxy when the Three Chapters were condemned by Justinian in

17 Ibid., 353.

18 In 1097, Yves de Chartres, who was consulted on the occasion of a controversy in 1097 involving Daimbert de Sens and Hugh de Die concerning the investiture of the primate by the sovereign, became the first to make a subtle distinction between the spiritual and temporal aspects of the investiture. He maintained that investiture, in the strict sense, only concerned the temporal assets of the bishopric, that it was not a sacrament and should be distinguished from "the sacrament of ordination through which the prelate receives his spiritual responsibilities." According to such a perspective, the investiture, since it only concerns the temporal, can be bestowed by a lay person—in this case, the king.

545. But does this not mean that, in the Christian tradition of the first millennium, the See of Rome disposed of a specific authority, distinct from its statutory position in the Church? In his conclusion to the collection, Dominique Julia recognizes the limits of the method used: "I am not sure that the consideration of the term 'orthodoxy' as something durable over a long period of time does not have its dangers. Are we really speaking of the same thing when we are in the fifth century and the 16th century?"[19]

Moreover, the method proposed for this collection, favoring a microhistoric and discontinuous focus in order to avoid a "linear history of orthodoxy,"[20] does not manage to convey the importance of events in dogmatic discourse. The study made by Helen Stillett of Theodoret of Cyr's analytical and non-chronological work on heresies, *Haereticarum fabularum compendium* (451), opens the perspective of rediscovering, by means of a more accurate classification of the different groups of believers, the mutually impregnating relationship between orthodox Christians and heretics. But only a historical and contextual approach can grasp the reasons and meaning behind a given delimitation of the boundaries of truth.

The "scientific analysis which rejects any confessional commitment," as vaunted by S. Elm, P. A. Fabre, E. Rebillard, A. Romano and C. Sotinel, is itself based on numerous a priori assumptions. Several authors, such as Jacques Lebrun, Alain Le Boulluec and Cécile Caby, make reference to Pierre Legendre and his 1974 book *L'amour du censeur, essai sur l'ordre dogmatique* in order to justify their juridical interpretation of the dogmatic record.[21] It is well known that Legendre's principal method consisted in "observing how submission is propagated and becomes desire of submission when the great task of Power consists in making itself loved."[22] One of the contributors to the collection, Cécile Caby, in an article on the Council of Florence, remarks that within every society there is an exigency of orthodoxy which contributes to its construction through a twofold phenomenon of appropriation and conformation. Thus, for example, the humanist Ambrogio

19 *Orthodoxie*, 394.

20 Ibid., xx.

21 A. Le Boulluec points out that under *dogmatic* Pierre Legendre includes "the opinions, theories, beliefs and practical decisions resulting from an ensemble of rules," in keeping with his understanding of the orthodoxy-orthopraxis rapport (*Orthodoxie*, 363). André Vauchez, however, believes that this representation is primarily medieval (*Orthodoxie*, 364).

22 P. Legendre, *L'amour du censeur. Essai sur l'ordre dogmatique*, Paris, Seuil, 1974, 5.

Traversari, who entered the Camaldolese order in 1400 and was a great philologist as well as a decisive presence at the Council of Florence, certainly defended Christian truth in his writings and used his religious status as a sort of self-censorship to avoid making translations of pagan philosophers. Nonetheless, in spite of his desire to devote himself to Christian philosophy, he agreed to translate works of pagan philosophy in obedience to an order of the bishop of Genoa.[23] Such an approach prioritizes the comings and goings between the ethical conscience and social conscience of people in search of the "*serenum veritatis.*" It also sheds light on the intellectual and sociological mechanisms at work in the formation of orthodoxy. Caby highlights the possibility offered by the humanist Renaissance for practical knowledge to be both "*religionis filii*" and "*sapientiae et doctrinae discipuli.*"[24] But this approach, inspired by Jacques Lacan, cannot explain the concept of orthodoxy from a historical or theological point of view.

Likewise, the use of the theses of Michel Foucault concerning the ideology of institutions as based on "the necessity of combat"[25] by J. Rebecca Lyman can shed light upon the heresiology of Epiphanius of Salamis, who became the bishop of Cyprus in 365 and is recognized as a Father of the Church. The "strategy" of Epiphanius consisted in identifying the Church with a biological body and arguing that only obedience to doctrinal authority would ensure the good health of the Church in any given degree of asceticism or of theological culture. According to Lyman, "the good health of orthodoxy required that it be constantly vigilant and justified its intervention in certain debates. This internalization of the exigencies of orthodoxy has made orthodoxy the prison of the Church—just as Foucault maintained that the control of the soul made the soul the prison of the body."[26] Even though she admits that Basil of Caesarea and John Chrysostom left room for negotiation and change in the formulation of orthodoxy, it is doubtful that such a scientific definition of orthodoxy would be able to convince Christian traditionalists of the reality of their confinement. Along the same lines, Virginia Burrus uses the concept of "apparatus" as articulated in 1977 by

23 http://www.persee.fr/web/revues/home/prescript/article/mefr_1123-9883_1996_num_108_1_3486.

24 Cécile Caby, "Entre observance et humanisme. Définition et pratiques dune orthodoxie culturelle dans l'Ordre Camaldule," *Orthodoxie, Christianisme, Histoire*, 21.

25 M. Foucault, *Surveiller et punir*, Paris, Gallimard, 1975.

26 J. Rebecca Lyman, "Ascetics and bishops. Epiphanius on Orthodoxy," *Orthodoxie*, 149.

Foucault: "an ensemble of narratives and institutions defined by a common strategic object." Burrus applies this concept to the history of Christianity in order to understand orthodoxy from a metadoctrinal perspective. This approach is stimulating but it does not rule out a narrative recital of the evolution of "orthodoxy."[27]

## THE NECESSITY OF A NEW UNDERSTANDING OF ORTHODOXY

In our view, it is possible to have a definition of the concept of orthodoxy which is both theological and scientific. Such a definition is necessarily, but not exclusively, historical; it cannot ignore the very content of Christian revelation. As our brief review of the acts of the colloquium of the Ecole Française de Rome shows, a study of orthodoxy should be complex, multidisciplinary, stressing the structural relationship between doxic and epistemic truth, between openness to transcendence and understanding of immanent realities. Many similarities can be found between the history of philosophic and scientific thought and the evolution of religious thought. Moreover, many of the mechanisms of religious orthodoxy are also found in the formation of contemporary secular orthodoxy, in the world of media and that of academic research. Just as orthodoxy is often enigmatic, ideology rarely presents itself as it is. The philosopher Nicholas Berdyaev has made a striking comparison between the Spanish Inquisition and the trials in Moscow during the 1930s. In the end, only a "second level of history" makes it possible to affirm the whole of this double exigency of using the scientific method and taking the content of revelation seriously. Pierre Nora defines this task as follows: "To create a 'second level of history,' which I think that the historian of contemporary reality must do, contributes to transforming historical criticism into a history which has become totally critical of itself and not just of its tools."[28]

By so doing, one discovers that the modern concept of truth as conformity to reality and the Christian vision of truth as participation in the life of a divine-human person travel side by side through the centuries. Interest in the sphere of the *doxa* coincides with Michel Foucault's ambition to detach the

27 V. Burrus, "Orthodoxy, Subjectivity and Institutionalization," *Orthodoxie*, 356–60.
28 Pierre Nora, *Présent, nation, mémoire*, Paris, Gallimard, 1975.

question of truth from the exclusive competence of logic or epistemology.[29] In a course at the Collège de France, Foucault sought a certain ethical impulse behind the desire to speak the truth, a personal engagement articulated in the expression "the courage of truth." By rediscovering the meaning of the *orthos*, of uprightness, of the curve of opinion towards what is beyond one's self, Foucault proposes a wisdom which is first and foremost a lifestyle. But there cannot be an absolute separation between the sphere of opinion and that of truth. This resonates with the final definition of orthodoxy proposed by Dominique Julia during the Roman colloquium: "The creation of orthodoxy can thus be envisaged as the effort or act by which each generation, in a reflexive movement which leads it to actively reinterpret its origins and traditions, alters this movement in order to make it living and actual. This reinterpretation, which explicitly denies innovation, is, at the same time, the work of enunciation by which it constantly appropriates and internalizes the history of its heritage within different *epistemes*."[30] For this definition to be workable, it must be complemented by an analysis of the contents of Christian revelation and the terms of their transmission. The study of the narratives of Church historians will enable an equilibrium between the two spheres of *doxa* and *episteme*. Historians are indeed the principal protagonists in this task of transforming memorial opinion into communitarian truth. The mission of Church historians is to anchor the ecclesial remembrance of revelation within the universal history of truth.

To begin our study of the second level of orthodoxy, of its historical evolution and its dynamic links with philosophical truth, we must first propose a presentation, both comprehensive and critical, of the institution which, in our times, most identifies itself with orthodoxy, the Orthodox Church. Specifically, we will question the legitimacy of the pretensions of the Eastern Christian Church, which has expanded throughout the world in our times, to identify itself, institutionally and doctrinally, with orthodoxy. Since the fall of the Berlin Wall the Orthodox Church has been confronted with an unprecedented identity crisis. Little by little, it is becoming aware that this crisis essentially concerns its very understanding of orthodoxy. According to John Zizioulas, Eastern Christian identity is profoundly eschatological. As long as it continues to see itself as the second Rome (for the church of

29 Aristotle defined *doxa* thus: "opinion refers to that which, be it true or false, can be other than what it is." *Posterior Analytics*, I, 33, 88b.

30 D. Julia, "La production de l'orthodoxie," *Orthodoxie*, 402.

Constantinople) or as the third Rome (for the church of Moscow), the Orthodox Church can only envisage the historical process of modern globalization as an attack on its own universal mission. This eschatological consciousness is of interest to the historian of orthodoxy, seen by R. Koselleck as being as much an observer of horizons of expectation as a witness of spaces of experience. It is for this reason that such a historian is not a stranger to what is at stake today. If one accepts that the Chalcedonian churches do not have a monopoly on orthodox Christianity and if, above all, the Orthodox churches recognize that they should integrate their own historical journeys into the constitution of their awareness of their identity, in the same way as Rome and Geneva should, they will necessarily be obliged to draw certain conclusions regarding the future Pan-Orthodox Council.[31]

The ongoing rediscovery of the concept of orthodoxy by postmodern philosophy and postconfessional theology offers a solution both to the Christian confessions that are striving to heal their internal and external wounds and to the different scientific disciplines that are becoming more and more atomized within the institutions which gave birth to them. In the second phase of our reflection, we will try to examine both the consequences of the ecumenical progress realized in the 20th century and the results of the philosophical reconstruction of truth, initiated by the great wave of Francophile deconstruction in the 1970s but now carried on principally within Anglo-Saxon universities. On a philosophical level, there will be an emphasis on the movement known as Radical Orthodoxy which originated in Cambridge in the late 1990s. The first years of the 21st century have also been the occasion to reap the fruits of ecumenical dialogue. Elsewhere we have dealt with the principal results of the ecumenical dialogue undertaken by the Orthodox churches with other churches.[32] Other authors have treated the same theme from the perspective of the Catholic and Protestant churches.[33] The task now before us is to analyze the consequences of these contemporary evolutions of the relationship between epistemic and doxic truth from an ecclesiological, philosophical and historical perspective.

31 At the time of writing (2012), the Holy and Great Council of the Orthodox Church had not yet occurred. It took place from 19 to 26 June 2016, albeit without the participation of the Churches of Antioch, Bulgaria, Georgia, and Russia. As a result, there is disagreement about its standing as a pan-Orthodox council.

32 A. Arjakovsky, *En attendant le concile de l'Eglise Orthodoxe,* Paris, Cerf, 2010.

33 Cardinal Walter Kasper, *Harvesting the Fruits: Basic Aspects of Christian Faith in Ecumenical Dialogue,* London, Continuum, 2009.

This history of orthodoxy until our present age concludes with an historical and semantic reinterpretation of the concept of orthodoxy in Christian historiography. We will use the four major paradigms of the notion of truth such as they appear in the narratives of Church historians. This history, if it is well understood, suggests that the secular age, which extends from the 15th century to the 20th, might well transform itself, as Charles Taylor postulates, into a new period of mutual and fruitful interpenetration between the temporal world and the spiritual world. Such a transformation can come about only if there is a significant evolution in the relation between *epistemic* and *doxic* truth: the transition from the Cartesian rupture between ecclesial faith and individual understanding to the synthesis, still uncertain, of true and fair knowledge.

# PART I
# *The Orthodox Church and Orthodoxy*

WHAT IS ORTHODOXY? WHAT IS "RIGHT TRUTH," currently the most favored translation of the term "orthodoxy"? Does the Orthodox Church have a monopoly on orthodoxy? Kallistos Ware, one of the most well-known bishops in the Orthodox Christian world, replies to this latter question in his book *The Inner Kingdom*. He defines orthodoxy as "the fullness of life in Christ" and adds that the Orthodox Church is not the exclusive repository of the truth. To those who want to find certain answers in the Orthodox Church, who oppose the truth of the Church to the truth of our contemporary world, who compare the orthodoxy of the East to the heresies of the West, Ware proposes a broader vision of orthodoxy:

> Why should anyone have to reject Dante, Montaigne, Shakespeare, Milton, Victor Hugo and all the others? Are they not part of our cultural heritage? The truth is not like a search engine which gives systematic answers to every question: it is a light. And, like all lights, it is surrounded by shadows and obscurity. Let us be humble enough to recognize that there are many questions which escape us and where the West, with its specific tradition, can help us to find the answers.[1]

How then do we define orthodoxy, the source that gives legitimacy to the doctrine, the spirituality and practices of the Orthodox Church? The traditional (i.e., confessional) presentations of this Church, be they historical, geographical or doctrinal, have a tendency, as John Erickson has

1 K. Ware, *Le royaume intérieur,* Paris, Cerf, 1993, 15.

pointed out,[2] either to ignore its earthly and institutional reality or, in the opposite direction, to amplify these to the point of excluding millions of baptized Christians from its sacramental life. In any case, several decades of ecumenical and interreligious dialogue oblige Christian Orthodox historians to rewrite their histories due to the fact that so many once-defining certitudes have been shaken, even deeply questioned. Many Catholic and Protestant theologians, such as Jean-Marie Tillard, who was president of the ecumenical commission of Faith and Order for many years, and former Archbishop of Canterbury Rowan Williams have recognized that they share the same faith and reasoning process as the Christians of the Orthodox Churches.[3] On the Orthodox side, John Jillions, the former director of the Institute of Orthodox Studies at Cambridge, recently posed the question directly: "The concept of the Church as a confessional entity (Orthodox, Anglican, Lutheran...) is, historically, a relatively recent phenomenon and it has complicated things to an alarming degree. Can we affirm that the Eucharist, which unites Jews and Greeks, men and women, whites and blacks, can also unite Anglicans, Lutherans and Orthodox in a given place?"[4]

Basing himself on the authority of John Zizioulas, one of the most respected contemporary Orthodox theologians, Jillions affirms that a confessional institution (which is what Orthodoxy has become today according to Zizioulas) cannot define itself as Church if it sees itself as a club sharing ideas and beliefs instead of incarnating itself in a given place, in a people made up of different cultures, including different ecclesial cultures.[5] The political, social and economic upheavals which have taken place in the world since the 1960s, when the principal syntheses on the Orthodox Church were redacted, only amplify this necessity. Paul Evdokimov sees the "sociological cemeteries" of the confessional churches swept by the strong winds of globalization, secularism and massive migrations.

2 J. Erickson, *The Challenge of Our Past,* Crestwood, St. Vladimir's Seminary Press, 1991.

3 *Confessing the One Faith,* Geneva, WCC Publications, 1991.

4 John Jillions, "Orthodox Christianity in the West: the Ecumenical Challenge," in *The Cambridge Companion to Orthodox Christian Theology*, ed. Mary B. Cunningham and Elizabeth Theokritoff, Cambridge and New York, Cambridge University Press, 2008, 276–293.

5 John Zizioulas, "Orthodox Ecclesiology and the Ecumenical Movement," *Sourozh* 21 (1985): 16–27.

# CHAPTER 1

## *History and Remembrances of the Orthodox Church*

IT IS NOT EASY TO ESTABLISH A CHRONOLOGY OF the Orthodox Church. Very few Orthodox authors (in the confessional sense of the term) have attempted to do so. Most of the classic manuals on the Orthodox Church do not even propose such a chronology. It is not to be found in the works of Kallistos Ware (*L'Orthodoxie, l'Eglise des sept conciles*), in those of John Meyendorff (*L'Eglise Orthodoxe, hier et aujourd'hui*), or in those of Paul Evdokimov (*L'Orthodoxie*). There are several reasons for this: for one, such a task means carefully distinguishing Orthodoxy as the inner life of the Church from orthodoxy as the experience of truth in all of life's dimensions. For example, should the birth of Islam be mentioned in a history of the Orthodox Church? Moreover, the establishment of a chronology of the Orthodox Church means distinguishing the life of the churches which mutually recognize one another as Orthodox from the life of churches who merely designate themselves as Orthodox. Should the Orthodox Church in America be included among the Orthodox churches, even though it still is not recognized by the Ecumenical Patriarchate of Constantinople? What is more, synthesizing the past signifies placing temporal limits on the consciousness of truth and thus implies an ability to distinguish between the actual consciousness of truth and the consciousness of truth in the past. Is it possible to integrate within the history of the Orthodox Church the narrative of the liturgical celebration at Saint Sophia in Constantinople in 1453 which united Greeks and Latins in the same prayer and Eucharist, when every baptized Catholic is condemned to hell according to Greek canon law (since 1775)? The chronology also poses real theological questions. When was the Church born? From the birth of Christ, if the Church is defined as the Body of Christ? From the outpouring of the Holy Spirit at Pentecost, if the Church is defined as the Temple of the Holy Spirit? Or is the Church eternal by its very nature since one of the Biblical figures of the Church is the Wisdom of God who was present to God from the creation of the world?

In spite of all these risks of a partial representation of the truth—that is, of heresy—in theological language, certain impetuous authors who call themselves orthodox have risked offering a unified presentation of the "Orthodox Church," of "Orthodox spirituality," or of "Orthodox Christianity." The rational simplification they have been obliged to make by selecting essential, inescapable and foundational events is very presumptuous. Such a chronology, because it is a synthesis, reveals the sources and mechanisms of remembrance in the Orthodox Church; in particular, it shows the conviction of the individuals that the truth is found through the logic of a succession of events in time. Yet, in spite of its objective and impersonal appearance, contemporary chronology has become a synonym for simplification and mystification, a mnemonic rather than a history aid.

The three sources we have chosen for the following chronology are all texts by recognized Orthodox Christian authors: Maurice Zinovieff (born in Paris in 1932, graduated from the Ecole National des Langues Orientales Vivantes, a doctor in political science), "Rappel de quelques grandes dates," in *La chrétienté orthodoxe* (Paris: Publisud, 1997); Placide Deseille (archimandrite of the monastery of Simonos Petra at Mount Athos, teacher at the St. Sergius Institute; was a monk at the Cistercian Abbey of Bellefontaine where he inaugurated the collection Oriental Spirituality), "Chronology," in *La spiritualité orthodoxe et la Philocalie* (Paris: Bayard, 1977); and Mary Cunningham and Elizabeth Theokritoff (Cunningham a theologian at the University of Nottingham, Theokritoff an Orthodox theologian and former secretary of the Fellowship of St. Alban and St. Sergius in Great Britain), "A Chronology of the Eastern Churches," in *The Cambridge Companion to Orthodox Christian Theology* (Cambridge: Cambridge University Press, 2009).

We have retained all the historic events singled out by these authors in the hope of being more objective. However, alongside each of the selected events we have noted the initials of the author (MZ, PD, MC-ET) so that the reader might be mindful of each particular author's intention. When the same event is included in multiple chronologies, we have chosen the more precise formulation of it and simply mentioned its presence in other sources by using initials. Following this triple chronology, we will demonstrate the eminently subjective character of a document which presents itself as the most objective tool imaginable. After this, using a history of our contemporary time, there will be an attempt to shed light on certain theological-political issues concerning today's Orthodox world.

## THREE BRIEF CHRONOLOGIES OF ORTHODOX CHRISTIANITY

1 Birth of our Lord Jesus Christ. (MZ)

33 Death and Resurrection of Christ. Pentecost. (MZ)

34 Martyrdom of St. Stephen (Stephanos), the first deacon. (MZ)

50–52 Mission of the apostle Paul in Greece. (MZ)

52 The Council of Jerusalem. Decision to convert the "gentiles" (pagans). (MZ)

64 Persecution of Christians by Nero and the martyrdom of the apostle Peter at Rome. (MZ)

64–313 Persecution of Christians by the Roman emperors and governors. (MC-ET)

67 Martyrdom of Paul at Rome. (MZ)

95 Exile of the Apostle John at Patmos. (MZ)

2ND–3RD C The gnostic and heterodox sects defy orthodoxy. (MC-ET)

112 Persecutions of the Emperor Trajan. (MZ)

116 Persecutions of the Emperor Marcus Aurelius. (MZ)

c. 130–200 St. Irenaeus of Lyons. (MC-ET)

c. 185–254 Origen of Alexandria. (MC-ET)

202 Persecution of Septimus Severus. (MZ)

c. 251–356 St. Anthony of Egypt, founder of monachism. (MC-ET)

258 Persecutions of Valerian. (MZ)

c. 270 St. Anthony withdraws to the desert. (PD)

c. 296–373 St. Athanasius the Great. (MC-ET)

c. 300 Armenia converts to Christianity (first Christian state). (MC-ET)

303 Persecution of Diocletian. (MZ) (PD)

306 Constantine becomes emperor. (PD)

312 Conversion of Emperor Constantine I. (MC-ET)

313 Edict of Milan promulgated by Emperor Constantine I. End of the persecutions against Christianity. (MZ) (MC-ET) (PD)

315 Amoun in the Nitrian Desert. (PD)

324 Constantine becomes the emperor of the West and the East. He decides to make Constantinople his capital. (MZ)

325 Council of Nicaea. First ecumenical council. Condemnation of Arius, who denied the divinity of Christ. Composition of the Nicaean Creed. (MZ) (PD)

326 Discovery of the relics of the Holy Cross by St. Helen. (MZ)

328 Athanasius becomes bishop of Alexandria. (PD)

329/30–389/90 St. Gregory of Nazianzus. (MC-ET)

c. 330–379 St. Gregory of Nyssa. (MC-ET)

330 St. Macarius of Egypt in the Scetic desert. (PD)

347–407 St. John Chrysostom. (MC-ET)

350 Foundation of the church of Georgia. (MC-ET)

355 St. Basil embraces monastic life. (PD)

356 Death of St. Anthony. (PD)

c. 360 *The Life of St. Anthony* composed by St. Athanasius. (PD)

361–363 Reign of Julian the Apostate. (PD)

370 St. Basil becomes Archbishop of Caesarea. (PD)

370–399 Evagrius Ponticus and St. Cassian in Egypt. (PD) (MC-ET)

376 Emperor Valens allows the Visigoths to settle in the Empire. (PD)

379 Death of St. Basil.

379–395 Reign of Theodosius. (PD)

381 Second ecumenical council at Constantinople. Condemnation of the Macedonians, who deny the divinity of the Holy Spirit; acceptance of the creed known as the "Symbol of Faith of Nicaea-Constantinople." (MZ) (PD) (MC-ET)

395 Death of Emperor Theodosius. Division of the Roman Empire into two parts, Eastern and Western. (MZ)

END OF 4TH C *Homilies* of Macarius.

c. 410 St. Honorat founds a monastery on the island of Lerins. (PD)

410 Alaric conquers Rome. (PD)

c. 420 St. Cassian at Marseilles. (PD)

431 Third ecumenical council at Ephesus. Condemnation of Nestorius, who denied that Mary was the Mother of God (Theotokos). The bishop of Constantinople, the Second Rome, is accorded the second dignity in the hierarchy of order after the bishop of Rome. (MZ) (PD) (MC-ET)

c. 450 Diadochus of Photice (PD). Born around 400, died after 446. (MC-ET)

451 Fourth ecumenical council at Chalcedon. Definition of the two natures of Christ (divine and human). Condemnation of Monophysitism (followed by separation of the Copts, Armenians, Ethiopians and Syrians). The repartitioning of the Church into five patriarchates (Rome, Constantinople, Alexandria, Antioch and Jerusalem). (MZ) (PD) (MC-ET)

476 The last Roman emperor in the West is overthrown by the Ostrogoth General Odoacer. (MC-ET)

c. 488 Death of St. Isaiah the Anchorite. (PD)

496 Baptism of Clovis. (PD)

c. 500 The Monks of Gaza: St. Barsanuphius, St. John the Prophet, St. Dorotheus. (PD)

c. 500 Composition of the works of Pseudo-Dionysius the Areopagite. (MC-ET)

527–565 Reign of Justinian.

537 The Church of St. Sophia is rebuilt by Justinian. (MC-ET)

553 Fifth ecumenical council at Constantinople. Confirmation of the preceding councils and condemnation of Origenism (i.e., the Platonic account of the preexistence of souls) (MZ) (PD). Constantinople is recognized as second see after Rome. (MC-ET)

555 Death of St. Romanus the Melodist, a hymnographer. (MC-ET)

c. 575–650 St. John Climacus (PD), author of *The Ladder*. (MC-ET)

580–662 St. Maximus the Confessor. (PD) (MC-ET)

582 The patriarch of Constantinople assumes the title of ecumenical (universal) patriarch, thus establishing a primacy of honor over the Eastern churches. (MZ)

589 Addition of the *Filioque* to the Creed in Spain following the Third Council of Toledo. (MC-ET)

622 The Hegira (PD). The Moslems conquer Damascus in 635, Jerusalem in 638 and Alexandria in 642. (MC-ET)

675–679 St. John Damascus (PD). Died in 750. Hymnographer, theologian, defender of icons. (MC-ET)

680 Sixth ecumenical council at Constantinople. Condemnation of Monothelitism (two natures in Christ but a sole divine will) (MZ) (PD). Affirmation of two wills in Christ. (MC-ET)

692 The "Quinisext" Council of Constantinople establishes 102 canonical regulations, including those that stipulate that married men can be ordained priests and deacons but bishops must be chosen from among celibates or widowers (MZ). Canons on sacred art. (MC-ET)

c. 700 St. Isaac the Syrian (PD), spiritual father, Bishop of Nineveh. (MC-ET) (MZ)

754–780 Iconoclast persecutions. (MZ) (PD)

759–826 St. Theodore the Studite (PD), hymnographer, theologian, defender of icons. (MC-ET)

717–718 The Arabs attack Constantinople.

732 Charles Martel vanquishes the Arabs at Poitiers. (PD)

751 Pepin the Short, King of France. (PD)

787 Seventh ecumenical council: Nicaea II. Approbation of the veneration of icons (images representing Christ and the saints). (MZ) (PD) (MC-ET)

800 Charlemagne becomes Emperor of the West. (PD)

813 Resurgence of Iconoclasm. (PD)

843 Triumph of Orthodoxy (PD). Restoration of icons by Empress Theodora. (MC-ET)

858/67–878/86 St. Photius as Patriarch of Constantinople. (MC-ET)

863–865 Mission of Cyril and Methodius in Moravia and the Christianization of the Bulgarians. (MC-ET) (MZ)

864–65 Missionary activity of Saints Cyril and Methodius among the Slavic peoples (MC-ET). Conversion of the Slavs to Christianity in 867–74. (MZ)

909 Foundation of Cluny in Bourgogne. (PD)

917 Establishment of the patriarchate of Bulgaria. (MC-ET)

949–1022 St. Simeon the New Theologian, hegumen, theologian, poet. (MC-ET) (PD)

962 Otto I founds the Holy Roman Empire. (PD)

963–64 Foundation of the Monastery of the Great Lavra on Mount Athos. (MC-ET) (MZ) (PD)

987 Hugh Capet, King of France. (PD)

988 Baptism of the Rus' of Kiev. Prince Vladimir of Kiev. (MC-ET) (MZ) (PD)

1000–1090 Nicetas Stethanos. (PD)

1027–1107 Pierre of Damascus, theologian and monk. (MC-ET)

1054 The "Great Schism": exchange of anathemas between Rome and Constantinople. (MC-ET) (MZ) (PD)

1055 St. Anthony of Mount Athos founds the Monastery of the Kievian Caves. (PD)

1090–1153 St. Bernard of Clairvaux. (PD)

1095–1099 First crusade: the crusaders occupy Jerusalem and Antioch and install a Latin hierarchy. (MC-ET) (MZ) (PD)

1098 Foundation of Cîteaux. (PD)

1204 The sack of Constantinople by the fourth crusade. (MC-ET) (MZ) (PD)

1237 The invasion of Russia by the Tartars. (MC-ET) (PD)

c. 1250 Nicholas the Solitary. (PD)

1250–c. 1320 Theoliptos of Philadelphia. (PD)

1255/65–1337 St. Gregory of Sinai, hesychast, Master of the Jesus Prayer. (MC-ET)

1255–1346 St. Gregory of Sinai. (PD)

1268 Michael VIII Paleologus reigns in Constantinople. (MZ)

1274 Council of Lyon: failed attempt to reunite Rome and Constantinople. (MC-ET) (MZ)

c. 1296–1359 St. Gregory Palamas, archbishop of Thessalonica, defender of the hesychasts. (MC-ET)

c. 1314–1392 St. Sergius of Radonezh, founder of the Monastery of the Holy Trinity near Moscow. (MC-ET)

1322–1390 St. Nicholas Cabasilas, lay theologian, hesychast. (MC-ET)

1325–c. 1395 Callistus Angelicoudes. (PD)

1340–1396 St. Stephan of Perm, intellectual and missionary to the Zyrians. (MC-ET)

1341, 1347, 1351 Councils at Constantinople concerning the teachings of Gregory Palamas. (MC-ET)

1346 Foundation of the Patriarchate of Pec (Serbia) by St. Savva. (MC-ET)

1380 Battle of Kulikovo. The Russian prince St. Dimitry Donskoi vanquishes the Tartars. (MC-ET)

1389 Battle of Kosovo. The Serbian prince St. Lazar is vanquished by the Turks. (MC-ET) (MZ)

1433–1508 St. Nil of Sora, Hesychast, "Non-Possessor." (MC-ET) (PD)

1438–1439 Council of Ferrara-Florence: official end of the schism between Rome and the Eastern churches (called into question in 1484). (MC-ET)

1439/40–1515 St. Joseph of Volokalamsk, hegumen, "Possessor." (MC-ET) (PD)

1448 Autocephaly of the Russian Church. (MC-ET)

1453 Fall of Constantinople to the Turks. (MC-ET) (MZ) (PD)

1459 Conquest of Serbia by the Turks. (MC-ET)

1480 End of Mongolian domination in Russia. (PD)

1517 The Ottoman Turks occupy Syria and Egypt. (MC-ET)

1572–1638 Cyril Lukaris, author of a pro-Calvinist confession. (MC-ET)

1573–1581 Lutheran scholars correspond with Patriarch Jeremiah II. (MC-ET)

1589 The first patriarch of Russia is elected. (MC-ET) (MZ)

1596 The Union of Brest: creation of a uniate church in Ukraine; foundation of lay "Fraternities" to defend the Orthodox Church. (MC-ET) (MZ)

1597–1646 Peter Mohyla, Metropolitan of Kiev. (MC-ET)

1625–1672 Proclamation of different "Orthodox Confessions." (MC-ET)

1652 The liturgical reforms of Patriarch Nikon of Moscow and the schism of the Old Believers. (MC-ET)

1682–1725 Peter the Great. (PD)

1683 The army of John Sobieski defeats the Turks at the gates of Vienna. (MZ)

1692–1767 Basil of Poiana Marului. (PD)

1700 Synod of Alba Julia: emergence of the Romanian uniate church of Transylvania. (MZ)

1721 Abolition of the patriarchate of Moscow by Peter the Great. (MC-ET)

1722–1794 St. Paisius Velichkovsky, translator of the *Philokalia* into Slavonic (1793). (MC-ET) (PD)

1724 Schism at Antioch: the Melkites enter into communion with Rome. (MC-ET)

1749–1809 St. Nicodemus of the Holy Mountain. Published the *Philokalia* in 1782 and the *Pedalion* in 1800. (MC-ET) (PD)

1759–1833 St. Seraphim of Sarov, monk and spiritual father. (MC-ET) (PD)

1762–1796 Catherine II. (PD)

1774 Treaty of Kutchuk-Kainardji. The Tsar of Russia becomes the protector of the Orthodox Christians within the Ottoman Empire. (MZ)

1789–1799 The French Revolution. (PD)

1793 Publication of the *Philokalia* in Slavonic. (PD)

1794 The Russian mission in Alaska: St. Herman. (MC-ET) (MZ)

1800 Napoleon becomes emperor. (PD)

1807–1867 St. Ignatius Brianchaninov. (PD)

1812 Napoleon's campaign in Russia. (PD)

1812–1891 St. Ambrose of Optina. (PD)

1815–1894 St. Theophan the Recluse. (PD)

1821 Greece frees itself from the Ottoman regime. (MC-ET)

1829 The Starets Leonid of Optino. (PD)

1830 French Revolution of July. (PD)

1840s Slavophile movement in Russia. Alexis Khomiakov (1804–1860). (MC-ET)

1846–1920 St. Nectarios of Aegina. (PD)

1850s Massacres by the Ottomans in Syria. Emigration of Christians. (MC-ET)

1848 Revolutionary movements in Europe. (PD)

1853–1930 Kallinikos the Hesychast (Mount Athos). (PD)

1853–1900 Vladimir Soloviev, religious philosopher. (MC-ET)

1861 Russian mission in Japan: St. Nicholas Kasatkin of Tokyo.

1866–1938 St. Silouan the Athonite. (PD)

1871–1944 Sergius Bulgakov, economist, theologian and ecumenist. (MC-ET)

1872 Council presided over by the patriarch of Constantinople in the presence of the patriarchs of Alexandria and Antioch. Condemnation of phyletism: national rivalries and quarrels among peoples within the Church of Christ. (MZ)

1877–1889 The Russian *Philokalia* of St. Theophan the Recluse. (PD)

END OF 19TH C Russian, Greek and Arabic parishes are established in Australia and North America. (MC-ET)

1882–1937 Paul Florensky, theologian and scientist. (MC-ET)

1891–1909 In the United States, the Archpriest Alexis Toth brings about the reentry of uniate parishes into the Orthodox Church. (MC-ET)

1893–1979 Georges Florovsky, Patristic theologian and Church historian. (MC-ET)

1899 Meletius Al-Doumani is elected patriarch of Antioch. The Arab hierarchy is restored at Antioch. (MC-ET)

1905 First Russian Revolution. (PD)

1914–1918 World War I. (PD)

1917 Soviet Revolution. (PD)

1917–1918 Council of Moscow: restoration of the patriarchate of Moscow and election of Patriarch Tikhon. (MZ) (MC-ET)

1918–1941 Persecution of Christians in the Soviet Union. (MZ)

1922 Persecution of Christians in Asia Minor and Thrace (MZ). Exodus the following year. (PD)

1926 Foundation of the St. Sergius Theological Institute in Paris. (MC-ET)

1938 Foundation of the St. Vladimir Seminary in New York. (MC-ET)

1939–1945 World War II. (PD)

1942 Foundation of the Orthodox Youth Movement at Antioch. (MC-ET)

1946 The Orthodox Church of Uganda is received by the Patriarchate of Alexandria.

1947 The extension of Communist regimes. (PD)

1947–1982 The Romanian *Philokalia* is published by Father Dumitru Stăniloae. (PD)

1953 Foundation of *Syndesmos*, the World Fellowship of Orthodox Youth. (MC-ET)

1959 Death of Joseph the Hesychast (Mount Athos). (PD)

1961 First Pan-Orthodox Conference at Rhodes. (MZ)

1965 Lifting of the anathemas of 1054 by Pope Paul VI and the Patriarch Athenagoras I of Constantinople. (MZ) (MC-ET)

1970 The Russian Metropolis of North America receives autocephaly from the Patriarchate of Moscow and becomes the Orthodox Church in America. (MC-ET)

1982 The Orthodox Church of Ghana is received by the Patriarchate of Alexandria. (MC-ET)

1988 Millennium of the Baptism of Russia. (PD)

1989–1991 Collapse of the Communist regimes. (PD)

1989 The dialogue between Oriental and Orthodox Chalcedonians results in a consensus agreement. (MC-ET)

1992 Msgr. Anastasios is elected Primate of the Albanian Church. (MC-ET)

1993 Death of the Starets Sophrony (Maldon, Great Britain). (PD)

## CHRONOLOGY OR MYTHOLOGY?

### *A Self-identifying Representation*

Memoirs always pretend to be objective histories. All the same, these narratives are very precious. They reveal the attraction, the vitality, even the predominance of certain aspects of orthodoxy over others in the mentality of contemporaries. Some believe that the great figure of the last part of the 19th century was St. Theophan the Recluse, a monk especially appreciated by the zealot stream of the Orthodox Church, while others venerate the Patriarch of Constantinople, who was known in proselyte circles for his opposition to religious nationalism, and still others look to Vladimir Soloviev as one of the principal authors of the spiritual current within Orthodoxy. The first group is attuned to the ascetics, the second group to the great missionaries, and the third to religious philosophy.

Each group pursues very precise goals without feeling obliged to justify them. Thus the reader can see that certain authors, for didactic reasons, begin their chronology of the Orthodox Church with the birth of Jesus Christ. Others, more preoccupied with spirituality, begin their narrative in the third century with St. Anthony the Great. This has the advantage of situating Christian monasticism as a novel phenomenon in history, but it risks losing the continuity of this Christian testimony with the ensemble of the Church's saints described in the Acts of the Apostles. The final group, in its concern to manifest the political character of the Church in its "history," dates its emergence to the first persecutions of the Roman Empire. This approach is equally risky, for it does not take into consideration that the Church is a baptismal, Eucharistic and pastoral assembly.

All these groups, however, want to justify a representational self-identity. This is why certain Orthodox churches appear in the chronology only when they separate from other dissident churches. For example, there is little mention of the ecclesial life of the Christians of the patriarchate of Antioch prior to the 18th century, yet their rupture with the Melkite Church in 1724 caught the attention of the Cambridge chronographers. Likewise, due to this same motive of self-identity, the chronographers, in spite of their concern for objectivity, cannot avoid putting forward the illustrious character of those ancestors whose heritage they have embraced. Thus it is that Father Placide Deseille presents St. Anthony of the Kievian Caves as simply a former "monk" of Mount Athos without any mention of the saint's Slavic roots. His Slavic background is, however, of great importance for the history of the Rus' Orthodox Church. In the 20th century, the Russian St. Silouan is similarly defined as "the Athonite."

It should be noted that certain authors adopt a confessing position when they consider that the moment of the death and resurrection of Christ is central to the history of the Orthodox Church. For others, however, the history of Orthodox spirituality is a synchronic narrative between internal events (such as the lives of great saints) and external events (such as the evolution of empires). From this perspective, Placide Deseille maintains that an event such as the life of St. Bernard of Clairvaux (1090–1153) still belongs to Orthodox memory despite ending after the schism of 1054. All three groups adopt a confessional posture by accepting certain ecumenical councils as orthodox and rejecting others, such as that of 879, which were recognized as ecumenical at the time of their convocation but would disappear from the memory of the Orthodox churches after schisms. In the first and third group, the history of the world is presented as if on the same level as the history of the Church. The second group, however, separates "general history" (essentially political, military and ecclesial) from the history of monks and hesychastic authors.

Aside from this internal logic, the chronologies often try to show lines of continuity between the present age and the foundational events of the past. A French Orthodox monk would be more likely to mention the baptism of Clovis and ignore the baptism of Mirian, the king of Georgia, in the fourth century—brought about in great part by St. Nina, who died in 335 and is venerated as "equal to the apostles" in the Orthodox Church. It should be noted that the mention of Hugh Capet as king of France in 987 brings a certain balance to the remembrance of the present Orthodox Church in Europe. This remembrance is most frequently centered on the baptism of the Rus' in 988 and forgets that the kingdom of France belonged to orthodox Christianity. After the schism of 1054, the Capet dynasty disappeared from the collective remembrance of the Church. The life of Joan of Arc (1412–1431), canonized in 1920 by the Catholic Church, is ignored.

### *The Impossible Neutrality of a Temporal Classification*

The Western "channels" of Eastern spirituality (such as St. Cassian and St. Paisius Velichkovsky) are seen as especially important. But not all of the intermediaries are mentioned. Father Placide Deseille has nothing to say about St. Irenaeus of Lyons, who was honored on account of his contacts with the first circle of apostles. One reason might be that the bishop of Lyons symbolizes an orthodox spirituality which does not fit in with the criteria of Philocalic spirituality. The bishop of Lyons fights against heresies but does not reject any concordance between faith and reason, between gnosis and Christian transcendental knowledge. St. Irenaeus did not compose treatises against the passions of the "flesh." He believed that human deification consisted, above all, in a circulation of glory between God and humanity.

This continuity (of which chronology assures us) between contemporary identity and the past also explains all the flagrantly unjust historical shortcuts. The transcription of terms is especially indicative of the chronographer's spiritual state. The chronographer will easily alternate between Byzantium and Constantinople, but ignore Istanbul. In the Cambridge chronology for 1237, the chronologist refers to the "Russia" of Kiev, which is an anachronism, and fails to distinguish the *Rus'* from the Muscovite. The name of Prince Vladimir of Kiev is given in its Russian form, ignoring the original transcription

(Volodymyr/Valdemar). The Orthodox historiographers are probably least aware of their bias in their account of the fourth crusade, which ended in the pillage of Constantinople. This has been unflinchingly maintained as an open and incurable wound by Orthodox historians, a bitter betrayal in the collective memory of the Eastern church, without these historians ever taking into consideration the crimes committed by the Byzantines against the Latins, even those against the papal delegates, prior to the sack of the city by the Crusaders. Robert Taft affirms that this selective memory among most Orthodox "historians" is a more direct cause of the division among Christian communities than dogmatic divergences or the traditional use of religious dissensions for political ends.[1] The victim mentality, always searching for a scapegoat, adamantly refusing to assume its own responsibilities, has been preserved through the centuries by "vectors of opinion." The most well-known case is that of the generation of intellectuals who focused on the neo-Patristic synthesis (G. Florovsky, J. Meyendorff, B. Bobrinskoy), for whom the crisis in the world of contemporary Orthodoxy, its internal divisions, the fragility of its academic and charitable structures and so forth, is due essentially to the chronic repetition—in the form of the treachery of the Latins, subjection to the Turkish invaders, persecution by Communist ideologists—of the catastrophe suffered by the Jewish people during the Babylonian Captivity.[2]

Due to their extreme simplification, the style of the chronologies gives us an idea within our own times of the disputes which have marked the history of the Orthodox Church. When one reads that the condemnation of Nestorius by the Council of Ephesus is linked to the fact that Nestorius did not recognize that "Mary was the Mother of God," one understands some of the reasons why those Orthodox communities which became divided in 431 have never yet succeeded in reconciling themselves. Certain 20th-century scholars, such as Professor Bethune-Baker, believe that "Nestorius was not a Nestorian."[3] It is well known that the Council of Ephesus affirmed that Mary was the *Theotokos*, that she gave birth to God. The theologians of Antioch would not have disputed this claim, yet they refused to reduce the divine

1 Robert Taft, "Perceptions and Realities in Orthodox-Catholic Relations Today: Reflections on the Past, Prospects for the Future" (paper presented at a conference on "Orthodoxy and the West" at Fordham University, The Bronx, New York, June 2010).

2 A. Arjakovsky, *La Génération des penseurs religieux de l'émigration russe*, Kiev and Paris, Dukhi Litera, 2000.

3 R. Graffin, F. Nau, *Patrologia Orientalis*, Brepols, 1916, vol. 13, fasicule 2, no. 63, http://gallica.bnf.fr/ark:/12148/bpt6k9111n.

humanity of Christ to a unique "nature." The Council Fathers did not use the expression "*mitera to theou*" ("Mother of God"); rather, they chose an expression which clearly affirms, in opposition to Nestorius, that He who took flesh in Mary can be called God, while conserving the similarly scriptural revelation that Mary, His mother, was perfectly human. The synthesis between Cyril of Alexandria and John of Antioch was realized in 433 by the following unifying formula: "Born or begotten of the Father according to His divinity, the same person is born of the Virgin Mary according to His humanity."[4] The Orthodox theologian Jaroslav Pelikan has defined the term *Theotokos* as "she who gives birth to Him who is God." Thus the popular translation of *Theotokos* as "Mother of God" is historically inexact and has only been retained by tradition on the condition of respecting the meaning of *deipare*. The Virgin is "truly the Mother of God" insofar as the reference is to the God-Man. The Virgin Mary cannot be considered to be the Mother of God if the reference is to the Trinitarian God. This semantic ambiguity was one of the reasons why Mohammed rejected Christian doctrine.[5] Present chronologies should at least keep in mind the semantic causes of theological-political disputes.

Surprisingly, the chronologies also seem to gloss over conflictive situations. For example, when Patriarch John IV of Constantinople (582–595) attributed to himself the title of Ecumenical Patriarch in 582, the chronologist explains this act as the affirmation of a simple "primacy of honor" over the Eastern churches, meant to silence the recriminations of Pope Gregory I (590–604) against the patriarch. This new title of ecumenical patriarch had political repercussions going far beyond a simple primacy of honor in the East. The title of ecumenical patriarch (*oikoumenikos patriarches*) appeared in the new laws (*Novellae*) of Emperor Justinian, promulgated beginning in 530. It thus has a political and juridical origin. It was translated into Latin as "*universalis patriarches*." This title, which associated the power of the bishop of Constantinople with the universal power of the Byzantine *Basileus*, could not be accepted by the bishop of Rome, above all at a historical moment when the pope had to confront the invasion of the Lombards and the questioning of his jurisdiction in the Balkans. Through a series of letters issued on June 1, 595 and addressed to Eastern patriarchs and the emperor, the pope made

4 Paul Galtier, *L'unité dans le Christ*, Paris, Beauchesne, 1939, 67.

5 Laurent Cleenewerck, *Methods in Ecumenical Dialogue: Lessons from Critical Thinking, Diplomacy and the Physical Sciences* (master's thesis, Institute of Ecumenical Studies, Ukrainian Catholic University, Lviv, 2011).

known his opposition to the title. These letters reveal the political significance which the pope attributed to the title of universal patriarch. It is for this reason that the pope began to question the apostolic foundations of the See of Constantinople (and thus its political presumptions). For Pope Gregory the Great, the patriarch of Constantinople, through this ecumenical title, would become "the only bishop" and the sole authority from whom other bishops would receive theirs. This was truly unacceptable both on the level of ecclesiology and on that of the earthly authority of each bishop. Such a concept was unacceptable in the Church, wrote Gregory, even when applied to the power of the bishop of Rome. The patriarchs of the East remembered this argument when the 11th-century popes attempted to attribute such a universal power to themselves.

The chronologists, however, only make mention of a simple primacy of honor suddenly ascribed to the Bishop of Constantinople. They can hardly imagine that, as the American historian George Demacopoulos has observed, it is precisely this claim to the title of ecumenical patriarch which later led the Roman popes to develop the rhetoric of a universal, monarchical power in the Church.[6] Even today the Vatican Congregation for the Doctrine of the Faith maintains that the defect in the ecclesiology of the Orthodox churches consists in the fact that they do not believe that membership in the Church of Christ depends, above all, on its unity with the Bishop of Rome.[7]

It is equally surprising that the chronology of Maurice Zinovieff shows the persecution of Christians in the USSR ending in 1941. It is as if the resistance of the Church to the German invasion was enough to convince the Soviet state of the social utility of the Orthodox Church. In reality, the persecution lasted until the collapse of the Soviet Union in 1991, half a century later. Is this an attempt to deemphasize the control the Soviet state exercised over the Church for three quarters of a century? It is true that in 1997, when Zinovieff published his chronology, numerous documents were appearing in the press accusing Orthodox hierarchs of central and eastern European countries of collaboration with the governments of the Soviet period.[8]

6 On this topic cf. G. Demacopoulos, "Gregory the Great and the Sixth-Century Dispute over the Ecumenical Title," *Theological Studies* 70 (2009): 600–620.

7 Congregation for the Doctrine of the Faith, "Responses to Some Questions Regarding Certain Aspects of the Doctrine of the Church," at the Vatican website.

8 For a detailed chronology of events concerning the Orthodox Churches of Eastern Europe since 1989, cf. H. Destivelle, "Chronique des chrétiens de l'Est depuis la chute du mur de Berlin," *Istina* 54 (January–March 2009).

There are, however, elements common to all these chronologies. The memory of the Orthodox Church recognizes that the Edict of Milan in 313 is an important turning point in its history. Likewise, all three chronologies mention the seven councils of Asia Minor between 325 and 787 which brought together the universal Church. The three chronologies, however, all "forget" several significant events. They make no reference to the 879 ecumenical council of union which reestablished communion among the different Christian Sees. Even though John Meyendorff, the eminent American Orthodox theologian, has proposed reinstating this council in Orthodox remembrance, many encyclopedists maintain that the churches have not retained this council as ecumenical. Would the true Eighth Ecumenical Council be the 869 Council of Discord, also ignored by the chronologists, where the Patriarch Photius was condemned and subsequently deposed?[9] The rupture with "Western" Christianity in 1054 is also an indisputable landmark in the forging of the identity of "Eastern" Christianity. Even though historians consider this formal rupture a moment among other moments in the long history of the estrangement between the church of Rome and the church of Constantinople, it has always been etched in memories as the primary cause of the separation. It is here that we must pose the question of the nature of the ecclesial influence on the remembrance put forward as history. If the "historians" of Orthodoxy

9 It is necessary to have recourse to another encyclopedia online (orthodoxworld.ru) to understand the true — in the historical and not the memorial sense of the word — Eighth Ecumenical Council: "Above all, we have to pay attention to the council convoked at Constantinople in 879–880 during the pontificates of Patriarch Photius and Pope John VIII. Both by its composition and by the nature of its decisions, this council had all the characteristics of an ecumenical council. All five patriarchates of the Church of that epoch were represented — including the patriarchate of Rome — making this the last council common to the Eastern and Western churches. There were 383 participants, the greatest number since the Council of Chalcedon. It was convoked as an Ecumenical Council and, in its acts, spoke of itself as 'the Great and Ecumenical Council.' It is true that it has not been officially recognized by the Church as 'ecumenical' because such a recognition would generally take place during the following council and there were never any more councils. Nonetheless, several ecclesiastical personalities refer to this as the Eighth Ecumenical Council. Among these are the celebrated 12th-century canonist Theodore Balsamon, Nil of Thessalonica (14th century), Nil of Rhodes (14th century), Symeon of Thessalonica (15th century), Saint Mark of Ephesus, Gennadius Scholarius, Dositheus of Jerusalem (17th century), etc. As Professor Dvornik has demonstrated in his well-known work *Le Schisme de Photius* and as is generally admitted by present historical research (even Roman Catholic), the Council of 879–880 was, up to the 12th century, also considered in the West as the Eighth Ecumenical Council." Francis Dvornik, *The Photian Schism, History and Legend,* Cambridge, Cambridge University Press, 1948.

want to acquire academic legitimacy for their narratives, and not simply communitarian acceptance, they should admit certain historical facts such as the Council of Florence in 1439 (which is mentioned only to state that it was rejected in 1484, a statement not valid for every Orthodox church) and avoid a systematic preference for remembrance over history. In the history of the reception of councils, there are numerous examples which show that a council cannot be effaced with the stroke of a pen. The recent history of the Christological reconciliation between Chalcedonian and non-Chalcedonian Christians nearly 14 centuries after the dispute of 451 is one of the best examples.

As a final characteristic example of the confessional hypertrophy of contemporary Orthodox remembrance, let us point out the absence, in all three chronologies, of any mention of the participation of certain Orthodox churches in the creation of the World Council of Churches at Amsterdam in 1948, a council in which the majority of Orthodox churches now participate. Thus there are several levels of consciousness of the "truth," according to the degrees of confessional affiliation with a remembrance tradition. The remembrance narratives vary with respect to the degree of *participation* in the historical truth. They vary in their particularities with respect to the degree of recognition of the work of historical purification brought about through the repentance of consciences.[10]

## CONFESSIONAL AND SOPHIOLOGICAL CHRONOLOGY IN OUR TIMES

In other words, there are several types of Orthodox historiographies. The historian of the confessional age, whether Christian or not, sees his mission as manifesting the identity boundaries of the truth. For such a historian, temporality is marked by an irreparable division between the past, the present and the future. This is why he supposes that the truth should present itself to him as beyond time and mutation; it is accessible by an intellectual operation of historical objectivation. Such an operation consists in arranging the space for an unfettered deployment of what is radically other than ourselves. Under the influence of Descartes and Locke, the modern historian "believes" that withdrawal from the world enables the world to manifest itself such as it is.

10 T. Hainthaler, "Réflexions sur la levée des anathèmes historiques," Congrès: Rencontre des Eglises syriaques. Colloquium n. 3, Mundelein, Illinois, USA (July 8, 1997); *Istina*, vol. 43, no. 2 (1998): 221–36.

The philosopher Michel Bitbol claims deep and legitimate reasons for this belief: the human intellect needs to distance itself from what it participates in so as to be able to share its experience. According to Bitbol, "the imperative of inserting oneself into what is common" can lead to narrowing the field of possible experiences, beginning with the experience of interpersonal relationship, which is never general.[11] In fact, the act of objectivation is not pure passivity, even though it tends to pretend to be. It is not a withdrawal but "an aspiration never realized" to distance oneself. Thus Bitbol makes an appeal to adopt a more "inclusive" position capable of restricting objectivation to just one aspect of the definition of truth — a position capable also of rehabilitating the respectability of empathic, contemplative, speculative and aesthetic thought.

From this perspective, a Christian historiography — one that is symbolic, comprehensive and eschatological — can once again appear legitimate to a modern historian. The Russian philosopher Nicholas Berdyaev has shown the path towards this new Orthodox historiography. For Berdyaev, truth does not enter into us as an object: "The Truth implies an activity of the human spirit . . . knowledge of the truth depends on the degrees of community which can exist among persons, on their communion in the Spirit."[12] This is the famous doctrine of the *sobornost*, of conciliarity, which Berdyaev drew from the writings of Alexis Khomiakov (1804–1860) but which, more fundamentally, characterizes Patristic thought. Since knowledge is by nature participatory, it is not dependent only on the *logos*; it is erotic. For this reason, it should be understood as "*kath'holic*," symphonic. From such a perspective, cognition cannot be opposed to being nor subject to object. Although Berdyaev recognized the importance of phenomenology, he defined his personalist philosophy as an existential philosophy. In 1934 he wrote:

> According to Husserl, real objects are found in the essences without mediation and the evidence is not a state of consciousness but the very presence of the object. What phenomenology describes is pure consciousness and what it gives is the vision of essences (*Wesenheiten*). But the vision of essences does not reveal the mystery of existence.[13]

11 Antoine Arjakovsky, "Objectivation, subjectivation et transcendement: Michel Bitbol, Nicholas Berdyaev, Jean-Marc Ferry," *Revue théologique des Bernardins,* no. 6 (Sep.–Dec. 2012): 10–20.

12 Berdyaev, *Cinq méditations sur l'existence,* Paris, YMCA Press, 1934; French ed., Paris, Aubier/Montaigne, 1936, 208.

13 Berdyaev, *Cinq méditations,* 61.

For Berdyaev, the existentiality of the subject, as one of the paths of the spirit, gives access to the discovery of the mystery of the existing being. Consequently, "cognition is no longer confronted with being; it functions at the most intimate level of being and conjointly with it . . . cognition is an illumination of being."[14] The operation which enables a surpassing of the objectivation-subjectivation dichotomy is that of transcending. Berdyaev writes:

> Within being there is an obscure depth with which thought does not identify and the function of thought is to clarify this obscurity which cognition should illuminate. Cognition stands at the edge of the obscure abyss of being; but it should be clear and lucid itself. It is true that cognition is immanent to being; but it also must be said that it is a *transcending* which takes place within being and with it, a plunge into the great depths far and beyond any given being. Knowledge does not reflect; it adds something of its own. Transcending any individual being is a being yet deeper still: *transcending* is the passage to this being.[15]

There are thus two attitudes towards the past, towards things and beings that have perished. First, there is the conservative attitude, which seeks to retain the past and return to it. For Berdyaev, this attitude is indispensable, and on this point he concurs with Bitbol in the defense of objectivation at a certain level of the formation of consciousness:

> To take the critical awareness of the production of the object by the subject is to deliver oneself from the domination that the subject accorded to the object by naively accepting the material world as it imposed itself on the self from without.[16]

This represents a manner of "doing history" which is post-confessional, personalistic and sophiological. The theology of *Sophia*, the Wisdom of God, elaborated by Sergius Bulgakov is another witness to this new awareness. In the sapiential representation of temporality, the beginning is a reality more personal than mechanical. Rejoining an ancient Talmudic tradition,

14 Ibid., 62.
15 Ibid., 63.
16 Ibid., 54.

Bulgakov interprets the "In the beginning" of Genesis as an expression of the Wisdom of God, present to the Creator at the moment of the creation of the world. This is, in fact, what is written in the eighth chapter of the biblical Book of Proverbs. For Bulgakov as for Berdyaev, temporality is a participatory reality. They do not consider memory simply a source of objectivation. It is, first of all, the meeting place of the past and the future. This is the whole meaning of the new historiography of the "places of memory [*Lieux de mémoire*]" initiated by Pierre Nora. For Nora, memory "is no longer that which must be retained of the past in order to prepare the future one desires; it is what makes the present present to itself."[17] This school of historiography has nothing confessional about it, but it rehabilitates the symbolic approach to historical truth.

The postmodern historian can observe the reality of the division among Christian confessions in the course of history. There is, above all, the realization that the truth towards which these different confessions tend cannot be confined within their community boundaries. The modern historian also notes a discrepancy between conceptual discourse, which represents the truth in a homogeneous and univocal manner, and dogmatic discourse, which represents the truth as the encounter, in time and in space, between humanity and God. In this second representation there is room for the criticism of sociomorphisms and anthropomorphisms, while in the first representation truth must be accepted or rejected as a whole. For confessional historians, the past is objective, distinct from the subject. It can be represented, but there is no participation in it.

On the whole, the Christian definition of truth is not conceptual and communitarian but personal and metacommunitarian. Conscious of the influence of the hierarchy of truths that define each person in quest of orthodoxy, the postmodern historian considers the narrative of what unites a community to have at least as much importance as the narrative of what divides it, of what has separated it intellectually, politically, socially and culturally from another community. Every narrative will thus be considered capable of transfiguring memories, capable of guiding these memories towards reconciliation and the forgetting of discords and prevailing over the recital of the traumatic repetition of ancestral wounds over confessional traditions identified with the historical boundaries of the truth.

17 Pierre Nora, *Historien public,* Paris, Gallimard, 2011, 412.

# CHAPTER 2

# *The Orthodox Church in the World*

## THE GEOGRAPHY OF THE ORTHODOX CHURCHES

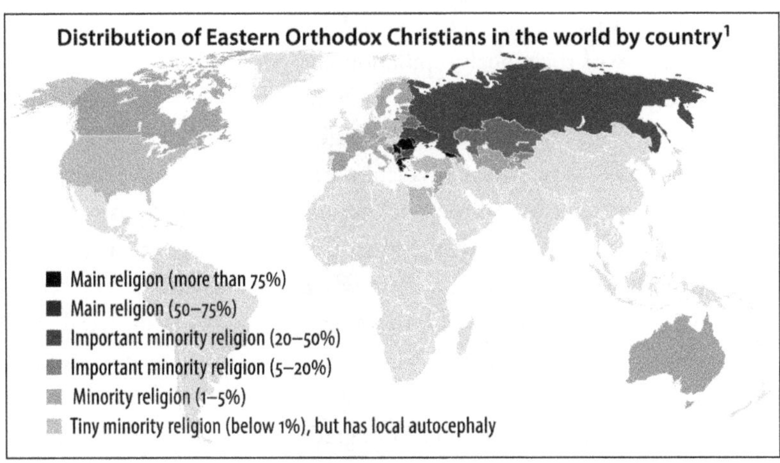


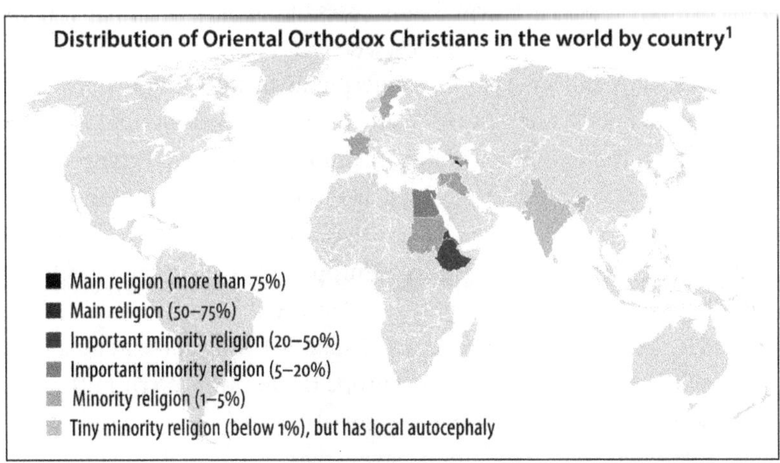


1 Source: http://en.wikipedia.org/wiki/Orthodoxy_by_country. Map created 2012; date of access: September 2018.

## EVOLUTION OF THE POPULATION OF CHALCEDONIAN AND NON-CHALCEDONIAN ORTHODOX CHURCHES[2]

The Orthodox population doubled over the course of the 20th century according to the new *Atlas of Global Christianity*, increasing from 124,923,000 in 1910 to 274,447,000 in 2010. Taking account of the accelerated growth of the human population, Orthodox Christians, who represented 7.1% of the total population in 1910, represented only 4% in 2010. The Orthodox faithful represent 12% of the Christian population, which numbers 2,292,454,000 (a third of the total global population). By way of comparison, Muslims represent 22.4% of the global population and count 1,549,444,000 adherents. Agnostics number 639,852,000 and represent 9.3% of the total while atheists make up 2% of the global population.

The majority of Orthodox Christians are found in Eastern Europe, with 177 million faithful or 61% of the total population of these countries. Moscow is the European city with the most Christians (more than London or Paris): 10,967,000 believers, 84% of whom are Christians. The center of gravity of the Orthodox world, however, has somewhat shifted during the past century from Northern Ukraine towards the region of Sebastopol. It should be noted that due to the decreasing birth rate, the increase in mortality and the phenomenon of immigration, several Eastern European countries have experienced significant losses in their Christian population, notably Ukraine, Romania and Bulgaria (as opposed to countries like China, Brazil, the USA and the Democratic Republic of the Congo which have had the most notable increases in their Christian populace). It is estimated that, in 2050, Russia will only have 91,117,000 Christians (as compared to 115,120,000 today) while China, which had 115,009,000 in 2011, could arrive at 225,075,000 in 2050, thus making it the second most Christian country in the world after the USA. Western Europe has only 2.2 million Orthodox Christians, 1.2% of the population. Northern Europe has 2.1 million faithful (2.1%) and Southern Europe 19.6 million (12.8% of the population). The total Orthodox population in Europe (including Eastern Europe) is 201,197,000 — 27.5% of the European population.

After Europe, Africa is the continent with the greatest number of Orthodox Christians, 48,286,000 or 4% of the African population. Oceania, essentially

2 *Atlas of Global Christianity (1910–2010)*, ed. Todd M. Johnson and Kenneth R. Ross, Edinburgh, Edinburgh University Press, 2009.

Australia and New Zealand, only has 928,000 faithful, but they represent 2.6% of the total population. The Orthodox have less presence in Asia (0.4% of the total), North America (0.3%) and Latin America (0.2%).

Whereas in 1910, 89.2% of the Orthodox population was situated in Europe, in 2010 this figure was only 73.3% (87,000 communities). The percentage of Orthodox living in Africa grew considerably, from 4.3% to 17.6% (17,300) of the universal Orthodox population. Kenya did not have any Orthodox churches at the beginning of the 20th century; it now has 620,000 Orthodox faithful. This is the most extensive growth of an Orthodox community in the 20th century, constituting an 11.8% increase. Several other African and Middle-East countries have experienced their highest rates of increase in Orthodox population: Libya (9.19%), United Arab Emirates (9.12%), Somalia (8.99%), Saudi Arabia (8.99%), Ivory Coast (8.78%), Nigeria (8.74%). There are now 93,600 Orthodox faithful in West Africa, whereas not a single one was counted here in 1910.

Asia remained stable (6.1–5.8%; 10,800 communities). East Asia, with 102,000 adherents, has experienced the greatest growth rate of Orthodox faithful in the world over the last decade at 6.83% (while the overall population only increased 0.57%). China, in particular, is the country which has seen the largest augmentation of Orthodox believers in the world over the last ten years (ahead of Norway and Iceland).

North America now represents 2.6% of the totality of the Orthodox world, with 3,500 communities. The number of Orthodox faithful in the United States is estimated to be about a million, with about 434,000 in Canada.[3]

Latin America (560 communities) and Oceania (460) are the continents with the fewest Orthodox Christians. The Caribbean nations, however, which counted only 58,000 faithful in 2010, had one of the strongest growth rates of the Orthodox population in the 20th century at 9.06% (whereas the general population increase was 1.66%).

The Russian Orthodox Church counts 119,973,000 members (of which 110,904,000 are in Russia), representing 43.7% of the Orthodox community and making it the largest Orthodox church. Next are the Ethiopian Church with 37,395,000 members (13.6%), the Ukrainian Orthodox Church with 30,397,000 (11.1%), the Romanian Orthodox Church with 19,305,000 (7%), the Greek Orthodox Church with 15,198,000 (5.5%), the Coptic Orthodox Church with 9,747,000 (3.6%), the Serbian Orthodox Church with 7,355,000 (2.7%), the Bulgarian Orthodox Church with 6,249,000 (2.3%),

3 http://www.cjoc.ca/pdf/vol5-W-2Stats.pdf.

the Armenian Orthodox Church with 5,913,000 (2.2%). The Orthodox Churches of Belarus make up 1.8% of the Orthodox population, the Georgian Church 1.1%, the Moldavian Church 1.1%, the Syro-Malabar Church 1%, the Antiochian Church 0.5%, the Macedonian Church 0.5%, the Syro-Antiochian Church 0.4%, the Polish Orthodox Church 0.2%, the Assyrian Church 0.2%, the Albanian Orthodox Church 0.1%, the Orthodox Church of Latvia 0.1%, the Estonian Orthodox Church 0.1%.

The countries where the Orthodox population is the national majority include, as of 2010, Moldavia (92.9%), Greece (92%), Romania (91.5%), Cyprus (84.9%), Georgia (82.9%), Bulgaria (81%), Russia (79%), Armenia (75.8%), Montenegro (70.9%), and Ukraine (69.9%).

## THE ORGANIZATION OF THE ORTHODOX CHURCHES

### *An Overview of the Chalcedonian & non-Chalcedonian Orthodox Churches*

Until quite recently, the distinctions among the Orthodox Churches were made according to their acceptance or rejection of the ecumenical councils which took place between 325 and 787. In particular, as late as 1960 a neat distinction was made between the churches which accepted the Council of Chalcedon in 451 and those which did not. Today the many ecumenical encounters among the churches and the phenomenon of globalization have made the dividing lines much more complex. These are now generally drawn according to the degree of reception of these councils by the churches and the degree of recognition of this memorable development of the one Church by the other churches. For example, the patriarchate of the Orthodox Church of Antioch (whose seat is in Damascus) is ready to recognize the Syrian Orthodox Church (whose seat is also in Damascus), and vice versa; but this will not be accomplished through solidarity with the patriarchate of Moscow, a late arrival to the ecumenical debate. Due to the lack of a new terminology recognized by all, and bearing in mind the fact that these churches have had divergent histories since the Council of Chalcedon in 451, French-speakers continue to distinguish the "non-Chalcedonian" churches (the Assyrian, Armenian, Coptic, Ethiopian, Eritrean, West Syrian and Syrian Malankara [Southern India] Churches) from the "Chalcedonian" churches. The English-speaking world prefers to use the term "oriental Orthodox churches" for the former and "eastern Orthodox churches" for the latter.

**The "Oriental Orthodox" or "non-Chalcedonian" Churches.**[4] Most members of the "non-Chalcedonian" Orthodox churches live in Ethiopia, Eritrea, Egypt, Armenia, India, Syria, and Lebanon. There are also important dispersed communities in the Near East, Europe, Asia, North and South America and Australia. The Oriental Orthodox churches are ancient churches, founded in apostolic times by the apostles themselves or by their earliest disciples. Their ecclesial stance is based, historically, on the teachings of the first two Ecumenical Councils (for the Assyrian Church) or the first three (for the six others), Nicaea in 325, Constantinople in 381, and Ephesus in 431.

The Oriental Orthodox churches, all of which are members of the World Council of Churches, represent approximately 60 million Christians. The Armenian Apostolic Church, which traces its origins to the apostles Thaddeus and Bartholomew, was established in the third century by St. Gregory the Illuminator. The Kingdom of Armenia became the first Christian state in 301 and, initially, avoided the "monophysite" crisis due to its struggles against the Persian invaders. The Armenian Apostolic Church is governed by the Catholicos of All Armenians, who resides in Etchmiadzine, near Erevan in Armenia, and is responsible for three centers of decision; the Catholicos of Sis in Cilicia, who was displaced to Lebanon after the Armenian genocide at the hands of the Turks in 1915; the patriarch of Jerusalem; and the patriarch of Constantinople. There are about eight million Armenians worldwide, with 3.7 million in Armenia.

The Oriental Assyrian Church is the heir of the so-called Nestorian Church. It uses the Syrian rite and reached into Mesopotamia by the sixth century. In the fourteenth century, it extended into India and China. At present it has about two million faithful in India, Lebanon, and Iraq, but widespread emigration to Sweden and Germany brought about the founding of several dioceses in the diaspora, including in the United States and Latin America. Within the Antiochian tradition there is a distinction to be made between the Assyrian Church and the Syrian Church, which is sometimes also called the Jacobite Church. The Syrian Orthodox Church, which was founded by the Apostle Peter in Antioch in 37, was united to the patriarchate of Antioch until the sixth century. It now counts about a million members who have

4 Cf. the writings of Christine Chaillot on these Churches: *The Coptic Orthodox Church,* Paris, Inter-Orthodox Dialogue, 2005; *The Ethiopian Orthodox Tewahedo Church Tradition,* Paris, Inter-Orthodox Dialogue, 2002; *The Malankara Orthodox Church,* Geneva, Inter-Orthodox Dialogue, 1996.

preserved the Syrian rite. Like the Assyrian Church, it is concentrated in Iraq, Lebanon, India and Syria. The diaspora is significant in Scandinavia and the United States. This church has had its seat near Damascus since 1959. Within Christianity of the Syrian and non-Chalcedonian tradition, a special place should be set aside for a third Church. The Syrian Malankara Orthodox Church had been in close relations with the Jacobite Church from at least 1665 until 1912; about a million of the faithful still maintain communion with the seat of Damascus. This church is found principally in India, in the province of Kerala. Tradition links the community to the Apostle Thomas, who supposedly evangelized the region beginning in the year 52. The Syrian liturgical tradition testifies to its ancient origin. Due to colonization and Latin influences, this community has suffered many vicissitudes.

According to tradition, the Coptic Orthodox Church was founded in Alexandria during the first century by the evangelist Mark. Progressively, from the fourth century on, this Church came to view the Byzantine Empire as its oppressor. Egypt was conquered by the Persians in 616. In 642, it greeted the Arabs as liberators. It was the Arabs who named this church "Coptic," a deformation of *aegyptos* (Egyptian). Today the Coptic Church counts around eight million faithful. The Ethiopian Orthodox Church claims that its first member was the eunuch minister of the Queen of Saba whose conversion to Christianity is related in the Acts of the Apostles (8:26–40). Since 1950, this church has become autonomous with respect to its "Mother Church," the patriarchate of Alexandria. Its current patriarch resides in Addis Ababa; it has 14 million members. While it experienced difficulties under a Marxist regime, it has now fully recovered. Since Eritrea was recognized as independent in 1993, the Orthodox Church of Eritrea has had a direct relationship with the Egyptian Orthodox Church and elected its first patriarch in 1998.

There is no Eucharistic communion between the Chalcedonian and non-Chalcedonian churches. The break came about in 451 due to the Christological teachings of the Council of Chalcedon.[5] The representatives of

5 "Following, then, the holy Fathers, we all unanimously teach that our Lord Jesus Christ is to us one and the same Son, the selfsame perfect in Godhead, the selfsame perfect in manhood; truly God and truly man; the selfsame of a rational soul and body; coessential with the Father according to the Godhead, the selfsame coessential with us according to the manhood; like us in all things, sin apart; before the ages begotten of the Father as to the Godhead, but in the last days, the selfsame, for us and for our salvation born of Mary the Virgin Theotokos as to the manhood; one and the same Christ, Son, Lord, Only-begotten; acknowledged in two natures unconfusedly, unchangeably, indivisibly,

the Oriental Orthodox churches believed that the Fathers of Chalcedon were introducing a division into the person of Christ when they spoke of his two "natures" or *physeis*. They preferred to follow the terminology of Cyril of Alexandria (†444), who did not yet make a distinction between the terms *physis* (nature) and *ousia* (substance) and spoke of "one *physis* of God the Incarnate Word." The Antiochian school of theology, which prevailed at the Council of Chalcedon, feared that the use of this expression would ultimately lessen one of the two natures, divine or human, of Christ. They thus treated those who were accused of recognizing only one nature in Christ as "monophysites." After the Council of Ephesus, however, John of Antioch had proposed a formula that reconciled the positions of both schools by insisting upon the personal unity of the two natures, divine and human, of Christ.[6] This formula won over the fathers of Chalcedon thanks especially to the intervention of Pope Leo of Rome. However, the political opposition between the patriarch of Alexandria and that of Constantinople, the latter being supported by the emperor, triumphed over theological considerations. There was a schism which, according to Christine Chaillot, brought about an upheaval even more profound: "If this schism had not happened, Islam would never have been able to penetrate and implant itself so easily and rapidly as it did in the East and all around the Mediterranean

---

inseparably; the difference of the natures being in no way removed because of the union, but rather the properties of each nature being preserved, and both concurring into one Person and one hypostasis; not as though He were parted or divided into two Persons, but one and the selfsame Son and Only-begotten God, Word, Lord, Jesus Christ; even as from the beginning the prophets have taught concerning Him, and as the Lord Jesus Christ Himself hath taught us, and as the Symbol of the Fathers hath handed down to us." From https://archive.org/stream/MN41552ucmf_1/MN41552ucmf_1_djvu.txt.

6 "We thus confess our Lord Jesus Christ, the only Son of God, perfect God and perfect man, with a rational soul and a body, born of the Father before all ages in his divinity and, at the end of days, for us and for our salvation, born of the Virgin Mary in his humanity; consubstantial to the Father in his divinity and consubstantial to us in his humanity. For the union (*henosis*) was accomplished; this is why we confess a sole Christ, a sole Son, a sole Lord. And because of this concept of a union without mixture, we confess that the holy Virgin is Mother of God because the Word of God became flesh and became man and from the moment of his conception he is united to the Temple which he took from her. As for the expressions used by the Gospels and apostles concerning the Lord, we know that theologians apply some indiscriminately because they concern the same person (*prosopon* and not *hypostasis*) but they concern the two natures and they attribute what pertains to God to the divinity of Christ and what concerns his abasement they attribute to his humanity." Cf. https://ia801408.us.archive.org/35/items/MN41552ucmf_1/MN41552ucmf_1.pdf.

from the seventh century onward."[7] It is well known that Mohammed only knew Christian doctrine in its monophysite tradition.

Over the course of the centuries, the relations between the Oriental Orthodox churches and the Chalcedonians have been marked by mutual distancing and confrontation, but also by dialogue and *rapprochement*. As Father Sergius Bulgakov had already understood in 1933, the opposition between the "monophysites" and the "dyphysites" was more a semantic than a theological problem. For Bulgakov, in the debates which followed the Council of Chalcedon "the reaction against the dogma (the different forms of monophytism) was not so much motivated by a heretical rejection as by a dogmatic and terminological misunderstanding.... In monophysite circles, people continued, as in the past (in the Cyrillian tradition), to identify the terms nature, hypostasis and person."[8] The rediscovery of orthodoxy as truth and not only as tradition has provoked an awareness among certain disciples of Bulgakov, especially John Meyendorff.

After centuries of isolation from one another, the "Orthodox" and "Orientals" finally came together in 1965 at Addis-Ababa. On the occasion of this historic meeting, the leaders of these churches reaffirmed their common faith. In 1985, after two decades of unofficial encounters, the two groups entered into an official theological dialogue which led to formal statements of Christological agreement in 1989–1990. In 1993, the two families of churches, at a reunion in Chambésy, proposed that the anathemas dating back to the Byzantine period be rescinded, a step which would lead to the immediate restoration of sacramental communion. This proposition was not followed up. The principal question which remains unresolved is that of the reception of the agreement by all of the churches concerned. The challenge which persists is that of giving more visibility and tangible expression to the unity of faith among the Oriental Orthodox Churches. Among the questions which call for a joint resolution are the influence of secularization, the resurgence of religious fundamentalism and the growing immigration of faithful who are leaving their country of origin to settle in other parts of the world.[9]

7 C. Chaillot, "Fidélité et vulnérabilité des plus anciennes Eglises d'Orient" in *Les richesses de l'Orient chretien,* Paris, St. Augustin, Sel de la terre, 2000, 139.

8 S. Bulgakov, *Du Verbe Incarné,* Paris, L'Age d'Homme, 1982 (1933), 62.

9 The Oriental Orthodox family does not have a joint organization. Since 1996, the heads of the three Churches of the Near East (Coptic, Armenian and Syrian) have held annual meetings to discuss issues and questions of common interest. Several committees have been set up to help the patriarchs in this process.

In addition to its dialogue with the Chalcedonian Orthodox, the Oriental Orthodox family has also entered into theological discussions with the World Alliance of Reformed Churches, the Catholic Church and the Anglican Communion. On June 23, 1984, the Syrian Orthodox Church arrived at an agreement of intercommunion with the Roman Catholic Church. Pope John Paul II and Patriarch Zakka I Iwas signed a declaration of common faith. The ninth point of this agreement contains the following discussion:

> This identity of faith, although incomplete, authorizes us to envisage pastoral collaboration in situations that frequently present themselves to us nowadays due to the dispersion of the faithful throughout the world as well as to the precarious pastoral conditions created by the difficulties specific to our times. It is not rare that it is materially or morally impossible for our faithful to have access to a priest of their Church. In our desire to respond to their necessities and in view of their spiritual well-being, we authorize them to request the help of the sacraments of Penance, the Eucharist and Extreme Unction, according to their needs, from the legitimate pastors of other Churches. A logical corollary of this pastoral collaboration would be cooperation in priestly formation and theological teaching. We encourage bishops to promote the pooling of the resources at their disposition for theological education wherever they judge this to be desirable. By so doing, we do not forget that we should still do everything within our power in order to arrive at full visible communion between the Catholic Church and the Syrian Church of Antioch and ceaselessly implore the Lord to grant us this unity which alone will enable us to give a fully unanimous testimony to the Gospel before the world.[10]

**The "Eastern Orthodox" or "Chalcedonian Churches."** According to Nicholas Lossky, the author of an entry concerning the Orthodox Churches for the *Dictionary of the Ecumenical Movement*, the Chalcedonian Orthodox Church "claims to descend directly, without interruption, from the Church of the Apostles."[11] This patrimony finds its expression in the

10 https://w2.vatican.va/content/john-paul-ii/en/speeches/1984/june/documents/hf_jp-ii_spe_19840623_jp-ii-zakka-i.html.

11 Nicolas Lossky, "Eastern Orthodox Churches," in World Council of Churches,

church's "faithfulness to the apostolic faith as it was expressed and made explicit by the seven ecumenical councils and in the patristic tradition." The Chalcedonian churches are thus united in faith, and "each one enjoys an internal autonomy under the primacy of the Patriarch of Constantinople who is *primus inter pares*."[12]

Since their separation from Western Christianity, the Chalcedonian Orthodox Churches have essentially followed the Syro-Byzantine liturgical tradition, whose evolution has been influenced by the Eastern Church Fathers and the great monastic centers of which Mount Athos in Greece, with its twenty monasteries and numerous hermitages, is now the most important. The "autocephalous" Chalcedonian Orthodox churches are those which elect their primate without having to refer to another autocephalous church. These number 14 or 15 (depending on their recognition by other Churches). The autocephalous churches include the Sees of Constantinople, Alexandria, Antioch, Jerusalem, Moscow, Serbia, Romania, Bulgaria, Georgia, Cyprus, Greece, Poland, Albania, the Czech Republic and Slovakia, and America. The autonomous Chalcedonian Orthodox churches, which have internal autonomy but whose primate is elected under the aegis of one of the autocephalous churches, number between four and seven, according to their degree of recognition. The autonomous Chalcedonian Orthodox Churches include the Churches of Sinai (Jerusalem), the Church of Finland (Constantinople), the Church of Estonia (Constantinople), the Church of Japan (Moscow), the Church of China (Moscow), the Church of Ukraine in America and Canada (Constantinople) and the diocese of Ochrid (Serbia).[13]

As of the time of writing [2012], the Orthodox Churches are made up of four of the five patriarchates which existed during the Byzantine period: Constantinople (under Patriarch Bartholomew I), which counts about two million members, of whom only several thousand reside in Turkey and more than half are in America;[14] Alexandria (under Patriarch Peter VII), numbering about 100,000 members, which accepted the Council of Chalcedon (rejected by the majority of Egyptians) and became a Greek-speaking minority as of the fifth century, although the patriarch exercises authority over all of Africa;

*Dictionary of the Ecumenical Movement,* Grand Rapids, MI, Eerdmans, 2002, 346. Cf. also https://www.oikoumene.org/en/church-families/orthodox-churches-eastern.

12 J. Meyendorff, *L'Eglise Orthodoxe, hier et aujourd'hui,* Paris, Seuil, 1995 (1960).

13 The most comprehensive web site in French on the Orthodox Church is www.orthodoxie.com.

14 http://www.orthodoxa.org/FR/patriarcat/documents/constantinople.htm.

Antioch (whose patriarch resides in Damascus, since the former See of Antioch has become a small Turkish village), which has about 450,000 faithful, of whom at least 100,000 reside in the United States; and Jerusalem (under Patriarch Theophilo III), counting about 50,000 members, whose hierarchy is Greek-speaking while the lower clergy is Palestinian and speaks Arabic. (The Church of Jerusalem is essentially dedicated to the guardianship of the Holy Places; it has an important real-estate patrimony which is a source of conflict with the Israeli government.) The Ecumenical Council of Chalcedon gave the patriarchate of Constantinople the right to receive appeal cases judged in other Churches (canon 17) and jurisdiction over missionary bishops in the extensions of the Roman dioceses of Thrace, Asia and Pontus (canon 28). Certain modern canon lawyers have interpreted the latter canon as granting a right of preeminence over the whole diaspora in "barbarian" countries.

Several autocephalous churches constitute a majority in their respective countries. Numerically, the most important is that of Russia, which was recognized as autocephalous in 1589 by the Ecumenical Patriarch Jeremiah II. In January 2009, a council of this church elected Cyril as patriarch. It counted about a hundred million members in 1917; in 2010 it had 106 million baptized faithful. As can be seen on its French language website,[15] the Russian Church has been especially dynamic since the collapse of the Soviet Union and now enjoys the reliable support of the Russian state. There is also the Serbian Church, founded in 1219 by St. Sava, with a patriarchate at Belgrade; its current patriarch is Irenaeus, and there are today about eight million faithful. The Romanian Church has been autocephalous since 1885; its current patriarch is Daniel and it counts about 14 million members.[16] The Greek Church, separated from the patriarchate of Constantinople since 1833, has its own primate, the Archbishop of Athens (currently Jerome), and counts around 7.5 million members. The Bulgarian Church was only recognized by Constantinople in 1945; Maximus is the patriarch, and there are approximately six million faithful. The Church of Georgia, much more ancient than the Russian Church, was founded in the fifth century thanks to the missionary activity of a woman, St. Nina, who is recognized as "equal to the apostles" in the Orthodox sanctoral; today the patriarch is the Catholicos Elias II, and there were 2.5 million members as of 1917. The Church of Cyprus has been autocephalous since the Council of Ephesus in 431; today it is under Archbishop Chrysostom, with about 450,000 baptized faithful.

15 http://mospat.ru.

16 http://www.mitropolia.eu/en/.

Certain autocephalous churches represent an Orthodox minority among other Christians in their respective countries. These are the Orthodox Church of the Czech Republic and Slovakia, recognized by Constantinople since 1998 (under Metropolitan Christopher, with around 350,000 faithful as of 1950); the Polish Orthodox Church, whose autocephaly was recognized by Constantinople in 1924 (under Metropolitan Sabbas, with about 350,000 faithful); and the Albanian Orthodox Church (approximately 210,000 faithful as of 1944), which has experienced a revival since 1991 under Archbishop Anastasius (Yannoulatos).

Among the autonomous Churches one finds the Church of Finland (70,000 faithful; under the jurisdiction of Constantinople since 1923), the Church of Crete (also under Constantinople), the Orthodox Church of Japan (36,000 members, under the jurisdiction of Moscow), and the Orthodox Mission in China (probably about 20,000 members). The archbishop of the monastery of St. Catherine on Mount Sinai has an autonomous status and is consecrated by the patriarch of Jerusalem. The non-autonomous missions should be treated apart; this is especially the case for the Orthodox Mission in Korea (dependent on the Greek Archdiocese of North America) and African Orthodoxy, founded in Uganda by dissidents from the Anglican Church and now present in Kenya, the Democratic Republic of the Congo, Ghana and Zimbabwe, under the jurisdiction of the Patriarchate of Alexandria. The autocephalous Ukrainian Orthodox Church in the United States and Canada has been recognized by the ecumenical Patriarchate of Constantinople since 1994.[17]

Finally, there is the Orthodox diaspora. Since the 19th century, many Orthodox have emigrated to Western countries for political or economic reasons, leading to an Orthodox presence throughout the world. A recent report on the Orthodox Church in America (OCA) estimates the number of its faithful in the United States at 797,600. This shows that the jurisdictional mosaic of the Orthodox Churches does not impede the gradual formation of a local American Church (English is used in 73% of the parishes).[18] This Orthodox diaspora, which involves several million members dispersed practically all over the world (with as many as 600,000 in France),[19] has, since

17 On the other hand, certain Orthodox Churches, such as the patriarchate of Kiev, are yet in 2013 not recognized by any other Orthodox Church.

18 http://www.assemblyofbishops.org/files/news/FiveFacts.pdf.

19 http://www.aeof.fr/.

the 20th century, called into question the structural organization of the Orthodox Church. However, before treating the reasons for this, a few words must be said about the contemporary identity crisis of the Orthodox world and the preparation for the upcoming Pan-Orthodox Council.

## *The Crisis in the Traditional Self-representation of the Orthodox Church*[20]

In 1973, the Assembly of the Orthodox Bishops of America declared that "the Orthodox Church is the visible and historical realization of the One Church founded by Jesus Christ on earth and entrusted to his disciples under the guidance of the Holy Spirit."[21] The Orthodox Churches see themselves as a community of communities united among themselves by bonds of mutual recognition and by the conviction, rooted in the same faith, Scriptures and tradition, that they constitute the one, holy, catholic and apostolic Church.[22] The Orthodox Churches are also united by their ideal of a living unity such as that depicted in the Acts of the Apostles (2:42ff.): faithfulness to the apostolic teaching, fraternal unity, the breaking of the bread, prayer and a common life where everything is shared. All the Churches which define themselves as Orthodox acknowledge the primacy of the Ecumenical Patriarchate of Constantinople (Istanbul) and reach common decisions through Pan-Orthodox synods and councils.[23]

20 A. Arjakovsky, *En attendant le concile de l'Eglise Orthodoxe,* Paris, Cerf, 2011. See also: http://www.patriyarkhat.org.ua/antoine-arjakovsky-on-the-great-and-holy-council/.

21 "The Orthodox Church is the visible, historical realization of the one Church" (SCOBA, *Guidelines for Orthodox Christians in Ecumenical Relations*, Chapter I, 12 [Nov. 1973]). Cf. ibid., 13: "Jesus Christ founded the one true Church on the firm foundation of the Apostolic testimony, not many churches. That Church is visibly present in the historic Orthodox community" (at http://www.assemblyofbishops.org/resorces/ecumenical_guidelines.html). Cf. also—for a more tautological definition of the Orthodox Church—chapter I of "Foundational principles of the relationship of the Orthodox Church of Russia with the non-Orthodox" (https://mospat.ru/en/documents/attitude-to-the-non-orthodox/i/); cf. also "Encyclical Letter of the Holy Synod of Bishops of the Orthodox Church in America on Christian Unity and Ecumenism" (New York, 1973; at https://oca.org/holy-synod/encyclicals/on-christian-unity-and-ecumenism).

22 For a discussion of the definition of the Orthodox Church, cf. Petro Vassiliadis, "The Universal Claim of Orthodoxy and the Particularity of its Witness in a Pluralistic World," in WCC, *The Orthodox Churches in a Pluralistic World,* Geneva, 2004, 192–206.

23 This type of organization should be improved in view of the June 2009 statement of the preconciliar Conference of Orthodox Churches: "The Conference has decided to create new Episcopal Assemblies in certain parts of the world in order to regulate the question of the diaspora, that is, the problem of Orthodox faithful who live in

These bonds of recognition are not homogeneous and static but can vary in space and time.[24] Orthodox ecclesiology thus makes a distinction between the Orthodox Church (understood as a reality of faith — the One, Holy, Catholic and Apostolic Church) and the Orthodox churches incarnated in history.[25] These Churches both incarnate the Church and tend towards her as the kingdom of the divine-human reality. As noted by Catholic and Orthodox ecclesiologists, "on one side the Church celebrates the Eucharist as the temporal expression of the heavenly liturgy. But, on the other side, the Eucharist builds up the Church in the sense that the Spirit of the Risen Christ shapes it into the Body of Christ."[26] There is, then, a relationship

---

areas situated outside of the traditional boundaries of the local Orthodox Churches. The first among the bishops in the region under the jurisdiction of the Ecumenical Patriarchate are the presidents of the Assemblies or, in their absence, the bishops next named in the Diptychs of the Churches. All the canonical bishops, recognized as such by the Orthodox Churches and exercising their pastoral ministry within existing communities in each of these regions, are members of these Assemblies" (https://www.centreorthodoxe.org/saint-et-grand-concile/). The territories which have priority for the convocation of Episcopal Assemblies are the following: North and Central America; South America; Australia, New Zealand and Oceania; Great Britain and Ireland; France; Belgium; Holland and Luxembourg; Austria; Italy and Malta; Switzerland and Lichtenstein; Germany; Scandinavia (apart from Finland); Spain and Portugal (http://churchby.info/rus/322/). The Pan-Orthodox council took place in Kolymbari, Crete, in June 2016. All the final documents are here: https://www.holycouncil.org/fr/official-documents.

24 List of autocephalous and autonomous Orthodox churches: The Sees of Constantinople, Alexandria, Antioch, Jerusalem, Moscow, Serbia, Romania, Bulgaria, Georgia, Cyprus, Greece, Poland, Albania, Czech and Slovakia and America (this last Church is not recognized as autocephalous by Constantinople but is recognized as such by Moscow, Bulgaria, Georgia, Poland, the Czech Republic and Slovakia, Romania, and Albania); the autonomous churches are the Churches of Sinai, Finland, Estonia (recognized by Constantinople but not by Moscow), Japan (recognized by Moscow but not Constantinople), China (recognized by Moscow but not Constantinople), Ukraine (recognized by Moscow but not Constantinople) and the archdiocese of Ochrid (recognized only by Serbia) (http://www.orthodoxwiki.org/List_of_autocephalous_and_autonomous_churches).

25 Msgr. Damaskinos (Papandreou), metropolitan of Switzerland, writes: "The future of ecumenism consists in the mission of the Churches which identify themselves with the One Holy, Catholic and Apostolic Church to seek Churches which are outside of their own canonical boundaries. Personally, I believe that the existence of a Church outside of a Church — in the strong sense of the word *Church* — can be recognized where there is unity of faith and, what is indispensably linked to the former, apostolic succession." *Les dialogues oecuméniques hier et aujourd'hui,* Chambésy, editions COPOE, 1985, 50.

26 Mixed Catholic-Orthodox Commission of Theological Dialogue, *Le mystère de l'Eglise et de l'Eucharistie,* Munich, Mesnil-Saint-Loup, Le livre ouvert, 1994, 22.

of tension between the Church and the churches as well as between the present-day Church, Tradition and the Kingdom to come.[27]

In insisting too much on the unity of the Orthodox Church, there is the danger of diminishing the reality of the ecclesial diversity within Orthodoxy by adopting an ahistorical and even Monophysite perspective. The first three chapters of the Book of Revelation witness to this diversity. The Orthodox Church is one, but it is not made of a single block. Moreover, as the Greek Orthodox theologian Nikos Nissiotis writes, "The term Orthodoxy is exclusive for those who deliberately turn their backs on the historical stream of the life of the One Church, but it is inclusive for those who profess their spiritual identification in this direction."[28] Even though all the Orthodox Churches adopted a common position in 1986 at Chambesy in which they expressed their reasons for participating in the ecumenical movement, each Church also separately adopted specific and sometimes differing texts for setting the terms of their participation in this movement. The Churches of Georgia and Bulgaria, for example, are the only Orthodox Churches that are not part of the World Council of Churches. The Church of Finland, unlike the Russian or Antiochian Churches, approved a liturgical calendar permitting the celebration of Easter at the same time as the Catholic and Protestant churches. At the heart of each church there can be several different viewpoints, which should not be suppressed in the name of the essential unity of the Orthodox world. The Patriarch of the Romanian Church, Daniel Ciobotea, has opposed certain bishops of his church by defending his concept of an open catholicity (*sobornicitatea*);[29] the monks of Mount Athos constantly oppose the viewpoints of the ecumenical patriarchate on which they depend. In the opinion of the theologians of the School of Paris (Bulgakov and Berdyaev, for instance) one must know and respect the consensus of the Fathers of the Church, at least as it has been interpreted by ecclesial tradition. However, it is also useful to be mindful

27 A "unitarian" definition of Orthodoxy can be found in the 1966 text of SCOBA: "Orthodoxy is the fullness of the people of God, sharing the same apostolic faith, proclaiming the wonderful works of God in history which have been totally revealed in the person and acts of Jesus Christ and confirmed by the sanctifying activity of the Holy Spirit who calls to unity in the One Body of Christ" (http://www.scoba.us/resources/ecumenical_guidelines.html).

28 N. Nissiotis, "Interpreting Orthodoxy," *The Ecumenical Review* 14 (1961): 26.

29 Patriarch Daniel of the Romanian Orthodox Church, *La joie de la fidélité*, Paris, Cerf, 2009.

of the specific contexts in which the churches live. Local traditions, often simply oral, also actualize, or have actualized, the orthopraxis of this faith. The living tradition of the Orthodox Church is nothing other than a permanent reflection by contemporary history on the memories that coexist in the Church.[30]

The Church is not primarily an institution. It becomes institutional because, historically, it shows itself to be an interpersonal and communitarian reality. There are several consequences of this development. First, the concept of community takes precedence over that of territoriality without, however, excluding it. The Church is incarnate in a given place, yet sees itself as extending to the uttermost confines of the *oikoumene*, and this imposes a choice between the territorial principle and pastoral exigencies. Secondly, the awareness of the identity of the local Church, capable of a certain degree of autonomy or even autocephaly, is only possible if there is a fidelity to the faith of the Orthodox ecumenical tradition, which is distinct from the particular traditions of each community, and this obviously implies a continual reflection by each Church on its own historical roots. Thirdly, this fidelity is not in itself sufficient, for it must be recognized as such by the other Churches.[31] This implies that there can be *degrees* of mutual recognition among Churches. In certain cases, this type of organization can give rise to situations of mediated communion among churches where two churches which are not in direct communion with one another are nonetheless united through their simultaneous communion with a third church.[32] In order to better understand the life and the complex mechanism of the Church in its twofold nature as non-confessional and institutional, one must realize that in the Orthodox tradition, the *lex orandi* has precedence over the *lex credendi*. As G. Florovsky has pointed out, it is prayer, that is the degree of spiritual dynamism, which determines doctrine and discipline and not vice versa.[33]

30 S. Bulgakov, G. Fedotov, et al, *Zivoe Predanie*, Paris, YMCA Press, 1937.

31 This has come into play in the reception by the Russian Church, without a special confession of faith, of the members of the Russian Orthodox Church Outside Russia or, by the same token, in the rejection of the Church of the Patriarchate of Kiev, a Church not recognized but sharing the same confession of faith as the Orthodox Churches.

32 This would be the case with the Churches of Moscow and Estonia which are not in direct communion but which are nonetheless united through the mediation of their common communion with the Church of Constantinople.

33 G. Florovsky, "The Elements of Liturgy," in G. Patelos, ed., *The Orthodox Church in the Ecumenical Movement*, Geneva, WCC, 1978, 172–82.

## *The Need for a Pan-Orthodox Council*[34]

Because of a certain number of worldwide developments, such as the progress of the ecumenical movement and the fact of numerous diasporas,[35] and taking into account the divergences which have arisen among the different local churches on certain issues, the Ecumenical Patriarchs of Constantinople have been trying to convoke a Pan-Orthodox Council since the 1930s.[36] From 1930 to 1960, however, these hopes of the Ecumenical Patriarchs bore little fruit. The project was revived after the death of Patriarch Athenagoras in 1972 by Patriarch Dimitrios of Constantinople. On the occasion of the first preconciliar meeting, which took place at Chambesy (near Geneva), the Orthodox Churches agreed on ten points on which to seek consensus:

1. The Orthodox diaspora;
2. Autocephaly and the process leading to its proclamation;
3. Autonomy and the process leading to its proclamation;
4. The diptychs;
5. A common calendar;
6. Marriage impediments;
7. The revision of ecclesiastical rules concerning fasting;
8. The relationship between the Orthodox Churches and the rest of the Christian world;
9. Orthodoxy and the ecumenical movement;
10. The contribution of local Orthodox churches to the realization of Christian ideals of peace, liberty, fraternity and love among peoples and the suppression of racial discrimination.

34 This chapter was written in 2012. Since then the Pan-Orthodox Council finally took place in Kolymbari in June 2016. For a presentation of the Pan-Orthodox Council see: Antoine Arjakovsky "Le concile de Kolymbari," *France Catholique*, Juin 2016: https://www.france-catholique.fr/Concile-panorthodoxe-de-Kolymbari.html; in English: https://publicorthodoxy.org/2016/07/01/the-fruit-of-the-holy-and-great-council/; all the documents adopted by the council are available at: http://www.holycouncil.org.

35 Between 1990 and 2010 the number of Orthodox Christians in France grew from 300,000 to 600,000. Yorgo Lemopoulos, "Orthodox Diaspora in Europe: An attempt to describe a range of old and new issues." http://www.deltapublicaciones.com/derechoyreligion/gestor/archivos/07_10_00_895.pdf.

36 Antoine Arjakovsky, *En attendant le concile de l'Eglise Orthodoxe*, Paris, Cerf, 2011. The Russian translation of the book is available online: http://www.ecumenicalstudies.org.ua/sites/default/files/publication_docs/Antuan_Arjakovskiy%20_%20v%20ozhydanii_Vsepravoslavnogo_%20sobora_0.pdf.

A certain number of consensual decisions were approved during three preconciliar conferences in 1982, 1986 and 2009. This preparatory work, which has spanned nearly 40 years, has not resulted in any major breakthroughs. It is for this reason that many observers, in spite of the announcement by Patriarch Bartholomew of an upcoming Pan-Orthodox Council, are opposed to such a convocation. They think that it would only aggravate the already tense relations among the churches with regard to the themes under discussion.[37] The preconciliar process was even interrupted for a long while (between 1996 and 2008) because of Moscow's questioning of the authority of Constantinople during the crisis regarding the Estonian Church. Another element is the fact that most of the churches which were persecuted by Communist regimes over a long period of time and which were divided among themselves during the Cold War are now desirous, above all, of stability and the preservation of their identities. The majority of them are not ready to change their ways of doing things for the sake of Pan-Orthodox homogeneity and even less in the name of Pan-Christianity, nor are they willing to adapt to the modern age.

Thus it is that the Churches have not been able to settle on any common position on the date of Easter (celebrated on different dates in Finland and Ukraine), on what constitutes impediments to marriage (mixed marriages among Christians are discouraged in Greece but tolerated in France), or on fasting regulations (with different dates for Lent in Russia and Kenya). In general, their attitudes towards the World Council of Churches and the ecumenical movement are also very disparate; the Bulgarian Church withdrew from the World Council of Churches, while the Serbian Church continues to be a member. The text approved in 1986 concerning the tenth point is so outdated that it now has to be rewritten. The various decisions taken concerning the diaspora and the attribution of autocephaly and autonomy are so contradictory that observers consider them as a reaffirmation of the authority of the Mother Churches more than a right realization of the shift in ecclesial balance brought about in the 20th century by the presence of Orthodox Churches in countries of Catholic or Protestant tradition. On the one hand, the Orthodox Churches establish Episcopal Assemblies which include all the canonical bishops of a territory under the presidency of the

37 Antoine Arjakovsky, "Can the Orthodox council be saved from shipwreck?," *The Wheel*, March 2016 (https://www.wheeljournal.com/blog/2016/2/20/antoine-arjakovsky-can-the-pan-orthodox-council-be-saved-from-shipwreck).

bishop of Constantinople while, on the other hand, these same Churches demand that these assemblies "not deprive their members of their administrative and canonical competencies and do not limit their rights in what concerns the diaspora." As proved by the problem of the proclamation of autocephaly by the Orthodox Church in America, which was the source of the falling-out between Constantinople and Moscow in 1970 and 1976, the preconciliar assemblies have still not resolved how, in practice, a new Church can attain autocephaly. In fact, they recommend a practice which was never used in the past millennium, that *all the Churches* approve the request of autocephaly by any Church. The Churches have not even been able to agree on the actual list of autocephalous Churches. As for the diptychs — that is, the order of precedence of honor of the Churches — there is total confusion. Certain Churches do not give equal precedence to the Church of Georgia (in the 9th place for Constantinople, 6th for Moscow), the Polish Orthodox Church (in the 12th place for Constantinople, 13th for Moscow) or the Church of Cyprus (which thinks it should have precedence over Georgia).

New difficulties became apparent in 2011. Metropolitan Hilarion Alfeyev announced that if the ecumenical patriarchate decided to no longer use the criterion of unanimity in its decisions, the Russian Church would require that the representation of the Churches be in proportion to the number of their dioceses. This would lead to an absolute domination of the patriarchate of Moscow over the council, something which is unthinkable for the other Churches.[38] It is also probable that, following the example of the Russian Church, other Churches might question the leadership of the Patriarch of Constantinople — in particular the patriarchate of Romania and the Church of Greece (which has many links with Mount Athos, where several monasteries are openly opposed to Bartholomew I). The Russian Church also seeks the representation of the Orthodox Church in America at the council (even though it is not recognized by Constantinople). A final

38 "Regulation, incidentally, is a theme which has still never been studied in the course of inter-Orthodox reunions. According to the rules established by the preparatory preconciliar commissions, two members of each Church participate. In other words, a local Church consisting of many millions of faithful is represented by two members, the same as a Church which has tens of thousands of members. Until the moment when the principle of consensus was questioned, this proportion of representation did not pose any problems on the part of the local Orthodox Churches since all of them had the assurance that their interests would be taken into consideration" (http://orthodoxie.typepad.com/Fichiers_2/Mgr._Hilarion.pdf).

difficulty risks putting an end to the conciliar aspirations of the Orthodox Church. The patriarchate of Moscow is demanding that the details of the staging of the council be made known in advance to all the churches. This will certainly delay the realization of the council even more since, in reality, the Moscow patriarchate denies the exclusive precedence given to the Ecumenical Patriarch. Bishop Alfeyev writes:

> Many other questions need to be discussed. For example: how should the primates of the Churches be ranked? In what order, according to which diptychs? It is very important that, on this occasion, there be an emphasis on conciliarity and collegiality in the administration of the Orthodox Church. The very image of the ruling authority of the council should make manifest to the whole world what Orthodox theologians, down through the centuries, have insisted upon in their polemic with the West: the Orthodox Church does not have an earthly head, for its sole Head is the Lord Jesus Christ Himself. It is only because the Orthodox Church recognizes Christ as the sole Head of the Church that it has the right to call itself the Body of Christ.[39]

## THE GEOPOLITICS OF THE ORTHODOX WORLD[40]

The crisis in the Orthodox world is not just internal; it is equally evident in its relations with the world. In addition to the impossibility of the restoration of communion between the Chalcedonian and non-Chalcedonian churches, and to the incapability of these Churches to resolve their differences in a conciliar manner, there is also the incomprehension of many states regarding the political positions embraced by the Orthodox Churches during the 20th century. Several experts of the Orthodox Church believe that the Orthodox world has been during the course of its history both a victim of violent persecutions and the cause of these persecutions, due to its inability to

39 http://orthodoxie.typepad.com/Fichiers_2Mgr_Hilarion.pdf.

40 For more information on the geopolitics of the Orthodox world see François Thual, *Géopolitique de l'Orthodoxie,* Paris, Dunod, 1993, and *Le douaire de Byzance, territoires et identites de l'Orthodoxie,* Paris, Ellipses, 1998. Cf. also "Cyprus: Geopolitics and Minorities" (doctoral dissertation, University of Paris 1 Pantheon-Sorbonne, L'Harmattan, 2012), at https://nicolaskazarian.com/cyprus-geopolitics-minorities-chypre-geopolitique-et-minorites/.

establish a reasonable cooperation between Church, nation and state. We will proceed with a brief summary of the views of François Thual, Olivier Clément and Isabelle Dépret on this issue. These three contemporary authors have attempted to explain, but not justify, certain "antimodern" positions maintained by the Orthodox Churches since the fall of the Berlin Wall. They have especially called attention to the proximity, and even the fusion, which has existed in the Orthodox world for several centuries between the concepts of Church, state and nation.

## *The "Legacy of Byzantium"*

The writings of political scientist François Thual, professor at the Ecole Pratique des Hautes Etudes in Paris and research director at the Institute for International and Strategic Relations, have shown that the Orthodox world is a geocultural space that is still heavily influenced by the long era of Byzantine civilization (from the 4th to the 15th century). In Thual's opinion, the fall of Byzantium in 1453 gave rise to a collection of national egoisms and egotisms, generators of hatred. For Thual, Orthodoxy has become a sort of ideology enabling the "survival" of the former Byzantine Commonwealth during Turkish domination and subsequently under Communist and post-Communist regimes.

In an interview with the newspaper *Le Monde* published on January 20, 1998, Thual defined the contours of this transformation of Christian faith into "Orthodoxist" ideology in countries such as Russia, Serbia and Romania. His point of departure is the fact that the Orthodox world has experienced a history very different from that of the Western Church. Most of the Orthodox peoples have had to struggle to liberate themselves from Ottoman occupiers, who were both foreigners and Muslims. During the Ottoman domination, especially in the Balkan Peninsula and the Caucasus region, the Church was a refuge for local language and identity. Once these peoples were liberated, a sort of genetic link between the confessional and the national persisted. The Church legitimizes the nation; conversely the national sentiment draws legitimacy from the Church. Thual is aware of the impressive revival of the Russian Church after the fall of Communism. In 1914 the Russian Church had 54,457 churches; the Communist persecution reduced this number to 6,800. Yet by 1998 it had grown again to 16,500. Thual, however, thinks that the policies of the Russian Church directed against Western missionaries and favoring the 1994 and 2000 campaigns against the Chechens have revealed the shortcomings of an elite in the Russian Church very much influenced by the Soviet era:[41]

> Let's take the case of the patriarch of Moscow. It must not be forgotten that Russia was liberated from the Mongol yoke. At the outset, the Mongols were mainly pagans; it was only later that they converted to Islam. The liberation of Russia from Mongol domination was also a *reconquista*. Even today the Russian Church sees itself as the protector of Russian identity, the guarantor of Russian breathing space and compatible with the future of Russia. As for geography: when, in 1992, there were a certain number of centrifugal movements, the patriarch affirmed that he would not accept a breaking-up of national territory. These are positions that surprise us. Imagine that, on the occasion of the referendums concerning the independence of Algeria or the status of overseas territories, French Catholic authorities came out in favor of maintaining the unity of an empire. . . . We are dealing with a system which functions in a different manner from the Catholic and Protestant systems.[42]

## *The Instrumentalization of Religious Power in ex-Yugoslavia*

Just as there was a sacralization of the state in Western Europe after the French Revolution, modern times have witnessed a sacralization of national identity in Eastern Europe on the part of the Orthodox Church. This led the traditional Orthodox Churches, seeing that the new national Churches were turning against them, to condemn the "ethnophyletist" heresy in 1872, but they were unable to propose an alternative model. The Serbian Church, in particular, believed that it had a duty to protect national identity, guarantee its territory, and assure its future. Prior to its conflict with Croatia in 1991, the Church of Serbia declared that it would never accept the partition of Serbia's "historical territory." It was only when representatives of the Orthodox diaspora in France spoke out at the beginning of the Croatian-Serbian War that the Serbian Church, through its new patriarch Paul (elected December

41 Cf. also Kathy Rousselet and Gilles Favarel-Garrigues, *La Russie contemporaine*, Paris, Fayard, 2010.

42 F. Thual, interview by D. Dhombres, *Le Monde* (January 20, 1998).

1, 1990)[43] categorically rejected all use of force in the name of God.[44] In 1994, the French Orthodox theologian Olivier Clément published his own analysis of the Yugoslavian conflict in the newspaper *La Croix*.[45]

For Clément, a significant element of what is called "Serbian nationalism" is the counterpart of the Western doctrine known as the right of peoples to self-determination. This nationalism, he argues, should be seen in a historical perspective — in the context of the genocide of the Serbian

43 "On December 1, 1990, Bishop Paul was elected patriarch by the plenary assembly of Serbian bishops to replace Patriarch German who, very old and sick, had been obliged to resign in December of 1990 after 14 months of hospitalization. During the 19 years he served as head of the Serbian Church, Paul, whom commentators on his election judged to be 'a transitional figure,' realized an important pastoral renewal while preserving the Church from pressures on the part of the State and striving to lead the Serbian people back to the sources of its spiritual tradition. During the epoch of the collapse of Communist Yugoslavia and the ensuing wars in Croatia and Bosnia, Patriarch Paul distinguished himself by his stance against any kind of violence and exaggerated nationalism — especially when this came from Serbia: 'Not Great Serbia nor Little Serbia, if either is brought about by a crime,' as he put it in 1994. In order to wipe away the aftermath of the conflict, he had several meetings with Franjo Cardinal Kuharic, the head of the Catholic bishops, and together they launched appeals for reconciliation and dialogue between Serbs and Croatians. Within Serbia, Patriarch Paul defied the Milosevic regime and resolutely separated himself from it, to the point of leading a protest march in Belgrade on June 2, 1992, the feast of Pentecost. Insisting from the beginning that 'the Serbian people were victims of Communist tyranny,' he proclaimed, after the rigged municipal election of 1997, his 'unreserved' condemnation of the Milosevic regime and called for respect of 'the freely formulated expression of the will of the people.' He equally denounced Belgrade's abandonment of the Serbs of Croatia and Bosnia. In April 1999, during the war over Kosovo and in the middle of the NATO air raids, Patriarch Paul went to see for himself what was happening in the province while the battles between the Serbian Armed Forces and the Albanian insurgents were raging on all sides and hundreds of thousands of people, both Albanians and Serbs were fleeing from the conflicts. After the Serbian Army withdrew from Kosovo, Patriarch Paul intervened on several occasions with the Serbian authorities and with the international community to avoid any 'ethnic cleansing of the Serbs or other non-Albanian peoples of Kosovo' and to protect the churches and monasteries of the province, of which more than 120 had been attacked and profaned by Albanian separatists. He likewise called for the departure of Slobodan Milosevic whose politics in Kosovo had shown themselves to be 'criminal and malefic'" (http://www.orthodoxpress.com/index.php?group=display&action=info&page=476).

44 In the November 27, 1991, issue of *Le Monde*, while the Serbian-Croatian War was in full swing, Olivier Clément, Elisabeth Behr-Sigel and other Orthodox intellectuals signed an appeal to the Church of Serbia urging it not to become "an accomplice of the National-Communist war machine."

45 Olivier Clément, "Comprendre les Serbes?," *La Croix*, January 1994; see also Olivier Clément, "Liminaire," *Contacts*, Oct.–Dec. 1993, http://www.revue-contacts.com/archives/contacts164.php.

people on the part of the Ustashe Croatians during World War II. Clément goes on to say that the "precipitated recognition" of Croatia by the Vatican and Germany in 1990 caused fear and panic among the Serbian minority. He does not try to justify the massacres subsequently carried out by the Serbs (especially that of Sarajevo), which "are a source of shame and call for repentance," but he insists that the atheistic and nationalist mentalities inherited from the Communist era must be taken into consideration. In the light of all this, Clément believes that the Serbian people should be neither demonized nor excused. He takes pains to point out four elements especially important for understanding the conflict tearing apart the peoples of the former Yugoslavia. He pleads for support for the "courageous Serbian Church," which, from the moment it elected Patriarch Paul, opposed the violence of the Communist regime of President Milosevic:

> a) These horrors have, first of all, been committed by the Federal Army, which sees itself engaged in a war of secession and has applied the methods of the Soviet school—preliminary bombings of cities, terrorist bombings, "memoricide" (Vukovar, Dubrovnik, Karlocav); one must not forget, especially in the case of Bosnia, that these abominations were committed by the dregs of a populace, those enrolled in irregular "Chetniks" or "white eagles" and the product of Communist "demoralization"; one must also bear in mind that two out of three Serbs and eight out of ten Montenegrians were never baptized.
>
> b) Croatians and Muslims carried out similar atrocities—on a lesser level, to be sure, but only because they were less well armed and occupied less territory. Serbians also suffered from the war: 200 Serbian villages were destroyed in Slavonia, 50 in Herzegovina. Serbian refugees numbered up to 500,000 and were neglected by humanitarian aid organizations.
>
> c) The Serbian people have been and still are conditioned by a totalitarian propaganda that denounces the "plot" against Orthodoxy and the alliance between the Vatican and Islam, and tirelessly repeats the atrocious memories of the country's history: in Croatia, the genocide of the Second World War; in Bosnia, the more than 500 years of Ottoman abuses in which certain feudal Serbs became accomplices by converting to Islam....

d) The confusion between the realms of politics and religion (as in Northern Ireland), in both "Catholic" Croatia and "Orthodox" Serbia. Although, in reality, all the combatants belong to the same ethnic group, the psychological and sociological factor of "religious affiliation" has created pseudo-ethnic groups which all seek to purify themselves through appalling displacements of populations.[46]

## *The "Glorious Concept" of the Greek Orthodox Church and the Question of the Leadership of the Patriarch of Constantinople*[47]

Isabelle Dépret is affiliated with the Center of the History of Political Sciences and also with the Center for Interdisciplinary Studies of Religion (CNRS, EHESS, Paris). She is a former member of the Ecole Française of Athens. Depret's doctoral thesis, which she defended at the Institute for Political Studies in Paris under the direction of Pierre Milza and in collaboration with the University of Athens, explores the complex relationship between the high clergy of the Greek Orthodox Church and political power since the beginning of the 19th century. Her book *Religion, nation, citoyenneté en Grèce* reveals the inability of the Greek Church to accept the modern act of distinguishing between belonging to a nation and belonging to a Church. On the occasion of the 1993 debate over whether EU ID cards should include one's religion, the Orthodox hierarchy made known its objections to the directives of the European Parliament by invoking the "consubstantial link between Orthodoxy and the nation." In spite of the opposition of Bishop Christodoulos, the archbishop of Athens, religion was expunged from the ID card as of January 1, 2001.

For Isabelle Dépret, Patriarch Bartholomew's more favorable reaction to the initiative of the European Parliament was one of the decisive factors in this polemic. Dépret observes the connection between Orthodox ecclesiology (which, as we have seen, questions, in practice, the real authority of the ecumenical patriarch over the other local churches) and the social doctrine of the Orthodox Church (in particular, its protest against states

46 Olivier Clément, "Liminaire," *Contacts*, Oct.–Dec. 1993, http://www.revue-contacts.com/archives/contacts164.php.

47 Isabelle Dépret, *L'Eglise orthodoxe et l'histoire en Grèce contemporaine. Versions officielles et controverses historiographiques*, Paris, L'Harmattan, 2009; Isabelle Dépret, *Religion, nation, citoyenneté en Grèce: L'Eglise orthodoxe et le conflit des cartes d'identité*, Paris, L'Harmattan, 2011.

which do not recognize its identification with the nation). The emergence of national churches would be nothing other than the consequence of the end of the political leadership of the Patriarch of Constantinople, who, even under the Turkish Empire, was respected as ethnarch by Orthodox Greeks:

> The Greek Orthodox Church can be viewed through the prism of an initial conflict between two sources of authority: a more recent prerogative—that of the civil authorities of the new state—and a more traditional one—that of the Patriarch of Constantinople. In one way or another, these two authorities can pretend to represent—or direct—the Hellenic national community, which, in its turn, has to redefine itself. In the early days of the new state, the authority of the King of Greece and that of the Patriarch of Constantinople tended to present themselves to the Greek Orthodox clergy as two opposing and mutually exclusive allegiances. The acceptance of the modern Greek state by the Orthodox clergy at the beginning of the 19th century was far from evident. The thorny fact that the first sovereigns of Greece were "foreigners" is an insufficient explanation of these conflicting relations. But, even in the early 19th century, certain concepts of Greek nationalism which recognized the religious tradition began to take form. In this context, the Orthodox Church was a crucial—even symbolic—focus of concentration of the tension between the logic of a nation-state and an imperial logic.[48]

The modern history of the Greek Church enables us to understand this fusion of the national principle with the ecclesial principle. Between 1453 and 1821, Greece was occupied by the Ottoman Turks. The Church of the Kingdom of Greece proclaimed its independence from the ecumenical patriarchate on July 23, 1833. From that time on, the rule of the Church was entrusted to a synod composed of five members along with a permanent procurator representing the government, all of whom were appointed by the king.[49] Henceforth, the Church was used by the state and at the same

48 Isabelle Dépret, "L'Eglise orthodoxe de Grèce et le 'combat' des cartes d'identité (2000–2001)," *Archives de sciences sociales des religions* (July–December 2005): 131–32, http://assr.revues.org/3254.

49 It was only 17 years later, in 1853, that the Greek Church was recognized by Constantinople.

time functioned as the source of this state control. The constitution of Greece, proclaimed in the name of the Holy Trinity, was interpreted by the Orthodox Church as the foundation of the latter's moral authority over the state. The state, however, wanted to use the Church to recover Constantinople and restore the glory of Byzantine Hellenism. According to this "glorious concept," the Greco-Orthodox world had a universal mission which involved rule over the Balkan Peninsula and the Near East. The difficulties in a territorial realization of this idealized destiny led to the formation of a new nationalist ideology which George Prevelakis named "new Hellenism."[50] This ideology was part of the framework of Greek history from 1830 to the expulsion of the Greeks from Asia Minor by the Turkish government in 1924.[51]

The Second World War, the Cold War and the entry into NATO alongside Italy and Turkey did nothing to extinguish the "glorious concept" of the reconquest of the Byzantine world. Patriarch Makarios III, an archbishop who was elected president of Cyprus in 1959, was a partisan of the *Enosis*, the integration of the island to Greece. The 1974 uprising which sought to reverse this process provoked an intervention in Cyprus on the part of the Greek armed forces. This in turn led to a Turkish invasion of the island and subsequently its partitioning between the Republic of Cyprus and the Turkish Republic of North Cyprus. The entry of Greece into the European Union in 1981 was, in many aspects, more a phenomenon of compensation than an occasion to embrace the principles of modern civilization (separation of powers, secularity, economic transparency). Even though its constitution guarantees religious liberty, Greece has yet to achieve a separation between the Church and the State.

For Isabelle Dépret, the future evolution of Greek identity—especially the possibility of the Greek Church abandoning its nostalgic vision of the "glorious concept"—depends, above all, on the clarification of the relationship between the Church of Greece and the Ecumenical Patriarchate:

50 Georges Prevelakis, *Les Balkans,* Paris, Nathan, 1994.

51 From 1830 to 1914, Greece extended northwards with the conquest of Thessalia, Macedonia, Thrace, Crete and the islands of the Aegean Sea, in part through the Balkan War of 1912–1913 and a second one later in 1913. The First World War offered Greece the Treaty of Sevres, but the Greco-Turkish War of 1919–1922 and the ensuing treaty of Lausanne invalidated the former treaty and provoked the "great catastrophe"—the provisional end of the "New Hellenism" project and the exchanges of populations between Greece and Turkey.

> The tensions between the Archbishop of Athens and the Patriarch of Constantinople at the close of the 20th century are nothing new. There have been open disagreements for several decades. The mistrust of the "ecumenical movement" by the Greek Church is a prime example. Since the early 1960s, the Patriarchate of Constantinople has promoted dialogue and even rapprochement with other religious communities—especially with other expressions of Christian dogma. The Orthodox Synod of Athens sees this as a submission and betrayal. During the 1990s, under Archbishop Seraphim, the gap between the two centers widened. Among the challenges confronting the new Archbishop of Athens, elected in April of 1998, was the improvement of relations with the Patriarchate. Between the years 1998 and 2001, the tensions persisted. . . . [52]

The confrontation between civil and religious power in Greece should be understood in the context of the other aspect of the Byzantine heritage represented by the international authority of the Ecumenical Patriarchate of Constantinople with its twofold dimension—political and religious (as the term "ecumenical" implies from a historical viewpoint). The Turkish government has refused to recognize Patriarch Bartholomew's title of Ecumenical Patriarch even though other European governments have done so:[53]

> The question of the presence of Orthodoxy in Europe—a presence which is spiritual and cultural but also institutional and ecclesiastic—is not just a factor of solidarity among the different Orthodox Churches of Europe. It also makes manifest differences, sometimes rivalries, among the churches who are searching for their place within a political process which is redefining itself. In the face of the dogmas that underline the fundamental unity of the Church, in its diversity and local expressions, there are the national or state-linked ecclesiastical structures, very much attached to their institutional expression and specificities and by no means ready to sacrifice their status or their right to make autonomous decisions. This possibility of conflicts of authority illustrates the

52 Isabelle Dépret, "L'Eglise orthodoxe de Grèce."

53 Antoine Arjakovsky, "L'oecuménisme en Europe, approche religieuse et politique," *La Revue des deux mondes* (April 2012): 126–38.

relationship between the Archbishop of Athens and the Patriarch of Constantinople. The very proximity of these two centers is a potential source of tension. The confrontation which came to a head in 2000–2001 concerning the ID cards should be seen in this context. The challenge issued by the Church to the Greek civil authorities seems to have had an underlying plan which was both personal and institutional: to affirm the authority of the Archbishop of Athens and this, above all, *within* the Orthodox Church.[54]

54 Isabelle Dépret, op. cit.

# CHAPTER 3

# *The Piety, Doctrine, and Practices of the Orthodox Churches*

## HOW SHOULD THESE BE DEFINED?

Just as most contemporary authors do not take into account either the discrepancy between history and memory in their conceptualist understanding of the past of the Orthodox Church or the risks of tearing apart the Orthodox Church through representations seeking a strict identity, 20th-century confessional presentations of Orthodox piety and doctrine suffer from the non-recognition of the frequent disparity between the proclamation of the truths of the faith and actual practice. Admittedly there exist numerous and remarkable works presenting the spirituality and the faith of the Orthodox Church. It suffices to mention those of Kallistos Ware,[1] Olivier Clément,[2] Paul Evdokimov[3] and Sergius Bulgakov.[4] It is not our intention to repeat here what has already been said so well elsewhere, nor to offer a résumé of Orthodox theology and spirituality. What we will try to do is take the hesychastic path — the heart of Orthodox spirituality — as a *starting point* rather than *as an object*, and use this to analyze the discrepancies between ortho-doxy and ortho-praxis. Orthodox intellectuals have produced an abundant literature on the art of the icon but have very little to say about contemporary art;[5] they have offered profound reflections on the Wisdom of God[6] but neglected practical wisdom in the domains of politics, economy and law.[7]

1 K. Ware, *Le Royaume intérieur,* Paris, Cerf, 1996.

2 O. Clément, *Sources, les mystiques chrétiens des origines,* Paris, Stock, 1992.

3 P. Evdokimov, *L'art de l'icône, la théologie et la beauté,* Paris, DDB, 1970.

4 S. Bulgakov, *L'Orthodoxie,* Paris, L'Age d'Homme, 1982.

5 Wladimir Weidlé, *Les abeilles d'Aristée: Essai sur le destin actuel des lettres et des arts,* Paris, Gallimard, 1954.

6 Sergius Bulgakov, *La Sagesse de Dieu,* Paris, L'Age d'Homme, 1982.

7 Archbishop Anastasios Yannoulatos, *Facing the World: Orthodox Christian Essays*

There are wonderful studies of Orthodox Christian holiness,[8] but few works concerning present-day living icons.[9] The *New Orthodox Encyclopedia*, edited by the patriarchate of Moscow[10] and comprising more than twenty volumes, focuses on Orthodox identity, as does the excellent encyclopedia published in New York under the direction of John McGuckin.[11] One would hope for an attitude more fundamentally ecumenical and interreligious on the part of Orthodox Christianity, putting forward the universal character of Christian anthropology.[12] Such an approach would allow for the integration of the global rediscovery of Orthodox Christianity which is taking place today beyond the confessional boundaries of the Orthodox Church, from Rowan Williams to Pope Benedict XVI.[13] An anthropological approach would also facilitate future reconciliations with the great religious traditions of the world and with modern humanism.[14]

We would like to show that Orthodoxy is more a *lifestyle* than a doctrine, rite, or way of envisaging the world. This lifestyle is characterized by a symbolic, epiphanic and eschatological relationship with the world. The famous accounts of the Russian pilgrim[15] sum up all the spirituality and ascetic teachings of the *Philokalia*, a collection of spiritual texts drawn from the writings of the Fathers of the Church.[16] In one of the narratives, the pilgrim, citing St. Peter of Damascus, affirms that uninterrupted prayer, the awareness of the

---

*on Global Concerns,* Crestwood, NY, St. Vladimir's Seminary Press, 2003.

8 Hieromonk Macairius of Simonis-Petra, *Synaxaire. Vie des saints de l'Eglise Orthodoxe*, vol. 2, Athens, Editions Indiktos, 2010.

9 Michael Plekon, *Living Icons,* Notre Dame, IN, University of Notre Dame Press, 2002.

10 *Pravoslavna Encyclopedia,* Moscow, Ruskaja Pravoslavnaja Tserkov, 1997–2012.

11 *The Encyclopedia of Eastern Orthodox Christianity*, ed. John McGuckin, New York, Wiley-Blackwell, 2011.

12 O. Clément, *Mémoires d'espérance,* Paris, DDB, 2003.

13 Cf. R. Williams, *Lost Icons: Reflections on Cultural Bereavement*, Bloomsbury Academic, 2002; trans. *Icônes perdues*, Paris, Cerf, 2005; Joseph Ratzinger, *Pilgrim Fellowship of Faith, The Church as Communion,* Ignatius Press, 2005; *La communion de la foi. Croire et célébrer,* Paris, Parole et Silence, 2008.

14 Cf. Mohamed Talbi, Olivier Clément, *Un respect têtu,* Paris, Nouvelle Cite, 1989; Harry Oldmeadow, *Henri Le Saux, christianisme et spiritualité indienne,* Paris, Almora, 2010; Antoine Guggenheim, *Pour un nouvel humanisme,* Paris, Parole et Silence, 2011.

15 *The Way of a Pilgrim and Other Classics of Russian Spirituality*, ed. G.P. Fedotov, Mineola, New York, Dover Publications, 2003; New York, Harper, 1965; London, Sheed and Ward, 1950.

16 *La philocalie,* tomes I and II, presented by Olivier Clément, D.D.B. and J.C. Lattes, 1995; *The Philokalia, compiled by St. Nikodimos of the Holy Mountain and St. Makarios of Corinth*, a collection of texts first published in Greek in 1782, Farrar, Strauss and Giroux, 1983.

interaction between the heavenly world and the earthly world, constitutes the very center of Christian existence: "One must strive more to invoke the Name of Jesus than to breathe—always, everywhere, at every occasion. The Apostle tells us to 'pray without ceasing'; by that he teaches us one must be mindful of God always, everywhere and in everything."[17] Paul Evdokimov observes that while the Fathers of the Church were well versed in the culture of their times and did not hesitate to use the technical categories of current philosophical and scientific thought, they never stopped at a "theology of concepts." They aspired to the science which becomes love. St. Basil writes that "true theology liberates the passions."[18] Theology cannot be pure meditation; it must be practical. It must lead to an effort of self-domination and a commitment to strive for the transformation of the world. Orthodox faith and piety thus tend to come together in the form of personal and contextual examples; they do not remain theoretical and disincarnate.

### *The Definition of Orthodoxy According to the Confession of Faith*

There are some Orthodox who try to define "the Orthodox faith" by the Nicene-Constantinopolitan Creed (381), which is common to the entire body of Orthodox Churches. This is the text:

> We believe in one God, the Father Almighty, Creator of heaven and earth, of all things visible and invisible. And in one Lord Jesus Christ, the only Son of God, born of the Father before all ages, Light of Light, True God of True God, begotten not made, one in Being with the Father, through whom all things were made; who for us men and our salvation came down from heaven and was incarnate of the Holy Spirit, born of the Virgin Mary and became man. He was crucified for us under Pontius Pilate, suffered death and was buried. On the third day he arose again according to the Scriptures. He ascended into heaven and sits at the right hand of the Father. He will come again in glory to judge the living and the dead and his Kingdom will have no end.

17 *Récits d'un pèlerin russe*, trans. by Jean Laloy, Paris, Seuil, 1996, 127; *The Way of a Pilgrim*, trans. Nina Toumanova, Dover Publications, 2012.

18 Paul Evdokimov, *La connaissance de Dieu selon la tradition orientale*, Paris, DDB, 1988.

> We believe in the Holy Spirit, the Lord, Giver of life, who proceeds from the Father, who with the Father and the Son is adored and glorified, who spoke through the prophets; we believe in one holy, catholic and apostolic Church. We acknowledge one baptism for the forgiveness of sins; we await the resurrection of the dead and the life of the world to come. Amen.

To define Orthodoxy by the profession of faith is the equivalent of identifying the Orthodox Churches with the Catholic Church, the Anglican Church as well as the Lutheran and Reformed Churches, all of which recognize the orthodoxy of this confession. In August of 1990, at Dunblane (Scotland) the Faith and Order Commission of the World Council of Churches, composed of representatives of more than 350 churches, including the Catholic Church, the Orthodox Church and the principal Protestant Churches (Lutheran, Reformed, Anglican, Pentecostal), agreed on a mutual acceptance of this creed. This agreement found its expression (and an updated commentary) in a text entitled Confessing the One Faith.[19] Among those who assisted at this meeting were the future Patriarch of Constantinople Metropolitan Bartholomew of Chalcedon, Jean-Marie Tillard (Catholic Church), Wolfhart Pannenberg (Lutheran Church), Mary Tanner (Anglican Church), and John Deschner (Methodist Church). Such a manner of defining Orthodoxy is not embraced by a great number of Orthodox theologians and hierarchs who seek to preserve the specific identity of their Church in an era of globalization where all sorts of deviant syncretisms are being diffused.

## *The Definition of Orthodoxy According to its Sacramental Life*

Others believe that Orthodox piety should be defined through the sacraments and the institutions which recognize them. This approach tries to identify the frontiers of grace with institutional boundaries. This approach is equally problematic. Certain Orthodox churches recognize the sacraments of other churches — the Greek Orthodox Church in Germany recognizes the validity of the baptism conferred by the German Evangelical Church — while others do not; the same Greek Church, in Greece, does not recognize the validity of baptism in the German Evangelical Church. Moreover, such an approach,

19 *Confessing the One Faith. An Ecumenical Explication of the Apostolic Faith as it is Confessed in the Nicene-Constantinople Creed (381)*, Geneva, WWC, 1991.

which attempts to put limits on the workings of the Spirit, has not been historically homogeneous. Whereas the Russian Church gave Eucharistic hospitality to Catholics between 1970 and 1984, it has maintained a different position since 1985. And if it is true that iconography plays an important role in the Orthodox liturgical tradition, be it Byzantine, Arabic or Slavic, it is also a fact that, more and more, holy images are being venerated in Catholic and Protestant churches as well.

A "conceptualist" approach is not adequate for a true understanding of Orthodox faith and piety. The Chalcedonian Orthodox churches are called "sacramental." But, according to John Meyendorff, one of the most eminent specialists in Orthodox theology and spirituality, "Byzantine theology does not employ the Western distinction between 'sacraments' and 'sacramentals' and never officially limited the sacraments to a fixed number.... The term *mysterion* was mainly used in a very large and general sense to refer to the 'mystery of salvation' and only secondarily to designate the particular 'actions' which bring salvation."[20] In other words, the Orthodox faith can be lived through its sacramental life but cannot be contained by it. The sacraments of initiation of the Orthodox churches are baptism (by immersion), chrismation (or the unction of the Spirit) and the Eucharist (communion to the Body and Blood of Jesus Christ — to which the newly baptized is immediately admitted irrespective of age). The other sacraments administered by these churches are marriage, ordination, extreme unction and confession. However, St. Theodore the Studite considered the monastic tonsure and burial also to be sacraments. Nicholas Cabasilas composed his famous book *The Life in Christ* as a commentary on the illumination, unique but constantly exercised by the faithful, of baptism, chrismation, and the Eucharist. Olivier Clément summarized Orthodox spirituality borrowing from St. Paul: "Make the Eucharist in all things."

## *The Definition of Orthodoxy According to the Notion of Hellenistic or Byzantine-Slavonic Civilization*

The geographical and cultural limits of a church cannot define its identity. Nor can the Orthodox faith, theology and piety be "restricted" to the Eastern churches. If the Orthodox faith is not universal, it is meaningless. After the Second World War, many Orthodox intellectuals living in the West were convinced that the crisis which the world had just suffered was linked to

20 J. Meyendorff, *Initiation à la théologie byzantine,* Paris, Cerf, 1975, 253.

a crisis in Western Christianity, and they tried to put forward a universal and positive image of the faith and piety of the Eastern Church. In his 1944 book *The Mystical Theology of the Eastern Church*, Vladimir Lossky became one of the first to emphasize the universal, and not just regional, relevance of this church: "Orthodoxy has been the ferment of too many different cultures to be considered as a cultural form of Eastern Christianity; these forms are diverse, the faith is the same."[21]

In practice, however, this post-territorial universalism of the Orthodox faith needed time to evolve into a post-cultural concept. Several intellectuals, such as V. Lossky, G. Florovsky, and C. Yannaras, have defined Orthodoxy through its opposition to modern Western culture. The Church, which formerly called itself the Eastern Orthodox Catholic Church, now defines itself as "*kat'holic*" in opposition to a Catholic Church characterized by its monarchical structure, its rationalist theology, and its individualistic mysticism.[22] The new Orthodox theologians were rather indignant at the way their faith was simplified and qualified as a "vague mysticism" by Catholics. V. Lossky criticized Yves Congar, one of the most ecumenical Catholic theologians, for his inability to appreciate the effective separation between the Orthodox churches and their national states. Paul Evdokimov affirmed the theandric (divine-human) dimension of the Christian faith in opposition to the "naivety of Harnack" and his Protestant disciples.[23] Paul Evdokimov and V. Lossky, caught up in their apologetic defense of the Orthodox Church, have arrived at generalities on the themes of "the mystic East" and "the moralistic West." Without taking into account all of the consequences of his simplifications, Paul Evdokimov identified all of Catholicism with Abelard and all of Orthodoxy with Gregory Palamas: "In the face of scholasticism, as a level of religious knowledge with its analytical and thereby rationalistic method, the East prefers a spiritual wisdom where dogma, mystical contemplation, theology and philosophy all come together."[24] In opposition to a Western theology charged with rationally deducing God's attributes from the concept of Being, Eastern theology was glorified, in the 1950s to the 1970s, for its radically transcendent representation of the essence of God: "only the Divine operations — the energies, grace — are immanent and admit of participation."[25]

21 V. Lossky, *Essai sur la théologie mystique de l'Eglise d'Orient,* Paris, Cerf, 1990.
22 Ibid., 18.
23 P. Evdokimov, *L'Orthodoxie,* Paris, DDB, 1979 (1965), 15.
24 Ibid., 17.
25 Ibid., 27.

This account of Eastern theology and spirituality as radically distinct from Western theology was questioned by the Catholic Father Marie-Joseph Le Guillou, a great friend of the Orthodox Church.[26] In his book *Le mystère du Père*, published in 1973, Father Le Guillou pointed out that Gregory Palamas, at the end of his life, became aware of the risks of a theology which made too radical a distinction between the intra-divine life of the Persons of the Trinity and their acts:

> [Gregory Palamas] realized that what distinguishes the works *ad extra* from the necessity of the Divine Essence is not an entitative or formal distinction but is based on the fact that they have their primal and gratuitous origin in the Divine Persons whose relationship is made manifest in the economy. In this respect, Gregory echoes the pre-Nicaean concept of the Trinitarian Council. It is in this same context that he adopts the Augustinian doctrine of processions according to the order of intelligence (Word) and according to the order of love (Spirit) through a need to defend the articulation of acts *ad extra* and the order of the consubstantial Trinitarian Life (*Capita physica*, ch. 37).[27]

Father Le Guillou's warning was not heeded by the successors of Lossky and Evdokimov. Even though he admits that it was only through Palamas that Platonism was finally transcended in the Byzantine Church, John Meyendorff affirms that the Greek saint and his disciples always maintained that "God is totally present in His Essence and energies." The generation of the neo-Patristic theologians led by George Florovsky, John Meyendorff, Alexander Schmemann and Kallistos Ware believed — anachronistically — that the debate which opposed Gregory Palamas and Barlaam of Calabria was symbolic of the longstanding opposition between "Orthodox mystical" theology and a

26 Father Le Guillou entered the Dominican order in 1941. He taught at Saulchoir and was on the theology faculty of the Institut Catholique. He was the director of the Institut Supérieur d'Etudes Oecuméniques and was a member of the International Commission of Catholic Theology. Among his other publications is a 1962 book entitled *L'Esprit de l'Orthodoxie grecque et russe*. He knew Father Sergius Bulgakov and was a friend of Olivier Clément, with whom he founded the Institut Oecumenique of the Institut Catholique de Paris. Cf. Patrick Chauvet et al., *Le Père Le Guillou, un maître, éveilleur de la liberté*, Paris, Parole et Silence, 2010.

27 Le Guillou, *Le mystère du Père*, Paris, Fayard, 1973, 106–107.

"Platonizing Catholic" theology.[28] But it is no secret that, over the centuries, the Orthodox churches themselves were tempted by monophysitism, as well as by Scholastic, Calvinist and Lutheran theologies.[29] Many Orthodox theologians dismiss such critiques by stating that the Orthodox world was affected by the germs of heresy only because of its contact with the Western world. They claim that "Orthodoxy contracted the disease of nationalism through the Enlightenment. To rid itself of this disorder would therefore require dewesternization and not the opposite."[30]

A colloquium held at Fordham University June 28–30, 2010, dedicated to the question of the *Orthodox Conception of the West*, proposed a more historical and less mythicized reading of the history of the church.[31] Most of the Orthodox assisting at the conference criticized certain anti-Western theses of Christos Yannaras and argued that, in modern times, the Orthodox churches were simply unable to mount an intellectual defense against the ideas of Darwin, Hegel and Marx. Moreover, in this epoch of globalization, the Orthodox churches are progressively discovering that they are more westernized than they had previously imagined.

In order to understand the piety, faith and commitment of the Orthodox churches, the anthropological approach is probably more appropriate than the confessional perspective. The former can be qualified as authentically neo-Patristic insofar as it is essentially theanthropic, philokalic and nonconfessional. There are three types of mentalities that can be found in all churches, regardless of the particular confession: the ascetic profile, the missionary profile and the spiritual profile.[32] Of course, the boundaries between these different ecclesial mentalities are not all that well defined.[33] It is preferable to refer to an ascetic, missionary, or spiritual *orientation* rather than attributing defined and exclusive identities to such things. These spiritual streams need

28 Few and far between are those who, like Michel Stavrou, acknowledge an experience of the uncreated Light in Western mysticism. See Stavrou, "Les énergies divines," in *Les richesses de l'Orient chrétien,* ed. P. Baud and M. Egger, Paris, Le Sel de la Terre, 2000.

29 Nicolas Kazarian, "L'Eglise dans la correspondance entre le patriarche Jeremie II et les luthériens de Tübingen," *Positions lutheriennes* 55/2 (2007): 111–24.

30 J. F. Colosimo, *Le silence des anges,* Paris, DDB, 2001, 157.

31 https://www.fordham.edu/info/25444/2010_orthodox_constructions_of_the_west.

32 A. Arjakovsky, "L'Eglise Orthodoxe et l'oecuménisme," in *En attendant le concile de l'Eglise Orthodoxe,* Paris, Cerf, 2011.

33 They are similar to the medieval fiefs. Princes ruled their territory, but this did not prohibit them from sometimes waging war on the territories of their neighbors, where they could eventually establish enclaves.

one another; otherwise asceticism would dry up and become traditionalism, the missionary spirit would degenerate into an aggressive proselytism, and spiritual understanding would be transformed into a naive optimism. A brief presentation of some of the works of famous Orthodox authors will help us to clarify certain characteristics of these different orientations.

## THREE FORMS OF ANTHROPOLOGICAL CONSCIOUSNESS

### *Piety, Faith and Ascetic Commitment*

Msgr. Anthony Bloom (1914–2003), metropolitan of Sourozh, was the head of the Russian Orthodox Church in England for several decades (1962–2002). Two of his books have recently been published in French. One consists of texts written between 1966 and 1984 and is entitled *Entretiens sur la foi et l'Eglise*. A second book, translated and introduced by Father Evdokimov, is entitled *La vie, la maladie et la mort*. It incorporates two interviews conducted in 1976 and several talks which date from 1984. These texts are preceded by an "autobiographical sketch" of this "doctor of bodies who became a doctor of souls."

Bishop Bloom was one of the masters of Orthodox ascetic spirituality. He was born in Lausanne; his father was a Russian diplomat stationed in Switzerland who had his son baptized into the Orthodox Church. His spiritual rebirth, however, came much later: in 1930, when he was a young Russian immigrant in Paris. Outraged by the degradation of his family, he declared himself an atheist. Yet following a chance meeting with Sergius Bulgakov, he decided to read one of the Gospels. This led to a powerful and personal encounter with Christ. He described this moment for the first time in 1973, when he was 60 years old:

> I sat down to read, and between the beginning of the first chapter of Mark and the beginning of the third chapter, which I read slowly because of its unusual language, I suddenly felt that Christ was standing opposite me at the table. . . . I was so shocked that I had to stop reading and look. I looked for a long while and saw nothing, heard nothing, perceived nothing with my senses. Yet still, when I looked straight in front of me, at this spot where there was no one, I could not escape the clear perception that there was no doubt that *Christ was present there*. I remember that I had the sudden intuition that "If the living Christ is here, then

> Christ is *risen*." Thus, I know, through a totally trustworthy and personal experience, that Christ is risen, that, therefore, all that the Gospels say of him is true. The first Christians followed the same logic: they found Christ and came to believe, not because someone told them about what had happened from the beginning, but through an encounter with the living Christ and, *because of this encounter*, the risen Christ became he of whom they had heard and thus all that they had heard was also true. I continued to read but everything had changed.[34]

The young Anthony Bloom thus decided to consecrate his whole life to the Church. His voice gained worldwide recognition to the extent that in the 1970s, he was rated among the 15 most popular personalities in Great Britain after the queen and the Beatles. In his numerous writings, he showed that the most authentic Christian Orthodox spirituality consists above all in the battle against the passions—pride, lust, gluttony, anger, etc.[35] In *Entretiens sur la foi et sur l'Eglise*, he reveals the ardor and capacity of the hesychast ascetics for the practice of the prayer of the heart, the prayer that unites

34 Metropolitan Anthony of Sourozh, *La vie, la maladie, la mort*, Paris, Cerf, 2012, 39.

35 Metropolitan Anthony of Sourozh was born on June 19, 1914, at Lausanne. His father was a Russian diplomat stationed in Switzerland. His paternal ancestors were of Scottish origin who moved to Russia during the period of Peter the Great. His mother was from the same family as the Russian composer Scriabin. Anthony Bloom spent his childhood in Iran where his father was consul. His family emigrated to Europe after the revolution and settled in Paris in 1923. Anthony received his medical diploma from the Sorbonne. He was ordained a lector at the parish of The Three Holy Doctors (patriarchate of Moscow) in 1931. On September 10, 1939, he pronounced his monastic vows just prior to his departure to the front lines as a surgeon in the French Army. In honor of Saint Anthony of the Caves, he was tonsured on April 16, 1943, on Lazarus Sunday, by the Archimandrite Athanasius (Netchaev). During the war, the monk Anthony participated in the Resistance. He was named metropolitan on January 27, 1966 but left his position as exarch in the Spring of 1974. He was a member of the Central Committee of the World Council of Churches from 1968 to 1975. Beginning in 1968, his writings began to be published in Russia in the journal of the patriarchate. He was very popular in England where he published several works on prayer and spirituality. He was a dynamic force within his diocese and received honorary degrees from several universities. During the 1990s, he became famous in Russia where millions of people were converted to Orthodoxy and often used his writings as a baptismal preparation. In 2002, Bloom found himself in conflict with the patriarchate of Moscow concerning the future of his diocese which was already well integrated into British social life. He died on August 4, 2003, at the age of 89 after he refused, in February, to preside over an autonomous metropolis in Western Europe proposed by the patriarchate of Moscow.

the heart and the mind. Bloom shows how the interior struggle enables one to save oneself from the world of passions, from a self-centered life (*bios* in Greek), and to discover that, in Christ, everyone can die to self and be reborn to true life (*zoe* in Greek). Bloom is also one of the most eminent proponents of Orthodox apophatic theology. This theology, which rejects any attempt to define God, is a militantly anti-Communist and anti-ideological theology. Bloom enjoyed great success in Russia through his radio programs broadcast in Russian by the BBC, in which he tried to combat atheistic ideology and announce the Good News of the Gospel. The apophaticism of the Christian faith, which refuses to reduce God to a concept or any purely human representation, was, at that time, the greatest threat to ideological thought. The systematic negation of concepts radically questioned the scientific atheism of dialectical materialism.

But the ascetic stream of Orthodox theology from the 18th century to the 20th often identified apophatic theology with all of theology. Such a perspective is unable to suggest that evil has no basis in creation, that it becomes a reality only when a person turns aside from his divine vocation. For Metropolitan Anthony, God created mankind free: "This freedom has within itself the possibility of either good or evil" (*Entretiens*, 27). He thus identifies created freedom with fallen freedom. Freedom as a gift, as participation, is reduced to the mere freedom of choice. In accordance with a certain tradition of biblical exegesis, Bloom imagines that God governs the world with good and evil as His weapons; the good for his glorification, the evil so as to put humanity back on the right path. He doesn't for one moment imagine that the all-powerful God might have merely created freedom for eternal life (*zoe*), for in this case, God would be an "inept mechanic" (29). He is afraid to recognize that the world might be unaccomplished, that it needs the participation of humans to realize the divine plan. He imagines creation ultimately as an act external to humanity, outside the divine Trinity.

This sort of reasoning leads Bloom to distrust all types of rationality. Faced with persistent questions from the atheist journalist questioning him, he was unable to explain the sufferings of Job and subsequently shifted his position. Suffering is not caused by God but by man: "A major part of the misfortunes, sufferings and torments of people are caused by sin, just by sin, in the sense that if a person is malicious, he engenders evil and suffering and, moreover, disfigures himself, becomes frightening and ceases to be human" (30). The whole relationship between God and humanity is presented by Metropolitan Anthony as an incomprehensible and inaccessible mystery, as an unobjectifiable sacrament. In fact, however, because of this apophatic representation of God, the sacraments come to be defined in an institutional context: "The sacraments are divine acts, accomplished within the heart of the Church, through which God gives his grace by the mediation of the material world in which we find ourselves" (107). Such an approach is certainly Orthodox, but it is also incomplete.

## *Piety, Faith, and Missionary Commitments*

This is one of the reasons why, despite the already abundant literature on the Orthodox Church, Hilarion Alfeyev decided to write an additional book on Christian doctrine: *La doctrine de l'Eglise orthodoxe.*[36] Msgr. Hilarion, born in 1966, is the metropolitan of Volokalamsk in Russia. As vicar-patriarch of the Orthodox Church and as a permanent member of the Holy Synod, he has been in charge of the Department of Foreign Relations of the Patriarchate of Moscow since March of 2009. *La doctrine de l'Eglise orthodoxe* is the second of his five-volume work entitled *L'Orthodoxie,* a collection considered in Russia to be a legitimate version of Orthodox doctrine. Alfeyev contends that the Church needs to offer a positive narrative concerning both God and itself; the Church needs a certain degree of rationality when one realizes that the struggle against the passions cannot be just an individual concern.

36 Metropolitan Hilarion Alfeyev was born on July 24, 1966, in Moscow. Between 1973 and 1983 he studied violin and composition at the Gnessin Musical Institute and subsequently enrolled in the Tchaikovsky Conservatory for composition classes. But in 1984 he was drafted into the army for two years. Upon completing his military service, he became a novice at the Monastery of the Holy Spirit at Vilnius. He became a monk on June 19, 1987, then hierodeacon and hieromonk in August of that same year. In 1990, Bishop Chrysostom appointed him priest at the Cathedral of Kaunas. He finished his seminary studies by correspondence in 1989 and, in 1991, his studies at the Moscow Theological Academy. On January 14, 2002, he was consecrated bishop of Kertch by the patriarch Alexis II. In 2002, after an assignment in London where he had a painful personal and public confrontation with Msgr. Anthony Bloom, he became bishop of the Russian Church of Brussels and an Orthodox presence to the European Union. On May 7, 2003, the Holy Synod named him bishop of Vienna and Austria. He remained in this function until March 31, 2009, when the patriarch of Moscow and his synod named him president of the Department of External Relations of the Moscow Patriarchy, patriarchal vicar, and a permanent member of the Holy Synod. This made him one of the principal official personalities of the worldwide Orthodox Church. He is the author of dozens of publications and the composer of several musical works—among which is a setting of *The Passion According to Saint Matthew.*

Alfeyev cannot accept the traditional apophatic approach; he seeks conceptual discourse. This leads him to an ahistoric and non-critical conceptualism.[37] "According to the Orthodox tradition,"[38] he asserts, the enigmatic Biblical figure of the Wisdom of God is "identified with Christ." In spite of dozens of studies which show the diverse ways the figure of Wisdom is interpreted by the Fathers of the Church, Alfeyev only mentions the fact that the Saint Sophia Cathedral of Constantinople identifies the Wisdom of God with Christ and that, for him, is decisive.[39]

This is one of the reasons he maintains that the Russian philosopher Vladimir Soloviev "cannot be classified as an Orthodox intellectual."[40] He is also unable to accept the complex and nuanced definition of the Wisdom of God articulated by Sergius Bulgakov, who distinguished between Created Wisdom and Uncreated Wisdom. Bulgakov also believed that the most extended and complete revelation we have concerning the Church, "insofar as it is 'humanity in the Theanthropy' and an unwedded spouse, is its identification with created Wisdom." This is why Bulgakov believed that Mary, the Mother of God, was the personal recapitulation of the Church, Wisdom itself, still created but entirely deified, the summit of creation. "She is the Pneumatophore, the Spirit and the Spouse who, through her very being, reveals the image of the hypostatic Spirit of God."[41]

In his first volume, dedicated to the history and canonical structures of the Orthodox Church, Alfeyev acknowledges that many works have already been written about Orthodox Christianity. He mentions in particular *L'Eglise des sept conciles* by Kallistos Ware. However, Alfeyev believes that the books, written by Westerners for a Western public in (for instance) the 1960s, cannot claim to be fully and legitimately Orthodox.[42] His own work

37 In this perspective, his plan of presentation of the "doctrine of the Orthodox Church" is eloquent: God, the world and humanity, Christ, the Church, eschatology. As if nothing historic or "human" should be part of theology, of the "divine." In this volume, the history of the Church is presented separately—as is the history of piety.

38 M. Alfeyev, *L'Orthodoxie,* Paris, Cerf, 2009, vol. 1, 216.

39 A. Arjakovsky, *Essai sur le père Serge Bulgakov,* Paris, Parole et Silence, 2006. Cf. also Maurice Gilbert, *Les cinq livres des Sages,* Paris, Cerf, 2003.

40 *L'Orthodoxie,* vol. 1, 215.

41 S. Bulgakov, *L'Epouse de l'Agneau,* Paris, L'Age d'Homme/Editeurs Réunis, 1984, 396–97.

42 He takes Ware's book to have been written for "ino-slavs"—a term which means "glorify differently" and is often interpreted, because of the phonetic similarity of the terms, as "non-Slavic."

is original in that it integrates many insights of 20th-century Orthodox thinkers without emphasizing their innovative character, probably in order to avoid accusations of modernism from the ultraconservative sector of the Russian Orthodox Church. Thus, on the very first page Alfeyev states that the Orthodox Church is founded on divine revelation—a revelation historically mediated by both Holy Scripture and the oral and written tradition. This hermeneutic had been employed by Father Sergius Bulgakov in Paris during the 1930s and would be taken up again in the 1950s, within the context of the theological commission of the World Council of Churches, by Georges Florovsky. This is an approach which has gained widespread acceptance in the West but is hardly understood within a Church which certain conservative traditionalists see as the Third Rome (after Ancient Rome and Constantinople).

The whole question, however, is to discover how this hermeneutic can actualize the truth of revelation. For the Russian theologian, the Church is not only a mystery, but also an institution. Alfeyev takes the position of most Orthodox theologians since at least the 9th century: that the dogmatic definitions of the ecumenical councils, such as they are received in the Orthodox Church, possess an absolute authority.[43] However, it must be observed that the author believes the final interpretative key to be not the "councils" as such but the "definitions of the councils, received in the Orthodox Church." For proselytizing theologians, this position has the advantage of pushing to one side certain ecumenical councils, such as the council of 1439, which has now disappeared from the memory of the Orthodox Churches; but in reality it destabilizes Orthodox identity at a very profound level. How can we tell whether one definition has been "received" while another has not? The definition of the Council of Florence on the procession of the Holy Spirit had been prepared, accepted and received by the Orthodox Church of Alexandria for more than 50 years. It was only during the epoch of Turkish domination that this Church wound up rejecting the consensus of Florence, as it did through the intervention of just one of the delegates it sent to the synod of Constantinople in 1484. Moreover, in this synod of 1484, the Greek Church decided to chrismate Catholics who desired to convert to Orthodoxy (which is not the case today; now the practice is to baptize them). How can the Orthodox Church base its rejection of the decisions of the Council of Florence on a synod whose decisions it does not respect?

43 Alfeyev, *L'Orthodoxie*, vol. 1, 29.

Moreover, today the Orthodox Church of America, in conformity with the Council of Florence, believes that the doctrine of the *filioque* is no longer a source of division between Catholic and Orthodox theology. On a larger scale, many Orthodox theologians believe that the Fathers of Florence were right when they thought it possible to say that the Holy Spirit, as a hypostasis, "proceeds" (*ekporeusis*) from the Father, while insofar as sent by Christ the Holy Spirit also "proceeds" (*processio*) from the Son incarnate in history.

From the brief presentation of the doctrine of the Orthodox Church provided by Alfeyev, we have learnt that if it is defined confessionally, or in other words, in a uniquely memorial manner, it becomes somewhat fragile. The Orthodox Church cannot be reduced to the various levels of consciousness of local Churches. It cannot be governed by the criteria of "reception" alone. The Orthodox Church has never accepted the monopoly of the democratic principle in ecclesial governance. Alfeyev is right when he tries to question the apophatic approach of that generation of Orthodox intellectuals which largely favored the "neo-patristic synthesis," such as Anthony Bloom, Vladimir Lossky, Georges Florovsky, John Meyendorff, and Boris Bobrinskoy. Alfeyev admits that "certain rules laid down by the Fathers of Antiquity . . . have fallen into disuse."[44] He believes that this should lead to "an urgent revision and actualization of the code of canon law," but he does not dare to question the identity of Orthodoxy with "faithful memory" of the tradition of the first seven ecumenical councils. He does not seem to be aware of the risks of an outlook which sees itself as nothing more than conformity to an objectified past. He cannot imagine Orthodoxy in a postconfessional perspective as "true and fair knowledge," as a synthesis of truth and justice, as unity of thought and action. Yet the liturgical and biblical traditions of the Orthodox Church point towards the possibility of a literal definition of *ortho-doxis*. In Psalm III, the Lord does not want people to merely "remember His miracles"; he is not just "faithful"; His works are "justice and truth."

## *Piety, Faith, and Spiritual Commitment*

Given his concern to articulate a positive and proselyte theology, it is understandable that Alfeyev wishes to distinguish justice and truth, right practice and right doctrine. However, such an approach does not resonate with those who see the Church as first and foremost the Temple of the Holy Spirit, nor

44 Ibid.

with those who understand knowledge of the faith as a participation in the life of Christ or as concern for the least powerful.

The eminent and respected French theologian Olivier Clément[45] represents a third stream of Orthodoxy. In 1970, in collaboration with Paul

45 Olivier Clément (1921–2009) was born November 17, 1921, at Aniane, in Languedoc, a land with a tragic religious history (the Cathars, the Camisards). He came from a dechristianized milieu (peasants and school teachers), was not baptized after his birth and did not receive any religious formation. After a long quest where he flirted with the esoterism of the Oriental wisdoms he encountered Christ, thanks in great part to the works of Dostoevsky, Berdyaev, Eliade and V. Lossky. On November 1, 1952, at the age of 30, he requested and received baptism in the Orthodox Church. His Master's thesis in history at the Sorbonne was on Peter the Venerable, the Abbot of Cluny. As an assistant at the University, he studied under Alphonse Dupront, one of the founders of religious anthropology. When war broke out in 1940, he was mobilized and saw combat. During the final years of the war, he collaborated with the Resistance alongside A. Dupront. After the war he became a professor at the Louis le Grand School at Paris and remained there for more than 30 years. He received the National Merit Award from the French government. During the era of the Soviet regime he and Pierre Emmanuel militated in favor of the Christians of Russia. In the 1960s he formed a committee "to make known the situation of Christians in the USSR." After his conversion, he followed courses in theology organized by the patriarchate of Moscow and whose faculty included Vladimir Lossky, Leonid Ouspensky and Father Sophrony. After the premature death of V. Lossky, he edited several of Lossky's unpublished texts. He also collaborated with Paul Evdokimov and Father Dumitru Stăniloae. He was in close contact with the French personalist school of thought, with Christos Yannaras and Gabriel Matzneff. In 1959, he assumed the direction of the review *Contacts* alongside Elisabeth Behr-Sigel, Nicolas Lossky, Jean Balzon, Germaine Revault d'Allones and Father Boris Bobrinskoy. He took a special interest in the preparation of the Pan-Orthodox Council and in 1970 he and Paul Evdokimov signed an appeal. He began teaching comparative theology and moral theology at the Saint Sergius Institute in 1962 through the intermediary of Leon Zander who was the first to introduce Clément to the Parisian Orthodox world. Thanks to the initiatives of Father Lev Gillet, he was also one of the founders and animators of the Orthodox Fraternity in Western Europe. In 1975, Clément, Evdokimov and J. Tchekan founded the *Service Orthodoxe de Presse*. In 1975, in collaboration with the Bellefontaine publishing house, the Orthodox Fraternity issued *Le Mystère Pascal*, a work by Clément and Alexander Schmemann. During the decade 1970–1980, Clément contributed chronicles on a regular basis to major Christian magazines such as *L'Actualité religieuse dans le monde* and assured the direction of the Theophany series of the Desclée de Brouwer publishing house which issued several books by contemporary Orthodox intellectuals. He also taught for many years at the Advanced Institute for Ecumenical Studies (notably with Father Marie-Joseph Le Guillou in 1975 regarding the charismatic experience), at the Cathedral School of Paris and at the Centre Sèvres. From 1976 until 1994 he was president of the Association of Believing Writers which reunited Christian, Jewish and Muslim authors. He was named "Grand Archon" by the Ecumenical Patriarchate and received the Cross of St. Peter and St. Paul from the Patriarch of Antioch. In 1994, he wrote a text for the Patriarch Bartholomew on the *Via crucis*—the Way of the Cross—which John Paul II read at Rome during Passion Week.

Evdokimov,[46] he published a text entitled "Toward the Council? An Appeal to the Churches." The decidedly ecumenical and postconfessional tendency

---

He received honorary degrees from the universities of Louvain-la-Neuve and Bucharest and, on February 16, 1997, an honorary degree from the Saint Sergius Institute of Paris for the entirety of his work. In 1999, he received the Saint Nicholas award from the Institute of Greco-Byzantine Patristic Theology at Bari (Italy). In 2001, he also received the prestigious award of the Aletti Center at Rome. In 1995, with the help of Father Boris Bobrinskoy who had already initiated the project with the Bellefontaine publishing house, he published the complete two volume text of *La Philocalie* translated by his friend Jacques Touraille; the publishers were Lattes and DDB. He traveled extensively in Lebanon, Italy, Israel, Japan, etc., where he gave many conferences and committed himself to various causes. He was deeply marked by Russian religious philosophy—above all by Nicholas Berdyaev and Sergius Bulgakov—and very soon began to contribute to making it known in the Western world—as he did in a colloquium at Aix-en-Provence in 1968. He participated in the preparation of the catechetical manual *Dieu est vivant* and addressed numerous assemblies of Orthodox youth (ACER, the Lebanese MJO) as well as groups of young people of all Christian confessions at Taizé. During the 1960s, he maintained a dialogue with Marxist intellectuals and, in the 1980s, with Muslim philosophers. In 1991, in the newspaper *Le Monde*, he denounced several Orthodox personalities whom he found guilty of mystifying the land of Kosovo but he supported the Serbian hierarchy in its efforts to bring about peace. Similarly, in July of 1998, after a voyage to Russia, he wrote an article for *Le Monde* which denounced an atmosphere of inquisition within the Russian Church and directly questioned Patriarch Alexis II. Olivier Clément was also a poet and a friend of poets (Pierre Emmanuel). He died at Paris on January 15, 2009.

46 Paul Evdokimov (1901–1970) was born on August 2, 1901, at Saint Petersburg. In 1905 a drama turned his life upside down; during a parade at which Nicolas II assisted, a Polish revolutionary soldier assassinated Paul's father, a colonel in the Imperial Army who had just returned from the War in Manchuria. At the assassin's trial, the widow, of aristocratic descent, asked that the murderer not be executed. In 1918 Paul began his studies at the Academy of Theology at Kiev but was soon mobilized by the White Army. In 1921, he left Russia, through Odessa, on a British ship and arrived in France, via Constantinople, in 1924. He studied theology with his brother at the Saint Sergius Institute and was part of the first graduating class in 1928. He also became involved in the Russian Students Christian Action Movement and was its first national secretary in France. In 1927, at Marseilles, in the chapel of a Russian merchant ship, he married Natacha Brunel whose father was from Nîmes and whose mother was Russian-Caucasian. Two children were born from this marriage, Nina (1928) and Michel (1930). In 1942, Evdokimov defended his thesis on "Dostoevsky and the Problem of Evil." In 1944, he published *Marriage as a Sacrament of Love*, a work in which he liberates all traces of a disincarnate esoterism from Soloviev's philosophy on the meaning of love. During the German occupation he joined the Resistance alongside his Protestant friends of the Cimade. After the death of his wife in 1945, he dedicated himself to caring for refugees and directed the reception house and, subsequently, the student foyer founded by Cimade. His ecumenical commitment was characterized by his participation, from 1948 to 1961, in the Institute of Studies of the World Council of Churches at Bossey. In the Spring of 1953, he played a role in the foundation of Syndesmos at Sèvres and in the Fall became a professor of moral theology

evident in this work is typical of a particular strand of thought purporting to represent Orthodoxy.[47]

The work of Msgr. Vladimir Ghika (1873–1954), a Romanian prince, born into Orthodoxy, who became a Catholic priest and died a martyr, is another notable example. His writings have been presented in a work entitled *Une lumière dans les ténèbres* by Mihaela Vasiliu, a laywoman of Romanian descent who has been living in Germany since 1990.[48]

---

and the history of Western Christianity at Saint Sergius. In 1954, he married Tomoko Sakai, the daughter of a Japanese diplomat, and began writing again: *La Femme et le salut du monde* (1958), *L'Orthodoxie* (1959)—his doctoral thesis in theology—*Les âges de la vie spirituelle* (1964), *L'art de l'icône* (1967–1970) as well as *Gogol et Dostoievski* (1961) and *Le Christ dans la pensée russe* (1969), his course at the Department for Ecumenical Studies at the Catholic University. He was invited as an observer to the third session of Vatican II and his influence is evident in certain passages of *Gaudium et Spes*. Along with Olivier Clément, Father Lev Gillet and Nikos Nissiotis, he collaborated with the review *Contacts*. He organized annual "theology days" which led to the creation of an Orthodox Fraternity of Western Europe. He received an honorary degree from the University of Thessalonica in 1968. His works were quickly translated into English, German, Spanish, Catalan, Greek, Polish, Flemish, etc. He died on September 16, 1970, at Meudon.

47 "Towards the Council, an Appeal to the Church" in Olivier Clément, *Orient-Occident, deux passeurs: Vladimir Lossky, Paul Evdokimov*, Geneva, Labor et Fides, 1985, 197–210.

48 Msgr. Vladimir Ghika was born on December 25, 1837, at Constantinople where his father, Prince Ghika, the Romanian Minister of War and Foreign Relations, had been sent on a mission. His great-grandfather was the last sovereign of Moldavia and his mother was a descendent of Henry IV, the king of France. He was baptized in the Orthodox Church. When he was 8 years old, his father died of pulmonary congestion. He studied law at the University of Toulouse. In 1899 he left for Rome where he obtained a degree in philosophy and a doctorate in theology. In 1902, without renouncing his Orthodox faith, he became a Catholic. In collaboration with a religious sister named Pucci, he brought the Daughters of Charity to Romania, organized the first free dispensary—Mary of Bethlehem—at Bucharest (1906–1914) and founded the Saint Vincent de Paul Hospital. He lived in Rome from 1914–1917. On October 7, 1923, he was ordained a priest for the diocese of Paris. He was part of the group of intellectuals who met at the house of Jacques and Raissa Maritain at Meudon. In 1924 he began to devote himself to pastoral and charitable activities at Villejuif while, at the same time, writing many articles for different reviews (such as *La Revue des jeunes*). In 1931, the Holy See bestowed upon him the title of Protonotary and Monsignor. He participated in many international Eucharistic Congresses. In 1933 he founded the first Carmelite monastery in Japan, at Tokyo. He returned to Romania in September of 1939 and was allowed to remain there by the local hierarchy. As a priest, he celebrated in both the Latin and Byzantine rites and was active in both the Greek Catholic parish and in the francophone community of the Church of Saint Vincent; in both parishes, his work was at the service of the poorest as well as with students and intellectuals. On November 18, 1952, he was arrested by the Communist authorities and condemned on October 24, 1953. He was abused and tortured at the Jilava Prison near Bucharest. He died on May 17, 1954, at the age of 81.

Olivier Clément belongs to a particular stream of Christian Orthodox thought that flows from St. Paul through St. Martin of Tours and John Chrysostom; it emphasizes that the sacrament of the altar has its prolongation in the "sacrament of the brother." In July 1970, Clément and Evdokimov composed a text that defined the piety, doctrine, and social commitment of the spiritual stream of Orthodoxy. They emphasize the social consequences of faith in a Trinitarian God in the light of Orthodoxy's refusal to elaborate a theological judgment against violence, as well as the need to purify people's thirst for justice and truth in the face of the idolatry of the "Revolution" which swept the world in the 1960s:

> The interpellation of the Biblical prophets, the example of the primitive community of Jerusalem and that of the great monastic communities, the questioning of property and inheritance by the Fathers of the Church, and the role of social innovation which they often attributed to love of one's neighbor, the fact that Orthodox Churches in Eastern Europe have accepted new social structures in order to bear witness to the Living God with spiritual simplicity: all these factors are elements which should liberate the Orthodox faithful from individualistic reflexes and lead them to collaborate in all types of creative research without, however, diminishing the absolute value of each person.[49]

This trend insists first of all on the need for "a return to the essentials" of Christian Orthodox identity. For Clément and Evdokimov, two mysteries constitute the foundation of the Church and of our own lives: that of a God who became man so that man might become God and that of the Unity in Trinity whose radiance makes us neither separated nor confused but unique and one, resurrected in the unutterable love of God for humanity, in the infinite love of the Father, Son and Holy Spirit, the consubstantial and undivided Trinity.[50]

Such a return to the dogmatic core of Christian faith, the authors argue, will make it possible to address the historical problems of the Orthodox Church, to recognize that the catholicity of the Church has been shattered and that this has caused a juxtaposition of nationalisms among the Eastern

49 O. Clément, *Orient Occident*, op. cit., 207–208.

50 Ibid., 210.

Churches. It encourages a "liberation from the fundamentalism of human traditions" which saps the energies of the Orthodox world. Unlike all forms of authoritarian Christomonism and sectarian Pentecostalism, this position is thoroughly Trinitarian. It holds that orthodoxy is inseparable from orthopraxis. This is manifest in a particular way through the recognition of the legitimate diversity of local traditions and by appeal to the liturgical and personal experience of the Resurrection of Christ in the dialogue with human sciences.

In opposition to the rationalist individualism which has marked modern thought since Descartes and Locke, Orthodox Christian thought emphasizes the historical fecundity of eschatology and the vocation of all of creation to participate in the Kingdom of God. Clément and Evdokimov affirm that in Christian anthropology "a person realizes his fullness in God by participating in the Trinitarian energies which make him consubstantial with all things, the visage and voice of a transfigured universe."[51] In view of this, the two theologians concur that "a time of disinterested sharing has arrived for Orthodoxy, so that it might hasten the ongoing emergence of an undivided Church." That is, it is necessary to work towards the reconciliation between the Chalcedonian and non-Chalcedonian Churches, since "there is no doubt of their fundamental unity in the faith." Another consequence is the need for a certain "economy" in the dispensation of the Eucharist in the measure in which the dialogue among Christians progresses. Consequently:

> Would it not be opportune to conclude the work of a Pan-Orthodox Council with a preliminary preparation for a Pan-Christian Council which would bring together Orthodox, Catholics, Anglicans and Protestants desirous of reviving the Tradition of the undivided Church and, in light of this, revise the traditions which subsequently emerged during the separation of the different confessions—distinguishing the essential from the contingent, incorporating formulations into the real life of the Church, giving special attention to the legitimacy of diverse local expressions, resolving, little by little but respecting the fullness of the mystery, the oppositions inherent in partial approaches which might, in the end, be complementary?[52]

51 Ibid., 204.
52 Ibid., 206.

Clément and Evdokimov, both professors at the St. Sergius Institute of Orthodox Theology, even developed a theology of interreligious dialogue based on what the Fathers of the Church called "the visits of the Word." Due to its philokalic way of knowing things and its method of striving for the unification of the heart and the spirit, Orthodoxy is very close to "religions which recognize the transcendence of the person," such as Judaism and Islam. However, it also has affinities with the "rhythms of Black Africa" and the "Japanese attitude of wonder in the face of creation." For Orthodoxy knows, through its cruciforming and crucifying wisdom, that absorption into any presence of the divine opens one to the movement of Trinitarian love, and that the abyss does not extinguish the person. After the death of Paul Evdokimov in 1970, Olivier Clément continued to develop this theme more deeply.[53]

53 Olivier Clément wrote about 30 books—among them his bestseller *L'Eglise Orthodoxe* which sold tens of thousands of copies. This book was first published in 1961 and by 1998 there were already 6 editions. There are works which approach the Orthodox Church from within (*ad intra*)—mostly published in the 50s and 60s and again after 1983. But there were also works with an *ad extra* approach (marked by a star * in our list), most written after 1968, which were consecrated to the encounter of Orthodoxy with Western Christianity, with modernity and with non-Christian religions: *Notes sur le temps à la lumiere de la tradition orthodoxe* (1959), *Byzance et le christianisme* (1964), *Dyonisos et le Ressuscité** (1968), *Dialogues avec le patriarche Athénagoras* (1969 and 1976), *Questions sur l'homme** (1972), *L'Esprit de Soljénitsyne* (1974), *La liberté du Christ ** (1974), *La révolte de L'Esprit** (1979), *Le chant des larmes, essai sur le repentir, avec une traduction du Grand Canon de Saint André de Crète* (1983), *Sources, les mystiques chrétiens des origines* (1983, 1989, 1992, 1999), *Orient Occident, deux passeurs (V. Lossky, P. Evdokimov)* (1985), *Les visionnaires, essai sur le dépassement du nihilisme** (1986), *Un respect têtu, islam et christianisme** (avec Mohamed Talbi, 1989), *Anachroniques** (1990), "Le Christ du Credo" in *Le Fait religieux** (1993), *L'oeil de feu, deux visions spirituelles du cosmos** (1994, text of the 1960s), *Via Crucis** (1994 and 1998), *Corps du mort et corps de gloire* (1995), *La vérité vous rendra libre, Entretiens avec le patriarche oecuménique Bartholomée I* (1996), *Rome autrement* (1997—a response to the 1995 papal encyclical *Ut unum sint*), *Taizé, un sens a la vie** (1997), Preface, dossier and notes for *Quatre Evangiles* in the translation by Hughes Oltramare* (Gallimard, Folio, 1998), *Christ est ressuscité, propos pour sur les fêtes chrétiennes** (2000). O. Clément also collaborated with the Gallimard encyclopedia, *L'encyclopaedia Universalis* and contributed to *L'Histoire de la sainteté*. He also wrote an introduction to *L'Eglise est une* by Khomiakov and to *Les fondements spirituels de la vie* by Soloviev (the Catalan edition). He redacted many texts of the patriarch of Antioch, Ignatius IV. Along with Msgr. Elias of Beirut, he represented the Patriarch of Antioch at Bari in 1987 on the occasion of the meeting of the mixed international Catholic-Orthodox commission on the theme "The Faith, Mysteries and Unity of the Church." In 1998 he published *Déracine-toi et plante-toi dans la mer*. His prophetic approach is evident in the more than 50 articles he published for the *Orthodox Press Service* and the journal *Contacts*. In 2003, in collaboration

In such a perspective, the Orthodox Church does not possess a monopoly over this spiritual wisdom; on the contrary, it rejoices in finding it outside its own boundaries. Today the veneration of icons is not unique to the Eastern Churches, any more than biblical exegesis and the works of charity are the exclusive domains of the Protestant and Catholic Churches respectively.

Msgr. Vladimir Ghika testifies to the capacity of the Catholic Church to integrate the most authentic spirituality and doctrine of the Eastern Church. Ghika, who graduated with Master's degrees in both law and philosophy as well as a doctorate in theology, was a friend of those intellectuals possessing an awareness of the need in the world for a spiritual commitment and not just a doctrinal one. Through his dealings with both East and West, he became associated with Jacques Maritain, Emmanuel Mounier, Nicholas Berdyaev, and Charles du Bos. He belongs to the tradition of those who see an inherent, orthodox link between Christian doctrine and service to one's neighbor. In what Ghika himself described as a "theology of need," there could be no separation between memory of the Lord's wonders, liturgical celebration, doctrinal reflection, and commitment to helping the very weakest. As M. Vasiliu wrote, "in the mind of Vladimir Ghika, the most important thing was, first of all, to know God, to have a knowledge of this God who is 'Love and Compassion' and who, in the tenderness of his heart, is attentive to all in their daily necessities. Knowing God deeply opens our eyes to the needs of our brothers, to their spiritual and material needs" (60).

In 1913, Ghika founded a dispensary of the Daughters of Charity in Romania. During the period between the two World Wars, he chose to dedicate himself to the very poorest in a slum of Villejuif on the outskirts of Paris. After the Second World War, he opted to live in Communist Romania to serve all those in need of pastoral support. He was arrested, underwent a sham trial, and died in the prison of Jilava. Throughout his life his prayer was: "Lord, smile at me through the eyes of your poor ones. Lord, receive me one day in the Holy Company of your poor" (69). The prayer of this "Orthodox" Christian, who became a Catholic without renouncing his loyalty attachment to "Orthodoxy," was adopted by Jean Vanier and the Community of L'Arche.[54]

---

with M. Rupnik (who had awarded him with the prize of the Aletti Center in Rome), he published a work entitled *Sillons de lumière, théo-anthropologie de la beauté*. That same year, in collaboration with Jean-Claude Noyer, he published *Mémoires d'espérance*.

54 http://www.jean-vanier.org/en/his_works/foundations/larche.

## THE PATHS OF THE ORTHODOX FAITH/SPIRITUALITY

The different anthropological types that we have presented are also distinguished by their definitions of the Church. For the ascetics, the Church is, above all, the "Ark of Salvation"; and for the missionaries, the Church is lived as the "Body of Christ"; whereas for the "spirituals" the Church is experienced as the "Temple of the Holy Spirit."[55] These three types of Orthodox Christian piety and corresponding ecclesiologies also find expression in their manners of relating to the world, in their practices, and in their styles. In his 1950 "Message to the Churches," Paul Evdokimov wrote: "King Midas turned everything he touched into gold. A Christian by his inner attitude can make all things transparent, can transform them into icons, images of their truth. Style, once it has become an authentic spiritual category, will become more naturally efficacious than sermons."[56]

Rather than seeking structural and insurmountable confessional differences between Christians of different affiliations, as is sometimes seen in treatments of Papo-caesarism or Caesero-papism, let us take the example of the Orthodox Christian doctrine of peace and war to indicate how the differences among Christians are due more to the geohistoric context and level of anthropological consciousness than to confessional theology.[57] In spite of their different external manifestations, the various types of spiritual consciousness always bear the marks of quietude and joy which are, for St. Paul, the fruits of the Spirit.

It can be said that, according to varying contexts (traditional society/modern society; city/countryside; world of finance/student milieu), periods (before, during or after the conflict) and spiritual profiles, there are three fundamental relations with violence. All three of these connections can

55 A. Arjakovsky, *En attendant le concile de l'Eglise Orthodoxe*, Paris, Cerf, 2011.

56 P. Evdokimov, "Message aux Eglises" (1950), *L'Amour fou de Dieu*, Paris, Seuil, 1973, 172.

57 Jim Forest, Hildo Bos, *Peace from Above, An Orthodox Resource Book on War, Peace and Nationalism*, Athens, Geneva, WWC, Syndesmos, 1999; Olivier Clément, "The Orthodox Church and Peace—Some Reflections," in *Peace from Above, An Orthodox Resource Book on War, Peace and Nationalism*, Athens, Geneva, WWC, Syndesmos, 1999, 172–79; *Orthodox Peace Ethics and Oriental Christianity*, consultation in Bucharest (cf. Marian Gh. Simion), Holy Cross, Peace Studies in Eastern Christianity, 2009; Preconciliar Orthodox Conference, October 28–November 6, 1998, "The Contribution of the Local Orthodox Churches to the Adoption of the Christian Ideals of Peace, Freedom, Brotherhood and Love among the Peoples of the World and the Elimination of Racial Prejudice"; "Un regard orthodoxe sur la paix," Chambesy, 1986; "Orthodox Perspectives on Justice and Peace" in *Justice, Peace and the Integrity of Creation*, Geneva, WWC, 1990, 16–27.

sometimes be legitimate and complementary if they foster the progress of peace and, consequently, according to a religious perspective, hasten the advent of the divine radiance (*shalom*) and cosmic harmony.

For the ascetics, the struggle against evil is a necessity, and thus allows for recourse to physical violence. The battle against the passions calls for a total engagement of the soul and the body turned towards the Spirit. St. Silouan of Athos continually referred to the words of Matthew 7:14: "Small is the gate and narrow is the road which leads to life and those who find them are few."[58] Moreover, the ascetics are aware that evil is an angelic reality possessing self-awareness. Their battle against the Evil One is conducted with different weapons according to whether it is a period of temptation or one of total domination.

For the "missionaries," the struggle against evil cannot be experienced merely by an individual. This is why the ecclesial institution can support a defensive war—the Orthodox Church even has a ritual for the blessing of weapons. War is nonetheless always an evil and, for this reason, the canons prohibit priests from bearing arms. Although the Orthodox Church refused to use force against the Tatars in the 13th century, St. Sergius of Radonezh gave his blessing to Dmitri Donskoi. Boris Zaitsev described this episode:

> Saint Sergius was pretty much a stranger as regards the things of this world. His refusal of ecclesiastical honors and his trouble with disobedient monks are sufficient proof of his preference "for purely spiritual activity, for the perfume of sawdust in the forest of Radonezh." And yet he was not one to run away from life's tragedies. He blessed the faction which, in his mind, possessed the truth. He never favored war but sided with the people, with Russia, with Orthodoxy. His role as consoler and defender of Russia could hardly leave him indifferent.
>
> On August 18, 1380, Dmitri, along with his cousin Vladimir and other princes came to the Laura. It was a grave and solemn hour: for the first time, Russia was assembling, every town was sending out its forces—not acting on a whim, but well aware of the significance of their actions. A *Te Deum* was intoned and yet the messengers continued to arrive, bringing news of the enemy whose movements

58 Archimandrite Sophrony, *Starets Silouane, Moine du Mont Athos*, Paris, Presence, 1989, 194.

required an immediate response. In spite of all this, Sergius asked Dmitri to remain at the Laura until supper. In the cloister, Sergius told Dmitri "You will not yet wear the crown of victory by descending into the eternal repose; but martyrs' crowns are already prepared for a great number of your warriors." After supper Sergius sprinkled holy water on the princes and their retinues yet, even at this decisive moment, he spoke words of peace—as if he felt pity for all these young and brilliant warriors. "Your duty, my lord, demands that you first defend your subjects, that you be willing to offer your soul and shed your blood for them. But first present yourself to the Khan as a vassal, try to make him stop by submission and truth. Scripture teaches us that if our enemies demand honor and glory, if they want to take our gold and silver, we can give them all this; but we will not offer our souls, we will only shed our blood in defense of our faith and in the name of Christ! Listen, my lord, give them your glory and riches and God will not allow you to be defeated. Seeing your humility, God will raise you up and he will abase their stubborn pride." The prince replied that it was already too late, that all his efforts to avoid war had been in vain. "In that case," said Sergius, "they will perish. God will assist you; may his help, his Grace and his Glory be with you all!" Dmitri knelt before Saint Sergius who traced the Sign of the Cross over him saying "Go, fear nothing, God will help you"—and, bending down over him, he whispered in his ear "You will triumph!" The eyes of Dmitri swelled up in tears.

This is credible even if the legend is inexact. Was he not preparing himself for a mortal combat? What makes this interview majestic and even tragic is that Sergius will give Dmitri two monks, Peresvet and Osliabe, as companions in battle. These two monks had been warriors when they lived in the world but they will not bear arms against the Turks; they will continue to wear their monastic habits and their veils with a white cross. It is obvious that these two monks believed that they were participating in a crusade. The warrior monks would not be associated with a civil war. Dmitri had already arrived at Kolomna on August 20; on the 26th and 27th he crossed the Oka River and headed for the River Don. On September 6th he was still hesitant between crossing the river or awaiting the Tartars. Whatever errors Dmitri might have committed during his reign, on the battlefield of Koulikovo he took heart and his enthusiasm swept away all obstacles. On this occasion he incarnated the genius of the newborn Russia. In the face of the huge army of Mamai, of Prince Oleg of Riazan and Lithuania, commanders who were older and more experienced than Dmitri spoke of compromising. But Dmitri crossed the Don River in spite of their urgings. The roads were blocked; they had to advance towards either victory or death. Saint Sergius, who felt himself inspired in the middle of all this, decided to send a message to the prince: "Advance, my lord, continue to advance, God and the Holy Trinity will help you." On September 8, 1380, an overcast dawn broke over the Don and the little river Nepriadva which bordered the plain of Koulikovo where the spirit of *The Song of Igor* still hovered. Russia had emerged as a whole to face up to the furious beast. The hour was extremely serious, pregnant with "moral tension." Before the battle, prayers were said and the letter of Saint Sergius was read to the troops. A black flag adorned with a golden image of the Savior floated above the camp of the prince in the Autumn mist at this late and chilly dawn shimmering in the morning dew. Indistinct sounds and groans were heard on both sides of the river. The soldiers were getting up, taking care of their horses, putting on clean shirts, fondling their swords one last time; they drew up their ranks. They were heading for death, for fatality; there was no turning back.

The battle of Koulikovo has a significance which surpasses its historical circumstances and has now become one of these legends where incoherent details abound but whose spirit is more faithful to the truth than official scientific analysis. Certain episodes are disputable—such as that which has Dmitri exchanging his princely mantle to fight in the garb of a common soldier and who, after the pursuit of the enemy, is found unconscious and wounded on the edge of a forest 30 versts from the battlefield. It may well be that no one knew exactly the size of Dmitri's army nor that of the Tartars of Mamai. But what is certain is that this battle determined the destinies of two worlds in conflict with one another.

The Tartars appeared around noon. According to custom, Dmitri advanced at the head of his army in the first assault. He was not wounded but his armor was damaged. The legend has it that, at the same time, a Tartar knight provoked the Russians and one of the warrior monks left the ranks to confront him; both of the adversaries

> died, pierced by the lance of the other. It was only then that the great battle began, spaced over an area of at least 10 versts—an immense area for that epoch. Saint Sergius was right when he predicted that the martyrs crown awaited a great number of the combatants. While the battle was going on, Saint Sergius, surrounded by his brethren, stayed in his church, relating all that was happening on the battlefield, naming those who were slain and praying for their souls. Near the end of the battle, he declared: "We have vanquished!"[59]

For the "spiritual," evil is vanquished only if one is prepared to take the attacks upon oneself, in other words, to take one's share of responsibility in the outburst of violence. This self-absorption of violence, of which the holy princes Boris and Gleb were examples in medieval Rus', is similar to St. Paul's recommendation to "hold firm." The rejection of all violence in the name of Christ is possible through the power of liberty and truth. This self-assumption of violence takes on different forms according to context. Certain exegetes hold that turning the other cheek, far from being a form of weakness, can be considered a form of humor and derision when it comes to a pseudo-power. Pardon is the capacity to reestablish peace by eradicating any traces of resentment. The martyr is a living witness of his faith, of the vision of God which Stephen experienced as recorded in the Acts of the Apostles. In Christian doctrine, the power of the sword is of the spiritual order; it is the ability to discern between what is true and what is false, what is just and unjust.

Thus, for Orthodox Christianity, peace is an experience of harmony and confidence received from Christ. It initiates an inner battle for the transfiguration of evil into truth; it implies a collective commitment to the triumph of justice and reconciliation and allows the Christian to participate in the eschatological mission of Jesus Christ by taking violence upon himself. The rediscovery of the orthodox Christian doctrine of peace is inseparable from the duty of earthly justice. The body of Christian churches belonging to the World Council of Churches, and in particular the representatives of the Orthodox Churches, gathered in Kingstone in May 2011 published an important declaration in which they put forward the notion that "just peace" necessarily implies an imperative for the reception, participation in, and construction of, such a peace.

59 "Saint Serge de Radonège," *Le Roseau d'Or*, 1928.

> History, especially in the testimony of the historic peace churches, reminds us that violence is contrary to the will of God and can never resolve conflict. For this reason, we are moving beyond the doctrine of just war towards a commitment to Just Peace. It requires moving from the exclusive concern for national security to that for safety for all. This includes a day-to-day responsibility to prevent—that is, to avoid—violence at its root. Many practical aspects of the concept of Just Peace require discussion, discernment and elaboration. We continue to struggle with how innocent people can be protected from injustice, war and violence. In this light, we struggle with the concept of the "responsibility to protect" and its possible misuse.[60]

It has been shown elsewhere that the ecumenical reunion of the Christian world has political, economic, and social consequences.[61] The theories of the French philosopher Jean-Baptiste de Foucauld concerning just governance, the economy of meaning, and the material, relational and spiritual development of each person are based on a Catholic culture of regulation, a Protestant culture of resistance and an Orthodox culture of utopia.[62] The social doctrines of the Orthodox Churches are themselves evolving in the face of confrontation with the modern world and other Christian confessions. The social doctrine of the Russian Church has changed considerably since the year 2000.

The declaration of the Russian Church in 2008 concerning human rights shows that a restoration of these rights is possible in Russia once such a perspective is assimilated among the Orthodox faithful. The Russian Church has indeed in the past often favored the mixture of legalism and anarchism characteristic of the Eastern mentality. This declaration actually legitimizes for the first time in a reasoned way one of the pillars of modernity, namely freedom of conscience. However, it includes the qualification that, since pure freedom of choice can lead to the legitimization

60 http://www.vaincrelaviolence.org/fr/ressources-du-coe/documents/presentations-discours-messages/message-du-roip.html; www.overcomingviolence.org; International Ecumenical Peace Convocation, Kingstone, Jamaica, 2011, WCC.

61 Antoine Arjakovsky, "Notre génération," in *Les Jalons, cent ans après*, under the direction of Antoine Arjakovsky, Paris, Lviv, IEOE/FX de Guibert, 2009.

62 Jean-Baptiste de Foucauld, *Les trois cultures du développement humain*, Paris, Odile Jacob, 2002, 152.

of the denial of all freedom, it is appropriate to associate a second freedom with the first, defined as a freedom of service. The Russian Church had already presented the theological foundations of such a system in a previous document in the year 2000.[63] This early document opposes the theory of natural law, the source of modern law, for failing to "take into account the fallen nature of mankind"; however, it is difficult to understand how, from this perspective, a person could enjoy rights at all in practice when the world has been so profoundly affected by the Fall. There are reasons to fear the reappearance of the ancient distinction between "tyrannical" and "responsible" representatives of the divine power and between "irresponsible" and "ethical" resistance.

Certainly, the Russian Church's 2008 declaration on human rights still has many defects. All the same, in spite of some reservations, Lyudmila Alexeyeva, the president of the Helsinki Committee in Russia,[64] was pleased with the text, as was leading democrat and intellectual Grigori Iavlinski.[65] The declaration does have the merit of deriving the inalienable rights of the human person from solid theological principles.[66]

The authors of this text—among whom figured Father Cyril Hovorun, one of the principal redactors, in close relation to the actual Patriarch Cyril—draw an illuminating distinction between the two terms which the New Testament uses to designate liberty: *antexousion*, which refers to

63 "With the advent of secularization, the inalienable principle of human rights has changed into the rights of the individual considered independently from any relationship with God. Moreover, the defense of freedom has been transformed into the defense of self-will (provided that it does not harm other individuals)—all of which leads to demand that the State give guarantees of a certain material level of existence for persons and families. The contemporary secular and humanitarian understanding of the rights of citizens sees the person not as an image of God but as a self-sufficient and independent subject. Yet, without God, there can only be a fallen humanity, radically separated from the Christian ideal of perfection manifested in Christ ('Behold the Man'). Also, for the juridical Christian consciousness, the idea of liberty and human rights is indefectibly linked to that of service. Rights are necessary for persons so that, by possessing them, the person can better realize his vocation of becoming the 'resemblance of God,' of carrying out his duties towards God and the Church, and towards others—the family, the State, the people and other human societies." Chapter IV, 7, *Les bases de la conception sociale de l'Eglise orthodoxe russe*, www.mospat.ru. A French translation was published by H. Destivelle, Cerf, 2007.

64 http://www.foma.ru/articles/182/.

65 http://ru.wikipedia.org/wiki, etc.

66 C. Hovorun, 'Neskolko zametchanie v deklaratsi o pravakh' in *Tchelovetcheskaja tselostnost i vstretcha kultur*, Kiev, Duh i Litera, 2007, 130–34.

freedom as the power of self-determination (1 Cor 7:37: "But he who has made a firm resolution in his heart, without any constraint, and who, *in full possession of his will*, has decided to respect his fiancée, this man does the right thing"); and *eleutheria*, which designates freedom in the face of evil, as the capacity to fulfill oneself in God, as the power to vanquish fallen nature with the help of God (Gal 4:22: "But the Jerusalem from above is *free* and is your mother"; cf. also John 8:36: "So if the Son sets you free, you will be free indeed"). The declaration asserts that if freedom of choice (*antexousion*) is not the ultimate value, it is nonetheless inalienable, since the image of God in humanity has not been obliterated by sin. Additionally, the declaration states that true freedom (*eleutheria*) cannot be imposed by law but must be realized progressively—in particular through the sacraments, beginning with baptism and culminating in "the resurrection of all." There are echoes here of the most ancient patristic doctrine which belie images of the Russian Church as a bastion of retrogression. One can also detect a return to the thesis of Sergius Bulgakov in favor of universal salvation put forward in his 1944 book *The Bride of the Lamb* (*L'Epouse de l'Agneau*).

The new participation of the Orthodox Churches in the ecumenical movement and their recent entry into dialogue with the modern world also anticipates the reconciliation between the religions announced in 1997 by Olivier Clément in his book *Rome autrement*. Clément argued that in the future there would be an encounter between the hemisphere of India, where an all-inclusive concept of unity dominates—a concept of the Same with its cyclic vision of temporality and the universality of the Self of each person—and the Semitic hemisphere, which affirms the transcendence of a personal God and where time is either linear (as in Judaism) or commemorative (as in Islam). For Clément, the important thing is to try continually to understand the mystery of "Uni-Trinity" better and diffuse it more widely:

> The Living God is such that He contains all reality within Himself, the pulsation of the other and, in the Spirit, in the Holy Breath, the surpassing of all duality; not by folding into an impersonal unity, but through the coincidence of absolute unity with absolute diversity. . . . To religions of the Oneness of transcendence, and without doubt through their mystics, we will speak of the Incarnation and the "kenosis." To the religions of a fusion with the impersonal, we will speak of the Uni-Trinity. To humanists who are more or less atheistic, we will remind them that humanity would be nothing

> if it were not above and beyond all its conditionings, if it were not an enigma, a secret that could only be penetrated through the revelation of love.[67]

## CONCLUSION

The frequent divergences between history and memory in works on the history of the Orthodox Church illustrate the actual incapacity of the Orthodox world to defend its confessional vision of the truth. The difficulties of the Orthodox Churches in convening a Pan-Orthodox council and in reestablishing their communion with the so-called "non-Chalcedonian" Churches also evidence the crisis in the modernist paradigm of Orthodoxy. Finally, the many contradictions between orthodoxy and orthopraxis within the Orthodox Churches support the growing process of secularization among Orthodox Christian peoples. To just mention a few recent examples, the divisions among different Orthodox Churches in Ukraine, in Estonia and in the United States have become increasingly scandalous. The conflicts between the Ecumenical Patriarch and the Patriarch of Moscow concerning church buildings, such as that which pits the Russian State against the Orthodox community of the Cathedral of Nice, France, which was under the Constantinople jurisdiction from 1932 until 2014 before it was put under the Moscow jurisdiction,[68] oblige states to no longer consider the Orthodox Church as a sole entity. More and more the media is taking a hostile attitude towards the Orthodox Churches.[69] It is also true that, from Jerusalem to Moscow, from New York to Athens, frequent scandals have involved members of the Orthodox clergy.[70] A devastating report has been published concerning the misappropriation of funds, embezzlement and bookkeeping violations which have affected the Orthodox Church in America over a period of twenty years.[71] The publication, in January 2012,

67 Olivier Clément, *Rome autrement,* Paris, DDB, 1997, 122.

68 http://www.lefigaro.fr/actualite-france/2010/01/20/01016-20100120ARTFIG00053-moscou-veut-recuperer-la-cathedrale-orthodoxe-de-nice-.php.

69 http://archives-lepost.huffingtonpost.fr/article/2011/09/18/2592792_le-scandale-de-l'enrichissement-de-l'eglise-greque-orthodoxe-en-periode-de-crise.html.

70 Ireneos I, the Patriarch of Jerusalem, was deposed in May, 2005, following a scandal involving real estate operations in Jerusalem. He is suspected of having sold (or of having allowed to be sold) lots to Israeli Jewish investors.

71 In the United States, the chancellor of the Orthodox Church in America has been accused of diverting funds to profit the Russian Church: http://www.ocanews.org/PlekonOnBeingtheChurch.html.

of the secret archives of the Communist era revealed that eleven of the fifteen metropolitans of the Bulgarian Orthodox Church were informers working for the state.[72] These are all signs of the crisis affecting the Orthodox world today.

As we shall see, a redefinition of orthodoxy is necessary, not only for the Orthodox Church but for the totality of the Christian world, and even for all people of good will seeking to rediscover the bonds between the true, the good and the beautiful above and beyond the ruptures and innovations of modernity.

72 httrp://www.lavie.fr/chroniques/matinale-chretienne/l'eglise-orthodoxe-bulgare-rattrapee-par-son-passe-15-03-2012-25242_167.php.

# PART II

# *The Redefinition of Orthodoxy*

# CHAPTER 4
# *The Definitions of Orthodoxy*

## FOREWORD: PHENOMENOLOGY OF ORTHODOXY

Orthodoxy is an equivocal term that deserves further analysis. At present, "orthodox" is popularly understood to be equivalent to "conservative," whether one is a Jew or a Christian, a banker or a lawyer, from the left or from the right. An economist, for example, might be accused of professing "unorthodox" theories, meaning opinions that differ from common liberal teachings on market mechanisms.[1] On the eve of the anniversary of the inauguration of François Mitterrand as president of the French Republic, the French media freely speculated about the fidelity, or lack thereof, of the party members to the socialist *doxa*.[2]

Numerous ambiguities can also be observed in the usage of the concept of orthodoxy throughout history. "Orthodox Jews" claim to be faithful to the most ancient traditions of Judaism, but it was only in the early 19th century that the Reformed Jews introduced this term to refer to a distinct movement within Judaism.[3] Since the time of St. Paul the term "orthodox"

1 Olivier Favereau, "La science économique entre orthodoxie et hétérodoxie," *Problèmes économiques* 2734 (October 2001): 31.

2 Thomas Wieder, "Thirty years later, the socialist *doxa* remains intact but it has become weaker. Interview with G. Grunberg." *Le Monde*, May 10, 2011, p. 20; the file, pp. 17–22, is entitled "Thirty years later, Mitterand has once again become the *icon* of the left wing"—another instance of use of a Greek term in contemporary rhetoric.

3 The central point of reference for Orthodox Jews is fidelity to a chain of transmission of the *halaka* (a code of rules established by oral tradition dating from the Talmud to present times) revealed to Moses and coming down to us through the composition of the Talmud and the subsequent commentaries. An Orthodox Jew is one who recognizes his duty to live according to the *halaka*. In this context, the work of Isaac Eisig Halevy Rabinowitz (1847–1914), a teacher at Vilnius, is considered "orthodox" since it is based on the oral Torah. It should be noted that Jewish historical science, as a whole, differs from the Greek concept of history in that it develops a vision of time which is both circular and linear. Cf. Alain Boyer, Maurice-Ruben Hayoun, *L'Historiographie juive*, Paris, PUF, 2001.

had been applied to Christians who recognize themselves as such, without necessarily the connotation of a conservative mentality. The reference to "walking correctly" in Galatians 2:14 could be considered the first appeal in the first century to the concept of Christian orthodoxy, although the word itself is not used: "when I saw that *they were not walking in line with the truth of the Gospel*, I said to Cephas in front of everyone. . . ."[4]

Clement of Alexandria took up this expression with the name *ortho-tomia*, a term taken from the book of Proverbs where it has the meaning of "making straight" your paths, and alluding to Paul's letter to Timothy (2 Tim 2:15) where the apostle asks his disciple to handle aright the word of truth. This is the *kanon* or rule—of reading the Scriptures, which must be understood consistently, or of conduct in the assemblies, which must respect the diversity of the gifts of the Spirit despite social or ethnic differences—that ensures the collective application of walking in line for the salvation of souls. As Alain Le Boulluec writes, in the face of an ancient culture that favored the rejection of innovation, and despite the reputation that Orthodoxy has acquired in modern times, "the tradition of Orthodoxy and its norms are originally innovative and the work of interpretation is inherent in them." Orthodoxy is in reality always in a relationship of continuity, but it is constantly confronted with an internal tension between fidelity to tradition and creative commitment.

Here, too, there is ambiguity: the boundaries of the path towards Christian truth do not necessarily correspond to identifiable historical realities. In applying the term "orthodox" to Christians, no distinction is made between the orthodoxy of Greek Ukrainian Catholics and that of Nigerian Anglicans. Very often, including in academic work, people speak (without sufficient regard to the definition of the term orthodoxy) of a return to the "orthodoxy" of the faith of Luther, of the "orthodoxy" of the Council of Trent or of hesychast spirituality, as if there had been a disconnect between the word and the truth of the reality that it signifies.

Moreover, since the 14th or 15th centuries this term has been commonly associated with a specific religious confession. When Orthodoxy is spelled with a capital "O" to designate a Christian confession which identifies its faith with a specific historical-institutional reality, it refers to the Orthodox Church or the communion of Orthodox Churches, the heirs of the Eastern

4 Author's emphasis.

Churches which have now spread throughout the world.[5] Here also, in public opinion, the Orthodox Church is often misunderstood or reduced to half-truths; it is common to speak of the lack of unity in the Orthodox world (in spite of the great degree of liturgical and doctrinal unity among the 274 million Orthodox Christians); of the various ways these Churches became politically compromised during the 20th century (even though not all Orthodox believers reacted to totalitarian governments in the same way); of the exterior form of the Orthodox church buildings (onion domes in Eastern Europe but not in Asia Minor; onion domes are also characteristic of the baroque churches of the Germanic Holy Roman Empire); of the iconostasis or wall of icons separating the people from the clergy during the liturgy (but these did not always exist), and so forth. It is true that the Orthodox have a tendency to present themselves as the sole Church to have preserved the Christianity of the first millennium, but, as the Russian Orthodox philosopher Vladimir Soloviev mischievously remarked in his work *A Short Tale of the Antichrist*,[6] at the end of time, the Antichrist will ironically offer the Orthodox an institute of Christian archaeology. This provoked a reaction from Olivier Clément: "In archaeology, there is the *archè* which designates what is fundamental and original and which both goes beyond history and renders it fruitful. During the second millennium, the Orthodox Church assembled many councils, raised up witnesses and Church Fathers who were open to new approaches to the mystery."[7]

The historical notion of orthodoxy has often been reduced to a concept. Orthodoxy has consequently been opposed to heresy, understood as a false doctrine. In the first volume of *Histoire du Christianisme*, a 14-volume work which appeared in France between 1990 and 2000, Alain le Boulluec, professor at L'École Pratique des Hautes Études, published an article entitled "Hétérodoxie et orthodoxie" in which he synthesizes the debate over this problem from Walter Bauer to H. D. Altendorf and Rowan Williams, arriving at the conclusion that it is necessary to "abandon concepts of heresy and orthodoxy in the study of distant epochs."[8] However, the whole question is

5 Cf. my definition of the Orthodox Church in Antoine Arjakovsky, *En attendant le Concile de l'Eglise Orthodoxe*, Paris, Cerf, 2011, 123.

6 V. Soloviev, *Trois entretiens: sur la guerre, la morale et la religion; suivi du Court récit sur l'antichrist*, trans. Bernard Marchadier, Geneva, Ad Solem, 2005.

7 O. Clément, *Présentation de l'Eglise Orthodoxe*, Paris, St. Sergius Institute, 1985.

8 Alain le Boulluec, "Hétérodoxie et orthodoxie," *Histoire du Christianisme*, I, Des origines à 250, Paris, Desclée, 2000, 268.

to know where to situate the notion of orthodoxy in our conceptualizations. If it is understood in a purely sociological sense, *doxa* loses the meaning it had acquired historically. *Orthodoxy* designates more than the doctrine that a majority group imposes upon a minority. It is for this reason, ultimately, that Alain le Boulluec proposes using the term *orthopraxis* to indicate the intrinsic link between faith and the social, moral, and ritual practices of the primitive Christian communities.[9] Yet this approach cannot be entirely satisfactory, for it sacrifices the essential dimension of glorifying knowledge implied in the notion of *doxa* in primitive Christianity.

Moreover, le Boulluec himself realizes that heresy, which he studies alongside orthodoxy, cannot be reduced to a sole meaning. This term has itself undergone an evolution; derived from *hairoumai*, which means "to choose," *hairesis* was translated into Latin by *secta* (from *sequi*, "to follow").[10] In the second century BC it signified a philosophical system or a school of thought as opposed to an institutional school. In the Acts of the Apostles (at 5:17 and 15:5), the term is used by Luke to designate the different streams or variants of Judaism. Here the French ecumenical translation of the Bible (TOB), for instance, speaks of the "party" of the Sadducees. The word takes on pejorative implications when Paul is accused of being the leader of the *hairesis* of the Nazarenes (Acts 24:6). This connotation is accentuated in the work of other Christian authors such as Justin Martyr's *Treatise Against All Heresies* (circa 100–165), now lost but cited by Irenaeus of Lyons in his own book *Against Heresies.* Henceforth the term "heresy" came to signify a partial truth or attitude which, affirmed in isolation, becomes an error. By the fourth century, through a process of simplification, it had become synonymous with "false doctrine."

Finally, at a more epistemic level, orthodoxy refers to a larger extent to the truth of doctrines than to the institutions which profess them. In the

9 The principal arguments Boulluec employs are the following: on the one hand, the notion of heresy is relatively recent. Prior to 150, it signified "dissent." It was only in the time of Justin, around 150, that the term began to take on consistency when "a system of representations built up around it in order to condemn and exclude it" (ibid., 269). As for the terms *orthodoxia* or *orthodoxos,* it is only in the 4th century that they took on the full significance which corresponds to the concept of orthodoxy as "specific regulation." At the beginning rectitude was associated with actions such as "walking correctly." On the other hand, it can be seen from the example of the conflict over the date of Easter that, in the 2nd century, there was still a care to avoid reducing the ecclesiastical norms to dogmatic assertions—without, however, falling into a confused relativism.

10 Jean-Pierre Mahe, "Le défi des gnoses," in *Histoire générale du christianisme,* v. I, Paris, PUF, 2010, 104.

philosophy of Parmenides, one of the meanings of *doxa* is a confused opinion concerning some aspect of reality as opposed to the right path leading to truth: the Being that *is*. In contemporary philosophy and sociology, *doxa* is more associated with a "network of values" concerning certain aspects and elements of the reality signified. In his 1957 book *Mythologies*, Roland Barthes highlighted this by contrasting the vague beliefs of *doxa* with epistemic and certain knowledge. For Pierre Bourdieu, doxic discourse, by transforming the nature of culture, is the fundamental disposition of ideology.[11] He considers *doxa* to be the image that the bourgeoisie has of the world and in turn imposes on the world. Charles Grivel tried to reconcile the two approaches by showing that *doxa* and *episteme* are in a dialectical relationship since all *doxa* presents itself as *episteme* and every set of structured knowledge contains an element of *doxa*.[12] In all cases the *doxa* is beyond language, but below the discourse on which it tacitly bases intercomprehension.

Contemporary scholarship tends to emphasize the presence of "doxic systems" which are characterized on the one hand vertically by axiologies (bipolar lines whose extremities are in mutual tension) and on the other hand, by semantic fields. These systems represent "ideologisms" and reflect the internal organization of societies. In her work *Le pèlerin et le converti*, the sociologist of EHESS in Paris, Danièle Hervieu-Léger, has drawn upon the lessons of the finalities of inherited religious identification to propose a new systematic model which brings the new religious paths into tension.[13] On this account, the definition of the concept of *ortho-doxy* cannot be strictly conceptualized. Definitions may associate this term with faith, worship, knowledge, truth, tradition, or social practice. These definitions bestow on their terms, according to context, the qualifications "correct," "right," "faithful," or "just."

11 P. Bourdieu, *La distinction, Critique sociale du jugement,* Paris, St. Sergius Institute, 1985.

12 According to Charles Grivel, along with the semantic-logical filtration of language, there is a "social" pre-comprehension based on preference and behavior. For a message to be acceptable, it should be in conformity with the imperatives of transmission of comprehensibility but also with the imperatives of utility and persuasiveness. This presupposes the sharing of a same speech, of "the same beliefs," i.e., a "community of faith" between those who participate in the communication. Charles Grivel, "Savoir social et savoir litteraire," *Litterature* 44 (Dec. 1981): 117–27.

13 D. Hervieu-Leger, *Le pèlerin et le converti*, Paris, Flammarion, 1999, 78. This model, which illustrates the disconnection in France between faith and community membership, can be applied to other European countries. Cf. *Identités religieuses en Europe*, directed by Grace Davie and D. Hervieu-Léger, Paris, La Decouverte, 1996.

These variations and imprecisions are reinforced by an important historical fact. When the Hebrew Bible was translated into Greek around 270 BC by the Septuagint, the Jewish word *kabod* (commonly meaning "glory") was translated by the Greek *doxa* (with "opinion" as one of its meanings).[14] In the New Testament, the *kabod YHVH* becomes the *doxa tou theou*. We will return later to this major semantic leap. However, we can propose a preliminary definition of orthodoxy on a general epistemological level (incorporating the historical evolution of the concept). The term orthodoxy is distinct from that of truth when the latter refers merely to the ability of human intelligence to arrive at the truth deductively. Orthodox thought reflects true thought when the logical discernment of reason adds to the expression of truth a decision of adherence from the personal conscience, that is, of the inner voice of the individual. For this conscience to be able to express its judgment without falling into arbitrariness, there are at least two conditions which must be present and which can potentially exclude one another. The conscience must be totally free, in the sense of independent, capable of making its own judgment, but it must also be connected to a community, a repository of knowledge and specific memory, which produces fields of communication. The orthodox definition of the orthodox truth therefore is not situated purely on the level of individual conviction and intuition.

Orthodoxy in the end is a journey, a way of life, mediated through a community in space and time, which symbolically formulates and precisely transmits its experience of truth in a grateful, rational, and faithful way. The history of thought bears witness to two major attempts, philosophical and theological, to further define this experience of the truth.

## THE PHILOSOPHICAL DEFINITION OF TRUTH

Truth "is not just an aspect of knowledge; it is, above all, a transcendental qualification of being as such."[15] In 1952, the Swiss Catholic philosopher and theologian Hans Urs von Balthasar published an important work entitled *Phénoménologie de la vérité*. In this study he demonstrates that, for the Christian tradition of the East and the West, the reduction of knowledge of truth to purely theoretical knowledge, independently of the vital decisions

14 C. Mohrmann, "Note sur Doxa," in *Sprachgeschichte und Wortbedeutung*, Berne, Festricht A. Debrunner, 1954.

15 Hans Urs von Balthasar, *Phénoménologie de la vérité*, Paris, Beauchesne, 1952, 9.

individuals are led to take when confronted by it, deprives the truth of its universality and true nature. Truth is integral, vital and existential; this is why, unlike the perception of truth which marks modern rationalism, in the ancient tradition the spheres of good and beauty cannot be radically disassociated from that of truth. These aspects cannot be rejected on account of private faith or individual taste.

In order to rediscover the truth in the post-rationalist sense of the term, there is need of a method, of criteria which enable us to formulate and evaluate judgments. This method is precisely what the history of philosophy has designated by the term orthodoxy. Von Balthasar defines his method in phenomenological language: "Describe the truth of the world by emphasizing above all what makes it belong to the world without, however, excluding the possibility that the truth thus described may contain in itself certain elements directly derived from a divine, supernatural origin."[16] This method is rooted in two major characteristics attributed to revealed truth throughout the history of thought, namely its capacity of self-revelation and its trustworthiness. In the tradition of Ancient Greece, the truth is an element of being, of being revealed, not-hidden (*aletheia*), whereas in the biblical tradition the truth is also *emeth*, fidelity, consistency, something worthy of confidence. For von Balthasar, truth thus defined puts an end to uncertainty through "the evidence of the unveiled gift" which offers a way of access to a myriad of new understandings.

The relationship of humanity with truth, however, has a history which must henceforth be taken into consideration through the narrative of the orthodoxy of truth. In modern rationalism, truth is understood as the abstract conformity of the idea with its object, as the adequacy of what one says or thinks with what is real, or what can be proven. Such modern definitions of the truth are not without consequences. For the Russian thinker Sergius Bulgakov (1871–1944), the modern individualistic representation of the truth is doomed to establish arbitrary, one-sided, and therefore heretical decisions in the etymological sense of the term. In his major work *La tragédie de la philosophie*, written in the early 1920s,[17] Bulgakov defined the relationship between philosophical thought and truth as a tragedy insofar as it seeks to disregard the relation of commitment that exists between the individual and the world:

16 Ibid., 16

17 S. Bulgakov, *Die Tragödie der Philosophie,* Darmstadt, Otto Reichl Verlag, 1927.

> The antinomies that devastate reason are those very ones which constitute and define it. The critical antinomianism in metaphysics and epistemology thus takes the place of dogmatic rationalism. This latter is only the infatuation of the reason with itself. Criticism, on the contrary, consists precisely in questioning the structures of reason and its foundations — not in order to overthrow it but rather to affirm it. In light of this criticism, the history of philosophy is merely a tragic history of heresies.[18]

Bulgakov bases his opinion on the following argument: the person who wants to arrive at the truth should first affirm himself as a conscious human being who declares "I am this someone." But this movement of the consciousness is based on antimonies. Indeed the "I" cannot be objectivized and is absolute, whereas the predicate "this someone" both determines and objectivizes it. This reality violates the two basic principles of logical reasoning — namely, the principle of identity and the principle of non-contradiction — and leads to the idealist philosophy of J. G. Fichte, which is characterized by the never-realized desire to attain awareness of the infinite. Similarly, the predicate "this someone," which represents the conceptual determination, the idea, the nature, requires the totality and universality of the Logos. This is the meaning of Hegel's philosophy conceived as a philosophy of the predicativity of being. Such a philosophy leads to an unbearable tension between the relative and the absolute. Moreover, in reality the verb "to be" signifies neither consciousness nor nature. The copula "am" is divided in two: one and multiple, motionless and mobile. We find here the instability of the monist pantheistic systems (which deny the distinction between subject and predicate) of Leibniz and Spinoza and the philosophy of the Absolute without distinction, of the philosophy of mythology and of the revelation of Schelling. According to Bulgakov, in these three cases human thought seeks to reduce the three terms to just one. The human mind, however, fails to reveal itself as subject in the predicate because there is no complete identity between the three moments of judgment of self-determination. Bulgakov concludes that philosophy must become critical of itself, that it must recognize an Absolute Spirit within which the three irreducible moments of the life of the spirit are reconciled. Pierre Hadot (1922–2010), a colleague of Michel Foucault's at the Collège

18 Ibid., 37.

de France, wrote an enthusiastic review of Bulgakov's book. He sums up the Russian philosopher's position in these terms:

> The dogma of the Unitrinity appears as a unique outcome, postulated by the human spirit but inaccessible without Revelation. What reason postulates when it becomes aware of its own enigma is an Absolute Spirit in which the self-revelation of the Self is exhaustive—that is, in which the self-determination of the predicate is not a Non-Self imposed from without or some pure idealistic construct but the I-Myself, going out of itself into another oneself, in a relationship in which I-Myself would experience the unity of self-to-self in a copular being which, in turn, would have the fullness of personal consciousness. In other words, there is need of a Self which is, at the same time, being and *Logos*, a *Logos* which is simultaneously Self and being—and all this within the unity of a sole self-affirmation of the Self.[19]

Thus, for Bulgakov, "the Trinitarian dogma enlightens reason and enables it to discover itself." This implies an important consequence: philosophy, which is heterodox at a certain level of sapiential tension, must tend towards Christian orthodoxy if it is to avoid modalist systemism and realize its quest for truth. Conversely, for him, theology can only be sapiential. It cannot include the divine unity in an abstract and impersonal manner, and it must not fall into the heresies of monarchism or pluralist Arianism. The consubstantiality of the Father, Son, and Spirit is the light of truth which shines over the human sciences of the future.

Even though many aspects of Bulgakov's analysis have become unacceptable in contemporary academic circles, probably because of these circles' abstract and fragmented representation of knowledge and their highly specialized organization of scholarship, one finds among certain thinkers a renewed interest for any thought associating the transcendental with the empirical. In 2003, the French philosopher Marcel Gauchet proposed his "transcendental anthroposociology" in his book *La condition historique*. The director of the magazine *Le Débat* no longer talks of expelling the religious element from sociology, as many are wont to do, but attempts to understand the evolution of "the religious structurings" of societies. For Gauchet,

19 Pierre Hadot, "La philosophie comme hérésie trinitaire," in *Revue d'Histoire et de Philosophie Religieuse*, Paris, PUF, 1957, 246.

societies are dependent on a gift [*donation*], and it is precisely this which enables them to have power over themselves, from which it follows that humans are not political "animals," as Aristotle would have it. Rather, what distinguishes them from animals is that their political consciousness enables them to invent ways of being together. Gauchet concludes that religion is the means by which the social person relates to the self. At this juncture, our reflection should focus on the distinction between "being one's self" and "being together." Thus, for Gauchet symbolic language is "before us." It is characterized by the ternary movement of self-awareness, by the distance in relation to one's self, and by the rediscovery of self through externality.

## THE THEOLOGICAL DEFINITION OF TRUTH

The history of Christian theology has led us to a contemporary definition of truth which is no longer homogeneous. According to the textbooks of dogmatic theology, the truth is first of all what has been defined by the Magisterium, what is in conformity with the Scriptures, or what is faithful to the traditions of the ecumenical councils. In spite of these rather schematic distinctions between the Catholic, Protestant, and Orthodox traditions, Christians share a common vision of the truth as a person. For them, Jesus Christ is the *hodos*, that is, the way of truth *and* the way of life. In the Christian *meta-hodo*-logy of orthodoxy, there cannot be anything that is true without life, nor life which does not aspire to truth.

Furthermore, in this tradition of thought, truth cannot be possessed, because it is a person. One can only belong to it. It is a gift inseparable from love.[20] This is why orthodoxy situates itself between faith — this disposition to live in God whom it seeks to serve by incarnation — and reason, which is its spiritual rudder. Faith is professed only insofar as it is demonstrated. The doctrine of faith is thus edification of meaning, interpretation. Orthodox Christian rationality implies, according to its tradition of scriptural interpretation, a relational and communal joining of people to Jesus Christ who is, in the Christian tradition, the *Logos* incarnate. In this sense, orthodoxy signifies the adequacy of faith and of reason, an accomplishment of rationality which attains the universal and the actualization of an encounter which

20 On this theme, cf. Fabrice Hadjadj, *La foi des démons, ou l'athéisme dépassé*, Paris, Salvator, 2009; cf. also the review of François-Xavier Putallaz, "Notes et lectures," *Nova et Vetera* (April–June 2011): 241.

gives meaning to it all. According to Christian doctrine, orthodoxy cannot be conceived as a static reality, something closed and finished. It is originally a journey in the Way opened by Christ. In patristic thought, orthodoxy appears where the Holy Spirit breathes, and it is always in continuity with the evangelical and apostolic tradition. In so far as its task is to bring the divine nature and human nature together, the function of orthodox thought is to bear witness to this encounter or to show the paths that lead to it. This can be translated into the discovery of the laws of the created universe, the teaching of spiritual truths, the guidance of people in their daily lives, the celebration of an exchange of gifts — in short by all that can lead human beings to tend, individually and collectively, towards the Kingdom of God, which is the plenitude (*Pleroma*) of Orthodoxy.

This is why the notion of personal consciousness, both individual and collective, is essential in determining orthodoxy. "Orthodox" thought, in the confessional sense of the term (as used by the School of Paris to designate a group of thinkers who worked mostly at the St. Sergius Institute and at the *Put* review), has borrowed the concept of conscience from German philosophy. The School of Paris reworked this concept in the light of Eastern tradition with the understanding that it was fundamentally catholic and conciliatory and not a self-consciousness turned in on itself (*Selbstbewusstsein*). In *A l'image et à la ressemblance de Dieu*, Vladimir Lossky defines catholicity of consciousness as follows: "The mystery of the catholicity of the Church is realized in the plurality of personal consciences as an agreement of unity and multiplicity in the image of the Holy Trinity which the Church realizes in its own life: three consciences — a unique Subject, a sole Divine Counsel or 'Counsel of the Saints' which is the divine catholicity."[21]

For Lossky, Orthodoxy is precisely this catholic ecclesial consciousness. Writers as diverse as Bulgakov, Lossky, Meyendorff, Evdokimov, and Clément have employed this concept of orthodoxy or ecclesial consciousness in order to arrive at an expression which is neither triumphalist nor sectarian, neither disincarnate nor closed in on itself. Insofar as this notion of orthodoxy has been reflected upon and enriched by Christian culture, orthodox Christianity (as a cultural phenomenon) can be understood in the following way: on the one hand, orthodox Christianity is a historical reality, symbolic in nature, characterized by *acts* which manifest the lives of men and women who follow the path of Jesus Christ, by specific *ways*

21 V. Lossky, *A l'image et à la ressemblance de Dieu*, Paris, Cerf, 2006, 191.

*of thinking* which represent the truth as personal, and by *organizational structures* which seek to realize the Christian kerygma. On the other hand, orthodox Christianity is a *self-awareness* which determines the identity of different communities who profess to be Christian.

Thus, the history of Christian orthodoxy is the narrative which tries to describe a Christian community's consciousness of itself in its sacramental, spiritual and civic life. The history of revelation brought about by faith does not coincide with its reception, which is never homogeneous and always contradictory. This is why Nicholas Berdyaev wanted to write a *Critique of Revelation* which would attribute to the Holy Spirit what Kant postulated of pure reason. The history of the Orthodox Church should be understood in its twofold significance as a historical institution and a symbolic space: house of the Father, body of Christ, temple of the Holy Spirit, Bride of the Lamb, and so forth. It is therefore at once the narrative of the various representations that its faithful make of God, of the coexistence within it of often different representations of the world, and of the expression of the degrees of communion existing among its faithful.

## THE NECESSARY HISTORICAL REDEFINITION OF THE CRITERION OF TRUTH

The love of wisdom, which takes into consideration the Trinitarian dimension of the human spirit and the tragic character of the history of philosophy, cannot ignore the theological process that posits the reality of God, radically other yet capable of self-revelation as person. Conversely, because of the very content of the Christian faith, the *ortho-doxy* of truth cannot be the exclusive property of institutional theological discourse. This of course has political consequences, as was agreed in the debate between Joseph Ratzinger and Jürgen Habermas on today's postsecular society held on 19 January 2004. The Catholic cardinal insisted that everyone should recognize that "the divine light of the reason" can purify and regulate religions, and yet that history teaches us that reason also is susceptible to violent pathologies (the atomic bomb, or the objectification of the person) if it is not reminded of its limits and if it turns a deaf ear to the great religious traditions of humanity. For his part, Habermas situated himself in the same logic of a necessary new alliance, in the public sphere, between citizens who are believers and those who are not. Habermas states:

> When secularized citizens assume their role as citizens, they have no right to deny a possibility of truth in the religious images of the world, nor to question the right of their fellow citizens who are believers to contribute to public debates using religious terminology. A liberal political culture can even expect secular citizens to participate in the efforts to diffuse, in public terms accessible to all, pertinent contributions originally expressed in a religious vocabulary.[22]

There is, therefore, a reason for trying to redefine, historically, the implications of the contours of the notion of orthodoxy as a criterion of philosophical, theological, moral and political truth. There are numerous publications in philosophy dealing with the truth, but few take into account the specific history of doxic thought in the margins of the progressive constitution of Western rationalism. In many respects, however, one can consider the history of the philosophical thinking of the twentieth century, from Martin Heidegger to Michel Foucault and Stanislas Breton, as an effort towards its rediscovery. On the side of the theologians, numerous studies have been published which seek to understand orthodoxy as a historical, confessional ecclesial reality. One thinks in particular of the pioneering study *Qu'est-ce que l'orthodoxie?* by the three monks of the Abbey of Chevetogne: Pierre Dumont, Feuillant Mercenier and Clément Lialine, published in Brussels in 1944.[23] Equally worthy of mention is Sergius Bulgakov's major postmodern work *L'Orthodoxie,* translated by Lev Gillet and published in Paris in 1932. This attempt at definition is taken up by many thinkers such as Paul Evdokimov, his son Michel Evdokimov, and many other authors. There are also many other comparable studies which seek to define the orthodoxy of the Magisterium or that of Protestant hermeneutics. But, to the best of our knowledge, there has never been a study which tries to define the place of orthodox thought in the entire history of Judeo-Christian civilization. The study of Orthodoxy (and orthodoxy more generally) is at the junction of philosophy, history, theology and the sciences. It is by following the semantic history of this symbolic notion that we will attempt to define a

22 Ibid., 60

23 For Jean Danielou, "What marks these pages is that they do not present us with a historical Orthodoxy, the object of retrospective studies, but with an Orthodoxy which has to live with the problem posed by the new political conditions of the Russian State and the encounter with Marxist philosophy." J. Danielou, *Dieu vivant*, no. 8, 144.

new synthetic intelligibility for orthodoxy. This is a daunting undertaking, since it is a question of nothing less than a new representation of the truth which synthesizes the understanding of Christian revelation, the narrative of historical incarnation and epistemological implications of that revelation, and certain developments in contemporary philosophical discourse.[24]

This is why it is fitting to first make mention of this question of the definition of orthodoxy and its place in the complex doxic system of modern thought. As a second consideration, our method for recovering the paradigmatic meanings of orthodoxy will be presented exposing a semantic history of the concept of orthodoxy, situated at the crossroads of two major axes of truth, the horizontal and cosmic and the vertical and transcendent. At this point emphasis will be placed on the *criterion* of truth in the history of Christianity. Finally, the third, more historical and more detailed part of the study will rely on a historiographical study of the orthodox consciousness in the works of the principal historians of Christianity, in both the East and the West, in order to demonstrate the constitution of four major paradigms of orthodoxy in the history of humanity since Jesus Christ.

24 The word orthodoxy or truth will not be capitalized given that, from the outset, it has been indicated that there is the possibility of elevating the meaning from that of a quality to that of a subject. The word will be capitalized only in specific cases when the concept is only clear in its institutional signification.

# CHAPTER 5

# *The Rediscovery of Christian Orthodoxy*

THE QUESTION OF ORTHODOXY, WHICH ASSUMES as we have seen the recognition of the link between philosophy and theology, is at the heart of the current debate on the nature of modernity and its ultramodern or postmodern outgrowth. Among the leading voices in this vast worldwide discussion are the Anglican John Milbank, the founder of the philosophical school known as "Radical Orthodoxy,"[1] which promotes a new dialogue between faith and reason and counts among its adherents personalities such as William Cavanaugh and Catherine Pickstock;[2] and on the other side a whole series of contemporary thinkers both living (Alain Badiou, Richard Dawkins, Jean-Luc Marion, Jürgen Habermas) and deceased (Gilles Deleuze, Michel Foucault, Paul Ricoeur) who have in common their refusal on principle to link philosophy and theology. Certainly, there are many details and nuances to be added.[3] More often than not, these authors are suspicious of any blending of genre that can lead to the worst excesses of fanaticism and ideology. Jean-Luc Marion rejects above all any theological discipline which seeks to prove the existence of God through purely rational logic.[4] Likewise, in his hermeneutical philosophy of religious language, Paul Ricoeur distinguishes between the act of discourse and its content, the speaker, the primitive audience, and the contemporary reader. He thus limits the

1 *Radical Orthodoxy? A Catholic Enquiry*, ed., Laurence Paul Hemming, Aldershot, Ashgate, 2000.

2 Rowan Williams, the former Archbishop of Canterbury, should also be mentioned as one of the sources of J. Milbank.

3 For Marion, "phenomenology refuses to admit the real possibility of a revelation since it establishes two limits to possibility in general: the self and the horizon." Jean-Luc Marion, *Le visible et le révélé*, Paris, Cerf, 2005, 30.

4 Jean-Luc Marion, *Le visible et le révélé*, 17.

role of hermeneutics to grasping meaning on the basis of the forms of the discourse.[5] This does not prevent the Protestant philosopher from admitting the possibility of an individual faith which constantly interprets, but only "for oneself," the events and signs attested by Scripture.[6]

Yet the proponents of Radical Orthodoxy consider that such an attitude of passive distancing and the search for an individualistic line of thought can lead to neglect of the very essence of the philosophical process: its loving, creative, and communitarian participation in created wisdom. Pickstock writes: "If we want to set ourselves on *the right path* and recover our freedom as human beings, we must rediscover this sense of participation and, above all, that of our participation in God's Trinitarian life. This is the faith of radical orthodoxy, the whole meaning of our struggle."[7] Such a call for a correct reasoning, which would be a new synthesis between the work of the intellect and an opening to the spirit, is not envisaged by the members of this school as a simple return to the truth of Thomas Aquinas. Indeed, this intellectual movement defines itself as postmodern. Catherine Pickstock sees the philosophy of radical orthodoxy as both enemy and ally of the thought of Derrida, Foucault and Barthes:

> the enemy because we believe that the differences, being real, should coexist and collaborate with one another; otherwise they will disappear due to their antagonism and the war they would wage on one another; the ally because we all think, like postmodern thinkers, that we are living on the surface of a world full of changing and mysterious symbols that we are constantly being led to decipher. This world is that which has been created *ex nihilo*, for, as St. Augustine states, things do not exist by themselves; they are only the fleeting reflection of God, their Creator. The postmodern thinker adopts

5 P. Ricoeur, "La philosophie et la spécificité du language religieux," *Revue d'histoire et de philosophie religieuses*, no. 1 (1975).

6 "Hope or 'unconditional confidence' would remain vain and empty if it did not rely on a continuously renewed interpretation of the event-signs attested to by the Scriptures — especially the liberation narratives of the Old Testament and that of the resurrection in the New Testament. These are the events which signify the ultimate possibilities of *my* liberty and thus become, *for me*, Word of God. Such is the hermeneutical determination of Biblical faith," P. Ricoeur, "La philosophie et la spécificité du langage religieux," op. cit, conclusion.

7 C. Pickstock, "L'orthodoxie est-elle radicale?" in Adrian Pabst, Olivier Thomas Venard, *Radical Orthodoxy, Pour une révolution théologique*, Paris, Ad Solem, 2004, 33.

> an almost nihilistic position; for him, there is nothing beneath this influx of signs. Radical orthodoxy tries to reframe this nihilism; the flow of signs escapes the nothingness to the extent that it is the reflection of God who is everything. . . . The nothingness from which we have been drawn is not the murky vacuum of postmodern thought but the inexhaustible plenitude of God which only appears somber to us because of an excess of light.[8]

The two previous popes, John Paul II, more philosopher, and Benedict XVI, more theologian, both participated in this interdisciplinary discussion on the new relationships between philosophy, science, and theology. This was in particular due to John Paul's 1995 encyclical *Fides et ratio*,[9] and a number of Benedict's addresses, for instance at the University of Regensburg in 2006, the Collège des Bernardins in 2008, before the British Parliament in 2010. In his speech at Westminster Hall on September 17, 2010, Benedict insisted on the political consequences of this ongoing international discussion on the definition of right reason:

> The central question at issue, then, is this: where is the ethical foundation for political choices to be found? The Catholic tradition maintains that the objective norms governing right action are accessible to reason, prescinding from the content of revelation. According to this understanding, the role of religion in political debate is not so much to supply these norms, as if they could not be known by non-believers—still less to propose concrete political solutions, which would lie altogether outside the competence of religion—but rather to help purify and shed light upon the application of reason to the discovery of objective moral principles. This "corrective" role of religion vis-à-vis reason is not always welcomed, though, partly because distorted forms of religion, such as sectarianism and fundamentalism, can be seen to create serious social problems themselves. And in their turn, these distortions

8 Ibid., 23.

9 George Weigel, more orthodox than radical, is one of the leading American intellectual conservatives. Making his own an expression of John Paul II (whose biography he wrote), Weigel believes that the alternative to a modernity sapped of its strength by "metaphysical ennui" is to be found in "the exalted adventure of orthodox Christianity." George Weigel, *The Cube and the Cathedral*, New York, Basic Books, 2005, 172.

> of religion arise when insufficient attention is given to the purifying and structuring role of reason within religion. It is a two-way process. Without the corrective supplied by religion, though, reason too can fall prey to distortions, as when it is manipulated by ideology, or applied in a partial way that fails to take full account of the dignity of the human person. Such misuse of reason, after all, was what gave rise to the slave trade in the first place and to many other social evils, not least the totalitarian ideologies of the twentieth century. This is why I would suggest that the world of reason and the world of faith — the world of secular rationality and the world of religious belief — need one another and should not be afraid to enter into a profound and ongoing dialogue, for the good of our civilization.[10]

After a brief presentation of this stream of philosophical and theological thought, which is now strongly redefined as orthodox, we will show the specificity of the contributions of Charles Taylor, a Canadian Catholic philosopher. Taylor admits the need for a new, subtle reconnection between philosophy and theology, while refusing Milbank's too radical denial of modern truth. It will be seen that the Russian religious thinkers of the 19th and 20th centuries, from Soloviev to Berdyaev and Bulgakov, also represent a necessary point of reference in this ongoing reconfiguration. Finally, special attention will be given to Jean-Marc Ferry, a French agnostic philosopher who in his later works has come to question the supposed neutrality of modern philosophy. He exemplifies a broader movement of European intellectuals criticizing the ostensibly "universal" foundations of secularity. A detailed presentation of these three positions can be found in a series of eight conferences, the *Stanton Lectures*, delivered by John Milbank in January–March 2011 at the Faculty of Divinity of the University of Cambridge,[11] in Charles Taylor's book, *A Secular Age*, published in 2007 by Harvard University Press,[12] and that of J. M. Ferry, *La religion réflexive* (Paris, Cerf, 2010).

10 https://w2.vatican.va/content/benedict-xvi/en/speeches/2010/september/documents/hf_ben-xvi_spe_20100917_societa-civile.html.

11 John Milbank's *Stanton Lectures* have been published on the internet site of the Center of Theology and Philosophy of the University of Nottingham.

12 Charles Taylor, *A Secular Age*, Cambridge, Harvard University Press, 2007.

## JOHN MILBANK'S REDISCOVERY OF ORTHODOX THOUGHT

In *Theology and Social Theory*,[13] published in 1990, John Milbank set forth his vision of a philosophy that would again be guided by faith — "again" because, for Milbank, this synergistic relationship is the hallmark of *philosophia perennis.* This restoration will come about not through submission but by respecting tradition. This is radical orthodoxy, a discourse anchored in the philosophical and theological tradition yet capable of self-criticism. It has its source in Christian revelation and thus constitutes a new "meta-discourse." For Milbank, as for the whole Western tradition which identifies itself as orthodox, from St. Thomas Aquinas to Henri de Lubac and John Paul II, faith and reason are not radically distinct, for both represent different degrees of the participation of the human spirit in the Divine Spirit. According to this tradition, faith is open to criticism when it claims to be complete and stands in no need of reason, just as reason can be criticized when it imagines itself to be independent of any relationship to the invisible and the unknown. According to Milbank, the non-recognition of this interplay between faith and reason is the principal source of modern violence, whether of religious or secular origin.[14]

13 John Milbank, *Theology and Social Theory,* Cambridge, Blackwell, 1990, 1; J. Milbank, *Théologie et théorie sociale,* Paris, Cerf, 2010.

14 Similar proposals can be found in the works of the Orthodox Christian anthropologist Stephen Headley. "Scotus argued for an original principle of individuation which he called the 'this-ness' of a thing, its *haecceity*; what the French call the 'chosification,' the materialisation of a person, constitutes the unity of a unique individual. Ultimately, this simply means his divisibility from other human beings. The atomizing axiom that only the individual exists dominates Scotus' understanding of reality. For the apprehension of individuals, a cognitive representation is required. No dialogical dimension of the *lien social* impinges on his vision. All that is external to oneself constitutes difference, hence the primacy for the subject of the perceived object. Here again there is no mutually established shared communion, but a unilateral hence subjective perception of the world. Here no primordial 'belonging' together is found, hence Heidegger's search for one. In societies undergoing modernization, heterogeneity was ordered through secularized compartmentalization and no longer encompassment through a sacred hierarchy. In traditional cosmologies, participation in divine creativity is renewed in time through different networks of exchange. In any secularized subject and object epistemology, every modification of my perception of the diversity of the outside world involves a partial deconstruction by *substitution* of a new illusory construct, which is why the difference is said to have a primordial association with *violence*." S. C. Headley, "The Crisis of Representation," publication forthcoming.

Twenty-one years later in Cambridge, after a multitude of debates on his principal thesis,[15] Milbank continues to criticize modern philosophy, which since John Duns Scotus[16] has come to consider itself emancipated from any religious perspective and focused on a better understanding of its own internal logic. This represents a response to the history of truth put forth by Michel Foucault in his 1966 work *Les Mots et les Choses*. The French philosopher, an heir to the Kantian heritage, described two great discontinuities in the *episteme* of Western culture: that of the classic age of the 17th and 18th centuries, which made the theory of representation coincide with language, natural orders, wealth, and value; and that of the modern age, from 1775 to the 20th century, during which the consciousness of finitude, historicity, analogy, and succession organized knowledge in a new discontinuous and functional manner. In the transition from the classical to the modern, "the obscure, repetitive violence of desire," writes Foucault, to signify the shift between the two periods, "comes to defeat the limits of representation."[17]

John Milbank recognizes the role of *eros* in our rationality, but this does not lead him to disqualify the symbolic representation of the world which constituted the foundation of truth during the Middle Ages. For him, many of the "rational" presuppositions and "neutral" ways of thinking

15 See Hemming, *Radical Orthodoxy?*

16 According to analytical philosophers, the thought of the Franciscan Duns Scotus represents a turning point insofar as it left the Aristotelian primacy of actuality in order to concentrate on the primacy of the possible. Whereas for the Dominican Saint Thomas, finite beings were not complete in themselves and only find fulfillment in the measure in which they participate in God, for Scotus, what is "transcendental" to all finite reality is no longer a participated existence in the Pure Act of God, but rather all the conditions of possibility contained in an actual existence (*Stanton Lecture*, 1, 7). This "possibilistic" and transcendental approach will be adopted by Kant who will transform metaphysics into epistemology. In the context of the European philosophy of the history of metaphysics, Duns Scotus also plays a pivotal role by introducing the onto-theological approach which consists in placing God in the transcendental realm of being. This leads to putting will and love above any intellectual effort of understanding. In this univocal ontology, being is affirmed, not by communion or mutual participation but by a unilateral mental act of conceptual definition. This philosophy, which reduces the person to the subject, will make possible the political theory of representation without participation and will weaken the intuition that a just governance is the result of interactions between persons who consider themselves dependent on a whole which surpasses them and which, consequently, unites them to one another.

17 M. Foucault, *Les mots et les choses*, Paris, Gallimard, 1966, 223.

of secular philosophy to some degree assume certain theological beliefs.[18] In particular, he shows that by detaching itself (under the influence of the Franciscans) from the pole of transcendence, modern civilization has lost the indispensable source of knowledge represented by the oscillation of the finite with the infinite, that can be expressed by participation of the created being with the uncreated Being. Without such an oscillation, one invariably arrives at either a Kantian finitism or a Spinozian infinitism. Both identify being with God, give precedence to possibility over actuality, to representation over participation; but while the epistemologists and logicians limit themselves to the possibility of meaning and reduce being to its knowledge, proponents of immanent ontology favor the reference to God-being and suggest that human intelligence is equal to the divinity. From this point on, in accordance with this modern logic, space is conceived by Newton through the prism of the new alliance of gravitational force, and evolution is interpreted by Darwin as dominated by the biological law of the survival of the fittest. The meta-concepts or chronotopes that are kingdom and eternity become ridiculous and useless.[19]

Milbank does not wish, however, to purely and simply return to the Middle Ages and to Dionysius the Areopagite. His objective is to make the heterodox signification of modernity intelligible to contemporary orthodox thinkers,[20] in order to enable them to rediscover the orthodoxy of their

18 Let it be noted that this return of metaphysics is a salient phenomenon of the beginning of the 21st century. Cf. C. Yannaras, *Postmodern Metaphysics*, Brookline, Holy Cross, 2004 (1999 in Greek); Rémi Brague, *Les ancres dans le ciel*, Paris, Seuil, 2011.

19 In France, the physician and theologian François Euvé is rediscovering the need of balancing the point of view of actuality and that of potentiality. "The horizon is the line that separates the 'known world' of the observer (the domain of actuality) from what is beyond this known world (the domain of potentiality). This approach distinguishes between the pole of 'actuality' (the apparent horizon, the phenomenological traces of reality) and the 'potential' level (the deep horizon, the ensemble of the logically possible modes of reality). Reality is neither just actuality nor just potentiality (the 'imaginary' world of theories). The real world can be envisaged as 'the place of all the possible lines of horizon' (Gilles Cohen-Tannoudji). It cannot be represented on a unique apparent horizon. The scientific method can never arrive at an immediate comprehension of everything; it will always be a state of coming and going between our apparent horizon — to which it constantly returns (this is the role of experimentation) — and the deep horizon which is opened by the imaginative power of theories." François Euvé, ed., *Science, Foi, Sagesse*, Paris, Editions de l'Atelier/Ouvrières, 2004, 51.

20 This implies showing the part of truth in the works of Kant, Hegel, Schelling etc., such as Sergius Bulgakov did in his 1927 book *La Tragédie de la philosophie*.

own tradition, often itself tainted by heterodoxy;[21] to rediscover the path of countermodernity traced by Meister Eckhart, Jacobi, Coleridge, Franz von Baader, and Johann Möhler; and to propose a postmodern synthesis that would embrace language, phenomena, mathematics, and life, not under the banner of virtual immanence or of a phantasmal externality but as the expression of "actual words," "actual things," "actual numbers,"[22] and "actual transcendence."

Milbank, faithful to his principle of oscillation, shows that the concept of evolution requires the doctrine of creation. Contemporary biologists such as Theodosius Dobzhansky have given priority to the notion of environmental adaptation over that of struggle for survival in order to understand evolution. This makes it possible to propose the model of self-organizational force (or that of *habitus* in the terminology of Ravaisson) and thus rediscover the concepts of actuality and participation. In this perspective, physical reality does not initially obey laws. It is governed by an impulse of self-created life, the vital impulse dear to Bergson (for whom "duration" was equivalent to God). In this vision, there is no life without resurrection. Life incessantly begets life, regardless of the power of death. Milbank endeavors to distinguishes his approach from that of postmodern and post-Spinozian philosophers such as Gilles Deleuze who identify life with the idea of immanence or of an abstract machine. For the Anglican philosopher, finite life participates in the unique transcendent life, not by way of fusion but as a gift. This is why he maintains that "true

21 Milbank especially pleads the case for the doctrine of *apokatastasis* which, in his opinion, is required by a "non-idolatrous monotheism" (*Stanton Lectures*, no. 3, p. 35). He also criticizes E. Levinas, M. Henry and J.-L. Marion who, faithful to the idea of the conformity between being and knowledge, refuse any type of mediation and participation (except in an indirect and non-recognized manner), give priority to the non-participated immediacy of the divine and thus ignore all religious philosophy and any theology of participation. Milbank explains that, for his part, "participation" is the better model for the gift. Marion is qualified as an "orthodox Catholic" but his theory of saturated phenomenon, which is based on a "doubtful dualism" between the intentional and the intuitive, is, in Milbank's opinion, closer to what Kant called the sublime than to patristic thought. Philosophy is only a propaedeutic to theology. This is why Milbank, who doesn't pay enough attention to the intellectual evolution of Marion, favors the concept of participation over that of distance, the concept that Marion considered primary. For Marion the ontological base of reality is gratitude and thanksgiving.

22 Mathematics can only be conceived on those plans which exclude either immanence or transcendence. The transfinite numbers bear testimony to this reality situated between the finite and infinite.

vitalism is a personalist vitalism."[23] To describe his representation of doxic truth, Milbank draws a cross.[24] The vertical axis unites humanity to God, the immanent to the transcendent. In this model of participated transcendence, finite realities partake of the eternal truth to varying degrees. The horizontal axis is that of the material universe, where there is a continuity between being and knowledge through the passage of ideas or forms of things into the intellect. Milbank suggests rethinking these ideas in terms of signs, numbers, and aspects. He also proposes considering these mediations between reality and reason, these three forms of understanding just mentioned, as products of feelings and imagination. Truth is not given to men by a distant glance, as Locke and Descartes believed. Milbank thus refers to the mediation of teleological desire, whose role Michel Foucault had shown to be crucial for understanding the crisis of classical *episteme*. Foucault's demonstration of this is based on Felix Ravaisson's *L'Habitude*. In this work, habitude, "a mixture of reception and reaction that coagulates effort," is presented as the link between movement and thought, existence and knowledge. Ravaisson also deemed that every natural habitude is the approximation of a supernatural habitude infused within man. For Milbank, who joins Foucault on this point, in all creation it is the human *eros* that forms the fundamental habitude, mediator, and organizer of knowledge. With Ravaisson, according to Milbank, Western thought has surpassed all Pelagianism; receptivity to grace is already a gift of grace.

Thanks to recent academic research, this rediscovery of Ravaisson allows Milbank to reintegrate the empirical thinkers Berkeley and Hume, whose orthodoxy he rediscovers, despite their dependence on Duns Scotus and William of Ockham. Berkeley had managed to escape both solipsist phenomenalism, denial of the reality of matter, and skepticism of personal identity through his rediscovery of the Cappadocian view that externality consists of finite images of divine ideas or divine language. For his part, Hume considered that in order to overcome skepticism, one has to trust the structures that make up the world and that are connected to thought, a trust that is in continuity with religious faith. Between the infinitist monism of Spinoza (which would survive up until Deleuze) and the finitist epistemology of Descartes (taken up by Locke, Kant, Husserl and Frege), Hume was still able to defend a "conservative ontological realism" because of his

23 *Stanton Lectures*, 2, p. 24.

24 J. Milbank, "The Habit of Reason," *Stanton Lectures*, no. 6, op. cit.

Aristotelian conviction that all reasoning is only "a modulation of feeling."[25] His "skepticism" was directed against the rationalist naturalism of nominalism and against all rationalist religiosity that makes God an idol, a kind of human reason carried over into infinity. For Hume, thought separated from feeling and sensation and therefore from incarnation, is threatened by solipsist confinement and risks closing itself up in solipsism. On the other hand, the more "objectively" a thought can be expressed, the more it can be considered as not requiring consciousness and can then be regarded as the product of natural forces.

Within this perspective, Milbank analyses not only the works of contemporary thinkers such as Badiou, Meillassoux and Zizek, but also those of Priest, Dummet and McDowell (representing the current of revised idealist speculation) in addition to the neo-materialist epigones of Quine and Davidson (namely Rorty, Laruelle and Dawkins) or the distant neo-realist heirs of Hume such as Latour, Harman and Lowe. He shows that the boundary between sterile immanentism and orthodox truth is tenuous and consequently proposes an understanding of the trinitarian ontology of Gregory of Nyssa according to which the *dynamis* is as fundamental as the *ousia.* In order to establish his metaphysics of participatory transcendence, which also implies an ontological hierarchy, Milbank restores the categories of substance (defined as our consciousness of the persistence of something in spite of the changes it undergoes), of relation (which cannot be a simple substitute for substance), and potentiality (understood as participatory transcendence). Thus, for him, "reality is more fundamental than being for it is both being and the power of being and this participation in reality as both actual and dynamic (as the self-generating force which is simultaneously art and life) is more fundamental than participation in being."[26] This echoes the turning point articulated by Nicholas Berdyaev in his 1935 book *Esprit et Réalité.*

Milbank argues that, if imagination is at the heart of human intellectual activity, it is because it is also at the heart of divine knowing. This is a truth found not only in Christian sophiology (Soloviev, Bulgakov, et al.) but also in the Islamic philosophy of the *alam-al-mithal* or the *mundus imaginalis.* It allows us to envisage the reality of the mediation of subtle bodies, angelic or demonic such as are found in all the great religions and in many fairy tales. This leads Milbank to propose an ontology of the imagination where

25 *Stanton Lectures*, no. 7, p. 7.
26 *Stanton Lectures*, no. 8, p. 26.

everything is described as a self-imagining force. But this reenchantment of the universe, already invoked by Vladimir Veidle in the 1930s, is not a justification of the New Age mentality. For Milbank, it is "the Trinitarian Logos who saves the reality of human reason by thinking about it as Infinite Imagination."[27]

According to J. H. Newman, the power of Divine Imagination has its corollary in human imagination. In his *Grammar of Assent*, the Catholic philosopher links his concept of real assent to that of religious imagination: "A dogma is a proposition; it stands for a notion or for a thing; and to believe it is to give the assent of the mind to it, as it stands for the one or for the other. To give a real assent to it is an act of religion; to give a notional, is a theological act. It is discerned, rested in, and appropriated as a reality, by the religious imagination; it is held as a truth, by the theological intellect."[28]

## THE RESPONSE OF CHARLES TAYLOR

It is characteristic of contemporary ecumenical *doxa* that a Catholic, in this instance Charles Taylor, should attempt to justify the work of the Reformation. This might have been in order to attenuate the bitterness of the Anglican Milbank who was alarmed by modernity's loss of metaphysics and the concept of participation, a loss to which Protestantism contributed greatly by uncritically accepting the works of the Franciscan nominalists. In *A Secular Age*, Taylor attempts to balance the historical narrative of the Intellectual Deviation (ID)[29] favored by Milbank and many Catholic[30] and Orthodox[31] Christians (in the confessional sense of the words), by means of a complementary narrative, the Great History of the Reformation (GHR).

While we will not go into the details of his narrative, Taylor's analysis enables us to understand the spiritual resilience of modernity. It centers on the appearance, in the 16th century, under the impetus of the Reformers, of a culture which sought to be humanistic, disengaged and autonomous. This culture sought to succeed a culture which, at the end of the Middle Ages,

27 Ibid., 40.

28 J. H. Newman, *The Grammar of Assent*, ch. 5, "Apprehension and Assent in the Matter of Religion."

29 A narrative found under different forms in John Milbank, Sergius Bulgakov and Marie-Joseph Le Guillou. Cf. especially Le Guillou, *Le Mystère du Père: foi des apôtres: gnoses actuelles*, Paris, Fayard, 1973.

30 Le Guillou, *Le Mystère du Père.*

31 Sergius Bulgakov, *Tragedia filosofii* (1927) in *Sotchinenia*, t.1, Moskva, Nauka, 1993.

had already lost the sense of eternity, the key to a divine space-time, deeper and more celebratory than that of the century (*saeculum=aion*=century) and the ability to participate in cosmic epiphanies. This secular and henceforth humanistic culture retained transcendence at the beginning but neutralized it in a natural law which became progressively impersonal. In the 18th century, modernity became frankly hostile to so-called "orthodox" Christianity, accusing it of offending rationality, proposing an unacceptable theodicy, being authoritarian and of threatening the new order of the social contract. However, for Taylor, this reaction of the Reformation, which he sees as rooted in the Greek Fathers,[32] liberated medieval society from a juridical theology of salvation,[33] from a notion of redemption that emphasized the satisfaction of the Father through the death of His Son, and tore down the barriers between the sacred and the profane — God sanctifying humanity reaching into everyday life (one's work, family life, etc.). The sacraments were rejected by the Reformers as belonging to what they considered a magical relationship with the world. Lived, however, as words of the Logos, in the personal life of each person, they enabled people to again give glory to divine justice.

32 C. Taylor, op. cit., 233.

33 Juridical or penitential theology of salvation found among "Catholic" as well as "Protestant" and "Orthodox" theologians. For Russian Orthodox theology, one has only to read the works of the bishops S. Stragorodsky and A. Khrapovitsky who were strongly influenced in this regard by the Protestant theologian Albert Ritschl (1822–1889). Msgr. Sergius Stragorodsky (1867–1944), states in *La doctrine orthodoxe du salut, Essai de dévoilement des aspects moraux et subjectifs du salut sur la base des saintes Ecritures*, Kazan, 1898 (in Russian, 254 pp., 5 editions) that God does not change, only human beings are subject to change. His soteriology of *kenos* and salvation is similar to that of Nestorius. He affirms the presence of Christ in two spirits — the human spirit which Christ hands over to God, "Father, into your hands I commend my spirit" — and the divine spirit which is not affected by the crucifixion. This extreme kenoticism denies the divinity of Christ when he was crucified. Metropolitan Anthony Khrapovitski (1863–1936) wrote *Le dogme du rachat*, Sremski Karlovtsy, 1926 (in Russian). He criticizes the theology of satisfaction. Through his battle, Christ reestablished the bond of love between God and Humanity. His perspective, however, is psychological and moral. Metropolitan Sergius criticizes Msgr. Anthony because his vision of Gethsemane overshadows that of Golgatha (where the corporal death of Christ took place but not that of his spirit). For Msgr. Anthony, it is the *Logos* and even the whole Trinity which suffers. Vladimir Iljine, in his review of the book, sees a nominalism and psychologism (V. Iljine, "Recension," *Pout'* 8, 1927, p. 156). In both cases, this is a far cry from the Good Friday sermon of Metropolitan Philaret of Moscow: "The crucifying love of the Father, the crucified love of the Son, the triumphant love of the Spirit through the wood of the Cross . . . it was in this way that God loved the world." Cf. Piotr Gneditch, *Russkaia Bogoslovskaia literatura o dogmate iskuplenia v period s 1893 po 1944, JMP*, 8/1962, pp. 68–72.

Secular culture, however, enclosed as it is in the sphere of immanence, gives rise to a number of dissatisfactions (solitude, moralism, utilitarianism). This provokes the romantic reaction with its rehabilitation of beauty, sentiment and symbolism. Taylor thus interprets the pietistic current in Protestantism as a movement of partial return to orthodox faith.[34] This reaction leads to the contemporary period that Taylor describes as "the age of authenticity," dominant since the 1960s, and characterized by the belief that each person disposes of his own way of realizing his humanity and that it is necessary to find it without yielding to conformity. According to the Canadian philosopher, the actual religious landscape still remains divided among those who, in order to belong, rely on an authority (the Bible, the pope, Tradition) and therefore some kind of self-sacrifice, and those who consider that the logic of authenticity leads to a liberation from all external authority.[35] Taylor quotes the Russian Orthodox philosopher Nicholas Berdyaev to suggest that the synthesis of the two currents is to be found in the ecclesialization, "from within, freely," of knowledge, morality, art, government and economy.[36] He also calls upon the Catholic Austrian philosopher Ivan Illich (1926–2002) in his search for an evangelical Christianity that would be lived not through moral obligation but as a transparent life style. Similar analyses can be found in the book *Le christianisme comme style* by the theologian Christopher Theobald, which, like Milbank and Taylor, challenged Marcel Gauchet's interpretation of the disenchantment of the world by noting that these interpretations did not give enough importance to the trinitarian dimension of Christian *doxa*.[37]

Taylor shares Milbank's preoccupation with articulating the spiritual logics at work in the framework of contemporary social and intellectual immanence. He examines what he calls Closed World Structures, narratives which pretend to be objective such as the discourse on the death of God or the incompatibility of human rights with Christianity. He also evokes the possibilities of opening up the frame of immanence on the basis of themes like human dignity, or the capacity of wonderment, or even fascination with violence. When the order of nature is no longer separated from the

34 C. Taylor, op. cit., 314.

35 Ibid., 509.

36 He cites a 2006 article of M. Epstein on the new "minimal religion" in Russia; Taylor, op. cit., 535.

37 C. Theobald, *Le christianisme comme style: une manière de faire la théologie en post-modernité*, Paris, Cerf, 2007.

order of grace, wonderment becomes possible again. When the wrath of God is no longer conceived within a juridical and penal context but is understood as the consequence of the rejection of divine love, the fear of hell can be transcended.[38] This is why Taylor believes that Christianity can offer unsuspected resources to modern culture to transfigure those energies that, most often, tend towards the mechanism of purification offered by the scapegoat. He also mentions certain itineraries of faith from within the depths of immanence, such as that of Péguy who rediscovered the Christian notion of eternity not as a divine time situated above human time but as a gathered time in which all the moments are reconnected to the same movement.[39]

When dealing with orthodoxy, however, Charles Taylor is more of a philosopher than historian. For him, orthodoxy is a concept that signifies "the theological correctness," the intact tradition of faith.[40] He does not notice that this Monophysite definition, incapable of discerning the two-fold source, human and divine, of truth in Christian doctrine, leads him to ignore the specific evolution of orthodoxy in the history of Christianity. He speaks of the spirituality of "theosis" or transfiguration as if it had always been inherent and dominant within Western "orthodox theology"[41] which, for Taylor, is to be found in the work of Thomas Aquinas and the Platonists of Cambridge.[42] In another chapter, however, he admits that the radical distinction between the natural and supernatural spheres was a reaction of the nominalists and, subsequently, of the Reformers, to the system of the Angelic Doctor and that it could have led to limiting God's sovereign power.[43] Rather curiously, he qualifies Dostoevsky as a "premodern" author. Taylor has difficulty integrating Methodism, which certainly,

38 Ibid., 656.

39 Ibid., 750.

40 C. Taylor, op. cit., 488.

41 N. Lemaître has shown that it is the theme of redemption and not that of deification which has most marked Western theology. N. Lemaître, "Le christianisme et son histoire," *Histoire du christianisme*, XIV, Paris, Desclée, 2001, 66–67. "Anti-gnostic Greek theology supposed . . . that the perfection of Adam was a terminus and not a point of departure. Adam was, after all, a man-child, brought to his definitive dimension by Christ, who recapitulated human history. . . . Saint Augustine who, for polemical reasons, chose to insist on original sin which destroyed the perfection of the first man instead of admiring the fundamental goodness and the interior dynamism of creation, definitively orientated Western Christianity on its specific path."

42 C. Taylor, op. cit., 736.

43 Ibid., 542.

in the 18th century, represented a reaction to the "impeccable intellectual orthodoxy" of the previous century,[44] as being itself a form of orthodoxy which reincorporated sentiment and emotion into the expression of faith. This is why, ultimately, it is difficult to understand how the secular age, already present at the end of the Middle Ages, succeeded in imposing itself on Western Christian culture without admitting the inherent weakness of Christian doctrine. Taylor suggests that the contemporary debate over religion is located between the "two extreme positions" of orthodox religion (be it Christianity, Judaism, Islam, Buddhism or other)[45] and atheistic materialism.[46] He does not, however, choose to completely ignore the work of John Henry Newman and Vladimir Soloviev. He comes close to the truth when he laments the "regressions of the Christian faith,"[47] when he admits the disastrous consequences of the "hyper-Augustinian" current in Western theology,[48] when he explains that atheism was more a rejection of impersonal providence (as in Voltaire's *Candide*) than of orthodox Christianity,[49] and when he denounces the process of excarnation, source of violence, peculiar to modernity.

For Taylor, author of *Sources of the Self* — as for Newman in his *Grammar of Assent*[50] — the emergence of the concept of self-awareness in Modern Times corresponds to the following rediscovery: there exists a good and an evil and one cannot avoid defining oneself in relation to them.[51]

44 Ibid., 488.
45 Ibid., 676.
46 Ibid., 598.
47 Ibid., 377.
48 Ibid., 652.
49 Ibid., 388.
50 John Locke was the first to reflect on the concept of what is called *assensus* in Latin or assent in English as a truth that implies action but on a scale of "degrees of assent." But Newman was opposed to Locke's theory of assent: "instead of seeing the human spirit such as it came forth from the hands of God, Locke fashions human beings as he thinks they should be; he makes them better and greater than they are and treats them like fools — if you'll pardon the comparison — should they prefer to jump overboard rather than entrust themselves to such an adventurous pilot." J. H. Newman, *Grammar of Assent*, op. cit., 134–35.
51 "Conscience does not rely only on itself; it tends, vaguely, to something beyond it and discerns, in its decisions, a sanction superior to oneself as evidenced by the intense sentiment of obligation and responsibility which impose themselves." J. H. Newman, *Grammar of Assent*, trans. Fr. *Grammaire de l'assentiment*, Paris, Bloud et Cie, 1907, 89.

## THE NEW APPROACHES OF JEAN-LUC MARION AND JEAN-MARC FERRY

The arguments of Milbank and Taylor—along with those of theologians such as John Paul II, Bernard Sesboüé, Benedict XVI, Olivier Clément, Rowan Williams and many others in favor of a new relationship between faith and reason which would respect orthodoxy—have permitted a certain evolution on the part of traditional philosophers who limit themselves to the realm of phenomena and communications. Independently of the dialogue between Milbank and Taylor, a good part of the contemporary philosophical community is participating in the rehabilitation of orthodox thought understood as the synthesis between the classical philosophical tradition and Christian revelation. It is common knowledge that Paul Ricoeur, near the end of his life, foresaw the possibility for the historian to free himself from the burden of debt by abandoning himself, above and beyond the exclusively hermeneutical approach, to the evangelical concept of Providence which alone makes possible the transformation of traumatic memory into an event of blissful remembrance.[52] The election of Jean-Luc Marion to Cardinal Lustiger's chair at L'Académie Française in 2009 is also testament to the academic world's recognition of his philosophical work on the heuristic merits of the conceptual fruits of the Revelation of the Spirit. This task, which he began in 1975 with his book on the ontology of Descartes, consists, in the philosopher's own words, of an attempt to "rediscover the original theological concept of *philosophia christiana* by following the path of a phenomenological demonstration, although never made manifest, of what Pascal (1623–1662) understood by the 'third order of charity.'"[53] In 1993, Marion summarized the philosophy of the French mathematician, philosopher and theologian in the following manner:

> In addition to its theological deployment, charity has specifically theoretical effects in the realm of reason. It opens a new theoretical continent to explore—what Pascal called "the order of charity as opposed to the order of carnal magnitude" (all powers concerning bodies, political, economic, imaginary, etc.) and to the order of "spirits" (science, the arts, etc.). The order of charity, which includes love in all its forms, dominates the other two orders but,

52 P. Ricoeur, *La mémoire, l'histoire, l'oubli*, Paris, Seuil, 2000.

53 J. L. Marion, *Le visible et le révélé*, Paris, Cerf, 2005, 186.

> for that very reason, remains less apparent and well known than they. Indeed, through an essential paradox, none of the orders can either know or see a higher order (even if an order knows itself and sees a lower order). Charity, the supreme order, remains therefore invisible in itself to the flesh and to the spirit, to all power and to all knowledge. It follows that charity opens up a field of new phenomena to knowledge, but that this field remains invisible to natural reason alone; that is why philosophy certainly needs an "indispensable auxiliary," a revelation. But, at this point, it is a question of what is revealed through charity which offers perfectly rational phenomena to philosophy even though these phenomena are specific to charity and as original as charity itself. This coincides with Etienne Gilson's definition of "Christian philosophy" but with one important difference: any philosophy which makes a formal distinction between the different orders (Pascal's terminology) considers Christian revelation (as revelation through charity; thus of the third order) as an indispensable auxiliary to reason. But henceforth "the auxiliary" furnished by Revelation not only helps provide a new interpretation of already visible phenomena; it introduces into visibility phenomena that would remain invisible without it.[54]

Jean-Marc Ferry, a professor at the University of Nantes as well as at the Sorbonne where he conducted a seminar in collaboration with Alain Renaut, proposes a moral reconfiguration of the relations between faith and reason. In 2010, he published a book entitled *La religion réflexive* and, in 2011, gave a conference at the Bernadines College on "The insertion of interreligious dialogue in a post-secular context." For the author of the book on *Habermas, l'éthique de la communication* (1987), even on the level of *episteme*, one finds a "dilution of the boundaries between reason and religion." According to Ferry, more and more people are talking about "religious reasons" and "secular convictions." The French philosopher accepts Milbank's thesis that the Church itself, by secularizing the concept of *corpus mysticum*, made room for Hobbes to invent the notion of the State as a "fictitious person." Hobbes radicalizes the concept by adding the work of Jean Bodin to the medieval sources of the modern political imagination (unity, indivisibility, the inalienable rights of divine and monarchic power as set forth in *Les Six Livres de la*

54 Jean-Luc Marion, *Le visible et le révélé*, op. cit., 108.

*République* which appeared in 1576). This political imagination, characterized by the concepts of personality, representation and sovereignty, had, from the times of Rousseau, replaced the divine sovereignty with the general will of the people. This leads Ferry to propose in his book, *La république crépusculaire*, an original model of governance for postmodern European societies, namely that of co-sovereignty. He takes up and corrects the analyses of Joseph Weiler, a South African-born scholar of Jewish tradition, director of the Jean Monnet Center and professor at the New York University School of Law, to imagine a political reconstruction of Europe where the religious foundations of social life would no longer be ignored or marginalized.[55] For Ferry, who follows Taylor in this, a European constitution does not have to refer to cultural norms but rather to reflexive convictions which can be translated into meta-standards authorizing cooperation in a regime of profound diversity.

Moreover, Jean-Marc Ferry makes the following observation: "at its critical point, philosophical reason establishes the possibility of a reconciliation with religious truth by the justification of practical presumptions such as the reality of the world, the effectiveness of an autonomous self, the existence of the other, all *creencias*[56] indemonstrable but almost indispensable — the image of the existence of God, the immortality of the soul and human freedom. The primary truths of existence, constitutive and, therefore, necessary are those that cannot be proven theoretically, but only postulated in practice."[57] Alongside the narrative, interpretive and argu-

55 J. H. Weiler, *L'Europe chrétienne? Une excursion*, preface by Rémi Brague, Paris, Cerf, 2007. Weiler proposes that the European constitution include "liberty from religion and liberty of religion." For him, there is no tolerance without convictions; there is only indifference. He specifically juxtaposes the Orwellian vision of French laicism and the model of the 1989 Polish constitution which integrates "those who believe in God as the source of truth, justice and beauty and those who do not share this faith but who respect these universal values." Cf. George Weigel, *The Cube and the Cathedral,* New York, Basic Books, 2005, 68. Following Josef Pieper and Servais Pinckaers, Weigel attributes the evolution of the concept "indifferent liberty" to the nominalism of Ockham in opposition to the Thomistic idea of "liberty in view of excellence." Liberty, for Thomas Aquinas, is the capacity to choose wisely and well, "as a matter of habit — or, to use an old-fashioned term, as a matter of virtue." Ibid., 79.

56 The term *creencias* is based on a phrase of José Ortega y Gasset which designates those vital certitudes which need no proof. Jean-Marc Ferry, *La République crepusculaire,* Paris, Cerf, 2010, 13.

57 Jean-Marc Ferry, "De l'insertion du dialogue inter-religieux dans un espace post-séculier," Collège des Bernadins, March 2011, manuscript, p. 3. I thank the author for having sent me his text.

mentative functions of philosophy, Ferry proposes adding a "reconstructive" function capable of dealing with these primary truths. For him, "religious truth, the true religion, the one religion," in brief, the ortho-dox truth, is a "work in progress," a project which is at the heart of the practice of inter-religious dialogue. In this respect, he explicitly follows the path of Charles Taylor for whom recognition, the foundation of identity, presupposes not only a social openness but also a "hermeneutic appropriation" of its roots and traditions. He also has recourse to the work of Paul Ricoeur for whom the new European ethos should be marked by three main characteristics: translation, cross narratives and forgiveness.[58] Cross narratives, in particular, allow us to engage in a process of reconstructive reconciliation in the course of which we open our own memory to that of former adversaries, "thus renouncing the autistic self-narrative and welcoming that of others."[59]

In arriving at this conclusion, Jean-Marc Ferry, in his own way, concurs with the teaching of John Henry Newman in his *Grammar of Assent* that posited the essential distinction between inferred truth and assented truth, which allowed him to imagine a double scale of abstract and experimental truth, ranging from the most mathematical inference to the most conscious belief.[60] Ferry prefers, more simply, to distinguish certitude from truth.[61]

58 Paul Ricoeur, "Quel éthos nouveau pour l'Europe?" in Peter Koslowski, *Imaginer l'Europe. Le marché européen comme tâche culturelle et économique,* Paris, Cerf, 1992, 107–16.

59 J. M. Ferry, op. cit., 8–9.

60 In the opinion of Jean Honoré, the argument of *The Grammar of Assent* "is based on the essential distinction, in the act of faith, between the approach of the intellect, which pronounces its verdict in the judgment of truth, and the approach of the conscience which, on the basis of this judgment, gives its adhesion (assent) to the truth of faith." On the one hand, there is the work of the spirit which examines a multiplicity of elements in order to arrive at certitude (illative sense) and, on the other hand, the personal decision to believe (assent). Jean Honoré, *Newman,* Paris, Desclée, 1988. This distinction is an indication of a pragmatic philosophy: "I'd prefer a thousand times to be obliged to demonstrate that it is reasonable to believe in the truth of Christianity than to deduce a directive and moral idea from the physical world. Life is made for action. If we want proofs before acting, we would never do anything; to be able to act, one must assume a responsibility and this responsibility is faith." J. H. Newman, *The Grammar of Assent.*

61 What in Newman could seem to be similar to the distinction that he makes between simple assent and complex assent — or between belief and certitude — is found here in the essential concept of *doxa*, on the borderline between theology and philosophy: "Assent is unconditional, otherwise it would be inadequate to the affirmation. Inference is conditional because a conclusion implies at least the presumption of its premises and, in the concrete — since this is what interests us — any demonstration is impossible. . . . [Moreover] we cannot give our assent to a proposition without having an intelligent

In this respect, the French philosopher subscribes to the tradition of the Reformation which pushed the distinction to the point of criticizing its own scriptural sources.[62] Ferry considers this point of departure, which is, admittedly not a point of arrival, as essential. He writes:

> It will therefore be posited that conviction, be it religious or secular, is that moment of certitude where a person affirms the truth, in the sense that he guarantees it, so to speak, through a proposition — although, as a result, this proposition is exposed to the refutation of counter-propositions and always in the name of an ever-evolving truth.[63] Therefore, fallibilism must not involve skepticism to any degree whatsoever. To fully assume the difference between certainty and truth is the minimal requirement for an intellect which knows how to recognize the distinct modalities between what is observed and what is prescribed; between what is prescribed and what is hoped for; between what is "asserted" as "being the case" and what one puts forth as "needing to be posited," that is, between a descriptive concerning the factual, and a regulative introducing the counterfactual — an "as if" practice of "reflexive religion" — if what is being sought is a *secuti Deus daretur* which does not imply any duplicity nor engages any degree of schizophrenia (for a person can genuinely *not know* if God exists

grasp of it, without understanding it, whereas we have no need to understand in order to arrive at a conclusion." Ibid., 7. Newman also distinguishes between notional assent (profession, belief, opinion, presumption, speculation) which can sometimes be erroneously confused with inference, and real assent, beliefs, convictions or certitudes given to moral objects. (Newman makes an amusing comparison regarding the assent of real belief between the "semi-Catholics of Russia" for whom "Heaven and Hell are as real as if they saw them" and the "religion of the Bible, the religion of England" which attaches so little importance to the acts of faith, to the catechism "and thus never felt the need of a very fixed instructional foundation."), Ibid., 46. It should be noted that, for Newman, *doxa* or opinion, is of the order of assent because "it explicitly gives its assent to the possibility of a given proposition." It is distinct, however, from pure faith (one is tempted to add from epistemic faith also) in the measure in which the latter "implicitly gives its assent to the truth within it." Moreover, belief is a reflexive act (we believe a thing that we consider true) whereas for Newman, as for the whole patristic tradition, "when we begin to analyze our belief, to weigh it, to compare it, to modify it, we begin to form an opinion." Ibid., 50.

62 Peter Berger, ed., *Between Relativism and Fundamentalism,* Grand Rapids, Eerdmans, 2010, 13.

63 One could also speak of a truth in perpetual development or permanent *syn-hodos.*

> or does not exist). Thus, those who choose to live accepting the idea of God, postulate, in practice, this God whose existence they cannot theoretically demonstrate.[64]

Jean-Marc Ferry goes a step further in his postmodern representation of orthodox thought. In his book *La religion réflexive*, religion is rehabilitated not only as an important symbolic element for philosophical architectonics in response to the question: what am I allowed to hope for? It also represents the critical point "from which the principle of duty and the principle of hope can be discerned."[65] For Jean-Marc Ferry, this unity is not of the realm of the *episteme* but rather depends on *doxa*; ortho-doxy is thus right morality. It follows the "narrow way, the path of righteousness" which does not lapse into either of the impasses of modern *episteme*: empiricism, "which dissipates the will" and idealism, "flight into the a priori which lulls the intellect into sleep." Ferry concludes with a definition of *ortho-doxia* that could well become the paradigm of a modern day synthesis between agnostics and radical orthodox thinkers: "To be right means that we do not surrender to anything other than what is just."[66]

## ORTHODOXY ACCORDING TO JOHN PAUL II AND BENEDICT XVI

How do you define truth when you are the pope of Rome? This is a question posed by Giovanni Miccoli, an Italian historian born in 1933 and professor at the University of Trieste,[67] in his book *Le pontificat de Jean-Paul II. Un gouvernement contrasté*, written in 2006–2007 and published in French in February 2012. This Italian Church historian, known in France for his work *Les dilemmes et les silences de Pie XII*,[68] tries to be prudent. When he gives a historical description of the acts and deeds of John Paul II, he does not question their legitimacy but centers on the magisterium's ability to define the truth for hundreds of millions of faithful. His method is historical — that

64 J. M. Ferry, op. cit., 6.

65 Ibid., 3.

66 J. M. Ferry, *La religion réflexive*, Cerf, 2010, 125.

67 http://www.istitutoveneto.it/flex/FixedPages/Common/academici_se.php/L/IT/IDS/92.

68 Paris/Bruxelles, IHTP/Complexe, 2005; http://www.ihtp.cnrs.fr/spip.php%3Farticle250.html.

is to say, in the author's mind, scientific and critical[69]—not theological, therefore "free," not dependent on an external authority that can influence his consciousness as a researcher of truth. In reality, this so-called critical liberty claimed by the Italian historian manifests the limits of the paradigm of modern truth. As Charles Taylor has demonstrated, since Locke and Descartes at least, Western thought sees reality as autonomous and thus alien to participation. Consequently, he who seeks the truth should disengage himself in relation to the world he observes and consider that his freedom of judgment is absolute. This modern perspective is clearly evident in the eminently subjective analysis which G. Miccoli makes of the postmodern conception of the truth according to John Paul II and Benedict XVI. This conception, vigorously affirmed in the conciliar declaration of December 7, 1965, *Dignitatis humanae*, posits that the right to liberty cannot be separated from a duty towards the truth.[70]

## *The Criticism of the Orthodoxy of John Paul II*

The very first pages of Miccoli's book *Le pontificat de Jean-Paul II, un gouvernement contrasté* make clear that, with such premises, the Italian historian is not disposed to participate in the chorus of praises which resounded when

69 This is how Miccoli described his method in his book on Pius XII: "It is above all as a historian that one must examine the relationship of Pius XII to Nazism and its crimes. So the problem is not to establish what the pope should have done and did not do or to maintain that he did what he should have done because he could not have done otherwise but to determine, above all, what he did and why, given the context in which he and his collaborators had to make decisions according to the ideas, expectations and judgments which alternately guided and motivated them. Indeed, it is only on this basis that we can then formulate a historical judgment—that is, seek to evaluate the consequences of the attitudes which were adopted during the course of events."

70 "It is in accordance with their dignity as persons—that is, beings endowed with reason and free will and therefore privileged to bear personal responsibility—that all men should be at once impelled by nature and also bound by a moral obligation to seek the truth, especially religious truth. They are also bound to adhere to the truth, once it is known, and to order their whole lives in accord with the demands of truth. However, men cannot discharge these obligations in a manner in keeping with their own nature unless they enjoy immunity from external coercion as well as psychological freedom. Therefore the right to religious freedom has its foundation not in the subjective disposition of the person, but in his very nature. In consequence, the right to this immunity continues to exist even in those who do not live up to their obligation of seeking the truth and adhering to it and the exercise of this right is not to be impeded, provided that just public order be observed." *Dignitatis humanae*, 2, http://www.vatican.va/archive/hist_councils/ii_vatican_council/documents/vat-ii_decl_19651207_dignitatis-humanae_en.html.

the Polish pope died on April 2, 2005, and which led to his beatification on May 1, 2011. Miccoli begins by explaining that as soon as John Paul II was elected on October 16, 1978, he chose to favor a "normalizing" reading of Vatican II in order to put an end to the disorders of the period between 1965 and 1978 which arose from interpretations of the council which were judged to be excessively liberal. Miccoli explains that this restoration of order manifested itself in the removal of Pedro Arrupe, the Superior General of the Jesuits (whose "fresh vision," however, was praised by the Pontiff) and in a radical criticism of liberation theology, which the Jesuits saw as being in the line of the Council's orientation towards the emancipation of the "people of God." G. Miccoli recognizes that John Paul II had his moments of brilliance, as when he invited theologians to reevaluate the place of the bishop of Rome in the Church. Fundamentally, however, he considers this sort of discourse as elegant window-dressing hiding a retaking of power in the Church by the Roman Curia after the turbulences of the Council. As proof, Miccoli offers the extension of papal infallibility, the lessening of the authority of the "particular Churches," the disappointing results of ecumenical and interreligious dialogue, etc. Certainly, Miccoli nuances all these affirmations. He accepts that the Polish pope initiated a different type of Roman dialogue concerning the Jewish people. Additionally, in 1985, the Muslim youth of Casablanca might well have heard the pope tell them that the differences between Christianity and Islam should be accepted with humility and respect. In essence, Miccoli believes that the ecumenical moment of the Magisterial discourse goes hand in hand with a "doctrinal hardening" and that the conciliar openness to interreligious dialogue ended in a "destruction of any theology of religious pluralism."[71]

The professor of Church History at the Universities of Pisa, Venice, and Trieste seeks to be "objective." He concedes that John Paul II had a few good points, especially in his ability to resist American imperialism at the moment of the invasion of Iraq or his reexamination of shadowy moments in the history of Catholicism beginning with the condemnation of Galileo. However, his "objectivity" does not allow him to be satisfied with these advances. He believes that the Church, under John Paul II, did not go far enough in denouncing the crimes of the Inquisition, anti-Judaism and the role of the popes in the terrible deviations of the Catholic Church. Similarly, he is pleased with John Paul's recognition of the decisive role of the United Nations in the resolution

71 Ibid., 202.

of wars in the world, but he regrets the attitude of impartiality adopted in the past by the Holy See when faced with conflict situations. The pope certainly was living out his mission when he proposed a new evangelization of Europe but this refoundation of European culture was, in Miccoli's view, nothing but a desire to restore the hierarchical structure of Medieval Christianity, typical of a son of the Polish people. As proof, the historian invokes the very use of the concept of "Christian civilization" by John Paul II, a concept Miccoli traces to the reactionary Catholic political thought prevalent during the 19th century. In the end, Miccoli lays his cards on the table. In his eyes, the work of John Paul II consisted only in the restoration of a "Church of the past, a Church of faith, devotions and models encumbered by the large amount of driftwood which history has deposited on its shores over the centuries."[72] For this reason, he concludes, the long reign of the Polish pope should be considered "a huge waste of vital energies which had nothing more to offer than a stubborn refusal and condemnation."[73]

All this, of course, is extremely subjective and illustrates all the difficulties experienced by Italian intellectuals trying to position themselves in relation to the Magisterium of the pope. It is also possible, given the personality of the translator, that the frustrations of the Jesuit order, which underwent a severe crisis after Vatican II, find their echo in the scathing prose of the professor of Trieste. Miccoli's book was, in fact, translated into French by Paul Gilbert, a French Jesuit, a specialist on the thought of St. Anselm, a professor of metaphysics at the Gregorian University of Rome, and a guest lecturer at the Catholic Institute of Paris. Miccoli has nothing to say about the historic agreements with Orthodox Christians on the procession of the Holy Spirit and with Protestant Christians on the question of justification. He denounces the Vatican's monarchical structure without acknowledging that, in 1995, John Paul II was the first modern pope to publicly request a reconsideration of the place of the Bishop of Rome in the Church. The Italian historian is also not particularly convincing when he states that John Paul II had a Eurocentric and conservative vision which contrasted with the global perspective and thirst for justice of the Jesuit Pedro Arrupe, the Superior General of the Society of Jesus. It is as if John Paul II had not worked throughout his life and multiple journeys for a new Western development policy in favor of the Third World. Miccoli's credibility also suffers by his all too brief mention of the decisive role

72 Ibid., 348.
73 Ibid., 347.

played by John Paul II in the fall of Communist ideology from 1989 onwards, an ideology most serious historians consider responsible for more than 80 million violent deaths in the course of the 20th century. There is no mention of the meetings between the Polish pope and Mikhail Gorbachev, Lech Walesa and Fidel Castro. On the other hand, the pope is criticized for not having extended his hand to the Trappist monk, Ernesto Cardenal, when the two came face to face in Nicaragua in July of 1983; at that time Cardenal was the Minister of Culture of the Sandinista Junta of National Reconstruction.[74] Miccoli reproaches the pope for not having recourse to the means offered by the Marxist analysis to denounce social injustices, thus demonstrating the "total self-sufficiency of the Church to work in the service of man."[75] The prophetic vision of the antihumanist evolution of liberal capitalism articulated by John Paul II in *Centesimus Annus* hardly receives a mention since it contradicts the author's central thesis: that the only legacy left by John Paul II was the restoration of the institutional Church over and against the vision of the Church as the people of God proclaimed by the Council.

## *The Criticism of the Orthodoxy of Benedict XVI*

Giovanni Miccoli added two chapters (120 pages) on the beginnings of the pontificate of Benedict XVI in order to bolster up his thesis. According to the Italian historian, the first decisions of the German pontiff only reinforce the structural tendency to concentrate the power of the Catholic Church in the hands of the Roman Curia, a tendency he has observed since the end of the Council and especially since the pontificate of John Paul II. The restorative utopia is now openly proclaimed by Benedict XVI, whose name is a direct reference to one of the Fathers of Medieval Christianity. The Italian professor notes how this same vision was already evident in the discourses of Cardinal Ratzinger whose common theme, faced with the naive enthusiasm of certain interpreters of Vatican II, was to oppose the Church and

74 When John Paul II visited Nicaragua in 1983, Ernesto Cardenal, an eminent figure in liberation theology, was publicly humiliated by the pope in front of the international media. The pope refused to shake his hand and instead chided him with his finger as if Cardenal were a little child. Cardenal was later officially suspended *a divinis* by Rome and could no longer celebrate Mass or administer the sacraments. Cardenal left the FSLN in 1994 in protest of the authoritarian leadership of President Daniel Ortega but remained firm in his "progressive" opinions.

75 Ibid., 60.

the world. Miccoli notes that if Ratzinger was one of the most active of the Council Fathers, one of the most effective opponents of what Congar called the "Supreme Gestapo" of the Holy Office and one of the promoters of the review *Concilium*, his period at the University of Tübingen at the end of the 1960s convinced him of the dangers of an overly naive and "beat generation" reading of the documents of the Council. He then became the great adversary of the ethical relativism of modern Western civilization and the great restorer of the ecclesial tradition. He participated in the foundation of the review *Communio* as a reaction against the excesses of the postconciliar period.

For Ratzinger, if at the time of the Enlightenment one might still have been able to imagine a morality that could disregard the living God thanks to a consciousness of the natural law, this is no longer the case today. For this reason, in a discourse entitled "Europe and the Crisis of Cultures," delivered at Subiaco on April 1, 2005, the German cardinal made the following declaration: "Whoever fails to find the way to accept God should, in any case, seek to live and direct his life *velut si Deus daretur*—as if God existed." It is not a question of limiting the freedom of man, but rather, that "all that is in him" would find, in the acceptance of God, at least as a hypothesis, "a support and criterion which he urgently needs."[76] Miccoli sees such reasoning as a "strange simplification" of the evolution of thought since the 18th century. He questions the idea of natural law, insisting on the fact that what nature reveals above all is the survival of the fittest. For him, Ratzinger pays little attention to the fact that it is the historic commitment of modernity in favor of justice that has allowed democracy and freedom of conscience to prevail. Miccoli considers Cardinal Ratzinger's assertion that "Christianity has, alas, against its nature, become a tradition and a state religion" to be insufficient, "marginal, quite imprecise, of an atemporal generality."[77] He points out that the Holy See, even in the 20th century, did everything it could in Latin America and Africa to retain its privileges as the State religion. The main fault of Cardinal Ratzinger, he maintains, is that he does not make mention of the Church as such in his historical considerations. He recognizes some erring from "historical Christianity" but does not dare to acknowledge the compromises of the ecclesial institution. For this would call into question the dogma of papal infallibility. The problem for Benedict XVI, as for the former Cardinal

76 Ibid., 360.
77 Ibid.

Ratzinger, is not, Miccoli states, an institutional one, but is above all of a spiritual and intellectual order. Benedict's priority, as can be seen in his first encyclicals and addresses, is to find the relationship between reason and faith, between the Roman and Patristic traditions. This approach is severely criticized by the Italian scholar, because it puts too much emphasis on philosophy in relation to history:

> The omissions and reticences of Ratzinger's address thus elude convergences and fundamental passages, as if the Church, in her conduct, in her manner of acting and structuring herself (with exorbitant claims as magisterium and institution, in the regulation of the lives of persons and societies) was not inextricably involved in the refusal to recognize her prerogative of a possession of the truth so total and exclusive that she could intervene in all spheres of human activity. As if her persistent resistance to the recognition of the historicity of "truths" (and of their research) was not a capital and preliminary question, posing a serious obstacle to any dialogue on this subject.[78]

The rest of the analysis of the pontificate of Benedict XVI simply elaborates on this preliminary criticism: persistent tensions with the non-ecclesial media, which is more and more likened to a totalitarian power because of its pretension to free itself from the judgment of God, and thus from the Roman magisterium; crisis with the Muslim world provoked by the Regensburg speech; rapprochement with the most conservative and most favorable ideas of the administration of George Bush, defended by Marcello Pera, the former president of the Italian council; etc. For Miccoli, the pope is unable to consider that his non-Catholic interlocutors have an authentic moral consistency since the Church, of which the pope is the true interpreter, is the sole reality which makes authentic knowledge possible. According to Miccoli, it follows that, for Benedict XVI, "it is the role of the Church and its magisterium to dictate to all humanity the moral rules which should govern their actions in order to avoid new disasters in human history."[79] *Miccoli locuta; causa finita.*

In reality, the remarks of Benedict XVI are much more nuanced than the Italian historian suggests. In his address in September, 2008, at the College of the Bernardins in Paris, the pope emphasized the importance of

78 Ibid., 369.
79 Ibid., 382.

history and culture for theology.[80] Miccoli qualified the pope's discourse on secularism as unconvincing. Yet what Benedict XVI had to say about an "open secularism" when he came to France in 2008, and in the course of his conversations with President Nicholas Sarkozy, changed certain perspectives within a French intelligentsia fascinated by social unrest and neoliberal globalization. Finally, the fact that Benedict XVI, in 2009, denounced pedophilia among the clergy and recognized the Catholic Church's responsibility in the crimes committed has shown that the pope is quite capable of vigorously condemning the limits of the institutional Church.

Micolli's book, more a personal memoire than a history, seeks to highlight two totally opposed readings of the legacy of the Second Vatican Council. On the one hand, there would be a tendency to restore the power of the Roman Curia, frightened early on by the liberal and even libertarian readings of the Council, and having definitively taken over the reins of the Church with Benedict XVI. On the other hand, there would be a silent majority enthused by the Council's recognition of the decisive and adult status of the laity and its vision of the Church as the People of God, but progressively moving away from the institutional Church in the measure in which the latter once again considers itself antithetical to this world and refuses to commit itself politically against the pro-capitalist military dictatorships in the name of the struggle for justice and solidarity. Even though it has its share of truth, such a patchwork interpretation seems to lack a sufficient foundation. It has been shown to what extent the interpretation of the Council has been complex and nuanced on the part of the two principal protagonists, John Paul II and Benedict XVI. Many arguments could be added to counter the representation of a Catholic Church which has been progressively deserted by its people and criticized by both modern institutions and the other confessions and religions of the world. One need only mention the success of the meetings in Assisi to recall the increasing authority of the Roman Magisterium among the principal religious leaders, and the growing popularity of popes around the world in particular due

80 "Scripture needs to be interpreted and has need of the community in which it develops and where it is lived. It is only in the community that Scripture finds its unity and it is within the community that it reveals the meaning which unifies the whole. To put it in another way: there are dimensions of the meaning of the Word and of words which can only be discovered in a vital communion with this Word that fashions history." http://www.eglise.catholique.fr/benoit-xvi-en-france/actualites/textes-et-discours/discours-de-benoit-xvi-au-monde-de-la-culture-college-des-bernardins-paris.html.

to the great journeys of the pontiffs, the World Youth Days, and the progress of Catholic ecclesial conciliarity, especially if compared to that of the World Council of Churches where most observers recognize a structural and financial crisis.

## *The Redefinition of Orthodoxy since the Second Vatican Council*

The following lines are an attempt to show that there are elements of truth in Miccoli's book in spite of its biases and many limitations. Since the Council, there has been a significant event, namely an ecumenical rapprochement, and its corollary, the reconciliation between faith and reason, of which the 1995 encyclical *Fides et Ratio* is a major milestone. This evolution has led us to reread together the different texts of the Council and to discover a coherence between the life of the Church *ad intra* and the life of the Church *ad extra*. Such a rereading tends to redefine the determining criterion of faith, orthodoxy, as true and right knowledge. However, participants in the Council and the postconciliar period were unaware of this. Some insisted on the exigencies of justice and the closeness between the Church and the world, which opened to the reform of those institutions whose principle of conservation is founded, above all, on a sense of tradition and responsibility. Others, however, defended the search for truth, as right knowledge, to legitimize the advances of the Council and the new relations between the Church and the world, two entities remaining fundamentally distinct.

Giovanni Miccoli is aware of the progressive emergence of this paradigm of justice in the language of the Magisterium. It dates precisely from the moment when the exigencies of justice imposed themselves on the personal consciousness of the Church. In the Spring of 1994, John Paul II addressed an important text to the cardinals entitled "Reflections on the Great Jubilee of the Year 2000." This text was the precursor to several other foundational documents such as "We Remember: A Reflection on the Shoah" (1998) and "Memory and Reconciliation: The Church and the Faults of the Past" (2000), issued by the International Theological Commission. On the occasion of the official penitential ceremony asking for forgiveness at St. Peter's in Rome on March 12, 2000, the pope remained on his knees while six cardinals sought pardon for six faults which they confessed publicly: faults against the service of truth; faults which wounded the unity of the Body of Christ; faults against the people of Israel; faults committed against love, peace, the rights of peoples and the respect due to other cultures and religions; faults against the dignity of women and the unity of the human race; faults affecting the fundamental rights of the person. Miccoli, however, who knows by experience how Church history is taught in the theology departments of Catholic universities, does not believe that this confession has avowed the essential, namely, the confession of the sin of the Church.[81] He also highlights the new perspective of the Magisterium on the subject of war, according to which it is no longer possible since the last popes to invoke God's name to justify recourse to violence. He surmises, however, that the ecclesial institution uses this type of discourse for its own ends whereas it should be a force of liberation for all peoples, Christian and non-Christian, who are victims of oppression and injustice.

Conversely, both John Paul II and Benedict XVI had great esteem for Archbishop Oscar Romero, the Archbishop of San Salvador who was assassinated on March 24, 1980, and the Uruguayan Jesuit Juan Luis Segundo (1925–1996), insofar as they tried to be very near to the poorest. They felt, however, that liberation theologians did not sufficiently base their social justice programs on a quest for truth. For this reason, both insisted on orthodoxy, on the importance of the search for right truth, which alone can change political regimes from the inside towards justice and peace. As Miccoli points out, even though he disagrees with his "univocal" definition of the concept of truth, Cardinal Ratzinger, in his 1999 conference at the Sorbonne, made a special effort to restore "a meaning to the notion of Christianity as *religio vera*" which focuses on "orthodoxy at the same time as orthopraxis": "True reason is love and love is true reason. In their unity they are the right foundation and the ultimate finality of all reality."[82]

It is possible that the synthesis between these two main schools of thought within the Catholic Church consists in a reappraisal of the notion of orthodoxy as true and fair knowledge. True and fair knowledge does not consist in a new epistemic representation of knowledge, to which moral considerations on social justice, which become the decisive criteria for political and social action, would be added. On the other hand, true and fair knowledge does not distinguish theological discourse from historical discourse. It affirms a fundamental and historical identity between orthodoxy and orthopraxy. It considers orthodoxy as a contextual and dynamic reality, and knowledge

81 Ibid., 276.

82 Card. J. Ratzinger, "Vérité du christianisme," *La Documentation catholique*, no. 2217 (January 2, 2000): 35; cited by G. Miccoli, op. cit., 367.

as a reality which determines meaning according to the quality of human relations within human communities. It is in the image of the Church whose divine-human reality is holy in the measure in which it is both tension *towards* and actualization *of* the Kingdom of God on earth. There is no relativism in all this but rather a keen intellectual awareness of the riches and diversity of the words of God to creation. Orthodoxy as true and fair knowledge includes papal infallibility as indefectibility insofar as the magisterial authority makes itself the interpreter of the unified tradition of the Church. It includes the Magisterium itself as a service of communion for the whole Church, able to diversify according to local and regional circles of communion. It possesses real authority but for the benefit of the growth of the different local Churches which, together, form the mystical and historical Body of Christ.

With this awareness of the emergence of a new paradigm of orthodoxy as true and fair knowledge, the recent history of the pontificates of John Paul II and Benedict XVI can be reread, reconciling the two very real tendencies of a right and left wing within contemporary Catholic thought. As Miccoli has shown, the pontificate of John Paul II put an end, once and for all, to a definition of orthodoxy as faithful memory which had been dominant in the Church since the 16th century. The historical works undertaken for the Great Jubilee of the Church in 2000 enabled an impressive criticism of the faults of the Catholic Church. G. Miccoli is probably right to note the inadequacies of the Church's self-criticism. All the same, this work of temporal justice is irreversible; today no serious theologian can simply affirm, without any explanation, the patristic adage according to which "outside the Church there is no salvation." The Catholic Church has clearly acknowledged its responsibility for the injustices committed during the Inquisition trials and the forced evangelization of the Indians in Latin America. This work of purification of memory has been prompted by the reconciliation that has been in place for half a century between faith and reason and the ecumenical rapprochement that has been unprecedented since the Council of Florence in 1439. This reconciliation has itself facilitated new syntheses among different branches of knowledge. We have thus witnessed dialogues which would have been unthinkable 50 years ago between John Paul II, Paul Ricoeur, and Olivier Clément, and between Benedict XVI, Hans Küng, and Jürgen Habermas.

Without a doubt, this evolution of Catholic ecclesial consciousness has led to a reevaluation, especially evident with Benedict XVI, of the concept of orthodoxy as right truth. Many apologists of the German pope have tended to interpret this rehabilitation, this particular definition of orthodoxy, as a necessary return to the old model of the Christian regime. As Marcello Pera writes, Europe, in spite of its present multicultural reality, should still call itself Christian today. "It is not agnosticism, secularity or atheism that nourish freedom. If we want peace, cohabitation and respect, we must believe in the values on which they all depend. The values of Christianity are still the best antidote against all types of prevarications, including those committed in the very name of these Christian values."[83] But just as the criticism of orthodoxy as faithful memory by John Paul II has not necessarily led to a questioning of the institutional nature of the Catholic Church (and this is one of the elements of truth in Miccoli's thesis—even though it is unfortunately distorted by his exaggerations), the rehabilitation of orthodoxy as right truth by Benedict XVI does not necessarily lead to an abandonment of the paradigm of orthodoxy as true and fair knowledge such as it was presented by the Council Fathers of Vatican II. On the contrary, the recent addresses and acts of Pope Benedict XVI testify to his growing awareness (perhaps due to the critical work of present-day historians) of the major importance of the paradigm of true and fair knowledge for today's world. This paradigm, this "resolute commitment to human dignity," leads the pope to recognize the need to go beyond a merely institutional vision of the Church. On October 27, 2011, the pope had this to say to the religious leaders and diplomatic corps assembled at Assisi:

> I said that there is a way of understanding and using religion so that it becomes a source of violence, while the rightly lived relationship of man to God is a force for peace. In this context I referred to the need for dialogue and I spoke of the constant need for purification of lived religion. On the other hand I said that the denial of God corrupts man, robs him of his criteria and leads him to violence.
>
> In addition to the two phenomena of religion and anti-religion, a further basic orientation is found in the growing world of agnosticism: people to whom the gift of faith has not been given, but who are nevertheless on the lookout for truth, searching for God. Such people do not simply assert: "There is no God." They suffer

83 M. Pera, *Pourquoi nous devons nous dire chrétiens*, preface by Benedict XVI, Paris, Parole et Silence, 2011, 112.

> from his absence and yet are inwardly making their way towards him, inasmuch as they seek truth and goodness. They are "pilgrims of truth, pilgrims of peace." They ask questions of both sides. They take away from militant atheists the false certainty by which these claim to know that there is no God and they invite them to leave polemics aside and to become seekers who do not give up hope in the existence of truth and in the possibility and necessity of living by it.[84]

This recognition of a necessary postconfessional definition of the Church leads Benedict XVI to discern the importance of non-Christian wisdom swirling around the Church. This wisdom has, in the first place, the great merit of imposing a labor of self-criticism upon Christians. It is here that we best observe the paradigm of true and fair knowledge working invisibly within the Church. The pope continues to describe what the role of persons in the quest for truth and justice can be for Christians:

> But they also challenge the followers of religions not to consider God as their own property, as if he belonged to them, in such a way that they feel vindicated in using force against others. These people are seeking the truth, they are seeking the true God, whose image is frequently concealed in the religions because of the ways in which they are often practiced. Their inability to find God is partly the responsibility of believers with a limited or even falsified image of God. So all their struggling and questioning is in part an appeal to believers to purify their faith, so that God, the true God, becomes accessible. Therefore I have consciously invited delegates of this third group to our meeting in Assisi, which does not simply bring together representatives of religious institutions. Rather it is a case of being together on a journey towards truth, a case of taking a decisive stand for human dignity and a case of common engagement for peace against every form of destructive force. Finally I would like to assure you that the Catholic Church will not let up in her fight against violence, in her commitment

84 http://w2.vatican.va/content/benedict-xvi/en/speeches/2011/october/documents/hf_ben-xvi_spe_20111027_assisi.html.

for peace in the world. We are animated by the common desire to be "pilgrims of truth, pilgrims of peace."[85]

This declaration disqualifies the fundamental thesis of G. Miccoli but, at the same time, it also gives it a partial validation. The time has come for a peaceful and reconciled rereading of the Second Vatican Council.

In the face of an interpretation of the Council which seeks to minimize the breach and makes attempts at reconciliation with the traditionalist minority, one can indeed share the Italian historian's fear of a new ecclesial schism, this time, from the left. In fact, as we are reminded by Miccoli, there are many voices in the Catholic Church militantly in favor of the recognition of homosexual couples, of married priests and of the ordination of women. Once again, because of an ahistorical vision of orthodoxy and an institutional representation of the Church, an evolution through rupture would occur. However, overstating the Vatican II divide does not correspond to a fair and true interpretation of the Council. It is precisely for this reason that Pope Benedict XVI was able to reconcile the Fraternity of St. Pius X with the Catholic Church in spite of their disagreements. Bishop Bernard Fellay, the superior of this community, also wanted to end the Lefebvrist schism and, on April 17, 2012, signed a doctrinal preamble presented by Pope Benedict XVI.[86]

It was thanks to the intellectual effort which took place under John Paul II that there was a return to the concept of the orthodoxy of the faith as true and fair knowledge.[87] Indeed, in this process of reconciliation between legitimist and traditionalist Catholics, it is not a question of simply returning to orthodoxy as faithful memory (to the Nicene-Constantinopolitan symbol) or as right truth (as adherence to the dogmas proclaimed by the Council of 381). This would have ignored centuries of ecclesial tradition. What took place was a legitimate distinction between three types of truth: "revealed truth," which is in itself irrevocable; "ecclesial truth," which is necessarily historical but guaranteed by tradition; and "juridical, so called 'definitive' truth which certainly has the authority of *res judicata* by the competent authority, but which in reality can always be annulled by the

85 Ibid.

86 http://www.la-croix.com/Religion-Urbi/Rome/La-Fraternite-Saint-Pie-X-a-repondu-au-Preambule-doctrinal-propose-par-Rome-_NG_-2012-04-18-795922.

87 https://w2.vatican.va/content/john-paul-ii/en/motu_proprio/documents/hf_jp-ii_motu-proprio_30061998_ad-tuendam-fidem.html.

historical-juridical process." Article 2 of the *Profession of Faith* proposed to the faithful by the Congregation for the Doctrine of the Faith takes up again this juridical category of "definitive truth": "I adhere with submission of will and intellect to the teachings which either the Roman Pontiff or the College of Bishops enunciate when they exercise their authentic Magisterium, even if they do not intend to proclaim these teachings by a definitive act."[88] In spite of what G. Miccoli thinks,[89] in the motu proprio *Ad Tuendam Fidem* of May 1998, John Paul II, helped at the time by Cardinal Ratzinger, had the genius of specifying what he understood by "definitive":

> I also firmly accept and hold each and everything definitively proposed by the Church regarding teaching on faith and morals. Those things are to be believed by divine and catholic faith which are contained in the word of God as it has been written or handed down by tradition, that is, in the single deposit of faith entrusted to the Church, and which are at the same time proposed as divinely revealed either by the solemn Magisterium of the Church, or by its ordinary and universal Magisterium, which in fact is manifested by the common adherence of Christ's faithful under the guidance of the sacred Magisterium. All are therefore bound to avoid any contrary doctrines.
>
> § 2. Furthermore, each and every thing set forth definitively by the Magisterium of the Church regarding teaching on faith and morals must be firmly accepted and held; namely, those things required for the holy keeping and faithful exposition of the deposit of faith; therefore, anyone who rejects propositions which are to be held definitively sets himself against the teaching of the Catholic Church.[90]

This definition makes it possible to distinguish between, on the one hand, revealed truth, transmitted by tradition and by the Magisterium, which is the object of faith and, on the other hand, doctrine *concerning* faith and morals that the Magisterium proposes as "definitive" and which, while being

88 Ibid., point 2 (http://w2.vatican.va/content/john-paul-ii/en/motu_proprio/documents/hf_jp-ii_motu-proprio_30061998_ad-tuendam-fidem.html).

89 Ibid., 149. M. Pera, *Pourquoi nous devons nous dire chrétiens*, preface by Benedict XVI, Paris, Parole et Silence, 2011, 112.

90 Ibid., point 4.

"firmly adopted," is distinguished from revealed truths. These nuances are important and, above all, they are legitimized by the notion of the "hierarchy of truths" found in *Unitatis Redintegratio*, the decree of the Second Vatican Council on ecumenism. Although the French Jesuit, Bernard Sesboüé, may have feared that the Roman Curia would like to extend in this way decisions relating to the infallibility of the Magisterium, he recognizes, following the analysis of L. Choupin and J.-F. Chiron, that "a judgment can be without appeal, that is, definitive in the juridical sense of the word, without being infallible": "this is true for the pope, the ecclesiastical tribunals, but also for the Holy Office and the Biblical Commission. The judgment is definitive because it wants to bring about the juridical termination of a debate. In this sense, definitive does not mean that the judgment cannot be *reformed*."[91]

This distinction of levels of consciousness of the truth provides a new space which opens discussion with respect to the authority of the Magisterium.[92] It is once again possible for the Church to restore to the heterodox who intend to remain in her their responsibility for promoting peace while reserving the possibility of having a specific word to guide the community of nations. It also becomes possible to hold together the memorial identities of Christian confessions and to make an irreversible commitment towards the recognition of the different Churches of Christ. It finally becomes possible, with this historical interpretation different from that proposed by G. Miccoli, to reread, in an ecclesial spirit and without tensions, the document entitled "For a Renewal of Pontifical Service in the Church at the End of the 20th Century," written in August of 1978 by Giuseppe Alberigo and his collaborators at the Institute for Religious Science of Bologna. This document, which is addressed to the participants of the conclave, calls for "unequivocal acts such as the effective realization of collegiality, another policy in the choice of bishops, the overcoming of the division between clergy and laity, the respect of choices made by local communities, with their impact on history, and the recognition of an effective pluralism in political choices."[93]

91 B. Sesboüé, "Magistère de l'Eglise et magistère de l'histoire," in *Le magistère à l'épreuve*, Paris, DDB, 2001, 179.

92 B. Sesboüé thinks that when Pope Paul VI found himself in the dilemma of choosing between infallibility and error, he could not admit that the Church had been wrong for such a long time and this led to his stand against contraception in the July 1968 encyclical *Humanae Vitae*.

93 G. Miccoli, op. cit., 12.

# CHAPTER 6

# *The Method for a New History of Orthodox Truth*

IT IS COMMON IN CHRISTIAN THEOLOGY TO ASSOciate the concept of orthodoxy with that of tradition. Father John Meyendorff, former dean of the St. Vladimir Orthodox Institute, insisted that "there can be no Orthodoxy without Tradition."[1] But is all tradition orthodox? And is all orthodoxy already in the heritage of tradition? As Vladimir Lossky has shown, there is a great risk of overloading the concept of Tradition by identifying it totally with orthodoxy.[2] For Meyendorff, Tradition is a living, historical and dynamic concept. The theologian Olivier Clément has synthesized several decades of discussion within ecumenical church bodies, explaining that the orthodox concept of tradition is to be understood in an "involutional" and non-evolutionary manner. The criterion of orthodox Christian tradition is, according to St. Vincent de Lérins, to live all that has been believed, in all places, always and by all (*ubique, semper, ab omnibus creditum est*). But this cannot be understood in light of the facts of creative theology, such as the dogmatic decisions of the councils or the invention of multitudes of various expressions of ecclesial faith in art and architecture, unless this permanent, universal and shared faith is understood in its most crystalline reality: as faith in the divine humanity of Christ and in the Trinity of the hypostases of the One God. Tradition is, therefore, involutional in the sense that it is given from the very beginning and unfurls progressively in human understanding and civilization.

In this perspective, Tradition is not a protected species kept under glass. As Father Yves Congar (1904–1995) demonstrated, it is more an

1 John Meyendorff, "Tradition and Traditions," in *Orthodoxy and Catholicity,* Sheed and Ward, 1966, 91–106. I thank Stefan Barbu for having called my attention to this text.

2 Vladimir Lossky, "Tradition and Traditions," in *In the Image and Likeness of God,* Crestwood, NY, St. Vladimir's Seminary Press, 1974, 141–68.

open-mindedness to every opinion that evokes the undivided Tradition and does not pretend to be unique.[3] It is for this reason that the representatives of the Catholic, Orthodox and Protestants Churches, at the 4th Conference of Faith and Order held at Montreal in 1963, affirmed that, even if there was a lack of mutual agreement in some cases, the ecclesial Tradition (with a capital "T" to denote this undivided character) cannot be in opposition to local or particular ecclesial traditions (with a small "t" to indicate the diversity of the sapiential expression of the orthodox faith).[4] This is also the reason why Tradition cannot be a "Talmudism," an expression used by Sergius Bulgakov, or a "repetitive theology," a formula coined by Kallistos Ware. During a 2008 consultation of the Faith and Order Commission in Cambridge, the 24 representatives of the Catholic, Protestant and Orthodox Churches adopted a consensus text on Tradition which prevents any exclusive identification of Tradition with a particular tradition because of the eschatological nature of this notion:

> We recognize that the traditions of faith and witness are constantly being received by us in all our Churches, and that it is better to receive these traditions ecumenically, as we come to understand one another better and are more willing to both receive and to give. . . . We have affirmed the most appropriate way to express and define the type of traditions God gives us is to speak of the Living Tradition to underline that these traditions are neither sclerotic nor static but rather impregnated by the dynamic energy of the Holy Spirit. We are aware that, for some, the very word "tradition" may imply something passed or outdated, conservative and static; but we want to affirm a conception of tradition that has an eschatological dimension and is animated by the Spirit. We also affirm that, in our opinion, the type of authority God gives to the doctors and witnesses of the early Church is not an authority rooted in something extrinsically imposed as a sort of political power (*potestas*); it is a form of authority rooted in integrity and

3 Yves M.-J. Congar, *La Tradition et les traditions. Etude historique* (Vol. I), *Etude theologique* (Vol. II), Paris, Fayard, 1960–1963; *Tradition and Traditions: An Historical and a Theological Essay,* London, Burns & Oates, 1966, 190.

4 http://www.oikoumene.org/en/resorces/documents/wcc-commissions/faith-and-order-commission/x-other-documents-from-conferences-and-meetings/cambridge-report-on-tradition-and-traditions.html.

> authenticity (*auctoritas*). It is from within its own depths that it imposes itself on us and draws us to it. For all of us, the authority of the doctors and witnesses of the early Church is derived from this latter conception rather than the former. We all rejoice in the fact that all participants share this point of view.[5]

Thus, because of its "involutional" character, the notion of ecclesial tradition cannot be separated from the notion of orthodoxy but neither can it be identified with it. Orthodox thought is the capacity to actualize the tradition of the ecclesial body according to the paradigms at work in specific times and contexts. Orthodoxy continually articulates, in a new and coherent manner, the relation between personal conscience, the testimony of the Scriptures and their interpretation in ecclesial history. This requires an epistemological and historical understanding of orthodoxy.

## THE EPISTEMOLOGY OF THE CONCEPT OF ORTHODOXY

Orthodoxy is a transdisciplinary concept simultaneously philosophical, scientific, theological and historical. Using a semantic historical approach, a definition of orthodoxy will be proposed which synthesizes these four disciplines. If reason is made, as Newman wrote, for truth and certainty, as conscience is for good and virtue, Orthodox thought is based on the awareness of a necessary connection between reason and conscience. Such a pretension might appear surprising when one considers the painful antecedent of the dominant, and eventually dominating, medieval theology which led to the creation, in 1530, of the Royal College by Francis I and the humanist Guillaume Budé. This institute was modeled on the *Collège des Trois Langues* founded by Erasmus in Louvain. Theology was finally expelled from the universities in the 19th century. Moreover, even though there is now a renewed dialogue between conscience (which seeks to discern the voice from deep within) and reason (which recognizes the existence of *creencias*, of necessary "leaps," and the incapacity of pure logic to respond to the totality of human reality), disciplinary boundaries remain compartmentalized and regulated. Yet it can be hoped that the model of orthodox thought proposed below will, after being verified by

5 http://www.oikoumene.org/fr/documentation/documents/commissions-du-coe/foi-et-constitution-commission-de/x-other-documents-from-conferences-and-meetings/rapport-du-colloque-de-cambridge-sur-la-tradition-et-les-traditions.html.

a historical analysis, have some sort of echo in this extensive interdisciplinary and transreligious discussion of which we have just presented certain aspects and which increasingly takes on a global dimension.

*L'archéologie du savoir*, published in 1969, earned Michel Foucault his entry to the Collège de France as Chair of "The History of Systems of Thought." In this work, Foucault sought to propose a new epistemology, in which the keyword *episteme* was defined by the conditions of speech at a given time. He also sought, by these means, to capture the historical moment in which he was participating. As he wrote in his introduction, written in 1968, "the problem is no longer one of tradition, of tracing a line, but one of division, of limits."[6] Since then, the notion of discontinuity has invaded the human sciences to the point of erasing any common referential horizon and making unintelligible to most any formulation of meaning. At the end of his life, Michel Foucault himself realized the limitations of his discourse which was too radically opposed to *doxa*, to simple human opinion. The French philosopher tended in a transcendent, almost inhuman, manner towards a scale of inflexible enlightenments that only evolve through successive breaks with the past. For this reason, Foucault moved from the question of truth to that of the bearer of truth and its place in society. This change of direction went hand in hand with a rediscovery of symbolism and its inherent semantic intelligibility. During a lecture at the University of California, Berkeley, in October 1983, Foucault presented the concept of *parrhesia* (free and authoritative speech) and its evolution of meaning in the Greek and Roman culture.[7] The term appeared in Greek literature in the 5th century BC. It played a decisive role in the earliest Christian writings, in defining a truth associated with the human qualities of courage, freedom and risk. St. Paul was faced with the extraordinary novelty of his "message of the Cross." He said to the Corinthians: "But we preach Christ crucified, a stumbling block to Jews and foolishness to Gentiles, but to those whom God has called, both Jews and Greeks, Christ the power of God and the wisdom of God" (1 Cor 1:23–24). In Acts 4:13 Peter and John "uneducated and ordinary men," spoke with "boldness" before the Sanhedrin, who could only recognize them as companions of

6 M. Foucault, *L'archéologie du savoir*, Paris, Gallimard, 1969, 12.

7 Foucault was probably influenced by Pierre Hadot in this respect. Hadot was an assiduous reader of Sergius Bulgakov; cf. P. Hadot, "La sagesse divine et la théanthropie," in Laffont Bompiani, *Dictionnaire des oeuvres*, t. IV, 1954.

Jesus.[8] The patristic definition of a prophet, or gnostic, as one who walks the Christian path, "God-bearing and God-borne" according to St. Clement of Alexandria (*Strom.* VII, 13, 82), corresponds to the Christian version of a *parrhesiast.* This person offers frankness. He does not speak like the scribes and Pharisees but risks his life in the name of what he says. Foucault's Cartesian discourse of truth has all too often come to conceive of truth as an undeniable reality. But truth can also present itself as an open, living reality which requires a choice to allow it to manifest itself. In this sense it approaches the idea of *doxa*, not in the sense of a prejudgment but in the sense of opinion which, due to its verticality, does not oblige or constrain. *Orthodoxia*, which envisages the correspondence between opinion and conscience, is free from any type of conformism, demonstration or position of dominance. It is based on a companionship with the truth. It leads to a joyous and grateful testimony of being penetrated by truth, which is shared, to the point of risking death. Symbolic intelligence is based precisely on this non-binding relationship of the referent to the signified and the signifier.

The radical spirit of the 1960s prevented Michel Foucault from presenting his epistemology in complementarity with that of his predecessors and from considering the phenomenon of self-transcendence on which today philosophers such as Jean-Pierre Dupuy and Vincent Descombes are working. The contemporary epistemological question is therefore to define a type of symbolic, mytho-logical rationality that cuts across the most diverse sciences, and manifests both "the sovereign unity of a subject, a spirit or an era and the set of relations that can be discovered, in a given period, between the sciences when these are analyzed on the level of discursive regularities."[9] As will be seen, the permanence and the evolution of the paradigm of orthodoxy answer this twofold requirement. But first of all it is necessary to retrieve a symbolic understanding of being.[10] As Jean Borella wrote, the correlation

8 Michel Foucault, "Discourse and Truth: The Problematization of Parrhesia," six lectures at the University of California at Berkeley, Oct.–Nov. 1983. http:foucault.info/documents/parrhesia/.

9 Ibid., 250.

10 What follows is taken from two pages of the introduction to our doctoral thesis, Antoine Arjakovsky, *La génération des penseurs religieux de l'émigration russe*, Paris/Kiev, Dukh i Litera, 2000. Antoine Arjakovsky, *The Way, Religious Thinkers of the Russian Emigration in Paris and Their Journal (1925–1940)*, trans. Jerry Ryan, ed. John A. Jillions and Michael Plekon, Foreword by Rowan Williams, Notre Dame, Indiana, Notre Dame University Press, 2013.

of the *logos* and *muthos* proves that "if every symbol requires, ultimately, the production of an intellectual apprehension, there can be no production of intelligibility, except under the action of the symbol."[11]

In his book *Philosophie sans rupture*, published in 1986,[12] the Greek philosopher Christos Yannaras continued and updated the reflections of the Russian philosophers on the history of the discussions concerning being, concentrating especially on the position of Sergius Trubetskoy as outlined in his essay on *La doctrine du logos dans l'histoire* which appeared in 1900.[13] C. Yannaras explained the distinction between mythical experience and logical experience in the following manner: in the different forms of relations mankind has with reality, both in the mythical experience and the logical experience, the logos signifies and reveals the event of a relationship of the spirit with the mode of manifestation of beings and of cosmic harmony, the fact that the human logos conforms and corresponds to the logical mode constitutive of Being. Indeed, in myth, which is always a narrative, the function of reason is not to merely describe an experience of the senses or serve as an intellectual approach to reality; reason tries to communicate the awareness of the mode in which life is realized. In this case, reason functions as judgment and imagination. C. Yannaras defines the myth as "the history of a fact produced by the imagination: it reproduces actions and relations which belong to the domain of the senses but in the way the spirit imagines by judging, that is to say, by separating the essential from the incidental so that life might be realized."[14] These actions of an existential order, reproduced in the myth and expressed in the same language through symbols, are relationships between persons.

In the same way, in the case of logical knowledge, essence is not something accomplished but rather a participation in becoming, in the development of life as both a cosmic and social phenomenon. Logical thought is a semantic of essence. Concept or definition determines the singularity of essence as a discourse that results from differences. The action of demonstrating, the declarative discourse, reveals not only the singularity of the being as universality, but also the mode of this singularity. It must be kept in mind, however, that it is in the framework of the city and not in an autonomous

11 Jean Borella, *La crise du symbolisme religieux*, Paris, L'Age d'Homme, 1990.
12 C. Yannaras, *Philosophie sans rupture*, Paris, Labor et Fides, 1986.
13 S. N. Troubetskoy, *Oeuvres*, 1900; republished by Mysl', 1994.
14 C. Yannaras, *Philosophie sans rupture*, op. cit., 28.

way that the agreement of individual reason with the common reason is realized, with the *logos* of the communion of the citizens.

The difference between mythical experience and logical experience consists in a difference of participation in communitarian reasoning and this is why it is so difficult for thought to synthesize them into a single expression. However, the history of thought shows that their growing separation has been a hindrance to the realization of life. Indeed, the personified image used by myth has a tendency to identify itself with what it seeks to signify since it no longer distinguishes the otherness of each intelligible reality. Equally, the abstract and impersonal concept can easily lose its semantic character and submit itself to the arbitrary interpretation of the individual, since it is no longer grasped as a word of Being.

At this point, using the separation between *muthos* and *logos*, between the image and the word as a point of departure, it is advisable to consider a detour towards the question of Being in order to be able to give, in a second step, the patristic definition of mythological thought. Ontology is discourse concerning Being, everything that can be said about the fact that one participates in Being. In the course of the history of thought, three discourses on Being can be summarily distinguished: the ontic conception, the rational conception and the personalist conception. The ontic conception of Being considers it a something, a certain being that really exists. The rational conception of Being moves from the sphere of *muthos* to the sphere of *logos* while remaining in continuity with the substantialist vision of the ontic conception. In a reflexive movement, the intellect questions the veracity of the discourse concerning Being and adopts the criterion of the conformity of the human logos (which becomes reason) with the logos of beings-in-themselves or beings in relation to us. This approach presupposes the same conception of the subject who knows and the object known as autonomous ontic individualities. Finally, while the personalist conception of Being (based on "the religious ideal of Judaism," as Troubetskoy[15] puts it) shares in different degrees the rational approach which distinguishes man from the cosmos more clearly than the ontic conception, it refuses the rationalist reduction of the truth to the conformity between the concept and what is conceived, and returns to the ontic idea of the truth as a universal, dynamic and social fact of life. Using the apophatic method, that is to say, the logic of freedom from all notional cognitive determinism,

15 S. Troubetskoy, *Oeuvres*, op. cit., 76–77.

the personalist conception of Being consists in a new reversal of thought towards the mythical relationship to Being.

For Cappadocian thought this personalist vision of Being is rooted in a revelation of the spirit which renders inconceivable the ontic conception of a "God-cause-of-the-universe" imprisoned in his essence and a "humanity-crushed-by-time-and-the-cosmos." The personalist perspective restores life to Being and integrates history as the space-time of a personal relationship between man and the God-Creator. For Gregory of Nyssa or John of Damascus, being and being-in-relationship become identical. For someone or something to exist, two things are necessary at the same time: "being-in-itself" (hypostasis) and "being-in-relation" (person). It is only in relationship that this identity reveals itself as having an ontological significance. This discourse derives from the new representation of the unique nature of God, not as substance but as the Father, as a person and hypostasis.[16] Far from separating the discourse on God and the love of wisdom, Gregory of Nyssa, Maximus the Confessor and Nicholas Cabasilas revived the initial intuition of the Greek philosophy of Being as a given living reality which can only be expressed by myth, but which becomes more intelligible through discourse. The Christian Church conferred the title of Fathers of the Church on them precisely because of their ability to communicate their revelation of the Triune God in logical terms.

The Cappadocian philosophers take up Aristotle's distinction between primary essence (the individual attributes of the subject), which for them then becomes hypostasis in the sense of self-awareness, and secondary essence (the modes of a common participation in Being), the *ousia*, and introduce alongside these first two terms, a third element, energy, because a nature exists only as a dynamic event (*energoumenon*) brought about as the realization of unique relations for each subject or similar relations for several subjects. "The energies of the essence of the human person are those capacities which characterize the common mode of humanity's participation in Being (knowing, willing, creating, loving) while at the same time, the releasing, the existential ecstasy with respect to this common mode, in other words, the existential otherness of each concrete person but also the knowledge-participation of the otherness of other essences and other individuals."[17] Faced with the question of Being, this way of thinking passed

16 J. Zizioulas, *L'Etre ecclésial,* Paris, Labor et Fides, 1981, 76–77.

17 Yannaras, *Philosophie sans rupture,* op. cit., 85.

from the question of "What?" to the question of "How?" This progression of thought envisaged Being, not as a substance but as a Person. Alongside the great genres of the Same and of the Other, a third category emerged from consciousness, that of the Self freely founding its own hypostasis. The Christian mythological discourse has its origins in the personalist ontology of the Cappadocians. Here mythological thought is the discourse orientated towards the universal agreement of humanity's logical faculties with Being considered as a Person, with a view to the realization of life.

This mythological thought was rediscovered in the beginnings of the 20th century by Russian religious thinkers. Berdyaev, Bulgakov, Florovsky — proponents of the personalist, sophiological or theocentric currents of Russian thought — agreed in their understanding of orthodox thought as symbolic, antinomic and eschatological.[18] These intellectuals helped to bring together the traditional philosophical systems of Christian thinkers of the East and the West, making a critical analysis of their own symbolic perspective by opening it up to more universality, and confronting it with the conceptual genius of the West.[19] They also helped Western thinkers distance themselves from a nominalist philosophy that had become totally disconnected from reality, and reminded them of the necessarily interpersonal and conciliar dimension of truth.

This work was also undertaken by contemporary Western thinkers, including Jean Borella, professor of philosophy at the University of Nancy, and Jean-Luc Marion, professor of philosophy at the Sorbonne. In his book *Le lieu du soi*, Marion, starting with St. Augustine, surveys the whole history of European philosophy in an attempt to rediscover the person, not just as a finite entity destined to die but as a being capable of self-transcending through love for others. At the end of his narrative he writes: "The *ego* is not by itself. It is neither by a self-apprehension in self-awareness (Descartes, at least as commonly understood), nor by a performative act (Descartes, as he is more rarely interpreted), nor by apperception (Kant), nor even by self-affection (Henry) or anticipatory decision (Heidegger). The *ego* does not even reach to itself *for* another (Levinas), nor *like* another (Ricoeur); it only becomes itself *by* another."[20]

18 Antoine Arjakovsky, *La génération des penseurs religieux de l'émigration russe*, Paris/Kiev, Dukh i Litera, 2000.

19 Antoine Arjakovsky, "Notre génération" in *Les Jalons, Cent Ans après*, Paris, Lviv, IEO/François Xavier de Guibert, 2009, 17–56.

20 J.-L. Marion, *Au lieu de soi. L'approche de Saint Augustin*, Paris, PUF, 2008, 383–84.

For his part, Jean Borella, in his book entitled *La crise du symbolisme religieux,*[21] has shown that the eradication of the *muthos* (everything related to symbolism) inevitably leads to the negation of the *logos* (the intellect that speaks within us). But the logos cannot be denied. Myth, therefore, cannot be expelled. Following Paul Evdokimov, Borella proposes the recovery of an epiphanic knowledge of reality. He writes: "If the symbol apparently only asks to be interpreted, if the sign seems to exist only to refer to the reality to which it points, more profoundly, by its very nature as symbol, it imposes on our intelligence an interpretation of cosmic realities which, under the influence of its disruptive (incongruous, unassimilable) presence, are transformed into visible signs of a transcendent Reality: what was sign becomes reality, what was reality becomes sign."[22]

## THE FOUR POLES OF ORTHODOX THOUGHT

The diagram of the "metaphysical cross" (two dimensions) or the "metaphysical pyramid" (three dimensions) which Borella outlines in his book[23] will be used, with some modifications and precisions, for our cross-disciplinary definition of orthodoxy. The purpose of this diagram is to exhibit "the transformation brought about by the internal semantic activity of the symbol and the enhancement it achieves in order to unite what was separated."[24] A unifying vertical axis should be drawn uniting, from bottom to top, man to the divine referent. The axis that unites them is called "symbolic and sacred." A horizontal axis should also be drawn uniting, from left to right, the sensory world to the intelligible world (for Borella the natural pole to the cultural pole). The axis joining the divine referent to the cultural and natural poles are respectively designated as "symbolic and metaphysical" and "symbolic and cosmic." At the heart of the pyramid is a focal point that unites all the axes in a semantic dynamism. This point is referred to by the figure of Wisdom. In Christian revelation, Christ, who is the truth, is precisely "the wisdom of God and the power of God." But as will be seen, the biblical and patristic doctrine of the Wisdom of God is addressed to humanity as a whole. The study of philosophical and religious systems

21 J. Borella, *La crise du symbolisme religieux,* Paris, L'Age d'Homme, 1990.
22 Ibid., 348.
23 Ibid., 239.
24 Ibid., 236.

lying outside of Christian theological discourse enables the latter to precisely both defend its representation of the truth and question a certain number of anthropomorphisms and sociomorphisms within its own beliefs.

Our hypothesis, the fruit of a historical observation of orthodox thought, is the following: the four poles of Christian consciousness (recognition/glorification, memory, law, justice) are in an antinomic relationship to one another. As Father Paul Florensky demonstrated in his commentaries on the antinomies of Kant, an antinomic relation, unlike a dialectical one, is not resolved by an exhaustion of opposites in a third term.[25] It should rather be understood as a permanent tension that permits one to hold simultaneously several equally true propositions which could be contradictory at a certain level of consciousness. This interpolar tension results in the formation of paradigms, or predominating figures of community awareness within a given space-time.

Upon this "metaphysical cross" or "doxic structure," it is possible to define the boundaries of the paradigms of truth according to the four principal meanings of *orthodoxia* expressed in the history of Christianity: worthy glorification (when the ecclesial consciousness is magnetized by the pole of recognition, of the other, or of the divine), right truth (when the organization of the pole of nature, or of the sensory world, becomes, by its universal law, the ethical priority of Christian thought), faithful memory (when it is the pole of memory, of identity, or incarnate humanity which structures the dominant discourse), and fair knowledge (when the pole of justice, of culture, or of the intelligible world becomes predominant over the other three poles of the consciousness).

Orthodoxy as worthy glorification is the "radical" or "eschatological" posture which enables a person to "achieve" the reality which presents itself to him, to consume it and turn it over in the mind. It is situated on the side of the vertical axis going from humanity towards God and vice versa (since it is a circulation of glory). It has its foundation in the Epistle of St. Paul to the Corinthians. It consists in worshipping God as Wisdom (*doxa-kabod*), as the "Lord of glory" (1 Cor 2:8), which presupposes love as the source of all knowledge (1 Cor 13). Glorification is source of truth only insofar as it is orientated towards the glory of God and is itself permeated with glory. As St. Irenaeus wrote, there is a circulation of glory in Christian revelation: "The glory of God is man fully alive."[26]

25 P. Florensky, *La colonne et le fondement de la vérité*, Paris, L'Age d'Homme, 1994.
26 Irenaeus of Lyons, *Against Heresies*.

On the other side of the vertical metaphysical axis connecting humanity to God, the source of truth, is the pole of identity, of memory, of habit which, when turning towards the Logos, develops first of all the virtue of fidelity. Glory is not just a source of praise; it is also memory, *anamnese*, that is, a remembrance that actualizes. But it is a memory which only accedes to truth through fidelity to a living encounter, to an existential person to person exchange, to a promise given. This definition of orthodoxy as faithful memory is based on the speech of St. Peter to the Jerusalem community the day of Pentecost. The proclamation of the good news (*evangelion*) is made in conformity with the promise (*epangelian*) of Scriptures: "Exalted at God's right hand, he first received the promised Holy Spirit from the Father, then poured out this that you both see and hear" (Acts 2:33). This historical fulfillment of the word given, of the promise made of old by God to the prophet Joel to "pour out his spirit on all flesh" has made its way over the course of time through the faithfulness of people to their Creator and through that of the disciples of Jesus to the recommendations of their master. It is the source of truth, the foundation of the Pentecostal explosion of "the Spirit of truth." Orthodoxy as faithful memory, or in its function as "guardian of the deposit of faith" (2 Tim 6:20) against the idle talk and objections of the "pseudognostics," is also a source of knowledge "with certitude" (Acts 2:36).

The horizontal axis is that of cosmic and pneumatic space-time. It is anthropocosmic or natural and cultural. It is intersected at its center, in Christian revelation, by him who called himself the "way," to which St. John adds, "*and* the truth *and* the life,"[27] and who announces the coming of the Kingdom of God upon earth as a kingdom of a living and lived truth. On the pole of the world of the senses (or the natural world) one finds the pole of knowledge which, by turning itself correctly towards the Logos, becomes moral awareness. This higher order knowledge comes from the exchange between the glory of God and humanity. It was, originally, the path of *gnosis*, in the Christian sense of the term, and of monastic asceticism.[28] According to St. Paul, this conformity is in the realm of moral law; it implies a respect for the created laws of nature (and not those of the fallen world). In his letter to Timothy, he writes that although the law was not given for the just, the

27 As Father George Tchistiakov has observed, the translation of the first "and" is generally overlooked. This leads to obscuring the fact that this way which Christ incarnates is, as it were, defined by this division into two elements. The way in Christ, with Christ and towards Christ is a way tending towards the truth and a quest of living truth.

28 Jean Borella, *Problèmes de gnose,* Paris, L'Harmattan, 2007.

"sound doctrine" is founded on the law (1 Tim 1:10). It cannot be accessed by being unruly, impious, or sacrilegious: "A time will come when certain people will no longer tolerate sound doctrine but, having itching ears, they will surround themselves with teachers to suit their own likings. They will stop listening to the truth and will wander off to fables. As for you, be steady and self-possessed; put up with hardship, perform your work as an evangelist, fulfill your ministry" (2 Tim 4:3–5). For St. Paul, *doxa* in the sense of *didaskalia* can only claim universality to the extent that it is lived in a personal relationship to the law. It is question of a "meta-knowledge" (*epignoseos* — 2 Pt 1:3) that is not found in ancient philosophy or in Jewish wisdom. This "way of truth" is, according to St. Peter (2 Pt 2:2), gradual. Its starts with faith (*pistis*), extends in virtue and knowledge, consolidates itself through self-control, tenacity, and piety and finds its fulfillment in fraternal friendship and in love (2 Pt 1:5–7).

The horizontal axis which unites the cultural and intelligible pole to truth defines orthodoxy as true and fair knowledge. It is no longer a question of an individual moral stance but a just conformity of the truth being professed to the reality lived in society. This fourth pole of orthodox consciousness is also rooted in Scripture. When they meet at Antioch, Paul reminds Peter and Barnabas that their words must be in conformity with their behavior. "When I saw that they were not being straightforward about the truth of the Gospel, I had this to say to Cephas in the presence of all: 'If you who are a Jew are living according to Gentile ways rather than Jewish, by what logic do you force the Gentiles to adopt Jewish ways? . . . But we know that people are not justified by the works of the law but only by faith in Jesus Christ . . .'" (Gal 2:14, 16). It is not a question here of an immoral attitude that would prevent truth from manifesting itself. According to the law there is nothing wrong with Paul's behavior and that of his non-Jewish friends when it comes to sharing meals with pagans. The problem is not one of moral law but of justice. What harms the testimony of the light is the unjust and timorous behavior of Cephas and his friends who do not dare to be publicly identified with pagans in the presence of Jews. In this case, it is not by the law that one arrives at truth but by justice. The truth should not only be celebrated, memorized and lived individually, it should also be incarnated socially — it cannot remain an abstract concept. An echo of such an approach can be found in the *Didache* — the teachings of the twelve apostles — a text written in Greek near the end of the first century which explains how the way of life is to be lived.

Orthodoxy is not, therefore, as was commonly believed for a long time, simply the opposite of heresy, understood as a partial knowledge of the truth.

Orthodoxy is a mode of relationship to the truth that prevents worship from emptying itself of the glory it seeks to proclaim, that prevents memory from ossifying itself by clinging to a remembrance as if it were an object, that refuses a moral testimony not lived out in practice, and that leads science, in danger of remaining merely at a purely theoretical level, back to its obligations of justice. It assures a relationship to the truth that is complex and embraces the fundamental metaphysical positions of worship, memory, ethics and justice.

Within such a perspective, it is understandable why the concepts of orthodoxy and ecclesiology are connected in Christian epistemology.[29] Ecclesiality, or the field of Christian consciousness, represents the space of truth as defined by orthodoxy. The truth is dependent on the degree of conciliarity among those who attest it. This symbolic space is conceived by the Christian tradition as a meta-rational framework in which there is communication between God and humanity but also within humanity itself. To express this corporeality, Christian tradition has relied on prophetic visions. These visions place the different symbolic poles of human consciousness in antinomic tension. The vision of the glory of God in Ezekiel 1:5 uses a symbolic tetramorphic language which has the originality of presenting a chariot-throne with, at its summit, "the resemblance of a man," a theanthropic divinity in motion.[30] In the prophet's vision of "the glory of the Lord" one finds both the intermingling of the four living creatures or holy animals and the reoccurrence of the notion of uprightness:

> As I looked, behold, a stormy wind came out of the north, and a great cloud, with brightness round about it, and fire flashing forth continually, and in the midst of the fire, as it were gleaming bronze. And from the midst of it came the likeness of four living creatures. And this was their appearance: they had the form of men, but

29 As early as 1921, Bulgakov envisaged the characteristics of the Church as revelatory of the tensions which structured the ecclesial body. In particular, he reflected on the link between the Virgin and created Wisdom and the relations between Peter and John. A parallel can be seen with the attempt by Hans Urs von Balthasar (1905–1988), in 1974, to schematize "the structure in tension" of the Church by an apostolic cross. For this Catholic theologian, the four "symbolic-real" apostles, Peter, James, John and Paul are situated at the four poles of truth. At the heart of the four apostolic missions is the *fiat* of the Virgin to revelation. H. U. von Balthasar, *Le complexe anti-romain, essai sur les structures ecclesiales*, Montreal, mediaspaul, 1998. This theme will be treated further on.

30 Ana-Maria Girleanu-Guichard, "Les quatre 'animaux saints' ou le Tetramorphe: Sources et élaboration d'un motif iconographique médieval," *Contacts*, no. 231, Paris, 2011, 275–316.

> each had four faces, and each of them had four wings. Their legs were straight, and the soles of their feet were like the sole of a calf's foot; and they sparkled like burnished bronze. Under their wings on their four sides they had human hands. And the four had their faces and their wings thus: their wings touched one another; they went every one straight forward, without turning as they went. As for the likeness of their faces, each had the face of a man in front; the four had the face of a lion on the right side, the four had the face of an ox on the left side, and the four had the face of an eagle at the back. Such were their faces. And their wings were spread out above; each creature had two wings, each of which touched the wing of another, while two covered their bodies. (Ezek 1:4–13)

Certain targums have associated the four letters of the divine name with the four creatures: Y for humanity, H for the lion, V for the ox and H for the eagle. Philo of Alexandria linked the twelve tribes of Israel, rearranged in four groups of three according to a common emblem, with the twelve signs of the zodiac. The patristic and iconographic tradition connected the cherubim of the vision of Ezekiel with the four Evangelists. For St. Jerome, the eagle must be associated with John (because of his piercing, visionary perspective), the man with Matthew (because of his narrative of the genealogy of Christ), the ox with Luke (his Gospel begins with the story of the priest Zacharias) and the lion with Mark (due to his prophetic spirit, evident from the beginning of his Gospel). It is this representation of the late fourth century that was retained by tradition.[31] The lion symbolizes royal functions, the ox sacerdotal activity, the eagle the pouring forth of the gift of the Spirit, while the man represents human activity. The Pantocrator of the Byzantine and Russian cupolas, surrounded by an eagle, a man, a lion and an ox, is the one who "maintains all things" and who, in this sense only, is the all-mighty (the Russian word *vsederjitel* is a precise expression of the Greek word *pantocrator*).

It is thus legitimate to associate the four poles of ecclesiality—that is, orthodox corporeality—with the four faces of the truth with a human face, walking straight forward. The vertical axis, of the image and of the resemblance between the subject and the referent, unites the two poles of unity

31 For St. Irenaeus, John should have been associated with the lion and Mark with the eagle. St. Augustine linked the lion to Matthew and the man to Mark.

and sanctity within this body. These two poles are united by Christ himself. In the Gospel of John (21:15–19), at his last appearance to his disciples on the shores of Lake Tiberius, Christ tells Peter to feed his sheep and, at the same time, urges him to follow the path of love ("Do you love me?"), a path that can lead to martyrdom ("Jesus said this to indicate the sort of death by which Peter was to glorify God") as Peter would later experience. In this way, the pole of divine and ecclesial unity joins the pole of worthy glorification. This can be associated with the symbol of the eagle in the Tetramorph of the Judeo-Christian tradition. The pole of sanctity is the pole of human activity which, if it finds a coherence between the past, present and future, provides the expansion of glory, that is to say, of clarity and radiance.

The horizontal anthrocosmic axis of knowledge unites the sensory pole and intellectual pole of creation. It brings together the poles of catholicity, or the universal/ecumenical aspect, of the social, institutional and human law brought about by activity which reflects the trinitarian unity (Jn 17:20–26) and that of social, institutional and human apostolic activity which is the "path of justice" opened up by John the Baptist (Mt 21:23–32). There can be no justice without reconciliation, nor reconciliation without justice. Right truth means understanding the *ekklesia* in its totality, that is to say, according to its capacity to embrace both Jews and pagans.[32] The term *kath holon*, in its root meaning, designates the part in its conformity to the whole and on the basis of the evangelical witness, the relation of the unity between humanity and God in the image of the relation of Christ with his Father. In his sacerdotal prayer, Christ presents this relationship as a circulation of glory between God and humanity.[33] Thus it is that, from a perspective of fair knowledge, the dimension of mission appears related to catholicity on the pole representing the social transfiguration of the world: "As you have sent me into the world, so do I send them into the world" (Jn 17:18). There can be no mission, no apostolicity nor any transformation of human culture without reference to the catholicity that sustains it. But this catholicity exhausts itself if it is not orientated towards what both surpasses it and at the same time resists it.

32 Cardinal Lustiger, who accepts this definition of catholicism, seems to be unfair, however, when he affirms that the Church of Jerusalem, symbol of the permanence of the promise made to Israel, "has been destroyed [prior to the sixth century] through the pressure of Byzantium." J. M. Lustiger, *La promesse,* Paris, Parole et Silence, 2002, 17. There are many other reasons which need to be considered.

33 André Laurentin, *Doxa, Problèmes de Christologie, Jean 17/5 et ses commentaires patristiques,* Paris, Bloud et Gay, 1972.

The Church is, therefore, according to the symbol of Nicea, one, holy, catholic and apostolic given that it is orthodox.[34] Conversely, the Church cannot claim to be orthodox if it loses a single one of these four poles or pathways on the Way.[35] J.-M. Tillard writes: "Because it came forth from the assembly of Pentecost (the memorial of the Assembly of the Desert) as *fulfillment* of that which the *Qahal* tended towards, the Church of Jerusalem is from the beginning born catholic since it brings fullness, integrity, and the *katholou* of the gift of God. It is thus the community where the divine *oikonomia* reaches its moment (*kairos*) of plentitude. It is not, therefore, just a question of geographical universality, of which the nations represented by the proselytes assembled for the feast (Acts 2:5, 8–11) would already be the prophetic core. It is the complete realization of what the call (or convocation) of God actually means."[36]

34 Avery Dulles, *The Catholicity of the Church,* Oxford, Oxford University Press, 1985. The meaning of catholicity has evolved down through the ages, as Cardinal Avery Dulles has shown. In the 2nd century, during the period of St. Irenaeus of Antioch, the term "catholic" Church was still simply used in opposition to a "particular" Church or the part of a whole (*Smyr.*, 7/2). The definition by Cyril of Jerusalem in the 4th century is interesting in that it reveals all the semantic riches the term had acquired in two centuries. For this Father of the Church: "The Church is called catholic because it is spread throughout the world, from one end of the world to the other, and also because it teaches, universally and completely, all the doctrines that humanity should know concerning things visible and invisible, in heaven and on earth; and also because it points out the proper worship to all of mankind, governors and governed, literate or illiterate; then because it universally treats and heals every sort of sin committed by the soul and the body; it possesses in itself all the virtues conceivable in words, acts or spiritual gifts of every sort" (*Works of St. Cyril of Jerusalem*, Catecheses XVIII, Washington, CUA, 1970, 132; translation from the Greek, Latin, and English by AA). It is notable that, in this definition, catholicity tends to identify itself, due to its power of universality, with ecclesiality as a whole and to thus integrate the four modes of access to the truth through worship, virtue, justice and teaching or memory. In modern times, Melanchton defines the Church as catholic "in that it is an assembly dispersed throughout the world and in that its members, wherever they might be and even though geographically separated, exteriorly embrace and confess the unique and same right doctrine, at all times, from the beginning unto the consummation of history" (definition given by Avery Dulles). Our contemporary period, marked by the effort of systemization undertaken by Avery Dulles, notably as it appears in the definition *Lumen Gentium*, conceives catholicity according to the five levels of meaning presented by their opposites, i.e., contraries: sectarian, particular, false, mystic/invisible, governed without a communion with the synod of bishops and the bishop of Rome.

35 A few decades ago, the Orthodox Church still defined itself as the Orthodox Catholic Church. Cf. Panagiotis Trembelas, *Dogmatique de l'Eglise Orthodoxe Catholique,* Chevetogne, DDB, 1966.

36 J.-M. Tillard, *L'Eglise locale, ecclésiologie de communion et catholicité*, Paris, Cerf, 1995, 34.

Since the outline we have sketched establishes a semantic logic of the symbolic that unites humanity with God and the sensory to the world of intelligibility, we must now undertake a historical study of the concept of orthodoxy. Our thesis here is that ecclesial consciousness has very quickly made one sense of orthodoxy prevail over others, to the point that this sense has become paradigmatic not only within the ecclesial consciousness but more widely in all the cultures permeated by the Christian kerygma. It is through the study of ecclesial historiography that we have chosen to illustrate the advantage of one definition of orthodoxy over another.

## TOWARDS A SEMANTIC HISTORY OF ORTHODOX CHRISTIANITY

### *The Outline*

It will now be necessary to specify our historical method. The establishment of a periodization largely determined the historical narrative. Let us take the example of the Middle Ages to measure the difficulty of a history of orthodox Christianity. For Father George Florovsky, an historian of the Orthodox confession, the great historical schism is that of the excommunication of 1054, between Cardinal Humbert and the Patriarch Michael, an event which, according to him, marked the end of the history of orthodoxy in the West. But for the Byzantinist and Orthodox priest John Meyendorff, it would be more fitting to retain a political and nonecclesial date in order to understand this phenomenon of the extinction of orthodoxy in the West, that of 1071, which marked the defeat of Byzantium by the Turks at Manzikert.[37] While for a third historian, the Catholic Guy-Marie Oury, the pivotal date is 1048 marking the advent of an energetic and reformist pope, Leo IX of Lorraine, who will engage Western orthodoxy on its path of renewal (cf. his *Histoire de l'Eglise*, Solesmes, 2001). These variations over a span of 25 years might appear insignificant. All the same, they reveal three different points of view of historians which thus determine the whole *contemporary* consciousness of Christians of the East and of the West. Suddenly, in the history manuals

37 This political vision of the history of Christianity explains the importance that J. Meyendorff ascribes to the Crusades from 1095 onward—especially the 4th crusade of 1202–1204—as the source of the estrangement which will disassociate the Churches of the East and the West.

of the Orthodox Churches, the West disappears from the life of the Church, just as the East is erased from Catholic history books in favor of the "battle of the two swords." Certainly, there are historians who are more or less realistic or diplomatic and who explain that the schism did not take place overnight. Some in the East have the Christian West suddenly reappearing at the moment of the Council of Florence, but that really doesn't matter. There is not a single manual of the Orthodox Church (in the confessional sense) which treats Western spirituality as a vital phenomenon intrinsic to orthodox consciousness; the same is true in the West but inversely. Most of the manuals tend to consider the Orthodox Churches as "particular cases," often "complicated," worthy, at best, of a specific chapter, but the vector of the life of the Church, whose axis extends between Rome and Geneva, is not questioned. So do these three pivotal dates signify three incompatible interpretations of the history of orthodox Christianity? The reality is that in both the "Catholic" historiography and the "Orthodox" historiography no attempt is made to probe the historical consciousness of contemporaries of these events (which would respect the definition of the Church as a body) nor the compatibility of such judgments with the dynamic of Christian orthodoxy (which would respect the definition of the Church as the way). This is the reason why conceptual or dogmatic histories of the Orthodox Church fail to account for the reality of orthodox Christianity beyond its strictly institutional boundaries. In the same way, but conversely, the more or less mystical narratives on the path of "Orthodoxy"—disconnected from the visible, and therefore institutional, incarnation of Christianity—condemn themselves to retract from the narrative (that is to say, from the orthodox consciousness) whole periods of the life of the Church.

In our view, it is the concept of historical consciousness which enables us together to grasp the truth contained in these different discourses. When perceived according to its degrees of corporality, from its individual horizon to its paradigmatic horizon, from its recognition of a tradition which precedes it to its discovery that this tradition belongs to it, then this consciousness allows us to understand the sequence of past events, to rediscover their internal logic, to break the barriers of objectification and thus participate in related events. Théologue de Foucauld, the author of a history of Orthodoxy, understood this theurgical dimension of the work of a historian of orthodoxy. He envisages his narrative not as an "act of burial," but, according to the expression of Paul Ricoeur, as an act of life. He writes: "We do not want to talk about the schism; we claim any definitive explanation of it to be harmful because the schism is an ongoing event and not a historical fact. It is not a question of relating an unfinished history; it is a question of bringing this history to a close and recognizing the starting points of departure for such a venture. First we need to go back to basics, to rediscover the same vision. . . . It is the lack of dialogue and the lack of charity which hardened the opposing differences."[38] The word for "event" in Russian is *sobytie*, which also means the meeting of two beings. The event is what happens between the actor and the narrator, between the narrator and the reader. It might well be that a paradigmatic schema uniting vertical temporality (that of the axis of the human conscience in its relationship to its Creator) to horizontal temporality (that of the axis of human conscience in creation) in a pragmatic synthesis both hermeneutical and communicational, does justice to the memorial historiography of orthodoxy (identity as difference, according to John Erickson)[39] while enabling a fully confessional, Catholic, Protestant and Orthodox (identity as unity) understanding of the history of Christianity.

Jean-Marc Ferry suggests that: "universal history occurs pragmatically as a world of communication among the different historical worlds."[40] His logic of transmission studies the communications that have to be established between one form of identity and another, so that the sequential order of meanings appears. To demonstrate this, the philosopher uses the concept of recognition. This is important for us because this is one of the possible translations of the scriptural term *kabod-doxa*. Indeed glory, the source of reputation, can be understood as recognition. Paul Ricoeur consecrated his final work precisely to the semantic and philosophical study of the term "recognition" (*reconnaissance*) which signifies simultaneously the glory of general consensus, confession, rediscovery, justification, etc.[41] It is only by being "recognized" by a foreign culture that a given culture can live and therefore grow. Due to this paradigmatic constitution, it is impossible to represent the historical world as being analogous with the physical world, at least according to its traditional rational conception. History is not a homogeneous and linear reality. It branches out in a network of paradigmatic notions which die on one slope and are reborn on another in function of

38 Théologue de Foucauld, *L'Orthodoxie,* Paris, Buchet-Chastel, 1979, 60.

39 John Erickson, "The Formation of Orthodox Ecclesial Identity," *Saint Vladimir's Theological Quarterly*, vol. 42, nos. 3–4 (1998): 301–13. Conference of the Orthodox Institute of Balamand, July 1997 on "La vie et le témoignage de l'Eglise Orthodoxe."

40 Jean-Marc Ferry, *Les puissances de l'expérience*, Paris, Cerf, 1991, 201.

41 Paul Ricoeur, *Parcours de la reconnaissance. Trois études*, Paris, Stock, 2004.

the mechanism of recognition. The heretics of the 5th century, excluded in this respect from history, can appear as orthodox to 20th century historiography, as demonstrated by the phenomenon of ongoing rehabilitation of the so-called "non-Chalcedonian" Churches. It is these links of recognition that connect the moments of a sequence, give them order (Ferry points out that Stravinsky could not come before Vivaldi) and determine their meaning for our time. Within the same culture, specific mentalities can be identified, spiritual types which, over the course of centuries, constitute a particular culture through the phenomena of conflict and mutual recognition. We can now define four spiritual types which have played an important role in the history of the Church for the defense or the promotion of orthodoxy and which, at the same time, have contributed to its crises and moments of weakness by hardening themselves or by fearing communication with the other models. There is a zealous model (situated on the pole of morality), a spiritual model (situated on the pole of glorification), a critical model (situated on the pole of justice) and a proselyte model (situated on the pole of memory).[42]

## *The Concept of Paradigm*

An orthodox history of Christianity should aim at establishing a just mutual recognition between the present times, the time past and the time to come. On the one hand, Christ, in Christian theology, is the One who is, who was, and is to come and it is the same truth, believed by all, in all places, which constitutes Christian Tradition. On the other hand, the history of Christianity is indisputably marked by an evolution of its doctrine, worship and organization. These two truths must be recognized in order to attain orthodoxy. Our hypothesis is that this unity in diversity is found in the very concept of orthodoxy which has remained the same over the centuries, taking on several different paradigmatic meanings according to time and culture. The question is how this can be demonstrated. We will draw on the concept of paradigm.

42 Lucien Febvre approaches this model in his studies on religion in the 16th century when he chooses a typological examination of the figures of Rabelais (the critic), Calvin (the zealot), Luther (the proselyte) and Erasmus (the spiritual) rather than the current *doxa* concerning the step by step formation of the "schism of the Reformation." Cf. Robert Mandrou, "Le renouvellement de l'historiographie de la Réforme: Lucien Febvre et la Réforme," *Historiographie*, op. cit., 343. Cf. also my studies on the typologies in "Les Eglises orthodoxes et l'oecuménisme" in A. Arjakovsky, *En attendant le concile de L'Eglise orthodoxe,* Paris, Cerf, 2010.

Even though we can agree with Thomas Kuhn that scientific theories are not rejected when they are refuted but when they can be replaced, the concept of paradigm cannot be understood in an empirical sense and according to the sociological reception given to it by the professor at the Massachusetts Institute of Technology.[43] For us, a paradigm is a level of consciousness attained by an organized community that becomes dominant over other levels of consciousness in the course of a certain period of time. It consists of a common memory, an identical representation of the truth, similar social practices and a selfsame understanding of ethical struggle. This paradigm may be marginal or dominant depending on the times and places of the cultures in which the communities that share it evolve. However, the paradigms of Christian orthodoxy have such a historical importance that they cannot be radically disassociated from the common consciousness of the cultures that they have encountered, that they have enriched, and from which they have been nourished. In many respects, the evolution of Christian orthodoxy also tells us something about the state and functioning of the paradigms specific to these cultures. A paradigm is not orthodoxy; it is rather a configuration of orthodox thought. The knowledge of orthodoxy is in this sense epistemological—that is, the study of different levels of paradigmatic consciousness and their interactions.

## *The Four Steps of the Narrative*

We have seen how traditional historiographies of orthodox Christianity have failed to provide a universal and truly catholic vision of orthodoxy as a concept, symbol and historical reality. Our thesis, based on the paradigmatic schema described above, is that only a semantic, and therefore contextual, history of orthodoxy furnishes a meaning that is both universal and participative to the history of Christianity, that restores an intelligibility to past events and brings spiritual logic to the growth of the ecclesial body during the course of history. This semantic history, from Jesus Christ to the present day, unfolds in four paradigmatic periods which also represent four levels of consciousness.

During the first three centuries of Christianity in the era of Hellenistic civilization, the paradigm of orthodoxy slowly and progressively established itself as worthy glorification. Strongly influenced by the eschatological exigency

43 Thomas Kuhn, *La structure des révolutions scientifiques*, Paris, Flammarion, 1983 (1962).

of openness to the Kingdom of God, the four poles of celebration, memory, morality and justice were ordered and configured to this individual and collective journey of Christian consciousness.

Dating from the legalization of the Church by the edict of Milan in 313, the Arian controversies and then the first barbarian invasions, it is the sense of orthodoxy as right truth which became dominant up to the Council of Florence in 1439 and the fall of Constantinople in 1453. The urgency of the emperors to incarnate the Christian religion in politics and the need of Christians to make the new law of the Gospel universal contributed heavily to making Christian doctrine the heart of the new paradigm both in the East and in the West.

In the second half of the 15th century, with the Renaissance, then the Reformation and Counter-reformations, extending up to the present period of ultramodernity, it is the sense of orthodoxy as faithful memory which becomes paradigmatic. It was the demand for unity between the political head and the community body that marked the paradigmatic development of this age of formation and expansion of nation-states.

It is possible that, since the beginning of the 19th century, a period which has seen a rapid acceleration of technology, globalization, unprecedented mixing of identities and, above all, a crisis of ideologies, a new period of representation of orthodoxy as true and fair knowledge has emerged and become important without as yet becoming paradigmatic. The anthropological turn constitutive of the modern era has emphasized the notion of conformity between doctrine and action.

Further on, we will justify the factors that permit us to demarcate these different periods and affirm their homogeneity. For the moment, we will limit ourselves to a few additional remarks. First, in our opinion, it is the incapacity to envisage these four modalities of truth, glorification, morality, memory and justice as a whole that is the source of the difficulties of Christianity in history. This incapacity is undoubtedly bound up with the breach brought about by the Christian definition of truth as a theanthropic person, and not as a transcendent divinity or as a self-revealing being. This break, which goes hand in hand with a new mode of personalist understanding integrating all four poles of the truth into a whole, upset the mechanisms of recognition among the different types of religious mentalities within a same culture or among cultures.

Secondly, it is not a question of setting up a rigid interpretation of the notion of paradigm. In the course of the same period, several different uses of the concept of orthodoxy can be found. For example, St. John of Damascus (c. 676–749), in the midst of the period of dominance of the paradigm of right truth, considers that a person who does not believe according to the tradition of the universal church is "an infidel,"[44] meaning thereby that his definition of orthodoxy was located on the memory and identity axis. It is indisputable that this logic had a paradigmatic resonance in the Muslim world being formed. On the other hand, in the Byzantine culture of the time, it was orthodoxy as right truth that organized knowledge, culture and social relation. What unified the Byzantine society of that era was no so much an enduring link to a tradition of the past, even if, a little later, the celebration of the triumph of orthodoxy in 843 still reinforced the paradigm of faithful memory in the more zealot monastic circles. But while a minority saw this victory over the iconoclast heresy as a triumph of their fidelity to the Fathers of the First Council who had themselves venerated icons, the majority interpreted this victory according to the logic of right knowledge. The Fathers of the Seventh Council of Nicaea II (787) made the intellectual distinction—that is to say here a spiritual and moral one—between the adoration of the image, which was reprehensible, and the beneficial veneration of the image of God. This latter consisted in a restoration of the image of God in man through the worship of Christ, "the icon of the invisible God" (Col 1:15). The creativity of Byzantine civilization at the time of Patriarch Photius (c. 810–893), an accomplished scholar and expert in ancient literature, bears testimony to the paradigmatic role of this second stream which understood orthodoxy mainly as right truth.

Thirdly, the presence of dominant paradigms does not impede the existence of temporalities specific to cultures whose participation in the dynamics of universal history is more marginal. Remaining in the context of the Medieval period, it must be recognized that it is as worthy glorification, according to the etymology of the word "pravo-slavie" that the Rus' Church of Kiev, in 988, received the Byzantine understanding of the truth. This reception, however, cannot be disassociated from its characteristic political context, which was precisely that of the period of orthodoxy initiated by the Edict of Milan. A proof of this is the marriage of Prince Vladimir with the Princess Anne, sister of the emperor Basil II, which took place at Chersonese, the place where Vladimir had been baptized. This demonstrates the necessity of representing history not as a homogeneous

44 John of Damascus, *Exposé de la foi orthodoxe*, IV, chap. 10, PG 94:1128.

and linear process but according to a logic of recognition, which might be disruptive but which is, nevertheless, coherent.

It is our hope that, through an historical analysis, our thesis will be able to resolve a number of aporias of previous historiographies in such a way that an Orthodox Christian, in the confessional sense of the term, might be able to represent the orthodoxy of Western Christianity beyond the first millennium. Moreover, an increasing number of Western Orthodox Christians assert their orthodoxy but without necessarily desiring to live in the first millennium. And an increasing number of Eastern Orthodox Christians are, secretly or unknowingly, as in the *Spiritual Combat* of L. Scupoli, assimilating the fruits of Western spirituality in such a way that significant parallels can be established between the history of Christianity and the history of humanity as a whole, between the truth of the gnostics and scientific truth, between *doxa* and *episteme*, between the "vision of the open gates of heaven" and "clear and distinct thoughts." The debate among Milbank, Ferry and Taylor gives hope that the modern secularized representation of the truth as conformity between idea and object will progressively give way to a redefinition of truth as radical orthodoxy. Everyone shall then be able to speak of the past as "memories of hope."[45]

## The Method

Orthodox Christianity is a historical reality that, as we have seen, is understood in a symbolic, hermeneutic and communicational manner. It can be defined as a mode of thought and action imbued with the Christian revelation, source of a specific cult and culture, manifesting the way of life of persons who have chosen to follow Jesus Christ and thereby forming an organic community united in a "visible" way,[46] in the image of a body. This body has a self-awareness which evolves over the centuries according to the changes in its own memory and the narratives of which it is the subject. Our thesis consists in the consideration that these great accounts of Christian self-awareness, although few on a topological level (Luke and

45 The title of the book by Olivier Clément for his second autobiography. O. Clément, *Mémoires d'espérance*, conversations with Jean-Claude Noyer, Paris, DDB, 2003.

46 The word visible is written with quotation marks due to the fact that phenomenology has shown that visibility depends on degrees of consciousness and that ecumenism which has manifested that visible unity can surpass canonical and confessional frameworks (as in the case of the recognition of the sacraments of other confessions).

John; Eusebius and Augustine; Flacius Illyricus and Cesar Baronius; Stephen Charles Neill, Olivier Clément and Guy Bédouelle), point out and reinforce a paradigmatic change of Christian orthodox thought.

There are four of these meta-narratives in the history of Christianity. In the first century AD, the apostles and evangelists represented the first historians of Christian consciousness. What they had in common was the presentation of the coming of the Kingdom of God on earth as imminent. They can thus be considered as a generation of historians whose thought was eschatological, turned towards the end of space-time at the level of consciousness of "this world." The telling of history consisted in providing a dazzling, engaging and sometimes discordant account of the acts of the Church in pursuit of its divine mission. It was the worthy vision of the glory of God that made these different narratives coherent and become dominant in the Christian consciousness of the first three centuries.

Greek and Latin historians of the 4th and 5th centuries constitute a second historiographic generation which can be qualified as political. In succession Eusebius of Caesarea, Sozomen, and Gregory of Tours took it upon themselves to rewrite the whole history of the world as a history of the Church. Through concern for universality, a characteristic of the pole of law, they also tried to fill the chronological gap separating the end of the book of Acts from their own time, an effort that was pursued without any major methodological changes up until the 15th century. This imperative of the account of origins, of the historical incarnation, of a political lieutenant of divine power and of missionary evangelization reconfigured orthodox thought as a moral and spiritual knowledge claiming to become the new *episteme* of the world.

The historians of the Reformation (Flacius Illyricus, Gottfried Arnold), of the Counter-Reformation (Cesar Baronius, Sébastien Le Nain de Tillemont) and those of the period called the Silver Age in Russia[47] (V. Bolotov,

47 This expression is often used only in reference to the history of Russian culture, but it was coined during a reunion by N. Berdyaev and used by him in *L'Idée russe* to designate a period of Russian history (1890–1918). It referred to a period of intellectual revival and spiritual renewal marked by the rediscovery of symbolism (from Vladimir Soloviev to Alexander Blok, from Carl Fabergé to Marc Chagall, from the formation of societies of religious philosophy to the recognition of the holiness of Seraphim of Sarov). It leads to the end of the synodal period of the Orthodox Church in Russia after the reestablishment of the patriarchate by the Council of 1917–18. It followed on the heels of what the symbolist poets of the time considered (without designating it as such) as the golden age of Russian culture, i.e., the early 19th century when the Russian

A. Lebedev) make up a third confessional page of the history of ecclesial consciousness, characteristic of a division among the Christian confessions and a rupture between the openness to God and the organization of society. In a different but analogical manner, according to the contexts, the Christian narrative, in the name of the struggle for faithfulness to its sources of transcendence, but also in the name of the unity of the Head to the Body, becomes a source of identity and of self-legitimization of the Churches in the face of the emergence of nation-states. This narrative does not neglect any critical sense; on the contrary, it calls forth a true critical science of the archives of the past. It directs, however, this critical approach to its primary objective which is the defense of religious and community identity.

Finally, a new historiography appears, prepared in the 19th century through the spiritual renewal inspired by the works of J. A. Möhler, J. H. Newman and V. Soloviev and relayed, since 1945, by a generation of historians such as F. Dvornik, O. Clément and Robert Wilken. With the extension of globalization, with the intermingling of populations and the failure of totalitarian ideologies, a new ecumenical awareness of the history of the Church is also emerging. This historiography tends to establish true and fair knowledge by not unilaterally disassociating the being and the person, the State and the Church, the heart and the intellect. It rejects the divisions of the preceding historiographical periods which separated *doxa* and *episteme*, theology and politics, East and West, the social and the national. Recent historiographical undertakings (*Histoire du christianisme* in France, *Histoire du mouvement oecuménique* in Switzerland, *Entsiklopedia Pravoslavie* in Russia, etc.) also bear witness to this new postconfessional manner of relating the history of Christianity. Although these narratives are often more analytic and encyclopedic than concise and ecumenical, these new approaches can be considered as representing a sign of a new age of ecclesial consciousness. It could well one day become paradigmatic and part of the teaching of the Churches themselves.

This typology of historiographic narratives allows us to propose a history of orthodox thought according to four periods: orthodoxy as worthy glorification (33–313), orthodoxy as right truth (313–1453), orthodoxy as faithful

---

language was being molded through the works of A. Pushkin and M. Lomonossov. G. Nivat, however, cites a phrase of Alexander Pushkin which manifests the awareness that he had of his times: "In the iron age, tell me, what will become of the golden age?" Cf. the colloquium of June 21–24, 2006, "L'Age d'argent dans la culture russe," University of Lyon III; *Tresors du siècle d'or russe de Pouchkine a Tolstoi*, Paris, Bodmer, 2009.

memory (1453–1948), orthodoxy as true and fair knowledge (1948 to present). Our history of Christian historiography aims to demonstrate the internal logic of orthodox thought, the dynamic tension between the poles of otherness and identity, of hierarchy and community. At a moment when the globalization of the world is dismantling many cultures and making many people fearful, when orthodox thought can turn nostalgically towards the so-called "confessional" or "secular" or "modern" era (a time considered safe thanks to the guarantee provided by the beacons of authority understood as the transcendent authority of the Pope, the Bible and the Tradition) where the new ecumenical understanding of the Church can appear "Gnostic" (in the pejorative sense of the word), orthodox thought can be led to fall back on its remembrance pole. On the other hand, if orthodox thought were understood as being, at the same time, a mystical theology, a participative philosophy, a political science of justice and moral understanding, then contemporary thought would be able to find new resources to face the new global age of its history and propose a more fair and peaceful civilization, one more respectful of creation. Such orthopraxic awareness of the truth would enable the Church to heal a very ancient wound in its relations with the Jewish and Hellenistic worlds. It could thus forge new links with contemporary philosophical thought and with the religions of the world.

# PART III
## *The Demonstration as Confirmed by History*

ORTHODOX CHRISTIAN DOCTRINE, AS WE HAVE seen from the meta-narratives of Milbank and Taylor, cannot be cut off from the rational representation of the world formed by humanity. Neither can it be "excarnated," in other words, cut off from the historical forms it has taken on through its ecclesial expressions. It is therefore necessarily dynamic, as demonstrated by J. H. Newman and V. Soloviev. It cannot be divided into a good and bad orthodoxy or a new and old orthodoxy without becoming totally meaningless.[1] Correct orthodox identity, "capable of overcoming a narcissistic and apologetic manipulation of communitarian remembrances," is, according to Jean-Marc Ferry, "all that much stronger insofar as it is capable of making agonizing revisions." It is fitting, therefore, to present, in the context of this vision of orthodoxy, a brief overview of the different contemporary historiographical traditions that relate the history of the Church and of Christian communities, which in their faith-rationality

1 There are historians who refuse to recognize that orthodoxy is a truth that transcends time. F. Laplanche, for example, writes of the "old orthodoxy, which implies the condemnation of sinful man and a pessimistic view of creation." Cf. Laplanche, "La Foi chrétienne, sources et développements," *Histoire du christianisme*, XIV, op. cit., 45. Further on, we will study the work of Jaroslav Pelikan, a Protestant historian who became Orthodox near the end of his life, author of the monumental *Histoire du développement de la doctrine. La tradition chrétienne*, Paris, PUF, 1994 (Chicago, 1989), which attempts to trace the history of the development of the doctrine of the Church. Pelikan constructs a history of "what the Church has believed, taught and professed basing itself on the word of God." But his representation of the evolution of beliefs does not take into consideration the definition of tradition as what has been believed everywhere and by all. For him, orthodoxy simply means the correction of doctrinal teaching with respect to a base that can itself fluctuate.

identity desire to be orthodox. But we must be careful not to go to the other extreme and identify orthodox faith, from the outset and totally, with its historical incarnations. John Locke, in his famous *A Letter Concerning Toleration*, written in 1689, noted that "Everyone is orthodox to himself" and "Every church is orthodox to itself."[2] In most cases, however, and up to the middle of the 20th century, the historians of the Church unilaterally accepted the principle of the adequacy of faith, necessarily orthodox, for ecclesial identity. There was no distancing as regards one's own confessional tradition or the Church's own discourse about itself. Even though the terms themselves[3] are very ancient, it is only in modern times that the terms catholic, protestant and orthodox acquired a precise institutional meaning. The Byzantine Church only became "Orthodox," in its actual institutional sense, after the synod of Constantinople rejected the synod of Florence in 1484. It was only at the time of the Council of Trent that the terms Catholic and Protestant were used to designate particular confessions.[4] In early Christianity, orthodox identity was not linked primarily to community membership, but rather to the bond of communion between the believer and Jesus Christ. This link was not rational, contractual or individual, but existential, ethical and communitarian. The Apostle John writes in his epistle that it is the *vision* of the "Word of Life" which leads him to bear witness. In order to "accomplish the truth" (1 Jn 1:6), one must walk "in the path on which he walked" (1 Jn 2:6). It is only by walking in the Light that Christians are "in communion with one another" (1 Jn 1:7).

Thinking and acting "in truth" was originally a service of remembrance and thanksgiving, a doxology, given by the apostles, which maintained the community in the path of salvation by the association of every gesture with prayer. The cross, resurrection and ascension of Jesus represent the three stages that enabled the birth of the *ekklesia*, of the community of the baptized. The consciousness of this community came about, above all, through the memory of these events in the eucharistic act of remembrance and thanksgiving. Father Alexander Schmemann and Father Marcel Jousse (1886–1961) agree when they view the institution of the Eucharist as the sacrament of the Church and when they see in the communion of the Body and Blood

2 John Locke, "Everyone is orthodox to himself, every church is orthodox to itself," *A Letter Concerning Toleration* (1689), Indianapolis, Hackett, 1983, 23.

3 Later on, we will consider the history of the meaning of these terms.

4 The word "catholicism" first appeared in the French language in 1598 and did not become standard until 1794.

of Christ, the actualization of the Word of God. Father Jousse offered this interpretation of the words of institution by Rabbi Jeshoua of Nazareth: "Whenever you do this again, as a reminder of me, you do it again."[5] The consequence of this liturgical understanding of remembrance was to focus the primitive Christian consciousness on the pole of worthy glorification. The fact that worthy glorification became the paradigmatic pole of orthodox consciousness does not mean that the other poles of consciousness were not also active at the same time. One cannot have a conceptualist reading of Christian history. In studying a system of thought, an anthropological approach should bring together, in a complex manner, both gestures and works, silent asceticism and external administration.

5 Gabrielle Baron, *Mémoire vivante, vie et oeuvre de Marcel Jousse,* Le Centurion, 1981, 45.

## CHAPTER 7

# *"Worthy Glorification" in the Historiography of the First Three Centuries*

### ORTHODOXY AS WORTHY GLORIFICATION

The institutional, existential and identifying self-awareness of the first Christian community described in the Acts is based on a doxological synthesis of gesture-thought-participation. During the period of the first three centuries of the Christian era, inaugurated at Pentecost, orthodox thought is fundamentally eschatological, orientated towards the catastrophic arrival of the Kingdom of God on earth (Acts 2).[1] Bishop Cassian Besobrazoff, the Russian Orthodox theologian who was dean of the St. Sergius Institute in Paris, has written that the "daily" bread in the translations of the Our Father is nothing other than the *epiousios* bread, the eminently essential bread, that is, the bread of the Kingdom of God on earth, at the same time anticipated and awaited. This acute awareness of a ladder which unites every moment on earth to heaven is accompanied by a desire to give thanks. In the primitive orthodox tradition, true knowledge is expressed through chant, doxology and the celebration of glory. In Russian, "reconciliation" (*soglassie*) means "singing as one" (*so-glassie*), something akin to "harmony" in English. As pointed out by Paul Evdokimov, "even the dogmas defined by the councils are conceived as doxological formulas and enter organically into the liturgy as part of it."[2] The sung profession of faith is preceded by

1 A bibliography in English, French, and German can be found in the book by H. R. Drobner, *Les Pères de l'Eglise,* Paris, Desclée, 1999.

2 Paul Evdokimov, *La connaissance de Dieu selon la tradition orientale,* Paris, DDB, 1988 (1967), 104.

the kiss of peace, the sign of the conciliar dimension of orthodox knowledge.[3] For the Fathers of the Church, the saint is the one who utters with his whole being: "I will sing to God as long as I live." This song of praise is the recognition of the vision of the glory of God. Although no one has seen God with his own eyes, Orthodox tradition bears witness to many theophanies and angelophanies. The only apostle it names "Theologian" is St. John since he is the visionary of the divino-human liturgy.

As is evidenced in the *Didache* or the Doctrine of the Apostles, probably composed at the end of the first century AD, moral formation and liturgical instruction are inseparable from the origins of Christianity. The book of the Two Ways shows that the way of life joins love of God and neighbor with a rigorous personal asceticism and social duties. The book of life ends with this phrase which unites moral consciousness and glorification: "You will confess your failings in the assembly of the faithful and will not go to pray with a bad conscience."[4] Baptism was only performed after moral instruction. Thanksgiving was offered after the Eucharistic meal with another prayer and the invocation "Come, Lord Jesus! *Maranatha!*"

In order to enter into the understanding of orthodoxy as worthy glorification, it is necessary to put aside the influences of the paradigm of orthodoxy as right truth, fair knowledge or faithful memory. In his research on Tertullian (c. 150–220), Jerome Alexander has shown that classifying in terms of orthodox/heretic or faithful/infidel one who is among the greatest theologians of his age is anachronistic. The essential is to understand the specific logic of the 2nd and 3rd centuries. Tertullian, who wrote in Latin, was of Berber and pagan origins and a convert to Christianity. For him, "flesh is a reality of God" and thus promised to glory. But what is real needs to be believed in order to be received in what it fundamentally is; it is the nature of things that determines perception and not the other way around. J. Alexander synthesizes Tertullian's thought: "The flesh, like language, acts as a sign. It signifies a reality that only trust can attain. This is why the substantial difference between soul and flesh is so important: the soul knows that the flesh attached to it is other than itself, that it can neither take full possession of it nor separate itself from it. It must hence resolve to trust it, respect it

3 "L'homologhia pros Theon," or the alliance with God is at the origin of the meaning of the term "confession" or the recognition of the truth by the ensemble of the faithful. Léonide Chrol, *Alpha et Omega, Essai sur le christianisme oecuménique intégral*, Montauban, 1967, 17.

4 *Les Ecrits des pères apostoliques*, presented by D. Bertrand, Paris, Cerf, 2006.

and love it."[5] This logic will lead Tertullian, according to J. Alexander, not to change his faith but to insist on discipline, the incarnation of doctrine, at the risk of no longer being understood by his contemporaries.

## THE SEMANTIC ROOTS OF *DOXA*

We must now focus on the semantic evolution of the notion of *doxa* and return to a decisive point, the apparently incongruous translation of the notion of *kabod* by that of *doxa*.[6] At the time of the Ionian philosophers, *doxa* had a metaphysical signification before taking on a secularized meaning of "popular opinion." For Parmenides and his milieu, *doxa* denoted the world of appearances, a world full of gods where the *dunamis* was in play. It covered all that could be grasped humanly through the senses (*kata doxai*) as contrasted with what could be understood by the intellect (*kata aletheia*). *Doxa* was thus defined by its two poles: the sensory world aspect and the opinion people formed of this world; or, to put it in another way, the pole of appearances as opposed to the pole of being, the pole of illusion as opposed to the pole of the contemplation of truth. *Doxa* implies a certain unity of being and appearance. In his study on Heidegger, Jean Wahl notes that "*doxa* signifies, primarily, fame and glory" as a reflection of the world of ideas; it then took on the meaning of "the simple point of view put forth and came to signify pure appearance and, finally, mere opinion."[7] Plato likewise considered that *doxa* was a matter of appearances as opposed to what is. It refers to truth but in an ambivalent way, mixing darkness and brightness. In this sense it is contrary to the *episteme* which signifies the intelligible truth in all its purity.[8] Consequently, one can understand the

5 Jerome Alexandre, *Une chair pour la gloire, L'anthropologie réaliste et mystique de Tertullien*, Paris, Beauchesne, 2001, 522.

6 We are following the argumentation put forth by André Laurentin who, himself, relies on the works of E. Paz, notably "Ex parmenide ad septuaginta. De notione vocabuli doxa," *Verbum domini* 38 (1960): 92–102, and M. Heidegger concerning the Presocratic doxa, *Einführung in die Metaphysik*, Tübingen, 1953, 79ff.

7 J. Wahl, *Vers la fin de l'ontologie. Etude sur l'introduction de la metaphysique par Heidegger*, Paris, 1956, 103–20, cited by Laurentin, op. cit., 223.

8 While for Homer *doxa* signified that which was received, Plato uses the term in the sense of opinion (false or true) and, as such, opposed to authentic knowledge. The meaning of *ortha doxa* is what is received and retained, the correct doctrine, accepted because it proceeds from a well-reputed source of knowledge. The other meanings are not put aside, for *doxa* still insinuates the opinion one has of another person or that another person has of someone else. In other words, *doxa* commonly designates, in classical Greek, opinion

Septuagint translation of the Hebrew term *kabod,* meaning glory, by *doxa*; both words imply two aspects, what is and what appears.

In Ancient Greece, for Plato and Aristotle, the notion of *doxa* was thus dissociated from that of *episteme.* If the former referred to opinion, the fleeting and contingent perception of the sensory world, the latter denoted knowledge, the stable and necessary understanding. But whether it is historical knowledge or physical knowledge, human thought takes place in the reality of the world. According to the contemporary philosopher Charles Taylor, knowledge occurs "when the action of the Forms that model reality coincide with their action modeling my intellect (*nous*)."[9] In his book *Philosophie sans rupture*, Christos Yannaras interprets these two modes of doxic and epistemic knowledge as mystical and logical thought and agrees with Taylor: "In myth as well as logic, knowledge is assured only insofar as it is a participation in common reason, in the *logos* of communion."[10] The Greek philosopher adds an important explanation on the function of these two modes of thought: "The difference between mythical expression and logical expression seems to center, fundamentally, on what could be called a 'unity' of participation, in common reason, in the *logos* of communion. If unity of participation in common reason, in the *logos* of communion of myth is principally the personified image, the unity of participation in common logic is principally an abstract and therefore impersonal concept."[11]

On the basis of the synthesis brought about by the first Christians and then by the Fathers of the Church, ortho-doxy is defined as *right praise* for it is centered on Christ, true Man and true God. In the Second Letter of Peter, which deals with the struggle against false gnosis in the name of "true science," *epignosis*, a Pauline expression,[12] signifies true knowledge centered not only on the figure of the Father but also on the divine person of Christ (2 Pt 1:3)[13] and growing, under the action of the Spirit, by faith, through

---

in the sense of reputation, of fame, of good name and, therefore, in the sense of glory, of renown (Philippe Arjakovsky).

9 Charles Taylor, *Les Sources du moi,* Paris, Seuil, 1998, 243.

10 Ibid.

11 Christos Yannaras, *Philosophie sans rupture,* Geneva, Labor et Fides, 1986, 58.

12 Philippians 1:9; also Romans 1:28: "and since they did not see fit to acknowledge God, so God delivered them up to their own depraved sense to do what is unseemly."

13 "The divine power has freely bestowed upon us everything necessary for a life of genuine piety, through knowledge of him who called us by his own glory and power. By virtue of them he has bestowed on us the great and precious things he promised, so that through these you who have fled a world corrupted by lust might become sharers of

works, towards love and perfect understanding. The Fathers of the Church, since they thought according to the ontic categories of their time, took up the idea of the conformation of the human intellect to the being of the cosmos as the source of knowledge. But, following St. Paul who desired to "know as I am known" (1 Cor 13:12), they could no longer consider knowledge in an impersonal way. According to L. Bouyer, what enabled Paul to think in such a way was that the great "mystery," the magnificent royal secret, was that of divine Wisdom finally revealed in the coming of Christ, the Davidic Messiah, the Suffering Servant and the Heavenly Son of Man.[14] But the attempt to identify Wisdom, both created and established before the beginning of the earth, was already an objectification of gnostic knowledge. Wisdom indeed does not depend on a confession of faith but on an openness of the spirit. Contemporary exegesis shows that Wisdom cannot be identified exclusively with a hypostasis; it is a figure of the "the in-between" where man and God mutually "contemplate one another," as Dominique Cerbelaud put it. The Dominican theologian has described how, very early on, Jews and Christians were tempted to identify the figure of Wisdom with the Torah, with Christ and also with the Holy Spirit.[15] Indeed, Wisdom, by its fluidity, presented a threat to a closed and schematic vision of religion. It is well known that Arius (256–336), in applying the figure of Wisdom to Christ, drew his conclusion on the created nature of Christ. The orthodox reaction was to put forth the twofold aspect of Wisdom as both created and uncreated[16] and then to trinitize with the Holy Spirit the affirmation of the *homoousia* between the Father and the Son, as is already

---

the divine nature. This is reason enough for you to make every effort to undergird your virtue with faith, your discernment with virtue, and your self-control with discernment; this self-control, in turn, should lead to perseverance and perseverance to piety, and piety to care for your brother, and care of your brother, to love."

14 Louis Bouyer, *Sophia ou le monde en Dieu,* Paris, Cerf, 1994, 33.

15 Irenaeus of Lyons, Theophilus of Antioch, Hippolytus of Rome have identified Wisdom with the Third Person. In their view, the Father acts through his Word and Wisdom. Cf. D. Cerbelaud, *Ecouter Israel, une théologie chrétienne en dialogue,* Paris, Cerf, 1995, 49.

16 In his struggles with Arianism, Saint Athanasius of Alexandria considered Wisdom not as a creature but as the Logos, the second hypostasis of the Trinity. In this context, it was no longer a question of linking Wisdom with the Holy Spirit. The patristic tradition, however, was aware that the whole Trinity, and not just the second hypostasis, had participated in creation and continues to do so. It is for this reason that Saint Athanasius distinguishes between created Wisdom (Yah've created me) and uncreated Wisdom (Yah've engendered me). Cf. Antoine Arjakovsky, *Le père Serge Bulgakov, philosophe et théologien chrétien,* Paris, Parole et Silence, 2006.

depicted in the Gospels (Jn 13:20; Mt 28:19). But this in turn contributed to dispelling the Sapiential theme.

Father André Laurentin has made an in-depth study of the history of John 17:5, "And now Father, give me glory at your side, the glory I had with you before the world began." His research has enabled us to recover the doxological nature of primitive Christian thought. The original initiatory understanding of this formula, at least until the third century, was revealed by this investigation. This French Catholic theologian has pointed out that the main source of difficulty in understanding this verse, which is part of the sacerdotal prayer of Jesus just prior to his arrest, is the notion of "glory" and, more specifically, "glory . . . before the world began." Does this refer to the created glory that Adam possessed before his fall? To the glory of the angels? To the power given to Christ for the sake of humanity? To the Holy Spirit, the power of God given to Christ for creation? To the uncreated glory, the bond of love at the heart of the Trinity? Did Christ ask for an actual and collective glorification or a personal and unique glorification? If it refers to a collective glorification, the emphasis will be put on the sacramental actions that actualize such a request (baptism, Eucharist, ministry, etc.). If it refers to an event concerning Christ, ecclesial thought will interpret this request according to its consequences (Resurrection-Ascension, the sending forth of the Holy Spirit, the Parousia and final judgment).

The ecclesial memory first of all turned towards the Scriptures and interpreted a certain number of ancient texts, notably Isaiah 11:10, in the light of this verse of St. John.[17] As demonstrated by Bishop Bezobrazoff, the Apostle John had a practical, mystagogical or initiatory understanding of the truth.[18] In his writings, most of the discourses or dialogues are commentaries on a sign, such as that of the multiplication of the loaves (Jn 6) or the resurrection of Lazarus (Jn 11), or on a liturgical symbol (e.g., water in Jn 3:4). It is the gesture, hence the rite, which interprets the word or event and makes it actual. Later, the *Diatessaron*, the Gospel in the Syriac language composed for liturgical use, influenced a sacramental interpretation of our verse because of the way it was translated ("Give me the glory that comes from you"), to the extent that the glory was no longer Christ's own, but rather given to him. This is the baptismal catechesis "prior to the last quarter of the second

17 "On that day, the root of Jesse, set up as a signal for the nations, the Gentiles shall seek out, for his dwelling will be glorious."

18 Bishop Cassian, *Khristos i pervoie khristianskoie pokolenie*, Paris, YMCA Press, 1939.

century"[19] which crystallized the sacramental understanding of the words of Christ. The newly baptized Christian donned a garment of glory by participating in the rite of the death and resurrection of Christ. The early gnostics valued the world-glory, opposition to which appears in this verse of St. John. In this reading, the glory was necessarily uncreated. Glorification consisted in ascending to the primordial glory where the soul returns to its source clothed with a new corporality. It is Christ who revives the primal spark and his garment of light is full of all those souls who return to their original unity. The pseudognostic text of Pistis-Sophia paraphrased this verse: "Come therefore in haste so that you might receive all the glory that is the glory of the first of mysteries."[20] For the gnostics, glory concealed a mystery, which is that of the pleroma composed of all the eons. But, according to Laurentin, the pseudognostics (the Mandeans, Simon the Magician, etc.) introduced a spirit-matter dialectic, a dubious understanding of glory as a garment, a place and a mystery uniting the Father and Christ, something very foreign to the original Greek text of the Gospel. Human history is a mere symbol. Christ becomes an emanation with a hundred faces. The divinity of Christ is thus called into question. André Laurentin explains that, in this way, in gnosis, "glory was taken away from our world on the hypertrophic wings of baptismal symbolism."[21] Origen, even though he sought to restore the divinity of Christ and consolidate the eschatological perspectives of the mystagogues, fell victim to the gnostic cyclic vision of salvation history. This had a threefold consequence. For Arius, the divinity of the Supreme Being dissolves into history. For Apollinaris, history no longer centers on God. For Nestorius, the original Christ and the Christ of history cease to coincide. Orthodoxy rapidly refuted the errors of the first gnostics. Irenaeus of Lyons recovered the initial vision of the circulation of glory between God and humanity. His work is enlivened with the famous formulas: "The glory of God is a living man, and the life of man consists in beholding God" and "The glory of humanity is to remain and persevere in the power of God."[22] For the heir of John, Christ as Logos has this glory before the creation of the world. Glory is the self-revelation of the Father in the Son and reciprocally. Jesus Christ asks for this glory as God incarnate who desires that mankind receive a participation in the glory which

19 A. Laurentin, op. cit., 213.
20 *Pistis Sophia,* in Laurentin, op. cit., 43.
21 Laurentin, op. cit., 217.
22 Irenaeus of Lyons, *Contre les Hérésies*, IV, 17, 1.

is the path to salvation. At the time of Irenaeus, the victory of orthodoxy consisted in making praise as exchange of gifts prevail over the praise of disincarnation advocated by the pseudognostics. Certainly, while the mystagogue is principally interested in the liturgical act and the glorification it generates, the theologian starts from the original, uncreated glory. But the thought of Irenaeus still associated glory with the Holy Spirit and power with the Son, the two hands that reveal the Kingdom of the Father. There was still a possibility of dialogue between orthodox and heterodox gnostics. Irenaeus did not reject the sapiential approach but only its misuse.

## A BIBLIOGRAPHICAL OVERVIEW

It is necessary to return to the contemporary historiography of the orthodoxy of the first three centuries of Christianity in order to understand the plurivocity of the notion of orthodoxy. Up until now, this historiography tends to favor the thesis that Christian orthodox thought is defined solely in opposition to heresy understood as false knowledge. It goes so far as to affirm that the very notion of orthodoxy should be abandoned in order to understand the course of Christianity over the first three centuries.[23] Orthodox thought is, however, as already mentioned, more complex than the notion of dominant religion. It encompasses the whole human being in his relationship to God and the world. It responds to the desire to confide and give oneself over to the Creator. It engages its *eros* to transfigure it into loving *gnosis*. It forms people by placing them individually and collectively in space and time.

At a tormented moment in the history of German Protestantism, when a great number of Lutheran theologians were turning towards the Nazi Party, and shortly after the death of the famous Adolf von Harnack (1851–1930) whose anti-Judaism, inspired by Marcion, was well known, the German historian and Protestant theologian Walter Bauer (1877–1960) published in Tübingen, in 1934, a landmark work in the history of early Christianity entitled *Rechtgläubigkeit und Ketzerei im ältesten Christentum* (Mohr/Siebeck, republished in 1964). This book was translated into English in 1971 and appeared under the title of *Orthodoxy and Heresy in Earliest Christianity*; it was subsequently published in French by Cerf in 2009, with the title *Orthodoxie et hérésie aux débuts de christianisme*. Contrary to the testimony

23 Alain le Boulluec, *La Notion d'hérésie dans la littérature greque (IIe–IIIe s.)*, vol. 2, Paris, 1985.

of Tertullian (150–220), who affirms in his *De praescriptione hereticorum* that orthodoxy came first and heresy later, Bauer's main thesis is that, in certain regions, notably Edessa and Egypt, heresy preceded orthodoxy. Bauer in particular showed that at Edessa, in the 2nd century, the Marcionites called themselves Christians, while the orthodox still chose to be called Palutians. This thesis arrived at the conclusion that there were no defined and legitimate doctrinal foundations for Christian orthodoxy, that it evolved according to the contacts it had with pagan cultures and that it was in adapting to its environment that it was renewed. What was called "orthodoxy" in the centuries that followed the conversion of Constantine was, for Bauer, just one form among others, the "ecclesiastical form" that had coexisted with other forms in the Christian life during the first three centuries. This thesis had the virtue of underlining the universality of Christianity at a time when the majority of German Protestants were attracted by Nazism and where the historical science of the Church had become totally secularized for at least four decades by scholars such as Harnack. At the same time as the French thinker Father Sergius Bulgakov (cf. *The Lamb of God*) developed a new understanding of the intellectual dynamics of the first three centuries of Christianity, Bauer was insisting that *hairesis* simply signified a partial opinion and that this could not in itself be put down to a wiping out of humanity's memory. His book does not settle for reevaluating heresies; it questions the historicity of orthodoxy.

The principal error in Bauer's methodology, as is evident right from his introduction, was to limit orthodoxy, in a strictly sociological sense, to "correct belief" and then to proceed to show that this definition could not correspond to primitive Christianity, which could not be represented socially according to these categories of "true" and "false," "good" and "evil."[24] In his article "The Reception of the Book," George Strecker presented all the errors noted by Bauer's commentators.[25] As early as 1934, James Moffatt of the Union Theological Seminary in New York explained that orthodoxy could not be defined sociologically in terms of true/false and that it was more judicious to use a "sense of the middle way" or balance to understand the orthodox position. More importantly, most of the commentators insisted that it was impossible to neglect the theological dimension of

24 W. Bauer, *Orthodoxy and Heresy in Earliest Christianity*, Philadelphia, Fortress Press, 1971, xxiii.

25 Ibid., 286–316.

Church history. Even if the concept of orthodoxy had not yet been solidified in the second century, one cannot deny the existence of a *regula fidei*, or a "Christian gnosis" according to Clement of Alexandria, shared by all communities that recognize each other as Christian. The French Jesuit C. Martin demonstrated in 1935 in the *Nouvelle revue théologique* of Louvain that, from the beginning, Christians favored the orthodoxy of ecclesial life over its quantitative development. As is evident from the letters of Peter, Paul and John against the false gnostics and magicians of their time, there is a scriptural apostolic movement that promotes *epignosis*.

The most complete critique of Bauer's work came from England in 1954 with the Brampton lectures presented by H. Turner of the University of Durham and subsequently published in book form.[26] Without denying the presence of heretics in Edessa, Canon Turner shows that Marcion cannot be considered as the founder of the Christian Church in that city. Similarly, he maintains that to rely on an absence of sources to consider Kûnéas the first bishop of the city in the 4th century is very fragile methodology. Turner is even more critical when it comes to Egypt. The anachronistic focus of Bauer prevents him from understanding why Origen could have been considered orthodox at one time and disavowed at another. Turner goes on to point out that the letters of Ignatius of Antioch, denouncing the presence of heretics at the very heart of the Church, indicate that orthodoxy, at that time, had already arrived at a self-awareness and, consequently, a sense of its limitations. Moreover, the work of Irenaeus, *Against Heresies,* shows that, in the 2nd century, one could not claim that there was no clear-cut distinction between orthodoxy and heresy within Christianity. In sum, in Turner's opinion, Bauer does not grasp the rich complexity of orthodoxy and this leads him to place, on one and the same level, things that are not comparable. Orthodoxy according to the British historian "resembles not so much a stream as a sea, not a single melodic theme but a rich and varied harmony, not a single closed system but a rich manifold of thought and life."[27] He suggests that if Bauer could see orthodoxy from this perspective, he would understand better how it was able to reject radical partial opinions in the same way as a body rejects a virus. Thus we find a certain autonomy of orthodoxy as regards heresy, even if partial opinions were integrated according to certain rules: as long as they

26 H. Turner, *The Pattern of Christian Truth: A Study in the Relations Between Orthodoxy and Heresy in the Early Church,* London, Mowbray, 1954.

27 Ibid., 80.

did not deny the apostolic tradition, as long as they were incorporated into the prayer of the Church and as long as they did not repudiate the ecclesial community. The Third Letter of John to Gaius shows that the organization of those who walk "in the life of truth" (3 Jn 3) is not only founded on questions of worship, justice or knowledge, but also on faithful recognition, since in this case, Diotrephes is not accused of false *gnosis* but of an appetite for power. Ultimately, for the Anglican canon, it is not external influences but rather an internal communal sense, "which is another name for the guidance of the Holy Spirit," which dominates the history of the development of early Christianity.

Turner succeeds in formulating a definitive conclusion for our thesis. He contradicts the idea that the concepts of heresy and orthodoxy are only effective to account for early Christianity.[28] In his opinion, it is the *lex orandi* which formed "the instinctive basis for that exercise of Christian common sense which enabled the Church to reject interpretations of her faith and dilutions of her life even before she possessed formal standards of belief."[29] In other words, it is because Christians lived trinitarily and shared in the worthy glorification that they were able to subsequently formulate Nicaean orthodoxy in dogmatic expressions. This thesis, which gives the *lex orandi* priority over the *lex credendi*, has been accepted by many scholars including those of the Orthodox world (in the confessional meaning of the term) such as G. Florovsky and A. Schmemann.[30] This adage, which affirms that the law of prayer determines the law of belief, is thought to have been formulated by the monk Prosper of Aquitaine (c. 390–c. 466), the secretary of Pope Leo the Great, disciple of Augustine, and by Pope St. Celestine I in the 5th century, but it goes back to the very origins of Christianity.[31] St. Paul

28 Alain le Boulluec, "Hétérodoxie et orthodoxie," *Histoire du christianisme*, op. cit., vol. 1. The author, a professor at the EPHE, proposes that these concepts be "abandoned" because, on the one hand, he believes that the notion of heresy came later and, prior to 150 AD only referred to dissensions and, on the other hand, the term "orthodoxy" did not take on the meaning of "specific regulation" until the 4th century. Although we think that "abandoning" these concepts is not justified, we share the author's opinion that in the 2nd century, as evidenced, for example, by the conflict over the date of Easter, there was an effort to avoid confusing ecclesiastical norms in opposition to one another with divisive pronouncements without, however, falling into a confused relativism.

29 Ibid., 28. This translation of Turner's words can be found in Nicholas Sagovsky, *Ecumenism, Christian Origins and the Practice of Communion,* Cambridge: Cambridge University Press, 2000, 141.

30 Alexander Schmemann, *Liturgy and Tradition,* Crestwood, NY, SVSP, 1990.

31 Cf. Paul de Clerck, "Lex orandi, lex credendi. The Original Sense and Historical Avatars of an Equivocal Adage," *Studia Liturgica*, 24 (1994): 178–200. This article especially

summed up this doxological attitude of primitive orthodoxy in his letter to the Corinthians: "What I have received from the Lord and transmitted to you: the Lord Jesus, on the night in which he was betrayed, took bread, and, after giving thanks, he broke it and said: 'This is my body which is given for you, do this in memory of me.' He did the same for the cup after the meal saying: 'This is the cup of my blood of the new Covenant; do this each time you drink of it in memory of me. For when you eat this bread and drink this cup, you proclaim the death of the Lord until he comes'" (1 Cor 11:23–26).

Orthodoxy cannot be reduced to its sociological expression. In order to understand the formation of the paradigmatic constitution of orthodoxy as worthy glorification, a closer study of the ecclesial memory of primitive Christianity is necessary. It is the structure and evolution of this memory that will enable us as a second step to understand the internal functioning of the paradigm of worthy glorification. As a third step we will see how this paradigm is expressed ad extra, ecclesially and politically.

## MESSIANIC HISTORIOGRAPHY

As we have seen in the introduction, the moment that triggers the intellectual "awareness," which produces a narrative, represents for the contemporary historian the principal tangible trace of the historical emergence of a new level of consciousness of orthodoxy. The established prevalence of the act of prayer over conceptualization in the early Christian consciousness brought about a new type of historical discourse. For the first Christian historians, the act of relating history and the act of participating in it became inseparable. In the first century AD, the apostles and evangelists were the first historians of Christian consciousness. Their vision of history will continue to be dominant in orthodox thought until the 4th century. Their common point was the consideration that, with the resurrection of Jesus Christ, the temporality of the world should leave room for a new form of spiritual temporality. For this unconceptualizable event was, however, understandable through reason,

---

highlights the work of Prosper of Aquitaine (who formulated the expression "*ut legem credendi lex statuat supplicandi*" to affirm that the law of prayer establishes the law of faith). Cf. Kevin Irwin, *Context and Text: Method in Liturgical Theology*, Collegeville, MN, Liturgical Press, 1994. This adage signifies, in particular, that the faith of the Church is prior to the faith of the believer—a theme echoed by the Catechism of the Catholic Church. This adage is also important in the Anglican Church, which founds its organization and theology on *The Book of Common Prayer*, published in 1662.

inasmuch as it had been announced long ago. It could be transmitted or told, but differently. Writing to the Corinthians, St. Paul sums up the good news of salvation: "I hand over to you, first of all, what I myself have received; Christ died for our sins, *according to the Scriptures*. He was buried, rose on the third day, *according to the Scriptures*. He appeared to Cephas and then to the Twelve" (1 Cor. 15:3–5). To consider that the promise of God's anointing announced to the Jewish people by the Scriptures had been kept amounted to affirming the fulfillment of the times. If humanity is not in effect "abandoned to hell" as promised by the Scriptures (Ps 16), then the coming of a new space-time is imminent, that of "the Kingdom of God on earth." This introduces a new way of writing history, neither cyclic nor linear, but vertical one could argue. The narrative already knows its theocentric outcome and must reclassify all the facts of this event. Henceforth, the whole history of the world is interpreted through the coming of the Messiah, the Anointed of God, promised by God in the Scriptures and who brings a way of salvation to all mankind and not just for the Jewish people. The first of the apostles was the first to be aware of this when, not far from a city symbolically named after Caesar, he declared the Christ, the Son of God (Mk 8:27–29).[32] Later, in his address to the Jerusalem community at Pentecost or during the healing of the cripple at the temple gate, Peter also insisted on the fulfillment of the Scriptures in Christ (Acts 2:16, 3:24). Unlike the Hegelians, who thought that the fulfillment of history consisted in the triumph of the State, Peter saw it as the end of Caesarism, brought about through the joyous transparency between the cultures and languages of the community assembled around the Virgin and accompanied by signs such as that of the man born lame.[33]

The Evangelist Luke can be considered the first historian of this new type of narrative that reconciles "history as a chronicle" with "history as action." Luke was of Greek origin, a physician from Antioch, born and brought up in paganism, who entered into "the way" through Paul whom he accompanied on his missionary journeys. As evidenced in the book of *Acts* from chapter six onwards, Luke was an eyewitness to the events of his narrative. It was from the apostles themselves that he learned of the words spoken by Christ at the moment of his Ascension.[34] His account of the Last

32 As regards the political context of this profession of faith, Luke also points out that the recognition of Peter took place shortly after Herod expressed his desire to "see" Jesus and when the tetrarch made intimidating statements such as: "John, I beheaded" (Lk 9:9).

33 C. H. Dodd, *According to the Scriptures*, Welwyn, James Nisbet, 1952.

34 Luke sojourned in Jerusalem somewhere around 57–59.

Supper shows that he had grasped not only the nature of the new temporality but also how it manifested itself. As Bishop Cassian Bezobrazoff, the former dean of the St. Sergius Institute in Paris put it: "It is in place of the Jewish Passover that Jesus institutes the Eucharist which is His presence in His body and blood, in the midst of His disciples. The context of Luke's narrative makes such an interpretation inevitable; the words on the Passover introduce the narration of the Eucharistic institution"[35] (Lk 22:14–20). The Jewish Passover, which commemorated the crossing of the Red Sea, was celebrated on the 14th day of the month of Nisan, at the time of the first full moon of the Spring solstice, when the earth is bathed in light both day and night. In his narrative, Luke seeks to make clear that, in reality it is Christ who illuminates the whole world. It is impossible not to see this as extending to all of history. As C. Mimouni has pointed out, in Luke's Gospel all Scripture should be read from the perspective of the messianic times, inaugurated by Jesus but in continuity with the chain of prophetic tradition.[36] Luke concludes his Gospel with the episode of the pilgrims of Emmaus (Lk 24:13–35), the appearance to the eleven apostles (Lk 24:36–49) and the Ascension (Lk 24:50–53). He testifies that the apostles learned from the Risen Christ himself to understand Scripture as a prophecy concerning him. Christ said to them: "everything written about me must be fulfilled"; for the "witnesses" this signified that henceforth their mission was to preach, in the name of Jesus, "repentance and forgiveness of sins to all the nations."

Early Christian historiography is based on an attitude of humility on the part of the historian. In Luke's second account of the Ascension in *Acts*, that is, when the definitive metamorphosis of the corporality of Christ takes place, the apostles were still fascinated by the chronotopic changes they had been experiencing since the Resurrection. They ask Jesus if the time had come when he would restore the Kingdom to Israel, but Christ answered: "The exact time it is not yours to know. The Father has reserved that to Himself. . . . " It is not, therefore, the task of the orthodox historian to predict the future nor to want to tell everything about the past of a civilization, but rather to witness to the works of Christ and the Spirit within the community of the baptized. Thus it is that Luke focuses the plan of

35 Bishop Cassian Bezobrasoff, "La prière dans le Nouveau Testament," in Bishop Cassian Bezobrasoff, Dom Bernard Botte, *La prière des Heures,* Paris, Cerf, 1963, 37.

36 Simon C. Mimouni, "Les representations historiographiques du christianisme au 1er siecle," in *L'Historiographie de l'Eglise des premiers siècles*, directed by B. Pouderon and Y. M. Duval, Paris, Beauchesne, 2001, 81.

his second book on the mission Jesus gave to the apostles at the moment of his Ascension (the continuation of the verse cited above): "But you shall receive the power when the Holy Spirit has come upon you; and you shall be my witnesses in Jerusalem and in all Samaria and to the end of the earth" (Acts 1:6–9). In fact, the first part of the book of *Acts* is devoted to Pentecost and its consequences (1–2), then to the testimony of the apostles in Jerusalem (3–12) and finally to the missions of Peter and Paul (13–28).

Before writing *Acts*, Luke devoted himself to writing a narrative of the life of Christ with many details that no other evangelist had yet reported. He knows that the decisive moments in the life of Jesus were marked by his prayer: his baptism (Lk 3:21), the choosing of the twelve apostles (6:12), the confession of Peter (9:18), the Transfiguration (9:28–29), etc. It is as if Luke, by his spiritual insight, saw what Matthew and Mark had not discerned, the angel who strengthened Christ on the Mount of Olives (Lk 22:43), the prayer of Jesus for his tormentors (Lk 23:34). Luke is aware that Jesus constantly recited the Psalms (22, 31 and 68 during his Passion) which substantiated the messianic consciousness that he had of himself. Marveling, Luke discovers that the events of the Passion accomplish the temporality of the Scriptures. When the soldiers divide the vestments of Christ, the narrator disappears. In wonder, he can only cite Psalm 22:18: "They divided my garments among them and for my raiment they cast lots." However, Luke's christocentrism and openness to the Spirit does not mean an irrational blindness.

Mark doesn't abuse the method of citing Scripture, he tried to discern, in the Spirit, between historical events and metahistorical events. His youth and the fact that he did not know Christ personally probably were a factor. According to Bishop Cassian (Bezobrazoff), Luke wrote his Gospel after the destruction of the temple in Jerusalem in the year 70.[37] Thus he knew that the old covenant had come to an end, but this was not the end of the world, for a new covenant had been offered to humanity by God in Christ. Unlike the first two Evangelists and the author of the Epistle to the Hebrews, Mark distinguishes between the destruction of the Temple and the end of time (of the *aeons*). He describes the destruction of Jerusalem by linking it with Deuteronomy 12:3 ("You shall tear down their altars, and dash in pieces their pillars"). Mark continues: "For in those days there will be such tribulation as has not been from the beginning of the creation which God created until now,

37 Bishop Cassian Bezobrasoff, "La prière dans le Nouveau Testament" in Bishop Cassian Bezobrasoff, dom Bernard Botte, *La prière des Heures,* Paris, Cerf, 1963, 35.

and never will be" (Mk 13:19). Luke writes more soberly: "These indeed will be days of retribution, when all that is written must be fulfilled" (Lk 21:22).

Luke, who is familiar with Greek historiography, notably Plutarch's *Parallel Lives,* structures his work in two parallel parts. The first is consecrated to Christ (in which one finds a parallelism between the infancy of John the Baptist and the infancy of Christ) while the second is dedicated to the Church led by the Spirit (where there is a parallelism between the preaching of Peter in Jerusalem and that of Paul at the synagogue of Antioch). This Messianic historiography departs from Hellenistic historiography in that Luke does not insert his personal commentaries. As Michel Quesnel has written: "The narrative alone shows that Paul is continuing the work of Jesus."[38] St. Luke does not idealize the past; he records painful moments such as the deaths of Ananias and Sapphira, the stoning of Stephan, the "lively discussions" between the apostles and the elders (Acts 15), the setbacks of Paul at Athens, and the dangerous foundation of the first Christian community in Samaria led by Simon the Magician (Acts 8). Nothing should be hidden from the light of truth. Luke provides the model for the historical eschatological narrative without any experience or horizon of expectation other than that of Christ.

This implies challenges. The narrative of Luke is not so much vague as enlightened. The French historian H. Leclercq has drawn attention to Luke's rigorous documentation. Luke knew in depth the geography of Asia Minor. Leclercq, on the basis of multiple sources, writes: "It is impossible to find fault with him concerning many other details: Paul preached in the synagogue of Corinth every Sabbath (Acts 18:4). The lintel of the gate of a Jewish synagogue in this city has been unearthed: it bears the inscription 'Synagogue of the Hebrews.' As regards Paul's stay at Corinth, we learn that there was a major altercation in the Jewish colony of this city when Gallio was proconsul of Achaia (Acts 18:12). The inscription . . . on the lintel refers to L. Junius Annaeus Gallio as proconsul of Achaia. . . . Luke's historical integrity has emerged victorious after his work survived all the traps set by archeology and philology."[39]

In the second century, Origen, Justin and the apologists Tatian and Athenagoras continue the discourse of the apostles and evangelists. These testimonies dominated Christian consciousness until the time of Eusebius of Caesarea. In his polemic with Celsus, Origen insists on the fact that the

38 Michel Quesnel, "Luc, historien de Jésus et de Paul" in *L'Historiographie*, op. cit., 57.
39 H. Leclercq, "Historiens du Christianisme," *Dictionnaire*, 2541–2543.

Hebrew prophecies were fulfilled in Jesus Christ.[40] This argument developed in the direction of the success of Christianity that spread with the apologists around the year 230.[41] Prior to this, Justin Martyr (103–165) had insisted in his polemic against the Jews and against Marcion, on the messianic identity of Christ and the Scriptural roots of the Gospel. He does this by indicating the correspondence between the words (*logoi*), in other words, the Scriptures (*grafai*) and the historical facts (*pragmata*) which the evangelists recorded in their Gospels.[42] Messianic historiography leads to worthy glorification, for the doxologies and liturgies are typical ways of expressing the *pragmata*. Faced with a phenomenon saturated with glory, conceptuality is praise, a participatory membership. It can be noted that for Justin, the memory of Christian origins was indissolubly linked to its worship practices. Emmanuel Luhumbu Shodu, who studied Justin's work, writes: "Justin Martyr sees baptism and the Eucharist already announced in the Jewish prophecies, associates them with the life and works of Jesus and demonstrates their continuity within the Christian community."[43] Paradoxically, Christianity, aware of its limits, understanding the distance that separated it from the Lord of glory, and knowing itself to be imperfect and in constant need of reform, became conscious that it had become a new force in history. In the face of persecutions and misunderstandings, Christian discourse needed to be defended. Justin Martyr was one of the first to define Christian religion. He understands it as "the school of divine virtue" (2 *Apology* 2.13; cf. also 1 *Apology* 4.7) with Christ as the teacher and the apostles and disciples as pupils.

Irenaeus of Lyons uses the term *aletheia* when he speaks of truth. He cannot imagine such a deviant truth and does not feel the need, despite his struggle with those who use the term *gnosis*, to speak of right truth. For him, there is no half-truth. Truth cannot be separated from the person who embodies it—Jesus Christ. Indeed, one has to fight against those who profess heterodox teachings but these are *doctrinas alienas*, doctrines from "outside" that cannot be justified "neither as regards credibility nor as regards truth."[44] He uses the

40 Origen, *Contre Celse*, Book VII, 2–17, VIII, 45–47.

41 Gilles Dorival, "L'argument de la réussite historique du christianisme" in *L'historiographie de l'Eglise*, op. cit., 55.

42 Emmanuel Luhumbu Shodu, *La mémoire des origines chrétiennes selon Justin Martyr*, Fribourg, 2008.

43 Ibid., 275.

44 Irenaeus of Lyons, *Contre les Hérésies*, Book IV, 32/1, ed. directed by Adelin Rousseau, Paris, Cerf, Sources Chrétiennes, 1965, 797.

expression "*epignosis aletheias*" to designate that surpassing knowledge of the truth which is awarded by the Spirit of God. He is referring here, with apostolic logic, to a verse in St. Paul's Epistle to Timothy ("[God] desires everyone to be saved and to come to the knowledge of the truth," 1 Tm 2:4). This knowledge is not found at the level of epistemic awareness. It is in the reading of the Scriptures "alongside the presbyters of the Church because it is with them that the doctrine of the apostles can be found"[45] that the faithful are assured of finding the truth, that is, of meeting God. Further on, he states that "the distinctive mark of the Body of Christ is the succession of bishops who are entrusted with each of the local Churches."[46] This represents a movement towards the institutionalization of truth, but the bishop's recommendation of faithfulness is ordered by the "true *gnosis*,"[47] that is, apostolicity. His rejection of heresies and his insistence that the God of Moses is the same as the Father revealed by Jesus Christ are therefore still under the sign of the correct apostolic vision which calls for a worthy glorification.[48]

## CHRISTIANITY THE PARADIGM OF RELIGION

One must remember here a determining factor for the history of religious consciousness contributed by Luke. Jesus Christ proclaimed news up until then unprecedented in the history of mankind: a cult without a temple. The God that created the universe and all that dwells in it "does not inhabit temples made by the hands of men." Luke is the only evangelist to give an account of the leper (the only one among the ten to have returned and also the only Samaritan) who thanks Christ for his healing. If, at the beginning of his account, Luke notes that Christ sends the lepers to present themselves at the synagogue, "Go and show yourselves to the priests" (Lk 17:13), and that this leads to a first healing ("they were cleansed"), at the end of his text when Christ regrets that only one turned back "to give praise to

45 Ibid., 799.

46 Ibid., 821.

47 Book IV, 33, 8, op. cit., 819.

48 This leads him to conclude, as did Paul, that it is God Himself who blinds the spirit of the non-believers (2 Cor. 4:4). This is, perhaps, one of the reasons for the spiritual crisis of the second century. The Valentinians, who could not accept that the anti-Christ had been sent by God as Paul affirmed in his Epistle to the Thessalonians (2 Thes 2:11–12), reacted by imagining a God of love above the God of justice—and thus introduced a disassociation within the divinity.

God," the evangelist lets it be known that at that precise moment Jesus realizes something. He no longer hesitates to heal the Samaritan foreigner, whose faith was not limited by the execution of rules but overflowed with thankfulness. Here Bishop Cassian notes that Jesus is opposed to the religious institutions: "the Temple is no longer, Jesus is there in place of the Temple." This news was subsequently proclaimed in Jerusalem by Stephen. His speech was of such strength that it was punctuated by the vision of the glory of God (Acts 7:48–50). The words of the one who is revered by Christians as their first martyr, that is as the first witness of the glory, were of such seditious force that they ended in his stoning. This form of religion was so incredible that when Paul made his speech to the Athenians it was met with sarcasm (Acts 17:24–25). This of course had immediate political consequences. The *Letter of Diognetus*, written around 190–200, witnesses to the radical difference between the Christian knowledge-existence and the life of the profane world, a difference which, nonetheless, allows Christians to not distinguish themselves externally from the other citizens of the Empire, while manifesting the extraordinary laws of this new "spiritual republic."

One can better measure what is meant by the expression "to travel along the Way" by what Jean Borella has to say: "Humanity ignored the general concept of religion before the advent of Christianity." In fact, no term existed in any language of early peoples, nor even among the Greeks or Latins, which corresponded to the contemporary concept of religion. The term *religio*, as universal reality distinct from all other social and cultural forms, was defined historically in the early period of Christianity as demonstrated by the work of Tertullian, Lactantius and St. Augustine. Prior to Christianity, none of the religions had any name with which to refer to themselves. Instead the word "Christian," which appears in the work of Luke (Acts 11:4), and the noun "Christianity" as opposed to "Judaism," which appears in Ignatius of Antioch (Letter to the Romans 3:3), seem to be in common usage by the end of the first century. Orthodox Christian historiography therefore brings a decisive reversal. By turning, eschatologically, the *doxa*'s sense of illusion to the notion of worthy glorification, Christian historians invented the notion of religion. Worthy glorification is where nothing can circumscribe a glory higher than man can imagine and that nevertheless gives and participates. Let us listen to what Jean Borella has to say:

> Accordingly, there is in the (relative) anonymity of the pre-Christian religions both a memory of the indistinctiveness of the Divine

> principle from which they arise, but also a certain "illusion" concerning their real nature, an innate incompleteness which prevents them from recognizing their own limits, making them live in a sort of infinitude preventing them from clearly perceiving anything beyond. To accede to self-awareness, and thereby to the consciousness of religion as such, thinkers needed to, with the message of Christ, experience something that exceeded all they could have known in the sacred order, that is not only sacred Greek, Roman or Jewish, but also Indian, Egyptian or Celtic. In order for the other religious forms to be constituted in the same formality, ceasing to be spontaneous modes of living, blind to themselves, like Monsieur Jourdain who spoke in prose without knowing it, it was required that they be defined by what classified them in their own order, in other words by what transcended them. Transcendence which at the same time resembles these forms and eludes them: a vertical relation which only proves the (relative) horizontality of everything else. Thus Christianity by its own emergence is the revealer of all the religions precisely as religions.[49]

However, one should balance the historiography of Luke with that of John. John like Luke teaches a cult without a Temple, both in his Gospel (the story of the Samaritan, Jn 4:23–24) and in his Book of Revelation (Rev 21–22). But this worship is always turned first to the Father, then to Christ. Bishop Cassian considers that the Gospel of John and his Book of Revelation are "a theocentric reaction against the extreme Christocentrism of St. Luke."[50] In the great vision of the heavenly liturgy the sense of eternity is the adoration of the Trinity and not of Christ alone. History for St. John is not only symbolic and eschatological, it also becomes liturgical. Men become aware that they participate in a vast movement of exchange of glory between the earth and the heavens. The worship of the Name is what gives meaning to the life of the local Churches as in the letters written to the angel of the Church in Sardis (Rev 3). It is a gnosis where the dimension of one's own moral work, applied at an individual and collective level, is paramount. John knows that despite being cast out from "heaven" (an expression that

49 Jean Borella, "Problématique de l'unité des religions," in Bruno Bérard, *Introduction à une métaphysique des mystères chrétiens,* Paris, L'Harmattan, 2005, 267–68.

50 Bishop Cassian, op. cit., 40.

refers to the chronotope of theanthropy in the Gospels), Satan has not had his last word. Fallen temporality, although already overcome by the resurrection of Christ, still seeks to harm humanity at some level in the course of history. From then on, the whole of the Gospel of John can be understood by this logic of the liturgy as a theanthropic battle. The famous priestly prayer of Christ is this worship of Christ offered to the Father in spirit and truth. John knows that the former glory of the world of which Christ speaks is a shared possession of all three Persons of the Trinity. It is a movement of glory and not a divine fire falling like lighting without any possible reaction. He also understands that the glory received by Christ in time is a good that Christ and humanity are called upon to share. Men are called to share this glory, and to unite in the same process. For Bishop Cassian, the theocentric and doxological logic of early orthodox thought is at the source of the Creed, the Trisagion and the Eucharistic prayers.

## THE ANTINOMIC COMPLEMENTARITIES OF THE FIRST HISTORICAL NARRATIVES

For Irenaeus of Lyons, it is the overall vision of the fourfold revelation of God—his glory, his law, the fragility of humanity and the heavenly spirit—that justifies the canon of Scriptures, composed of the four Gospels of Matthew, Mark, Luke and John. This vision reveals a new conception of history made of different temporalities. The verticality of the work of the Father through his two hands, Word and Wisdom, directs history towards great characters such as Moses and Jesus Christ. This Trinitarian act shatters the identifying boundaries since each person who loves God "according to his time" is worthy of salvation. Irenaeus writes:

> There is only one and the same God the Father and His Word, present to humanity throughout all the ages although through diverse "economies" and multiform operations, saving, from the beginning, all those who are to be saved, i.e., those who love God and who, in the context of their time, follow His Word, and condemning those who are forgetful of God and who blaspheme and offend His Word.[51]

51 Irenaeus of Lyons, *Contre les hérésies*, Book iv, 28/2, ed. directed by Adelin Rousseau, Paris, Cerf, Sources Chrétiennes, 1965, 759.

According to this vision, Irenaeus esteems that the historian should be a "spiritual" person, someone who has received the Spirit of God "who, from the beginning, was present in all 'economies' of God, foretelling the future, revealing the present and narrating the past."[52] Such a gift enables the historian to judge the heretics, "all those who are outside of the truth, that is who are outside of the Church."[53]

Although it might appear astonishing to our current mentality, the consciousness of the early Church did not see any major contradiction between the historical, apocalyptic and liturgical discourse of John and the narratives of the synoptic Gospels, the Pastoral Letters and the Acts of the Apostles. The canon of Scripture for both the Old and New Testaments, essentially agreed upon near the end of the second century AD,[54] was not fixed according to an intellectual logic but on the basis of a logic glorifying the event of the Incarnation and Resurrection of the Son of God. Jean-Marc Prieur writes: "in the process of the formation of the canon, worship played an important role insofar as it was felt necessary to determine what could be read in the assembly and what could be used as a basis for preaching."[55] Contemporary perception, acknowledging its attempt to retrieve the historical coherence of Scriptures, after centuries of questioning their authenticity, has led several 20th century intellectuals, such as Sergius Bulgakov and Hans Urs von Balthasar, to reconsider the establishing of a scriptural codex according to a logic that is complex, symbolic and antinomic.

52 Ibid., 803.

53 Ibid., 817.

54 It is by no means certain, as Jean-Marc Prieur affirms ("Les Ecritures chrétiennes au IIe siècle," *Histoire générale du christianisme,* op. cit., 89), that the Christian canon was a replica of the canon of Jewish Scriptures established at Jamnia around 90–100. A different scenario could be possible—that since the rabbis refused the revelation of Jesus Christ, they attempted to close their Scriptures because of the propagation of the new Christian Gospels. The canon of Muratori, published in approximately 1740, which enumerates 22 of the 27 canonical books, is doubtlessly a list established at Rome around the year 200. The only books which do not appear are the Letter to the Hebrews, the Epistle of St. James, the two Letters of Peter and the Third Letter of John. On the other hand, the list also includes The Book of Wisdom, the Letter of Jude, the Apocalypse of Peter and the Pastor of Hermas (which could be read, but not in public). "The New Testament canon of the Greek Church is found, for the first time in its definitive form, in the 39th Easter Letter of Athanasius written in 387." Hubertus Drobner, *Les Pères de L'Eglise, Sept siècles de littérature chrétienne*, Paris, Desclée, 1999, 24. This is the listing accepted by Augustine.

55 "Les Ecritures chrétiennes au IIe siècle," *Histoire générale du christianisme*, op. cit., 94.

Father Sergius Bulgakov, in his 1923 book, *Les saints apôtres Pierre et Jean,*[56] demonstrated the interapostolic dynamism in the development of orthodox thought. For him, the Church is not simply pastorally constituted on the basis of Peter's faith. It is also generated by the filial bond between Mary, who ponders everything in her heart, and John the Evangelist. Mary can be symbolically considered as the burning bush of theanthropic history, the metahistorical figure who acts through her openness to the Spirit. In 1970, the theologian Hans Urs von Balthasar, following the path of Bulgakov, also proposed envisaging the Church as "a structure in tension."[57] Later, contemporary theologians (Anton Houtepen) and sociologists (Danièle Hervieu Léger) drew certain conclusions from this doxic system that brings together unity and holiness, catholicity and apostolicity.

For our purposes, we consider the idea of perceiving the personality of each apostle as a symbolic model, and interpreting his acts as a reflection of metahistorical mental structures, a historically valid and hermeneutically justified procedure. Both the first and second covenants speak of a judgment in which the twelve tribes of Israel will participate. By giving bynames to some of his apostles ("Rock" to Simon, "Son of Thunder" to John) Christ expressly indicated the metahistorical mission he had given to these disciples.[58] Judas himself fulfilled or achieved the type of the traitor-friend, a structure foreseen or announced in the Psalm (Ps 41:10, cf. Jn 13:18). This is why the spiritual insight of Irenaeus of Lyons discerned that the four Gospels actualized the prophetic vision of the divino-humanity.

Thus, on the vertical axis that we have traced, the Apostle James can be associated with the pole of remembrance and unity (tradition and law according to Balthasar), while the Apostle John would be found on the pole of worship and holiness (enduring love in Balthasar's vocabulary). On the horizontal axis, the Apostle Peter symbolizes the pole of moral knowledge and catholicity (pastoral responsibility for Balthasar) while the Apostle Paul represents the pole of justice and apostolicity (freedom in the Holy Spirit). At the intersection of these two lines are Mary, figure of created Wisdom, and John the Baptist, cousin and friend of the Spouse (cf. Jn 3:29), the two figures who surround the orant or Wisdom of God in primitive iconography.

56 S. Bulgakov, *Dva pervoapostola,* Minsk, Lutchi Sofii, 1996 (1923).

57 Hans Urs von Balthasar, *Le complexe antiromain, essai sur les structures ecclésiales,* Paris, Montreal, apostolat des éditions, éditions Paulines, 1976.

58 The importance of the bestowal of a new name in the Old Testament is well known (Abram/Abraham, Jacob/Israel, etc.).

The relationships among the apostles are thus symbolic, both structurally and historically significant. The tensions between unity and holiness have been resolved by Christ himself by his exaltation of the authority of service—the only viaticum allowing participation at the last judgment—when He responds to the request of the mother of James and John. The tensions between catholicity and apostolicity have found their historical synthesis in the relationship of trust that had been established between Peter and Paul all the way to their martyrdom in Rome. We can also find instructive aspects in the tensions between Peter and John on the one hand, and Paul and James on the other.

In his book *Les saints apôtres Pierre et Jean*, Bulgakov starts with the Scriptural recurrence of the mission of Peter, James and John with Jesus Christ. Within this central trinity of the apostolic college, the function of unity and proclamation is counterbalanced by that of love and fraternity. After his betrayal, Simon will not become Peter again until he discovers that Christ wants to have a relationship with him that is based on friendship. While on the cross, Christ makes John his brother and through him the whole apostolic college. After a meticulous analysis of the gifts received by each of the apostles as well as their weaknesses, Bulgakov points out the importance of their interaction for the ecclesial body. Here are a few examples: Peter's call to follow Jesus goes through John and Andrew (disciples of John the Baptist); the preparation for the Last Supper is only possible because of the faith of Peter and John, whom Christ sent to prepare the Passover meal (Lk 22:8–13); the gesture of Peter to John at Christ's last meal with his disciples concerning the betrayal of Jesus witnesses to a mode of circulation of authority which is far from unilateral. Bulgakov also reminds us that on the day of the Resurrection John was the first to arrive at the tomb (and immediately believed, an indication of his eschatological intuition) but lets Peter enter first (providing a sign of the necessity of history); on the occasion of the miraculous catch of fish, it is John who recognizes Jesus, and Peter who jumps into the water; during the meeting with the Risen Jesus, Peter is again entrusted with the keys of the Kingdom (this we know since it is confirmed by John's description) but John also calls to mind his own autonomy with respect to Peter; the first miracle in the Church, the healing of the cripple, is only made possible through the combined action of Peter and John; both apostles win their case by jointly defending their freedom of conscience to confess Christ in the presence of the Sanhedrin (Acts 8:14–15); together they decide to lay hands on the Samaritans.

This description illustrates that the primacy of external authority is subordinate to the primacy of freedom, of internal authority. Conversely, the genius of John yields to the positive and incarnate charism of Peter. In fact, for Bulgakov, there is only one primacy, but double and complex. One of its aspects is responsibility, continuous and visible, able to bind and to loose. The other is freedom, discontinuous and invisible, able to send a bolt of lightning when this is necessary. Only the mutual union of priesthood and prophecy is able to reveal the ministry of the kingship of Christ.

In a similar way, von Balthasar has pointed out the decisive role that the unity between James and Paul played for the Church, both historically and on a metahistorical level. Memory can, in fact, easily become identity and withdraw into itself. Justice can quickly lose patience and negate itself by not taking into consideration humanity's spatio-temporal limits. This is why the relationship between the two apostles is a decisive episode in the history of the Church (Acts 21:24). James, the first leader of the Church in Jerusalem, not only recognized Saul as a disciple of Christ in spite of the fact that he had persecuted the followers of the Way, but also accepted Paul's openness towards the Hellenists. He does not try to verify whether Paul really had asked the pagans not to circumcise their children. He requests that the Jewish community of Jerusalem, which practiced circumcision, be recognized as orthodox in this practice by Paul. Paul, on the other hand, according to Luke's narrative, does not try to convince James of the merits of his attitude but rather accepts, without discussion ("the next day..."), the social-historical legitimacy of the argument of James and conforms to the rites of the Judeo-Christian community of Jerusalem. While this didn't prevent him from being seized by the Jews and handed over to the pagans, the principles of social-historical reconciliation were laid forever.

The orthodox Christian thought of the early Church, which was both complex and interactive, was formed around its pole of worthy glorification. It progressively became doxological and mystagogical. We have seen that the other three poles of thought—right truth (morality), faithful memory, and fair knowledge—contributed through a sort of internal chemistry to the building of this paradigm. It may be added that they were also influenced by the attraction of this cultic pole but for external reasons this time: the persecutions suffered by Christians at the hands of the Roman authorities very quickly pushed them to reject political power as something unjust; the traditionalist trend of their original cultural milieu suffered from the rapid loss of important figures such as the Apostle James and from the dispersion of most of the apostles; lastly, the first synthesis with Hellenistic culture produced, by the very shock of the encounter, a *gnosis* which soon became a *gnosticism*, a mask which both reflected and betrayed the original *epignosis*.

CHAPTER 8

# *"Right Truth" from Eusebius of Caesarea to Sylvester Syropoulos*

RIGHT, BASED ON A UNIVERSAL LAW, IS ONE OF THE components of orthodox consciousness. It is the sign and revelation of the framework of a culture. By definition, it is the visible sign of the state of verticality of a society and its discursive regimes. This understanding can evolve in the course of time according to the mechanisms of recognition or non-recognition among cultures. During the same period and within the same culture, there can be different representations of the truth according to the social milieus and, above all, according to mentalities or spiritual psychologies but without compromising the dominant representation which defines the paradigm. The paradigm here is the dominant representation of truth-forming orthodoxy according to which people and societies live at a given time and place. In the Patristic tradition, dogma defines the boundary of the truth within which people can maintain an existential relationship with their Creator. According to Tocqueville, "dogmatic beliefs" (i.e., doxical beliefs) are self-evident truths that people take on trust and without discussion. This is what Pierre Legendre, using Tocqueville's questionable terminology, calls the "dogmatic base" of a society, the "place of legal truth, postulated and socially staged as such."[1] Alain Supiot writes: "The dogmatic, the key concept of the history of science (notably medicine) is now considered, in popular parlance, as antithetical to reason. And yet, today as in the past, human reason bases itself on dogmatic foundations."[2] Right, the locus par excellence of the common representation of justice,

1 Pierre Legendre, *Sur la question dogmatique en Occident,* Fayard, 1999, 78.

2 Alain Supiot, *Homo juridicus, Essai sur la fonction anthropologique du Droit,* Paris, Seuil, 2005, 21.

is itself founded on such beliefs and constitutes, according to Louis Gernet, a "secularization of the Word." For Alain Supiot, one of the beliefs in Western civilization is that man has been created in the image of God. This is why all people are necessarily equal. The law professor asserts that Christian culture is the only one to have fully conferred upon individuals the quality of subject which in the Muslim tradition belongs only to God, and in the Jewish tradition, on earth, belongs only to the people of Israel. Supiot concludes: "With the Right, man becomes the architect of his own laws, whether it is a matter of common law, founded in a democratic regime on a sovereign people or contractual law, founded in a liberal regime on the sovereignty of the individual."[3] The medieval period, inaugurated by the Edict of Milan in 313, was an experiment in nomocanonical thought which sought to establish a link of continuity between the Kingdom of God and earthly kingdoms.

## ORTHODOXY AS RIGHT TRUTH

In his *Introduction to the History of the Church* (*Introduction à l'histoire de l'Eglise*), Vassili Bolotov bluntly declares that "one must be born blind not to see that the time of Constantine opens a new period in the history of Christianity."[4] The conversion of the Emperor Constantine to the Cross of Christ in 312, followed by the Edict of Milan in 313 proclaiming the right "for Christians and for each person to embrace the religion of their choice," shook the political theology of the Roman Empire. Constantine's concept of freedom of choice was not, however, that of the Christians. A new period of ecclesial awareness would emerge from this painful ambiguity. From the time of the schism of the Donatists in Africa, Constantine involved the Roman State in the resolution of a case until then considered internal to the ecclesial body. His blunders and persecutions, which made the schismatics seem like the Christian martyrs of old, worsened with the Arian crisis. Following the Council of Nicaea's condemnation of Arianism in 325, Constantine expelled Arius and his supporters, thereby confusing, as writes Alexander Schmemann, "the judgment of the Church and the judgment of Caesar."[5]

3 Ibid., 57.

4 Vassili V. Bolotov, "Vvedenie v Tserkovnoujou Istoriou," *Prilojenie k Khristianskomou Tchteniou*, Spb, 1913–1918, vol. 1, 226.

5 A. Schememann, *Le chemin historique de l'Orthodoxie*, Paris, YMCA Press, 1995, 100.

During this period extending from the Council of Nicaea to the Council of Florence in 1439, two councils with both the personal participation of the emperor and a mutually recognized ecumenical character in common, orthodox thought underwent a transformation. There is a transition from the paradigm of worthy glorification to that of right truth. It was as if *doxa* had gone beyond its degraded signification of "personal opinion" and now aspired to embrace the truth of the world (this is the implication of the "limit" or "frontier" of the dogmatic definition promulgated by the *horoi* of the councils)[6] to become *episteme* or compelling knowledge.

Aside from the new political order, the struggle against Arianism in the East during the 4th century and the debate between Augustine and Pelagius (c. 415–418) in the West played a significant role in the evolution of the meaning of orthodoxy. The political context of the 5th century was dramatic for Roman civilization. The sacking of Rome by the Visigoths took place in 410. For Augustine, this signified the end of a world, that of Roman pagan ideology. To the polytheistic vision of the body, which, according to the Platonists, called for a necessary separation of soul and body, the Catholic bishop opposed the Christian vision of a body called to incorruptibility and resurrection. Augustine strived to use Plato's *Timaeus* to show that the universe is a body that does not die but which needs human consciousness. The demiurge (God in Augustine's vision) creates other divinities (the angels) but refuses to give them immortality; this provokes a reaction from the angels and the Divine Council subsequently grants them immortality. Augustine then attempts to rethink everything, especially the meaning of history, often in a radical way. This is the moment when the Fathers of the Church sought to clarify all points of doctrine still unresolved, especially the place of the Wisdom of God, a mysterious figure which appears in the Book of Proverbs. Was she the Logos (Athanasius)? Or the Spirit

6 The Greek word *horos* initially designated a stone boundary marker. Later on, this word was used to qualify the decisions of the councils. Cf. G. Papathomas "Praxis et theorie au sein de la theologie ecclesiale," *Nouvelles de Saint-Serge*, n. 20 (1996): 22–24: "The Church preserves and protects the event of Revelation and the perspective of the divine economy. But the life of the Church consists in what it lives, in its ecclesial experience, manifested in practice and only subsequently expressed in 'theory.' It follows that faith is an event before becoming a teaching, even before taking the form of a notion. It is a process and an encounter. The formulas of faith (e.g., the *horoi*) are brief maxims whose content theological systems fail to express. Faith implies a conversion, a turnaround; it cannot, consequently, be reduced to any rational normalization." http://www.orthodoxa.org/FR/orthodoxie/theologie/praxisFR.htm.

(Irenaeus)? For Augustine it was Jesus Christ. Augustine's polemics were not only with Aristotle and Porphyry. When he was writing the 12th book of *The City of God* he was also doing battle with Pelagius who believed that humanity, created in the image of God, possesses grace. Consequently, from his perspective, the fault of Adam was not a *fatum*; the grace of God is bestowed upon mankind, because of personal merit and not through the sacraments; he opposes the baptism of infants because grace is the fruit of the individual will. Augustine reacted vigorously by affirming that in a first instance humanity's nature, as St. Paul writes, is corrupted by original sin and needs the grace of God for its salvation. However, driven by polemic, he arrives at the new idea according to which God grants "predestined" grace arbitrarily. Pope Innocent supported Augustine and excommunicated Pelagius in 417. Subsequently, Augustine formulated the theory that uncontrolled physical desire (outside of marriage), *concupiscentia*, is the source and the propagator of original sin. In a letter addressed to Sixtus, a Roman priest in 418, he gives the impression that only the grace of God, unearned and unmerited, predetermines the destiny of an individual, even without any personal participation. Augustine died in 430 during the siege of Hippo by the Vandals.

During the first four centuries of Christianity, truth as the progressive exchange of gifts in Christ was experienced as the correct understanding of the Gospel teachings. Its redefinition as an intellectual and institutional boundary (*horos*) allowing a free encounter between God and humanity had in turn consequences for the very representation of relations between Church and State. The Church, which only considered itself as Catholic during its confessional period, now discovers that it is "ecumenical." This evolution began with the First Council of Nicaea in 325, presided over by the Emperor Constantine, and consolidated itself with the attribution of the title "ecumenical" to the Patriarch of Constantinople by the Council of Chalcedon in 451. In the East, with the Byzantine "symphony," then in the West with the doctrine of the "two swords," the emperor and the pope thought of themselves as the exclusive mediators between Christ and the people of God. This politicization of the ecclesial identity was the source of controversy between the seats of the old Rome and new Rome (and later in the 16th and 17th centuries with Moscow which, according to the same political theology, considered itself as the third Rome). The political meaning of the term "ecumenical" as found in the *Novellae* of Justinian was translated into Latin by "universalis." Gregory I, in 595, took this as unwarranted pretense on the part of Constantinople to set itself above the other seats. This was at the root of the first serious controversy between Rome and Constantinople and led to the seat of Rome in turn developing a new conception of its primacy in the Church.[7]

At the Council of Chalcedon, the new symphony between the Empire and the Church is also the source of the formation of a dissident political identity, that of the Syrian Jacobites who set themselves up in opposition to the Melkites (i.e., to the Chalcedonian Christians of the Syrian or Coptic tradition). Their theological divergences, as significant as they might have been due to the gap between their intellectual and religious mentalities, appear, particularly in hindsight, as a sort of undeclared justification of a distinct political identity rather than the principal cause of discord.

In this way there occurred a gradual transformation of orthodox thought from a celebratory consciousness to a body of doctrine aimed at embracing, in a catholic manner, the whole of truth and all people living under the aegis of the emperor (or, later on, the pope). A brief presentation of the formation of canon law in medieval times will confirm our thesis. In the West as in the East, Roman law opened up to Christian truths while seeking to integrate them into its own logic; this concerned primarily ecclesial issues. The major difference with the preceding period (which had experienced internal dissentions among Christians over questions such as the *lapsi* or the date of Easter) was that the meaning of what constituted the "law" was no longer understood in the same way. As John Erickson explained, the application of conciliar juridical decisions had in the Church's early canon law the same pedagogical and medicinal meaning. In the Constantinian age, however, divisions among Christians had a far more important impact than in the period of the first three centuries. They could call into question the unity of the Imperial State, which was not the case when, for example, the conflict over the date of Easter was resolved in the 2nd century. Henceforth the Church had a moral personality recognized by public law.

The Greek theologian Vlassios Phidas briefly presents the sources of canon law in the new Byzantine mentality of the 4th century:[8]

7 George E. Demacopoulos, "Gregory the Great and the Sixth-century Dispute Over the Ecumenical Title," *Theological Studies* 70 (2009): 600–621.

8 Vlassios Phidas, "Droit canon, une perspective orthodoxe," *Analecta Chambesiana* 1, Orthodox Institute of Advanced Studies, Orthodox Center of the Ecumenical Patriarchate Chambesy, Geneva, 1998.

> Holy Scripture (the Old and New Testaments), holy Tradition (patristic, liturgical, sacramental, conciliar and customary) and the holy canons thus constitute the inexhaustible source and diachronic criterion for the historical manifestation of ecclesial consciousness at each place and each time. However, while Holy Scripture and Tradition mainly determine the inexhaustible source, the holy canons present primarily the diachronic criterion for the true function of ecclesial consciousness when adapting the Christian message to the changing spiritual needs of each era. The holy canons of the ecumenical councils, and those of the local councils which have been ratified by an ecumenical council, have acquired force of law, namely, the coercive character (obligatory, imperative) of the principles of law, applicable not only to the constitution and correct function of each local ecclesial entity, but also to the relations among the local Churches throughout the world.[9]

However, it was equally necessary to invent a law that married the ecclesial canonical tradition and the civil legislation established by the *Corpus iuris civilis* (529), the *Digest* (533) and the *Novellae* (535–556) of Justinian (483–565).[10] Justinian considered himself the supreme leader of the Church. For this reason, he shut down the Platonic Academy of Athens in 529, sentenced Theodore of Mopsuestia, Ibas of Edessa and Theodoret of Cyr in the hope of rallying the Churches that rejected the Council of Chalcedon (adopted by the 5th Ecumenical Council of 553) and legalized the control of the bishops over local civil authorities. Byzantine nomocanonical law was a synthesis of Eastern canonical collections grouping ecclesiastical texts of both secular (*nomoi*) and religious origin (*canones*). These mixed collections are based on the fact that, in the Byzantine Church, an important part of ecclesiastical regulation came from secular authority. The term *nomocanon* itself only appears in the 11th century, but collections of this type existed as early as the 6th century, for example, the *Nomocanon with 50 Titles* or the *Nomocanon of John the Scholastic*, named after the Patriarch of Constantinople from 565–578 to whom the collection was, for a long time,

9 V. Phidas, op. cit., 1.

10 Justinian was glorified by the Orthodox Church which considers him as a saint and celebrates his memory on August 2 and November 14 and 15 together with Theodora, his wife.

wrongly attributed. This collection or *Synagogue* includes a grouping of ecclesiastical canons put together by John around 550 while he was still at Antioch and texts extracted from the compilation of Justinian. It dates from the second half of the 6th century and became a fundamental source for all subsequent collections of the East and for the Latin translations in the West, such as the first systematic Latin translation by Dionysius Exiguus, otherwise known as Denis the Small.

The Council of Trullo (691–692), convoked by Justinian II, was especially important.[11] As Father Alexis Kniazev has pointed out, the 102 canons of the council already revealed "the harm that the Church was suffering from at that time." Thus, the third canon prohibited priests from marrying a second time, an indication of the decline of morality within the Church, but more importantly, the institution tends to become more inward looking. As the dean of St. Sergius rather maliciously notes, canons 64 and 70 forbid preaching to laypeople and to women.[12] These canons were never abolished; on the contrary, the *Nomocanon with 14 Titles*, which went through three revisions between the 9th and 11th centuries, the *Synagogue* of John the Scholastic and the *Synopsis* (an abridged text of the canons) were transmitted to all peoples evangelized by Constantinople (Russians, Serbs, Bulgarians, Romanians). These Byzantine compilations formed the basis for the Russian collection (*Kormtchaia knigua*) as well as the Romanian compilations (*Pravila, Codes* of Basil the Wolf and Matthew Bessarab). Illustrious canonists such as Alexis Aristene, John Zonaras and Theodore Balsamon wrote commentaries in the 12th century with the purpose of updating these canons for their particular era.

At the same time, in the Latin Church, the monk Gratian wrote his *Decretum* or *Concordea discordantium canonorum* at Bologna. His work was resumed and continued in particular by Popes Gregory IX, Boniface VIII and Clement V. In the 14th century the *Corpus Juris Canonici* contained all that the Roman Catholic Church had decreed during 14 centuries in the field of canon law relating to both ecclesial and temporal affairs. In the 14th century, at Constantinople, Matthew Vlastaris also composed a *Constitution according to Subject Matter* (*Syntagma kata stoikheion*) which organized the now voluminous Byzantine corpus by alphabetical order.

11 Rome refused this canonical collection because the 36th canon confirmed the 28th canon of Chalcedon (which affirmed that the precedence of Rome was only one of convenience since it was the imperial city). Pope Leo protested this assertion.

12 A. Kniazev, *Cours de Droit Canon,* Paris, Institute Saint Serge.

However, jurists gradually lost interest in nomocanonical law, as orthodoxy was no longer understood as right truth for the majority of Christian citizens. For the post-Byzantine canonical tradition, and even today in the Greek world, it is the famous 18th century compilation of the monks Nicomedius and Agapios, the *Pedalion* (The Rudder), which serves as a reference work. At the beginning of the 20th century, Pope Benedict XV replaced the old code with a *Codex Juris Canonici* (1917).

This evolution of orthodox consciousness also had its effects on the theological tradition. The politico-ecclesial crisis provoked by Arius (c. 256–336) from 318 testifies to a new need in the Church to universalize the boundaries of truth through dogmatic decisions. As we know, Arius, priest of Alexandria, influenced by neo-Platonism and attempting to follow Origen's thinking on the unity within the Trinity, declared that "the Son had not always existed." The success of Arius's theses led Constantine to convene the first ecumenical council at Nicaea in 325. Reacting to this heresy, the 318 Fathers in attendance issued a Symbol of Faith in which the Son is declared to be begotten by the Father, True God of True God, begotten, not created, of one essence with the Father. As Bernard Sesboüé points out, the teaching of the Symbol of Nicaea was introduced by a simple "that is to say" (*tou'estin*): "the Only-Begotten of the Father, *that is to say*, of the substance of the Father." For the theologian of the Groupe des Dombes, this "that is to say" expresses the essential relationship between the word of Scripture and the word of dogma. By this explanation, which is also a translation, the council decided in the debate "on the meaning to be given," here and now, in the Greek cultural milieu, to the main Scriptural affirmations on God, Christ and the Holy Spirit.[13] Orthodox thought as right truth is therefore initially a semantic effort to incarnate the Scriptural Truth transmitted by the Church. We are not yet in a position to define truth in the sense of the word *horos,* rendered in English by the term dogma, but rather we try to translate the truth into the context of the community experience of faith. Against the traditionalism displayed by Gnosticism, the Fathers of the Council showed intellectual creativity by coining the concept of *homoousios* to refer to the inter-Trinitarian relations.

A shift took place, however. In the first centuries of Christianity the knowledge given by the Christian faith embraced all the aspects of life. The

13 B. Sesboüé, *L'Evangile dans l'Eglise. La tradition vivante de la foi,* Paris, Centurion, 1975, 46.

Christian gnostic walked with the truth and marveled at discovering its interpersonal dynamics. With the polemics of the 4th century, the essence of the vision of God, and thus the Christian faith, was questioned by people who called themselves Christians. A consequence of the defense of the orthodox faith consisted in the safeguarding of the vision of the apostolic tradition but by giving priority to the ontological or mystical dimension of the truth over the personal experience of *gnosis*. This thesis put forward by Marie-Joseph Le Guillou in 1973 in his book *Le Mystère du Père* received a fairly broad consensus. According to Marie-Thérèse Nadeau, in the course of the Middle Ages, in spite of a few exceptions, faith was primarily understood, institutionally, "as doctrines, truths to be believed, defended and taught" more than as lived experience and personal inner development.[14] Irenaeus of Lyons associated the *fides ecclesiae* with a content. This meant first a body of doctrine opposing heretics. In *De Trinitate* (356–359) Hilary of Poitiers affirmed that the orthodox faith of the Church is the faith of Nicaea. Augustine (354–430) spoke of the "right faith of the Catholic Church."[15] In the case of Vincent of Lérins (†450), it is the recourse to the authority of the Fathers, and not just the criteria of apostolicity as Irenaeus asserted, that allows control of a doctrine.

It is only in the West with Anselm of Canterbury (1033–1109), according to Marie-Thérèse Nadeau, that the dimension of a living reality of faith in the Church became manifest. This was occasioned by the Church's magisterial teaching regarding infant baptism. In his sermons, the Archbishop of Canterbury insists on the fact that it is through the faith of those who belong to the Church that infants still without intelligence can receive the sacrament. It is as if an understanding of orthodoxy as right truth was beginning to lose sight of its roots in orthodoxy as worthy glorification and was subsequently confronted with the problem of rationalism. Indeed, since it had not been sufficiently lived and interiorized, the faith of the Church became identical to the law of individual reasoning. In such a context, infant baptism represented an absurdity. St. Thomas Aquinas (1224/25–1274) sought to correct this deviancy by once again calling to mind the ontological dimension of truth. For him, the heretic who correctly observes the rite of the Church communicates, through the faith of the Church which he thus

14 Marie-Thérèse Nadeau, *Foi de l'Eglise, évolution et sens d'une formule*, Paris, Beauchesne, 1988, 36.

15 Augustine, *In Johannis Evangelium*, tract. XXXIV, 2, CCSL, XXXVI, 311; PL, 35, 1652.

respects, in the Passion of Christ, the source of the efficacy of the sacraments. This, however, signifies putting on the same level the unworthiness of any believer to participate in the holy mysteries and the more complex question of the ecclesial community's recognition of a conscious disassociation on the part of one of its members between the faith of the Church and lived faith.

In the East, after the peace of Constantine, there was a similar evolution of ritual unification centered on a progressively stabilized doctrine. The Council of Ephesus (431) fought the heresy of Nestorius and defended the clergy who professed "orthodox sentiments" (3rd canon). But it was forbidden to alter the text of the Nicene formula.[16]According to the German liturgist Anton Baumstark, the Rite of the Great Church of Constantinople united towards the end of the 7th century with the Rite of Jerusalem, just as the Roman Rite merged with that of Gaul. The great centers of Orthodoxy fell progressively into the hands of Islam at the same time that the monophysite movement severely weakened the Orthodox Church in these patriarchies. The Eastern Church withdrew into its Byzantine identity and confronted the worst internal crisis of its history with the iconoclastic controversy. In the 8th century the interpretation of the liturgy as a cosmic and participative event, still dear to Maximus the Confessor (c. 630), gave way under the influence of Patriarch Germanus I (c. 730) to a more narrative vision of the liturgical *historia*. The unfolding of the liturgy became more literal, more incarnate, with fewer risks of gnostic interpretations. This liturgical reform was prepared by St. Theodore, the Abbot of Stoudios (†826) and became predominant near the end of the 9th century. According to Migual Arranz, this stabilized the liturgy at least until the 14th century.[17] The Byzantine Neo-Sabaite Rite subsequently formed was a synthesis of the Studite Rite and that of the Palestinian monastery of Saint Sabbas. Simpler than the Rite of Constantinople, enriched by hesychast spirituality in the 14th century, it became the dominant rite in the majority of the Eastern Churches.

The Sunday *Synodikon* of Orthodoxy was written in 843 to celebrate the abolition of iconoclasm. It is a perfect illustration of this semantic evolution

16 "The Holy Council has decided that it is not permitted to publicly proclaim, write or compose a symbol of faith other than the one defined by the Holy Fathers united at Nicaea under the guidance of the Holy Spirit." *Actes du concile d'Ephèse*, canon no. 7, cf. Adolphe Charles Peltier, "Dictionnaire universel et complet des conciles" in Jacques-Paul Migne, *Encyclopédie théologique*, vol. 13, 1847.

17 According to modern liturgists, the studite and neo-sabaite rites are only variations of the same basic tradition.

of orthodoxy towards the "correct doctrine of immaculate faith" according to the words of the *Synodikon* itself.[18] This text was significantly inaugurated by a procession led by the Empress Theodora (842–856) from the Church of the Theotokos at Blachernae to the Cathedral of St. Sophia, followed by the imperial court, Patriarch Methodius, the iconodule clergy and the crowd. Since that time the text is read in Orthodox churches on the first Sunday of Great Lent:

> What the prophets saw, what the apostles taught, what is proclaimed by the tradition received by the Church, what the doctors defined, what the universe unanimously acknowledges, what grace has made to shine forth, that deception has been expelled, that Wisdom has spoken with assurance, that Christ has triumphed, this is what we think, what we say, what we preach thereby honoring Christ, our true God, and his saints, in word and writing and thought, by sacrifices, by sanctuaries and by images, giving honor and reverence to our one God and Lord, honoring the others, his saints, because of their relationship with this same God and as worthy servants, offering them worthy honor. Such is the faith of the apostles, such is the faith of the Fathers, such is the faith of the orthodox, such is the faith which upholds the universe.[19]

Alexander Schmemann considered that the *Synodikon* was a testimony of the Byzantine ideal formulated after the iconoclast revolt, of the negation of history in favor of eschatology. He wrote:

> A crystallization of tradition began within the Byzantine Church, a tendency to define the Tradition and consider it as closed and immutable. In this sense the Byzantine mentality considered the "triumph of orthodoxy" as a decisive and total victory of orthodoxy, the end point of its historic development. Henceforth the Orthodox Church is defined as "the Church of the Seven Councils and the Fathers" and the Byzantines would regard any heresy as a repetition of former heresies and condemn it almost automatically by

18 *Synodikon de l'Orthodoxie*, trans. Jean Gouillard, *Travaux et mémoires 2*, editions E. de Boccard, Paris, 1967, point III, "Usage of suffragant bishopric of Athens," 12.
19 Ibid., 4.

> referring it to decisions taken in the past. This fundamentalist and conservative attitude, which is still one of the most characteristic traits of the orthodox mentality and which bestows an absolute importance on the most accidental details of the life and cult of the Church, can be traced to this deeply anti-historic attitude of Byzantium.[20]

The logic of worthy glorification is visibly lost at Byzantium in the 9th century for, when the feast of the Triumph of Orthodoxy replaced that of the memory of the prophets, which until then had been celebrated on the First Sunday of Great Lent, no one dared touch the very texts of the liturgy of the day.[21] It is therefore always the Gospel of St. John on the call of Nathaniel that is read on this Sunday even though it has no relation to the new feast. This text is followed by benedictions for the blessed defenders of Orthodoxy but also maledictions on the heretics who are declared anathema. It can therefore be seen how, in the absence of an understanding and thus of an active participation in the celebrated event, Christian mentalities in the East shifted first from an understanding of the mysteries celebrated as right truth to a faithful memory of the liturgical ordo, and then to a gradual loss of understanding of what would then be experienced as an allegorical presentation. Even though the rite of the prothesis was introduced late into the Byzantine liturgy, and was practiced by the clergy behind the iconostasis, many theologians, even to this day, want to interpret it as an allegory of the Paschal sacrifice. In 1958, Paul Evdokimov explains further: "Already the first act or prothesis, the preparation of the bread and wine, is a small very condensed realistic drama that reproduces the immolation of the Lamb thus imparting a succinct sacrificial schema that is to be accomplished in the course of the liturgy."[22] This evolution of the paradigm of orthodoxy

20 A. Schmemann, "La théocratie byzantine et l'Eglise orthodoxe," *Dieu vivant*, no. 25 (Sept. 1953): 50.

21 A. Kniazev, "La lecture de l'Ancien Testament et du Nouveau Testament dans le rite byzantin," in Bishop Cassian, Dom Bernard Botte, *La Prière des Heures*, Paris, Cerf, 1963, 231. According to the dean of the Saint Sergius Institute, who references the work of the liturgical historian Karabinov, the choice of the pericopes of Isaiah which the Byzantine Church uses during Great Lent manifests the intention of "reproducing a whole glorious chapter of Byzantine history, i.e., the recital of the principal events which marked the brilliant military campaign of Emperor Heraclius (611–42) against the Persians." Ibid., 239.

22 P. Evdokimov, *L'Orthodoxie,* Paris, DDB, 1979, 254.

during the medieval and modern periods also resulted in a growing complexity of the typikon or Byzantine ordo. This was recently reported by A. Schmemann and R. Taft.[23] Today it is the object of a real "decryption."[24]

The dominant paradigm during the political period of Christianity was thus an understanding of orthodox faith primarily as the "content of the truths to be believed." Such a representation of orthodoxy has, as we have seen, its advantages as well as its limits. Many individual cases indicate, however, that the orthodox faith was also lived in a Trinitarian manner as life in Christ in the Spirit tending towards the Father, thereby integrating doctrine as a principle of life and salvation. But it was not until the 20th century that this sense of orthodoxy as true and fair knowledge, differentiated as incarnate tradition, assimilated and adapted according to the contexts, was gradually incorporated into the magisterial teaching by Christian theologians of the East and West. In 325, the orthodoxy of the faith, threatened by a *gnosis* that strayed from a correct vision of God, and pressed by the need to preserve the political unity of the Empire, still managed to prevail at Nicaea over heterodox gnosticism through a creative effort of conceptualization. This reaction did not obliterate the ancient eschatological and liturgical representation of the orthodox way. The latter did, however, become marginalized. The new political, spiritual and intellectual context led the ecclesial consciousness to redefine orthodoxy as the new body of doctrine of the Empire. From the 4th to the 15th century, the definition of doctrine was inseparable from its social and political implications. The result of all this was the strengthening of the tradition of apostolic doctrine understood as a reservoir of orthodoxy rather than as a path towards a doxological openness to the Spirit.

## A POLITICAL HISTORIOGRAPHY

The very term *orthodoxia,* as a synonym for right opinion in the order of reasoning, appears at a late date in the writings of the Fathers. Its use is first detected in the Arian and Monophysite polemics, as in the 4th century with Athanasius of Alexandria (*Letter to the Bishops of Egypt*) and Methodius of Olympus (*The Banquet of the Ten Virgins*), in Pseudo-Justin Martyr of the 5th century (in *Questions and Answers for the Orthodox*) or in the works of Anastasius the Sinaite, a monk from Syria or Palestine in

23 R. Taft, *Le rite byzantin,* Paris, Cerf, 1996.

24 Job Getcha, *Le typikon décrypté,* Paris, Cerf, 2009.

the 7th century who settled on Mount Sinai where he wrote the *Hodegos* (Guide) against the Eutychians.[25] It is in the 4th century that *orthodoxos* is first used as an adjective to qualify the faith of the Church. Around 371 Athanasius of Alexandria uses the term to designate the authentic doctrine of the Church. In his letter to Adelphius he defines "correct faith" as that "which proceeds from the apostolic teaching and the tradition of the Fathers and is strengthened by the New and Old Testaments."

The life and works of Eusebius of Caesarea (265–340) are characteristic of the new paradigm of truth that imposes itself with the legalization of Christianity. Recent research on Eusebius moves very much away from the point of view that consists in making this Father of the Church a sacred authority (as with P. I. Maier),[26] which had already been disputed in the 9th century by the Patriarch Photius, those of the former approach seeing in him only a servile caesaropapist (J. N. D. Kelly).[27] In a reunion of scholars dedicated to research organized by the Inter-Disciplinary Center of the Université Libre de Bruxelles on March 3, 2008, S. Inowlocki and C. Zamagni propose that the time has come to bring forth other Christian narratives of the history of the Church eclipsed by the "orthodox" version of the history of the Church of the bishop of Caesarea. The common point of these authors is therefore the study of Eusebius as a "full-fledged author" and his contextualization.[28]

Eusebius was a pupil of the presbyter Pamphilus of Caesarea, who died a martyr during the reign of Diocletian, and who introduced him to the works of Origen. He was ordained bishop of the Metropolis of Caesarea in Palestine around 313. Victim of the Diocletian persecution, Eusebius became a close friend of the Emperor Constantine for whom he composed

25 G. Lampe, ed. *A Patristic Greek Lexicon,* Oxford, Clarendon Press, 1961, s.v. orthodoxia, op. cit., 971–73.

26 Eusebius, *The Church History,* Translation and Commentary by P. I. Maier, Grand Rapids, Kregal, 2007.

27 J. N. D. Kelly, *Early Christian Doctrine,* London, Black, 1977.

28 Sabrina Inowlocki and Claudio Zamagni, eds. *Reconsidering Eusebius, Collected Papers on Literary, Historical and Theological Issues,* supplements to *Vigiliae Christianae* 107, Leiden, Boston, Brill, 2011; cf. A. Cameron and S. G. Hall, *Eusebius, Life of Constantine,* Oxford, Clarendon Press, 1999; S. Inowlocki, *Eusebius and the Jewish Authors: His Citation Technique in an Apologetic Context,* AJEC 64, Leiden, Brill, 2006; S. Morlet, *La Démonstration évangélique d'Eusèbe de Césarée: étude sur l'apologétique chrétienne à l'époque de Constantin,* Etudes Augustiniennes, serie Antiquites, 187, Paris, Etudes Augustiennes, 2009.

a panegyric homage. He was the theorist of the Christian Empire and of the divine mission entrusted to Constantine. His masterwork, the foundation of the new orthodox memorial, *Ecclesiastical History*, covers the period of the birth of Christ to 323. In many respects, Eusebius of Caesarea was instrumental in making the meaning of right truth prevail over that of worthy glorification; we find him using the term on many occasions.[29] For him, orthodoxy designates the universal and traditional doctrine of the Church opposed to heresy.[30] Eusebius was wary of the pseudognostics who abandoned the world to destiny and proposed an alternative "spiritual" way to go to heaven. In the 23rd chapter of his Church history he writes of "ecclesiastical orthodoxy" to designate two witnesses, Irenaeus and Clement of Alexandria. However, he wrote prior to the Council of Constantinople in 381 which defined the Trinity as three Persons sharing a same nature. For him, the nature of Christ is twofold. He quotes Irenaeus to affirm that Christ is both God and man, he is simultaneously man and "the Word of Wisdom existing from all eternity." Such a profession of faith can be considered a victory over Arianism, and the reason why Eusebius supported the Council of Nicaea in 325. Yet Eusebius also presided at the Council of Tyre in 335 which proved to be a revenge by the Arians against Athanasius of Alexandria. Because Eusebius used the Septuagint translation of the Book of Wisdom, for him Wisdom is a reality created by God.

For Eusebius, the Son is God only by participation in the Father, which logically authorizes the emperor to become his vicar on earth: "The emperor is an image of the Logos who is an image of the Father."[31] Later, in the 8th century, on the occasion of the so-called "Donation of Constantine," the legend which had Constantine acknowledging Pope Sylvester as the primate of the universal Church was based on the same logic.[32] In both cases the vicar of God becomes the chief of the Empire and the Church (caesaropapism or papocaesarism). Eusebius designates the emperor as the bishop of those who are outside the Church (*Vita Constantini*, IV, 24), a title that echoes back to that of the ancient *pontifex maximus* which the

29 G. Bardy, P. Perrichon, eds., Eusebius of Caesarea, *Histoire Ecclesiastique*, SC 31, 41, 55, 73 bis, Paris, Cerf, 1952–71. Vol. 4, 23.2.

30 Ibid., 3, 23, 2.

31 F. Winkelman, ed., Eusebius, *Vita Constantini*, GCS Eus 1/1, 1975; *De laudibus Constantini*, I.

32 Paul Veyne, *Quand notre monde est devenu chrétien (312–394)*, Paris, Albin Michel, Bibliothèque Idées, 2007.

Christian emperors continued to carry up to the time of Theodosius. For Constantine this concept of an emperor vested with a sacred power, validated by Eusebius, authorized him to intervene in the affairs of the Church. It was the same logic of an imperial unifying role that led Emperor Theodosius in 381 to make Christian orthodoxy the obligatory faith of the Empire. For Eusebius, the great doxological vision of the circulation of glory between God and all humanity created in His image gave place to a vertical representation of the transmission of glory between God and humanity through the mediation of the emperor.

As an example, Mark DelCogliano has shown that the text of Eusebius, *On the Feast of Easter*, written in 335, was primarily an endorsement of the agenda of Constantine after the decision in 325 of the Council of Nicaea on the date of the celebration of Christ's resurrection. This was settled to fall on the first Sunday following the first full moon after the Spring equinox.[33] It therefore represented a synthesis of the lunar and solar calendars so that Easter might be celebrated when the whole world is illuminated, the night by the full moon and the day by the sun. The Conciliar Fathers also made an amalgamation of the Old Testament calendar (calculated on the 14th day of the month of Nisan in memory of the Exodus from Egypt) and the dominical event of the resurrection. The emperor's first priority, however, was the liturgical unification of his Empire. He fought, just like the Fathers of Nicaea, the protopaschite practice that calculated the date of Easter according to the Jewish lunar calendar rather than the Julian solar calendar.[34] In order to justify his position, Constantine brings forth arguments condemning the Jewish people as a whole for Christ's crucifixion. Eusebius fuels the emperor's discourse. He dedicates his treatise on Easter to Constantine and thanks him for his solicitude towards the Church. In this text (PG 24, 693–706), translated into English by M. DelCogliano, Eusebius applies himself to further widening the growing gap between Jews and Christians. He insists that Christ himself refused to celebrate the Pascha with the Jews and points out that in Christian theology every Sunday liturgy is paschal. Following the emperor's lead, Eusebius shares in the polemic by treating the Jews as criminals and liars.

33 M. DelCogliano, "The Promotion of the Constantine Agenda in Eusebius of Caesarea's *On the Feast of Pascha*," *Reconsidering Eusebius*, op. cit., 39–68.

34 L. Duchesne, "La question de la Pâques au concile de Nicée," *Revue des questions historiques*, no. 28, Paris (1880): 5–42.

As Sébastien Morlet has shown, Eusebius, considered by the Orthodox tradition as the Father of Church history, wanted to synthesize the ancient representation and the Christian representation of history.[35] Like Thucydides, Eusebius, in his introduction to the history of the Church,[36] seeks to trace back to the very origins of history. In this way, before describing the human reality of the Church, the bishop of Caesarea, having read *On the First Principles* of Origen, wants to prove the divine origin of Christ. However, while Origen identified the Christ with Jesus, Eusebius associated the Word, the subject of the unction, to Christ.[37] Due to this imbalance introduced into the divino-humanity of Jesus Christ, the representation of God could once again take on the characteristics of all-mightiness which the ancient world attributed to the divinity: "God, who watches over all things, sent down upon men who did such things floods of water, torments of fire as upon a savage forest extended over the whole earth; He exterminated them by continual famines, plagues, wars and thunderbolts."[38] Time is represented as an arrow, that of salvation, lurking on the horizon. As a remnant of this first secularization of early messianic historiography, and an openness to the ancient cyclic temporality, one finds in Eusebius a Golden Age of Christian origins. This was not the case with Justin who knew that a false *gnosis* had always threatened orthodoxy.[39] In his *Chronicle*, Eusebius was also preoccupied with proving the antiquity of Moses to demonstrate the superiority of Judeo-Christian history over Greek and Roman history. Eusebius, however, no longer sets a date for the end of the world. He no longer seeks to draw attention to the approaching end of time as in primitive historiography. On the contrary, in the opinion of Hubert Drobner, Eusebius tries to "show that the Empire of Constantine marks the apogee of the world, as predicted and whose end is not foreseeable."[40]

35 Sébastien Morlet, *L'introduction de l'Histoire ecclesiastique d'Eusèbe de Césarée (I, II–IV): étude génétique, littéraire, et rhétorique*; mémoire Paris IV — Sorbonne, sd.

36 The date of the composition of this work is an object of debate. H. Drobner suggests that Books I–VII were first written and published prior to 303 and that they were revised in later editions. Books VIII–X cover the period between the persecution of Diocletian and the victory of Constantine over Licinius (324).

37 Eusebius, Book V, chapter XXVIII.

38 Eusebius, *Ecclesiastical History*, op. cit., chapter III.

39 One can agree with Enrico Norelli that, on this point, Eusebius was dependent on Hegesippus. Cf. B. Pouderon and Y. M. Duval eds., *L'historiographique de l'Eglise des premiers siècles*, Paris, Beauchesne, 2001, 19.

40 H. Drobner, op. cit., 255.

The narrative is therefore that of a succession of human events, of illustrious personages but also of ravaging wolves threatening the Christian flock, interrupted only by the heterogeneous and violent intervention of God in history such as in the destruction of the Temple which for Eusebius meant the end of Israel's mission in history. The role of a Christian historian is not that of a witness or a spiritual person, even though he recognizes that the Risen Lord confided his "gnosis" to Peter, James and John who passed it on to the other apostles,[41] but that of a judge whose task it is to separate the truth from the counterfeits. Eusebius is aware that in this perspective he is the first historian of the Church. This leads him to be extremely precise, and to base himself on the word of witnesses. In the narrative of Luke, orthodoxy is understood as "the truth with certitude" owing to the contacts of the evangelist with Paul and the other apostles.[42] With Eusebius, it is no longer participative obedience in Christ which is the criterion of orthodoxy, but rather the witness of the Church. This explains the extreme rigor with respect to his own subjectivity that Eusebius introduced into the work of a historian. Eusebius thus becomes the first historian of antiquity to continually cite the oral and written sources on which he bases his narrative. The canonicity of the Scriptures that accurately determines the truth of a testimony is of decisive importance in the work of Eusebius. The work of a historian becomes that of a director who introduces his characters according to a chronological order and not a theophanic one. The originality of Eusebius's method, of significance for understanding the paradigm of right truth, is that he follows the political agenda of the reigning years of emperors and pontiffs, whereas Luke simply followed Paul who acted according to promptings of the Spirit. With Eusebius, history passes from a pneumocentrism to an ecclesiocentrism, hence his insistence on chronicling the succession of bishops for each Church.

## THE HISTORIOGRAPHY OF AUGUSTINE

In the opinion of Glenn F. Chestnut, this history was the only serious alternative to the theology of history that St. Augustine developed in the following century.[43] Augustine (354–430) was born at Thagaste in Numidia.[44]

41 Ibid., Book II.

42 Ibid., chapter XXIII.

43 Glenn F. Chestnut, *The First Christian Histories,* Paris, Beauchesne, 1977.

44 Etienne Gilson, *Introduction à l'étude de saint Augustin,* Vrin, Paris, 1989; Lucien Jerphagnon, *Introduction à La Cité de Dieu*, Oeuvre de Saint Augustin, t. II, Gallimard,

He was baptized in Milan at the age of 33 in 387 and became bishop of Hippo around 396. The year after his death, Pope Celestine pronounced him to be *inter magistros optimos*, "one of the best teachers of the Church." He is considered one of the four Fathers of the Western Catholic Church and one of the thirty-six Doctors of the Church. The Eastern Orthodox Church considers him "blessed." *The City of God*, a new philosophy of history in Christian historiography, was written by Augustine between 413 and 426 and is divided into twenty-two books. The very title of the work is polemic: *De Civitate Dei contra Paganos*, in other words *The City of God in Opposition to the Pagans*. In the first ten books, he demonstrates that Roman decadence dates from paganism and that it is the God of Christians who is the source of the greatness of Rome. In *The Retractions,* II, 43/1–3, St. Augustine summarizes the second part of his work: "Of these last twelve books, the first four (11–14) contain an account of the origin of the two cities: the city of God and the city of this world. The second four (15–18) treat their progress and development; the third and last four (19–22) of their deserved destinies." In books XI–XIV, written before 418, Augustine explains that the earthly kingdom is separated from the eternal kingdom because of the proud will of the fallen angels. The Incarnation of the Son of God shows that the love of God is the way towards the City of God. "The two cities are entangled together in this world, and intermixed until the last judgment effects their separation."

Augustine, like Eusebius, was influenced by ancient historiography, namely, that of Herodotus or Thucydides. His doctrine of predestination and grace has its roots in the ancient concept of *fatum*. He had experienced the end of a world when Rome was first conquered by Alaric and the Visigoths on

---

coll. Pléiade, 1998–2002; Henri-Irénée Marrou, *L'Ambivalence du temps et de l'Histoire chez Saint Augustin,* Paris, Vrin, 1950; Henri-Irénée Marrou, *Saint Augustin et la fin de la culture antique*, 5th ed., Paris, DeBoccard, 1983; H. Holsiein, "Le peuple de Dieu et la cité de Dieu" in *Hiérarchie et peuple de Dieu,* Paris, Beauchesne, 1970; F. Donnely and M. Sherman, *Augustine's De civitate Dei, An annotated bibliography of modern criticism, 1960–1990,* New York, 1990; H. Burleigh, *The City of God, A Study of St. Augustine's Philosophy,* London, 1949; J.-C. Guy, *Unité et structure logique de la Cité de Dieu de saint Augustin,* Paris, 1961; P. Piret, *La Destinée de Dieu, La Cité de Dieu. Un commentaire du "De Civitate Dei,"* Bruxelles, 1991; G. Demacopoulos, A. Papanikolaou, *Orthodox Readings of Augustine*, Crestwood, SVSP, 2008; Sergius Bulgakov, *L'Epouse de l'Agneau*, Paris, L'Age d'Homme, 1987; Sergius Bulgakov, *L'Echelle de Jacob,* Paris, L'Age d'Homme, 1987; Jean-Luc Marion, *Au lieu de soi, l'Approche de Saint Augustin*, Paris, PUF, 2008; Victor Yudin, "Refuting Porphyry with Plato. Augustine's reading of the *Timaeus* 41 ab."

August 24, 410. His doctrine of the two cities rejected any possibility of historical progress. In his narrative he continues to make mention of the circulation of glory between heaven and earth. He still associates the Heavenly Jerusalem of the Apocalypse with created Wisdom or created Glory, which brings him closer to early Christian *gnosis*. But for the bishop of Hippo, the earthly *civitas* was destined to remain infested with evil until the Incarnation of the Son of God. In the meantime, the two kingdoms only coexist in the world:

> Accordingly, two cities have been formed by two loves: the earthly by the love of self, even to the contempt of God; the heavenly by the love of God, even to the contempt of self. The former, in a word, glories in itself, the latter in the Lord. For the one seeks glory from men; but the greatest glory of the other is God, the witness of conscience. The one lifts up its head in its own glory; the other says to its God, "You are my glory, and the lifter up of mine head." In the one, the princes and the nations it subdues are ruled by the love of ruling; in the other, the princes and the subjects serve one another in love, the latter obeying, while the former take thought for all. The one delights in its own strength, represented in the persons of its rulers; the other says to its God, "I will love You, O Lord, my strength."[45]

This pessimistic vision of a foreign city of God on earth was partly inherited from early Christianity. It ignores, however, the eschatological element of the doxological vision. It does not take into consideration the Church as mystical body and as a source of theanthropic action. For Eusebius, on the other hand, human beings have free will to act in history, which means that the social order can be reformed according to a Christian perspective. Free will had not been destroyed by the sin of Adam and Eve. It was therefore not human emotions that controlled history, but rather the victory over the passions. Moreover, whereas for Augustine the Almighty God intervened directly in history, for Eusebius such a God was unobjectifiable. Only the Logos, the Image of the Father, could participate in the life of the world.[46]

45 Saint Augustine, *The City of God*, XIV, 28, 1, trans. Marcus Dods.

46 Eusebius also opposed the Stoics who relied on oracles to prove that the world was determined by powers of which humanity was ignorant. For Eusebius, prophecy did not compromise the free action of the human will. By the same token, man's participation in the divine plan did not compromise the Almightiness of God.

At this point, it is appropriate to draw lessons from this Augustinian historiography to clarify our thesis on the evolution of the paradigm of orthodoxy during the period of late antiquity. An analysis of Book XII, in particular chapters IX to XXII, of *The City of God*, shows Augustine's evolution of orthodoxy as right truth (*sana doctrina* or *via recta* in paragraph 12, XIV 1) at the expense of losing the old definition of orthodoxy as worthy glorification (*debita laude Creatoris* in XII, 9).[47] Therefore, to rediscover Augustine beyond the centuries that separate us from him, to bring forth the different semantic strata of the *doxa* from the text under consideration, we must combine the four definitions of truth as: worthy glorification, right truth, faithful memory and true and fair knowledge. Our method attempts to be empathic (with a return to certain contemporary theses of Jean-Marc Marion on Augustinian anthropology) and synthetic (complementing the necessary chronological context with a sapiential and Trinitarian anthropology). It consists in distinguishing three temporalities that together can manifest the truth in all its depth. For Augustine this was a confrontation beyond the boundaries of space and time: the moment of extraction/*extentio* (the truth that Augustine sets out), the moment of distraction/*distentio* (the shift in the meaning of truth that Augustine experienced with his readers and commentators) and, finally, the moment of attraction/*intentio* (the truth in which he participated and sought to explain).

### *What Augustine said*

Book XII of *The City of God* is concerned with the origins of humanity. In the introduction, Augustine affirms the unique nature of the angels, both good and bad, the distinction being linked to the demonic will which is a failure in respect to good. This true good is, for the angels as for humans, for the living as for the dead, to be united in the City of God, to join with God. The book concludes with the theory that God foresaw the sin of the first man and also predicted which part of the human race would enjoy the glory of the reward and which part would be condemned to punishment. Between the introduction and the conclusion, the second section of Book XII deals with the temporal creation of mankind. Augustine begins by criticizing (Part A) the myths of the eternity of the human race, the

47 My thanks to Antoine Guggenheim for having invited me to give a conference on this theme at the Bernadine College in the context of his seminar "Theology and History."

cyclical return of events and the existence of innumerable worlds such as taught by Epicurus. This thesis, he believes, contradicts Scripture whose chronology narrates a story with both a beginning and an end. This leads Augustine on the one hand to criticize with the help of documentation the rival chronology of the Egyptians, and on the other hand to relativize, in the face of the immensity of eternity, the fact that humanity was created late in comparison with the creation of the world. Finally, he rejects as unsatisfactory, both morally and rationally, the cyclical conception of the world that does not allow for a true beatitude for humanity, since people must constantly fear falling again, and because it admits the possibility that "something occurs in time that does not end in time." Augustine admits that the words of Ecclesiastes affirming that there is nothing new under the sun can be interpreted as a "*praedestinatione Dei.*" But the death and resurrection of Christ are unique events enabling us to understand time as ever-new. Augustine writes:

> The philosopher Plato, having taught in the school at Athens which is called the Academy, so, numberless ages before, at long but certain intervals, this same Plato and the same school, and the same disciples existed, and so also are to be repeated during the countless cycles that are yet to be—far be it, I say, from us to believe this. For "Christ died once for our sins; and, rising from the dead, He dies no more. Death has no more dominion over Him" (Rom 6:9) and we ourselves after the resurrection "shall be ever with the Lord" (1 Thess 4:16), to whom we now say, as the sacred Psalmist dictates, "You shall keep us, O Lord, You shall preserve us from this generation" (Ps 11:8).[48]

For Augustine, there is an angelic "prehistory" of human consciousness. Moreover, the principle of time is the Word of God, eternal life. He explains (in Part B) the paradox of God creating mankind in time without a new act of will. Since there cannot be a before and after in God, for He is eternal, time and mankind had to be created simultaneously ("from some sort of beginning time and humanity came forth"—*ab aliquo tamen initio exorsus est tempora et hominem*).[49] In this way, and in continuity with Book

48 Augustine, *The City of God*, XII, 13.

49 In Augustine's mind, the world was not made within time but with time (cf. p. 51). But Augustine understands "in the beginning" as "in the Word"; the expression "in

XI, Augustine also shows that creation, which could only be good, had to come about according to two temporalities — that of the angels, created out "of nothing" from the first day (in other words "before all time"), and designated by the notion of "heaven," which has always existed,[50] and that of man who was created "in time," the sixth day, after the creation of astrological temporality on the fourth day when the simultaneity of parts was excluded. This thesis concerning immortal but non-coeternal creatures is all the more necessary to Augustine's thought in that if God has always been Lord, then there have always been creatures to serve Him, but this does not solve the aporia according to which on the one hand time has "existed from all eternity" and on the other hand "time has been created." He even recommends a certain humility on the subject, while suggesting his own theory on "the eternal life promised before the beginning of time," of which Paul speaks in his letter to Titus (1:2–3) — that God has settled through "predestination"[51] what had to happen in his time, the incarnation of the Word who is eternal life.

In the third part (C) he rejects the separation between faith in creation (which proclaims that God is not repetition but infinite) and reason (which could posit that science, which must necessarily be certain and accessible to all, cannot grasp anything of infinity).[52] For Augustine — who relies on reason (even Plato imagines the demiurge using numbers to create the world), on the revelations of Scripture (Psalm 146:5), and on the experience of the eternal life of the saints — the "*vero et recto itinere*" is that God is transcendent and cannot be anthropomorphized, that his creation is proof of his goodness and not the fruit of necessity (p. 213) and that being himself infinite, the knowledge of God embraces the infinite. The expression "for ever and ever" cannot be understood, according to Augustine, as the justification for a cyclic nature of time. In conclusion (12, 21), he frankly admits

---

the beginning" does not mean that here it is a question of what was created first of all, because even before God created the angels, He created all things in Wisdom, in His Word (*The City of God* XI.32).

50 For Augustine, the angels were created on the first day ("in the beginning God made heaven and earth") as participants in the eternal light which is the immutable Wisdom of God, which he calls the only-begotten Son of God.

51 Augustine, *The City of God*, op. cit., 209.

52 For if there was a beginning, then it would mean that God's goodness was inactive before this beginning, which would contradict the definition of God as Love. And if God Himself was ceaselessly engaged in this infinite, constantly making and remaking his work, then this would reveal a strange god, acting unexpectedly, therefore outside of all science.

his hesitations. He believes that either God can create without changing because He is creation from all eternity (and the number of new souls progressively increases in this divine infinity) or that God creates without a new act of will since from all eternity there exists a set number of blessed souls. This hesitation helped to obscure the understanding of Augustine's work and complicated the interpretations of his writings.

### *How Augustine was interpreted*

Let us now turn to the contemporaries of the bishop of Hippo and also to two 20th century commentators on Augustine's historiography to show the inevitable misunderstandings that arose during the evolution of the paradigm of orthodoxy.

Among the Pelagians, Julian of Eclanum understood Augustine's thought as a form of Manichaeism.[53] In 418 Pope Zosimus issued an *Epistula Tractatoria* (a decree of excommunication) against Pelagius. Julian of Eclanum was one of the eighteen Italian bishops who refused to subscribe to the document. As a result, he was deposed from his bishopric by an edict of the Emperor Honorius (March 418) pronouncing the banishment of all "Pelagians." Julian sent two letters to Pope Zosimus, one of which circulated in Italy. Around the same time, he also addressed a letter to Rufus, bishop of Thessalonica, in which he accused the adversaries of Pelagius and Celestius of being "Manichaeans." This is one of the two letters Augustine responds to in his *Contra duas epistulas Pelagianorum*. According to François Refoulé, Augustine was "incapable of grasping the significance of the Aristotelian notions of nature and free will as elaborated by the Aristotelian school, nor could he recognize the value of the objections of Julian Eclanum."[54] Likewise, Augustine's response was rejected in turn by the monks of Gaul, Prosper of Aquitaine, John Cassian, Vincent of Lérins, who considered that man's freedom of self-determination (*autexousion*) could not be nullified by the freedom of grace (*eleutheria*). However, this reaction was considered semi-Pelagian and was condemned by the Council of Orange in 529. This same council rejected their "semi-Pelagianism" and gave a theological definition of grace as advocated by Augustine of Hippo.

53 François Refoulé, "Julien d'Eclane, théologien et philosophe," *Recherches de Science Religieuse* 52 (1964): 42–84 and 233–47.

54 Ibid., 247.

The question thus remained unresolved until it reappeared in the debates on free will during the Reformation and Counter-Reformation.

Moreover, Augustine thought that for Porphyry the demiurge was omnipotent. Porphyry, however, distinguished between the demiurge which he identified with the soul of the world and the supreme god.[55] Augustine was not well acquainted with Plato's *Timaeus* (which he probably read in an incomplete translation by Cicero) or with the milieu of the neo-Platonists, from Plotinus to Porphyry, whom he identifies with the school of the Platonists such as Celsus. The Ukrainian theologian V. Youdin thinks that this is the reason Augustine was unable to bring the neo-Platonists to accept orthodox Christianity.[56]

In the 20th century, Father Sergius Bulgakov, Dean of the Orthodox St. Sergius Theological Institute, synthesized the criticisms directed against the "Blessed Augustine" by the Eastern Orthodox Church. In his masterpiece *The Bride of the Lamb*, published in 1944, he wrote an excursus on "Augustinianism and Predestination." According to the Russian Orthodox theologian, in his first treatises (388–395) against the Manichaeans, Augustine asserted that the source of evil is the fruit of human will (which contradicted the notion of an anti-god). He distinguished between prescience of God and necessity (God does not force evil upon us). For Augustine, human will was the first cause of sin. But in *De civitate Dei* (*The City of God*) the Father of the Church is now in his anti-Pelagian period. His doctrine becomes deterministic and pessimistic. The center of gravity of history is deferred to God's action: human freedom is merely subjection to sin. It only becomes true freedom for good when it is enlightened by grace. For Augustine, Bulgakov writes, "the only freedom that exists is that of grace."[57]

55 V. Youdin, op. cit., "The main thrust of Augustine's attack on Porphyrius is the former's insistence on the omnipotence of the demiurge. However, this emphasis is absolutely counterproductive. Porphyrius never claimed that the demiurge was omnipotent, nor did he think of the demiurge in terms of the supreme god. As is clear both from Proclus's evidence and from *De consensu*, the demiurge according to Porphyrius is a hypercosmic soul. In fact, he is subordinated to the intelligible paradigm, i.e., the world of ideas, which is the subject of the soul's contemplation."

56 V. Youdin, op. cit., "It would indeed be interesting to know what Augustine would have had to say on hearing that neither Porphyrius nor any other Neoplatonist ever identified the demiurge with the *summus deus*. . . . Celsus must have believed that according to Plato the demiurge was the creator of the world as well as the most supreme divinity. Yet the fourth-fifth century Platonist-Christian controversy definitely had limits of mutual understanding."

57 S. Bulgakov, *L'Epouse de l'Agneau*, Paris, L'Age d'Homme, 1984, 419.

Humanity has freedom of choice only before the Fall; after it is lost, "the salvation of fallen humanity is realized not through freedom but in spite of it." Grace is imparted by God without regard to a person's merits. God can even use the works of the devil to realize his plan. Augustine believes that the angels were created on the first day and that the separation between light and darkness corresponds to the creation of the angels and demons, of the heavenly city and the earthly city (*City of God,* XI, 19). God has therefore, although Augustine would deny such an interpretation, created evil! According to Bulgakov, Augustine mitigates this reality by saying that God created the good angelic nature and by affirming that He left the will free. Admittedly, this will can turn towards evil, towards pride, but that is the responsibility of the one who was homicidal from the beginning (p. 167, Book XII, 6). For Augustine, this pride is not a positive ontological principle but rather a deficiency. One slides towards what has less being. In spite of these nuances and although he admits that God's ways are unfathomable, for Bulgakov man knows for certain that God's paths can only be just and he cannot accept an eschatology which is so unjust. In Bulgakov's thought, created Wisdom does not replace divine Wisdom but rather reflects it and manifests it.[58] All this has its consequences in terms of historiography and political theology. Bulgakov sees an antinomic relationship between the City of God and the earthly city; or, rather, between the heavenly Jerusalem and the earthly Jerusalem. The descent of the holy Jerusalem does not replace the old but it points to the transfiguration of the world and accomplishes the synthesis of world history. The earthly city, symbolized by Babylon in chapters 27 and 28 of the Apocalypse, will indeed be destroyed, but this destruction will not annihilate mankind's creative work. Chapters 21 and 22 of the Apocalypse show that history will become a manifestation of theanthropic action: "Behold, the dwelling of God is with men. He will

58 S. Bulgakov, *L'Epouse de l'Agneau*, 360: "To be created presupposes change or temporality which has its origin in the creative act and which has no end, for the work of God is imperishable. It is only in this sense that we can speak of a created eternity, *aeveternitas*, as opposed to the true *aeternitas* of God which knows no change. Created or temporal eternity, subject to change, and the divine eternity are not only different — they are opposed. This does not mean that time, founded in eternity (of which it is 'the mobile image' according to Plato) does not have any contact with eternity. Nor does it mean that it cannot reveal eternity. But, in this contact, temporality does not lose its essential characteristic — that of change and mutability, nor is eternity diminished in its immobility and immutability. The two categories come together antinomically in the concept of 'eternal life' accorded to the creature."

dwell with them, and they shall be his people" (21:3). In the Apocalypse, this heavenly city is the Bride of the Lamb, the holy Jerusalem full of the Glory of God, "the Mother of God in her Glory," the personal recapitulation of the Church. It is created Wisdom completely deified, it is "the Spirit and the Bride." Bulgakov writes:

> The intelligibility (*sophianité*) of the created order, which is the living and permanent revelation of God, is the foundation of this alliance of the love of God and the love of the world in the unity of divine Wisdom and the Wisdom of the creature. This corresponds to the words of St. Paul: "All is from Him, by Him and for Him"—*from* Him in the divine Wisdom, *by* Him as creation depending on Him, and *for* Him as union of the divine Wisdom and created Wisdom. Thus it is that "God is all in all," the divine in created being, the divine Wisdom in the Wisdom of the creature.[59]

In the opinion of the Orthodox theologian, Augustine has identified the Wisdom with the Word too exclusively, especially in Book XI, 32. The Russian theologian speaks of the "essential fault of patristic theology... its interpretation of Sophia in terms of the Logos." The Logos has become Sophia, a second god, a mediator, whereas Sophia "as non-hypostatic divinity in God manifests the whole Trinity." Bulgakov understands the limits of Pelagius, who has lost sight of the ontological dimension of the narrative of the fall. But he supports the Irish monk's defense of the idea of humanity's self-determination. Augustine, driven by polemic, substituted man with a robot, the terrestrial city with tolerance. The incarnation has become a *deus ex machina*. Augustine thus tended towards Eutychianism and monothelitism. This predestinarianism was in reality an anthropomorphism. He included God in the process of time. Everything happens, even if Augustine hesitates on this point, as if God had started out with a pre-established plan.

Henri-Irénée Marrou (1904–1977), a renowned specialist of Augustinian thought and professor at the Sorbonne, had quite a different point of view concerning the Father of Western ecclesial historiography. For Marrou, the history of the Church and, ultimately, the history of the world, bear witness to the fact that sight has been lost of the originality of the work of

59 S. Bulgakov, op. cit., 393.

the bishop of Hippo.[60] For Augustine, this concept of a beginning and an end implies an idea of progress. Marrou admits that what was retained in the West of *The City of God* during the Middle Ages was the notion that civilization only had meaning and durability within the context of the Church. The Church, however, has been understood as an institutional body where faith and reason form a monolithic whole, where the earthly city, "the city of evil," is condemned to degradation, where the justice of God sends the damned to Hell. "If history has a positive value, if the time lived is the instrument of progress, these attributes do not come from the order of nature but from that of grace. By itself, time cannot achieve anything good."[61] It can only be redeemed by the action of God. The City of God will be a time of stability.

Political Augustinism can be dated back to Pope Gregory the Great (590–604): political power is at the service of spiritual power. This implies specifically that the public good and Christian virtues are identical and that Augustine's earthly city of perdition becomes the temporal and political city. Such a monistic vision was rejected by the Renaissance. For Michelangelo, Wisdom reappears alongside the Creator at the moment man is fashioned. But with the passage of time, Augustinian historiosophy was replaced by an inverse monism, by a pessimistic vision of the original violence wrought upon the earthly city, by the exclusive defense of the rights of the human person and of the nation-states (Machiavelli, Hobbes, Rousseau).[62] The French Revolution founded a political autonomous city with respect to the Church. The Roman Catholic Church reacted by opposing an Augustinian approach (cf. *Quod Aliquantum* of Pius VI in 1791). The vision of the mystical body of the Church has thus been secularized. In Marrou's view, "these difficulties are of little importance"[63] in relation to Augustine's identification of the City of God with the Church and the earthly city with the city of the devil. He believes that it is simply a question of returning

60 Henri-Irénée Marrou, *L'Ambivalence du temps de l'histoire chez Saint Augustin*, Paris, Montreal, Vrin, 1950.

61 H.-I. Marrou, op. cit., 71.

62 In Augustine's text, there is a surprising trace of modernity's rebellion against the idea of two antagonistic cities created by God. A "translator's note" discreetly points out that the theses of Augustine lead to the belief in "eternal punishment for the wicked" (218). A bit further on (219) he tries to show, with little historical support, that Augustine does not give enough consideration to purgatory.

63 Marrou, ibid., 39.

to the Augustinian representation of the heavenly city as the progressive building of the City of God. On the other hand, in his book *The Secular Age*, Charles Taylor demonstrates that one of the characteristics of our times is the rejection of a static Augustinian monism, be it the model of medieval Christianity or that of modern contractual society.

### *What Augustine would have wanted to say*

According to the scholar Jean-Luc Marion, the author of a recent book entitled *In the Self's Place* (*Au lieu de soi*) which presents Augustine's conception of time, it is necessary to rediscover the logic of saturated phenomenon in order to understand the thought of the Father of the Church. Such an effort coincides with Augustine's own struggles against those whose "subtle reasoning is only intended to exclude the infinity of beings."[64] Marion's quasi-psychoanalytic interpretation of Augustine coincides with a phenomenology of donation. Marion writes:

> More importantly than a judgment on things (true or false), more importantly even than the manifestation of the phenomenon itself, the truth produces a verdict on myself; accordingly I can accept it or can only challenge it—love it or hate it. In this context, my ultimate relationship to the truth can no longer be based on theory but on practice.[65]

The rediscovery of truth should come about according to the mode of worthy glorification or confession. The French philosopher offers this definition of saturated phenomenon: "Neither a sermon on things, nor the manifestation of the thing, but the event of an obviousness which reveals itself only as much as I tolerate its excess."[66] One must love truth to accept knowledge. Let us take an example. In Book XII of *The City of God* Augustine considers the expression "ages of ages" (XII, 20, p. 217). He does not affirm anything; he is not sure ("I dare not decide"). Yet the idea of a Divine Wisdom interacting with a created Wisdom is present here as a potentiality. He speaks about ages that "remain unchangeable in God's

64 Augustin, *La Cité de Dieu*, op. cit., 229.
65 *Au lieu de soi*, op. cit., 159.
66 Ibid., 195.

unwavering wisdom, and are the efficient causes, as it were, of those ages which are being spent in time." He even goes so far as to make a comparison with the expression heaven of heaven, *caelum caeli* found in Psalm 148. The notion of "heaven of heaven" is also found in Book XII of the *Confessions*. It is the place where the knowledge of God becomes evident and manifest (but not adequate). In Marion's opinion, the "heaven of heaven" is the equivalent of created Wisdom.[67] It is certainly not the Divine Wisdom, the eternity of God, as it is for Bulgakov. For Augustine, it is about the New Jerusalem which descends from heaven to earth. Augustine had meditated on St. John's apocalyptic vision without necessarily finding interlocutors, allowing him to formulate this vision in theanthropic terms.

Let us first consider the Trinitarian anthropology of Augustine in its relationship to his conception of temporality. Several expressions are indicative of his meditation. He argues that the soul will be the seat of a new beatitude (XII, 21). It is not destined to a "fatal return to the same miseries." Augustine elaborates a trinitarian and sapiential anthropology, unexpected by his commentators because of this saturated phenomenon. For him, temporality is to be found within, not outside, the person. This is why Augustine in his *Confessions* (XI, 20, 26, 14, p. 312) refers to "the present of things past, memory; the present of things present, sight; the present of things future, expectation."[68] In Marion's opinion, there is also "an intentional present" in Augustine's thought which is the condition for the possibility of past, present and future. Time is the distension of the soul, *distentio animi*. The relationship between I and self mirrors this relationship between created and uncreated wisdom. For this reason, Marion criticizes G. Combes' translation of "*hominem temporalem*" as "temporal man" and proposes instead "man immersed in time." Here is his new translation of Chapter XII, 15 of *The City of God*: "Who could investigate this uninvestigable depth, scrutinize this inscrutable depth, that God, of a will without change, created in time a temporalized man before which there were none, and made of humankind, from one man, a multitude?"[69] From this, Marion draws some important phenomenological conclusions:

67 Ibid., 337.
68 Trans. J. G. Pilkington.
69 J.-L. Marion, *Au lieu de soi*, op. cit., 271.

> If time only comes into existence with the world and with the act of creation, if the difference between time and eternity can only be defined by a delay which would itself be temporal, the precedence of God over the ego as well as over the world is before time. The difference between the ego and God—finitude, therefore—consists precisely in the fact that the I alone differs from myself because I temporalize myself. My difference has a temporal expression but does not consist in temporality. My *différance* expresses, in time, my separation from myself but attests my *différance* with what does not differ from self.... The temporalization does not characterize the human person, it defines him as such, *homo temporalis*, who differs from God in that he temporally differs from himself, is behind himself.[70]

Thus, Augustine intuited that time does not imitate anything. It opens the *creatum tempus* (*De civitate Dei* XII, 16, 35, 202) of my absolutely personal decision. For Marion, this is not subjectivism:

> If the distention of the soul temporalizes well the clarity of the passing moments, measuring by an intuition it does not temporalize itself by itself. Its own temporalization happens as an event, but temporality is not only of the distension (*distentio*) of the soul (time of distraction, time of defeat); it can also include attraction (*intentio*) and extraction (*extensio*), that is to say, the time of conversion.[71]

Augustine found in Paul's epistle to the Philippians (3:13–14) this ability of the soul to rediscover itself by extending beyond itself: "I give no thought to what lies behind (*distraction*) but push on to what is ahead (by *intention*). My entire attention is on the finish line (*extension*) as I run to the prize to which God calls me—life on high in Jesus Christ." This is the capacity of the converted soul, of a desire that has been transfigured in Christ Jesus to participate in "the things that remain."

We can now conclude our analysis of the evolution of the paradigm of orthodoxy through the historiographical work of Augustine. According to the American historian Carol Harrison, Augustine had to sacrifice the

70 Ibid., 271.

71 Ibid., 304; 310.

*recta jubilatio* of the *Confessions* to the *recta fides* of *The City of God*.[72] This judgment needs to be clarified. Against the cyclic visions of antiquity, Augustine "rightly rejoices" in the eternity of a God who is always present in the most intimate depths of every person. But he is also "faithful" to Scripture even where understanding is lacking, and to its dimension of truth, to its "right truth," its historical truth, to the realism of the Scriptural narratives. But Augustine argues badly, whether about the Greek chronology (from a fanciful representation of the beginning of history) or the *Timaeus* of Plato (that admits to the beginning of the world but attributes it to a demiurge very different from the God-Creator of Scripture; cf. *Timaeus* 28ab). Influenced by his polemic with Pelagius, Augustine can go as far as to imagine a theodicy without the representation of a just God who, according to the Letter of St. James, has not created evil.

As is increasingly understood today, especially due to the coming together of Christian and Jewish thinkers, the orthodox interpretation of Scripture in the sense of "true and fair knowledge" (which takes into consideration the righteousness of God) can be found in the Christian *gnostic sense* of metahistory, in the recognition of the realistic symbolism of the letters and numbers. It can also be found, and Marion shows that Augustine experienced this, in the trinitarian logic of the human soul which, when turned towards its Creator, actualizes, in Christ by the Spirit, the coming together of created Wisdom with divine Wisdom. According to this eschatological interpretation of Scripture, creation is not complete. There is a continuous-discontinuous interrelation between created Wisdom (light and darkness, time of the accomplished and unaccomplished) and the uncreated Wisdom (Wisdom of God), between the earthly Jerusalem and the heavenly Jerusalem. This is the time of beatitude, of the 8th day, which begins and does not end, of the encounter of the musical scale of created Wisdom and the unique voice of divine Wisdom.

## ECCLESIAL HISTORIOGRAPHY AFTER EUSEBIUS AND AUGUSTINE

As we have seen, the Augustinian knowledge of the divine mysteries is situated between the purely doxological approach of the first centuries of

72 G. Demacopoulos and A. Papanikolaou, eds., *Orthodox Readings of Augustine*, Crestwood, SVSP, 2008.

Christianity and the strictly rational approach which will later be progressively characteristic of Western medieval theology after Hugh of St. Victor. Eusebius can also be said to be a transitional figure. He uses the concept of *eusebia* to signify an aspect of his new representation of orthodoxy. This term, which denotes the correct manner of living one's faith, becomes central not only in the writings of Eusebius but also in those of the Church Fathers. *Eusebia* opposes *asebia*, that is to say, heresy. Since, because of the polemics with Arius, the *doxa* was magnetized by a sense of correct opinion (knowledge is henceforth associated with faith, *pistis*, rather than the progression of the preceding period), it was necessary that its worship reemerged with a different meaning. The dimension of piety associated with orthodox thought took from Eusebius a sense of the fear of God. It is not yet a question of fear as was often the case, at least on the level of popular piety, in the West from the 14th century and in the East from the 16th century.[73] It is more a sense of responsibility towards the Pantocrator. For the line that divided the saved and the damned passed between those who had this fear and those who did not know it.

For Glenn Chestnut, it is the pious life of the emperor that represents as of the 4th century the paradigm of right truth. That is why the emperor was expected to be a model of piety, committed to the defense of doctrinal orthodoxy.[74] The vision of a cosmic Eucharist preserved by the liturgy was then sustained by the concept of piety. Since *gnosis*, in the sense of right glorification producing knowledge, was no longer understood, since it was the source of dangerous heresies, and especially and above all since the emperor imposed an official *doxa* which was to be homogenous for all, a disassociation took place between the worship of the heavenly things and the understanding of them. The consequence of all this was to put the *eusebia*-cult in context as one of the characteristics of the Catholic religion, and to transform orthodox thought into a sacred knowledge of the divine mysteries, necessarily apophatic, based on dogma, capable of understanding and therefore organizing both the visible and invisible worlds. This led to the disintegration of the gnostic synthesis of Christians of the first three centuries. Traces of this evolution can be found in the writings of Cyril of Jerusalem (c. 315–387), one of the

73 Jean Delumeau, *Le péché et la peur: La culpabilisation en Occident (XIII–XVIII siecles)*, Paris, Fayard 1983; Nicholas Berdyaev, "Deux compréhensions du christianisme (Au sujet de la discussion sur l'ancien et le nouveau dans le christianisme)," *Put'*, no. 36, 12/32, 17–43 (in Russian).

74 G. Chestnut, op. cit., 123.

most venerated Fathers of the Church in both the East and the West. His definition of the Catholic Church is worth a mention:

> The Church is called catholic because it is spread through the whole world, from one end of the earth to the other, and because it teaches, in a manner both universal and complete, all the doctrines [*dogmata*] that a person should know concerning things visible and invisible, in heaven and on earth. It is also called catholic because it brings all of humanity, the governors and the governed, the literate and the illiterate into correct worship [*eusebeiai cultui*] and because it is a universal treatment and cure for every kind of sin committed by the soul or the body, and possesses within it every conceivable virtue, be that by its deeds, or words, or in spiritual graces of every description.[75]

The works of Eusebius have left an impressive legacy even till this day, but they were especially influential in the period prior to the 16th century. Jerome (340–410) became aware of the *Chronicles* of Eusebius during his stay in Constantinople in 380/381 and began translating them into Latin.[76] The *Chronicles* also became the model for the chronicles of the Gallic priest Sulpicius Severus (c. 360–420), who also wrote a *Life of St. Martin*, and those of Prosper of Aquitaine, Isidore of Seville (c. 570–636), et al. *Ecclesiastical History* was translated and extended up until 395 by Rufinus of Aquileia (c. 340–410), by Sozomen (c. 400–443) until 425, by Theodoret of Cyrus (393–c. 460) until 428, and up to 439 by Socrates the Scholastic (c. 380–c. 450). H. Leclercq considers that after these writers and until the modern age there were "only chronicles, annals, episodic narratives or national histories."[77] Similarly, the Russian historian V. Bolotov affirms that after Eusebius and Socrates and until Nicephorus Calliste Xanthopoulos, a Byzantine monk and historian who died around 1350 and who authored an *Ecclesiastical History* (covering the period up to 610) in 18 volumes, one does not find in the East a history of the Church which distinguishes in a

75 J.-P. Migne, Cyril of Jerusalem, *Opera Quae Existant Omnia*, PG 33, *Catechesis* XVIII, Petit Montrouge, 1857, 1044 (trans. AA).

76 An Armenian translation discovered in Jerusalem in 1787 made the two sections available.

77 H. Leclercq, "Historiens du christianisme," op. cit., 2565.

specific manner the Fathers of the history of the Church.[78] The principle characteristic of this new orthodox history is that the political and the religious are so interwoven that the narrative does not differentiate between the history of the Church and that of the State. Thus the *History* of Nicetas Choniates (1155–1215/16), which covers the period between the reign of John II Comnenus and the fall of Constantinople in 1204, was a pro-Latin history, favorable to the resistance of the Lascaris dynasty. It is for this reason that the author of *The Treasure of Orthodoxy* used negative terms to depict the patriarchs compromised with Byzantine decadence.

In the West, according to Bolotov, "histories became local," but the Russian historian does not consider that they brought anything new to the model proposed by Eusebius. Gregory of Tours (c. 538–c. 594), Venerable Bede (637–735) and Paul Warnefrid (797) will merely unite their people, or simply their monastery, to the post-Carolingian period and to the overall history of Christianity. The *Liber Pontificalis* at Rome preserved the remembrance of the successors of Peter. Generally, however, such histories only recorded isolated events. Leclercq makes this severe diagnostic of medieval historiography: "By a strange coincidence, the Middle Ages proved to be as inept at conceiving and executing an historical synthesis as it was incapable of representing an artistic perspective. The frescos and paintings which this period left behind depict episodes and individuals on the same plane, buildings encroach upon one another, bodies flow into each other in combinations that are absolutely impossible. Any overview is absent."[79] This judgment should be nuanced, however, for if there was a weakening of historical consciousness, there was, on the other hand, a deepening of juridical awareness. *The Book of Sentences* by Peter Lombard is an anthology of patristic texts that had a considerable influence on Western medieval law. Even though Western authors are widely preferred over Eastern writers, Lombard points out the consistency between Augustine of Hippo (cited 680 times) and John Damascene (cited 26 times) according to the principle that "no one Person of the Trinity surpasses the other in grandeur."[80] Only a few historians of any talent can be found in the 13th century. In the East, Gregory Bar Hebreus (†1286) is the author of an *Ecclesiastical Chronicle* which allows one to become better acquainted with the history of the

78 Vassili Vassilievitch Bolotov, *Letski po istorii drevniei Tserkvi*, vol. 1, Petrograd, 1918.

79 H. Leclercq, op. cit., 2600.

80 P. Lombard, *Sentences*, first version of 1155, Book I, Distinction 19, chapter IX.

Western and Eastern Syrian Church. In the West, Geoffrey of Villehardouin wrote a *Chronicle* which narrates the 4th Crusade and Joinville produced a *History of St. Louis*. After this brief burst of energy, Christian historiography seemed to die out during the 14th and 15th centuries. Leclercq's judgment is even more terse: "nothing more is left . . . theology has invaded everything and dried up all that is not itself."[81] There will not be another return to history until the Reformation. But for that to happen, there has to be a new configuration of the relationship between faith and reason, between the poles of knowledge, cult, memory and justice.

## THE END OF A STAGE OF HISTORICAL CONSCIOUSNESS

Before turning to the historiographical renewal inspired by the Reformation, a few words should be said about the *Memoirs* of Sylvester Syropoulos dedicated to the Council of Florence.[82] This work marks the end of a period in the historic consciousness of orthodox Christianity. Eusebius of Caesarea had been identified with the first ecumenical council and its debates, unresolved in his opinion, on the relationship between the Father and the Son within the Trinity. The Council of Nicaea, as we have seen, influenced the political representation of the history of the Church which disassociated the life of the world from the life of the Christian community while unifying everything around the figure of the *basileus*. In a similar way, the incapability of Sylvester Syropoulos to accept the decisions of the Council of Florence from 1438–1439 is characteristic of this essentially political representation of orthodoxy. This had a decisive influence on subsequent historiography. But if Eusebius became the thurifer of caesaropapism, Syropoulos, along with other intellectuals of that generation, went so far as to favor "the turban to the tiara."[83] At the beginning of this political period of the Church, when piety and doctrine started to dissociate, Eusebius became the long-term historian of the ecclesial progression from the first apostles to the imperial council of Nicaea. At the end of this period, at the point when, in the West, the nation-states were beginning to conspire against the power of the pope

81 H. Leclercq, op. cit., 2610.

82 V. Laurent, *Les Mémoires du grand Ecclesiarque de l'Eglise de Constantinople Sylvestre Syropoulos sur le concile de Florence (1438–39)*, Rome, Oriental Pontifical Institute, 1971.

83 This is a famous phrase which the chronicle compiler Doukas attributes to Loukas Notaras prior to the fall of Constantinople. V. Grecu, *Ducas. Istoria turco-byzantina (1341–1462)*, Bucharest, 1958.

and when, in the East, the Church was brutally discovering the consequences of a de-ecclesialized State, Syropoulos was the short-term memorialist, the last witness, of the "symphonic" model of medieval orthodoxy.

The personality and most important writings of the "Great Ecclesiarch of the Church of Constantinople" have been made known thanks especially to the work of the Assumptionist Vitalien Laurent, a research scientist at the Centre National de la Recherche Scientifique and an expert in the Vatican for the Congregation for the Doctrine of the Faith. Syropoulos was born around 1400 in a renowned family of ecclesiastics attached to the Great Church of Constantinople. After his theological studies, he became an executive of the patriarchal administrative apparatus rather than a true theologian. Around 1430 he became a Grand Ecclesiarch, one of the highest patriarchal offices within the patriarchal curia. From 1438–39, he actively participated in the Council of Florence and signed the decree of union. In spite of what the Byzantine historian Ducas[84] reports, in the years that followed the council, there were no mass protests or any organized resistance in Constantinople to the decisions of the council. There were certainly anti-unionists, with Mark of Ephesus as a leading figure. Syropoulos, who, on his return from the council, regretted having signed the act of union, wrote his *Memoirs* of the council from 1444–1445 to justify his position. But, as V. Laurent writes: "on the eve of the Turkish conquest, the movement was not as widespread as the polemical literature of the time would have us believe."[85] It seems, however, that the respect accorded by the new emperor Constantine XII (1449–1453) to the anti-unionists precipitated Scholarios' anti-unionist turnaround as one of the main actors of the council. The latter resigned from his office as high judge and first secretary of the Patriarch and became a monk under the name of Gennadius in 1450. Syropoulos, anticipating that the political situation was about to change, also left office. However, on December 14, 1452, ten metropolitans and a great many clergy still participated in the liturgy at St. Sophia and proclaimed the decree of unity in the presence of the emperor and the constituted bodies. There are conflicting accounts of the fate of Sylvester Syropoulos after the fall of Constantinople. Some historians say that he died during the taking of the city. V. Laurent, however, points out

84 Ducas, *Historia*, XXXI, 9 (ed. Bonn, 120–210). The unionist historian attributes the fall of Constantinople to the renunciation of the Council of Florence and proceeds to purposely demean the bishops who participated in the council by accusing them of simony and giving an exaggerated description of their postconciliar maneuvers.

85 Ibid., 13.

that a patriarch by the name of Sophronius Syropoulos appears in the years after the fall of Constantinople (most certainly from the summer of 1463 to July of 1464) and, on the basis of a synodal document of 1488, considers it very plausible that this is our historian.[86] He died at the age of 65 from a "tragic fall," probably after having been dismissed from the synod.

The *Memoirs* of Syropoulos was transcribed by Theodore Agallianos who was also archon and friend of the author, who Vitalien describes as a "primary and unconditional Orthodox." They were published in Leiden in 1660. Catholic historiography was severely critical of these writings while Orthodox historians, such as Georges Coresios (†1660), Patriarch Dositheos of Jerusalem (†1707) and A. Diamantopoulos[87] heaped praise on them in an equally monolithic manner. A few Orthodox theologians and historians such as Sergius Bulgakov and Professor D. Geanakoplos, distanced themselves from Syropoulos if only by arguing that a virulent anti-unionist who had signed the decree of union could hardly have a perfectly objective perspective concerning the events he narrates.[88] On the Catholic side, the analysis of V. Laurent is also more nuanced. Although he appreciates the tremendous value of the testimony of Syropoulos as a protagonist and direct witness of the events he describes, the French historian cannot but note the approximations, the omissions and the excessive subjectivity of this testimony. Confronted with the fundamentalists of his time, Syropoulos had to plead the cause of those who, like himself, signed the decree of union out of weakness. Only 15 pages of the 250-page text are dedicated to the public sessions of the Council of Florence, and mainly due to the many indignities Syropoulos suffered in his own milieu for having been a signatory, he does not hesitate to introduce falsehoods which J. Gill and V. Laurent have unmasked with authority. When there is a contradiction between the *Memoirs* and the *Acts* of the council, Joseph Gill gives preference to the

86 V. Laurent, "Les premiers patriarches de Constantinople sous la domination turque (1454–1476). Succession et chronologie d'après un catalogue inédit," *Revues des études byzantines*, vol. 26 (1968): 229–63.

87 Adamantios Diamantopoulos, "Guennadios Scholarios" in *Hellenika*, IX, Athens (1936): 285–308. He had previously published a book on Mark of Ephesus at Athens in 1899.

88 S. Bulgakov, *U Sten Khersonisa*, Yalta, 1923, in *Troudy po sotsiologui*, Moscow, Naouka 1997; *Sous les remparts de Chersonnèse*, French translation by B. Marchadier, Paris, Ad solem, 1999. The Russian theologian esteemed that the Council of Florence was the 8th ecumenical council, recognized as such by the Orthodox Church, since no subsequent ecumenical council had rejected it; D. Geanakoplos, "Edward Gibbon and Byzantine Ecclesiastical History," *Church History*, XXXV (1966): 170–85.

*Acts* and explains why.[89] In the view of V. Laurent: "The materiality of the facts is actually most often irreproachable; their presentation and their interpretation alone are problematic, not only for the Catholic, but also for the scholar freed from any confessional constraint."[90] In this chapter, the *Memoirs* of Syropoulos are, above all, characteristic of a paradigm of orthodoxy which effectively led to the submission of spiritual power to political power in spite of its recognition of the separation between sound doctrine and *raison d'Etat*. The reasons Syropoulos gives for putting his own signature to the decree of union, even though it was written five years after the events, are significant in this respect:

> Since this is the command of our Master the Emperor and given that everyone believes that this will benefit the City and promote the unity of Christians, I do not want to seem to not desire the conservation and flourishing of our motherland or oppose its best interests, its progress, its usefulness for Christians and all the other advantages that are expected to be gained for the City. Therefore, out of necessity, I follow the majority and obey the order and will of the Emperor but I still protest that it is not out of conviction nor by free choice that I give my opinion that what I am going to approve represents the sound doctrine of our Church. God knows the dispositions of my soul, that I do not accept what is happening and am not going to sign willingly. I submit this affair to His Mercy! I am acting in this manner for the moment, but there is always the possibility of doing what I really want to do later on.[91]

Whatever may be said, there was an in-depth encounter between orthodox Christians of the East and the West in Florence. Contemporary historiography has shown that, in spite of their differences, the overwhelming majority of the participants in the Council of Florence considered that what united them was far greater than what divided them. According to Emmanuel Lanne, a monk and scholar at Chevetogne Abbey, "the Council of Florence realized, at least theoretically, unity in diversity to an extent never before

89 J. Gill, *The Council of Florence,* Cambridge, 1959, 4–8; and *Personalities of the Council of Florence,* Barnes and Nobles, 1964, 144–77.

90 V. Laurent, op. cit., 32.

91 The *Memoires* of S. Syropoulos, ed. V. Laurent, 493.

realized in previous councils and gave it a certain ecclesiological foundation."[92] Admittedly, theological concerns probably counted for less in this unity of view than did political considerations. One side was preoccupied with the advances of the Ottoman troops in certain regions of the Byzantine Empire while others were concerned with pretensions of superiority over the pope on the part of the delegates from the Council of Basil (1431–33). E. Lanne has a point when he asserts that the ecclesiology of the papal Bull *Laetentur Caeli* was still very monolithic and reluctant to admit a plurality of liturgical expressions. For Cécile Caby, the problem was essentially cultural. She states: "Basically, neither of the two sides understands the other, not only because they do not speak the same language (hence the unceasing work of the translators, including Traversari) but also because they refer to two distinct traditions as the foundation of orthodoxy (the Greek Fathers are no longer read in the West, apart from in a few anthologies), and they attribute a different role to each in the formation of orthodoxy: hence the need to resort to people not only familiar with both traditions but also convinced of their continuity." But one has to be wary of anachronisms in terms of ecumenical expectations. The proceedings of the council bear witness, above all, to the long and profound discussions among the Byzantine and Latin delegates. The reason for the failure of the council can be found more in its reception by peoples who had progressively distanced themselves from one another on a cultural level rather than because of any hypothetical structural incompatibility between the Eastern and Western Churches. Moreover, the non-reception of the Council of Florence

92 Emmanuel Lanne in "Uniformité et pluralisme" points out that, both on the question of the *Filioque* and that of papal primacy, the Council of Florence recognized a pluralism or legitimate diversity between the Greek and Latin positions. On the crucial question of the *Filioque*, the participants at the council had a real theological discussion where the two points of view, that of the Eastern Church and that of the Western Church, could express themselves. The Bull of Union, however, affirms that "with different formulas, all understood the same reality." Certainly, Roman primacy was strongly affirmed but "all the rights and privileges of the patriarchs" were maintained. The pope could not convoke an ecumenical council on his own and could not judge a patriarch in a Roman court. In addition, the Greeks succeeded in obtaining that the recognition of Roman primacy was accompanied by a clause that this primacy be interpreted "according to what is contained in the acts of the ecumenical councils and the holy canons." On the minor question of unleavened bread, local customs were recognized. As for the beatific vision, a watered-down version of the Latin formula was approved but the Latins did not impose on the Greeks that the blessed contemplated God face to face. G. Alberigo, ed., *Christian Unity: The Council of Ferrera-Florence (1438–39)*, Leuven, 1991, 364, 359.

must itself be relativized. In Muscovy, for example, the Church rejected the council. But, as A. Houssiau, the bishop of Liège, has pointed out in his article "Reception and Rejection of a Conciliary Consensus,"[93] the desire for national autonomy was more important than the preoccupation with affirming catholic unity.[94] One must also take into consideration, a fact emphasized by W. Hrynewicz, that Metropolitan Isidore received an enthusiastic welcoming at Kiev in 1441 on his return from the Council of Florence.[95] Thus, the memory of the council was not as homogeneous as the 19th century historians tended to believe. As late as 1498, the patriarch of Constantinople, Joachim I, could confirm Joseph Bolharinovitch as metropolitan of Kiev even though the latter was the author of a proposal to restore the unity of Florence. Bolharinovitch's position was supported by some eminent personalities, at least until the confessional and exclusive soteriology of the Council of Trent (outside of the Catholic Church there is no salvation) became more widely known. In Poland, the philosopher and theologian Stanislaus Orzechowski (†1566), the son of a Catholic father and Orthodox mother, was one of the principal promoters of the concept of double loyalty which would enable the communion of one Church with other Churches not in communion with each other, and he was also one of the founders of political science in the Slavic language.

Let us take some examples of the new syntheses between Eastern and Western Christians which took place at the time of the council and shortly afterwards. Nicholas of Cusa (1401–1464), a diplomat, mathematician, astronomer and philosopher, was a brilliant and ecumenical figure. He was the first to question the authenticity of the *Donation of Constantine*, which handed over the Papal States to the pope. In his *Catholic Concordance*, he proposed a far-reaching program of political and ecclesiastical reforms which prefigured the end of the political paradigm of orthodoxy. Nicholas of Cusa was well-acquainted with the Greek world, and was sent to Constantinople in 1437 by Pope Eugenius IV to invite the emperor and patriarch to participate

93 In *The Council*, op. cit., 516.

94 As I. Pavlov has shown, the humiliating treatment that Metropolitan Isidore received in Moscow after the council was due more to his Greek roots than to his pretended betrayal of the orthodox faith. "If he had occupied the seat of Kiev-Moscow a few decades earlier, he would have left an entirely different impression on the Russians." I. Pavlov, "The Ferrara-Florentine Union. A View from Moscow," *The Council*, op. cit., 503.

95 W. Hrynewicz, "The Florentine Union Reception and Rejection," *The Council*, op. cit., 522.

in the Council of Ferrara.[96] While at sea, returning from Greece, probably influenced by the theology of uncreated energies, he had the intuition of *learned ignorance*. His treatise, the first draft of a theanthropic religious philosophy, ended with a new representation of Church unity, not as a body subjected to a pontiff or emperor, but as "the hypostatic unity of natures in Christ."[97] His rediscovery of apophatic theology enabled him to establish an important distinction between the Church militant, marked by human divisions, and the Church triumphant, always one in Christ, a prophetic vision which unites all humanity in God in the Eucharist, including the philosophers of Antiquity.[98]

> And when we detach ourselves from the Church militant at our resurrection, we can arise only in Christ, so that in this way there will also be *one* church of those who are triumphant, each remaining in his own order. And at that time the truth of our flesh will exist not in itself but in the truth of Christ's flesh; and the truth of our body will exist only in the truth of Christ's body; and the truth of our spirit will exist in the truth of the spirit of Christ Jesus, as branches exist in the vine—so that there is by Christ only one humanity among all men, and one spirit, that of Christ, in all spirits—so that each one will be in Him, just as there is only one Christ formed from the reunion of all. And then whoever in this life receives any one of all of those who are Christ's receives Christ; and what is done to one of the least of His is done to Christ. By comparison, whoever injures Plato's hand injures Plato; and whoever injures the smallest part of a man injures the whole man.[99]

The Italian humanist Lorenzo Valla (1407–1457), who participated in the council, bears witness to the renewal of Christian orthodox thought in Italy which was no longer satisfied with the work of Thomas Aquinas and

96 He had as a disciple in France the humanist Lefèvre d'Etaples who edited his works in 1514.

97 N. de Cues, *De la docte ignorance*, Paris, ed. De la Maisne, PUF, 1930, Book III, chapter XII.

98 This vision also inspired his *De Pace Fidei* which shows that the divisions among the Churches are to be found on the plane of customs and rites but cannot affect the mystical unity of the Church.

99 Ibid., Book III, chapter XII, 55.

by extension with a scholasticism overly dependent on Aristotelianism.[100] Favorable to a new humanistic theology in which "*ars bene vivendi*" would be inseparable from "*ars bene dicendi*," he proposed a return to the theology of Basil of Caesarea and Ambrose of Milan.[101] He served as a great model for Erasmus (1466 or 1469–1536) who, like Valla, gave rhetoric precedence over metaphysics insofar as the former was able to convince, exhort, and finally to act orthopraxically.[102] Erasmus himself was a product of the *Devotio Moderna*, a movement founded by Geerte Grote (†1384) who, influenced by the mystical theology of Henry Suso, Tauler and Eckhart, called for a renewal of piety among lay people, for the reading of the Bible in the vernacular and for a rejection of scholastic dialectics in favor of an inner spiritual life. Following Thomas à Kempis, the author of *The Imitation of Christ* (c. 1407), Erasmus urged a return to the reading of the "patres orthodoxi," namely Jerome, John Chrysostom, Augustine, and Dionysius the Areopagite.[103]

Tommaso Parentucelli (1398–1455) also participated in the Council of Florence. In 1447 he was elected pope and called upon Lorenzo Valla to serve as apostolic notary. Together they made Rome the center in the West of patristic studies, a work continued by Popes Pius II (1458–1464) and Sixtus IV (1471–1484).[104] But the Bull *Romanus pontifex,* issued January 8,

100 As early as the 14th century in the West, Petrarch (1304–1374) wrote of a "*docta pietas*," which eloquently combined piety with wisdom, whereas in the East, Gregory Palamas (1296–1359) revived the teachings of the Church Fathers and developed a theology of uncreated energies to imagine humanity's participation in the work of God.

101 Charles Stinger, "Italian Renaissance Learning and the Church Fathers," Irena Backus, *The Reception of the Church Fathers in the West*, Leiden, Brill, 1997, 473–510.

102 In the opinion of J. Chomarat, Erasmus always preferred "piety to dogmas, eloquence to dialectics and realities to systems," J. Chomarat, *Grammaire et rhétorique chez Erasme*, Paris, 1981, 543.

103 Even though there are differences between the theology of Suso and that of Meister Eckhart, this generation of mystical masters had recourse to the pre-scholastics who "still used the term imitation as much as they did that of participation." P. Javelet, *Image et ressemblance au XIIième siècle de saint Anselme à Alain de Lille,* Strasbourg, 1967, 9.

104 The article by C. Stinger gives an idea of the extraordinary patristic renewal and intellectual creativity of the Byzantine and Latin humanists of this period. We can cite Marsilio Ficino who took an interest in sophiology, Giovanni Pico della Mirandola who did a commentary on the Kabbalah, Giles of Viterbo who composed a whole theology based on the Divine Names. John O'Malley esteems that this patristic renewal led to an "incarnational soteriology" among the Roman humanists. The rediscovery of the dignity of the person made deification possible as well as the providential interventions of God in human history. For the humanists, who were marked by the spiritual fervor

1455 by Nicholas V, revealed the hold that the old paradigm maintained over people of the Renaissance. As Vicar of Christ, the humanist pope continued to want to act as arbiter of the Spanish and Portuguese empires and gave the King of Portugal the authorization to reduce the Saracens to perpetual servitude. The popes did not want to listen to the warnings of the people of the Quattrocento. Half a century later, on May 23, 1498, the Italian Dominican and reformer Girolamo Savonarola (1452–1498) was burned at the stake. His criticism of the Roman Curia, which he called "a proud and lying whore," was not heard. But Savanarola's own attempt at theocratic dictatorship in the city of Florence (1494–1498) failed. The medieval political model was to collapse shortly after.

Thus, the attitude of both Sylvester Syropoulos and Tommaso Parentucelli during the years following the council show that, despite the intellectual renewal and the liturgically sealed reunion in the Cathedral of Florence on July 6, 1439, the unity of Christians was not possible without calling into question the political theology of Caesero-papism or Papo-caesarism. As we have seen with Eusebius and Augustine, this political theory was closely linked to the same paradigm of orthodoxy as right truth. Such a representation of orthodoxy, understood as progressively independent of other poles of orthodoxy, namely worthy glorification, faithful memory and true and just knowledge, left free rein to the most indefensible excesses of the representatives, considering themselves exclusive of God on earth, be it the pope, the emperor or the dictator of a city. The historiography of the ensuing confessional period of orthodoxy will rewrite, over the ashes of wounded memories, a polemic and proselyte history of the council. At the beginning of the 16th century, there no longer existed any trace of the Latin version of the *Acta* of the Council of Florence.[105]

---

of the Fathers of the Church, the reform signified, above all, a moral and personal reformation which should culminate in more social justice.

105 cf. Ihor Sevcenko, "Intellectual repercussions of the council of Florence," *Church History* 24 (1955): 291–323. Marie-Hélène Blanchet, "La question de l'Union des Eglises (13th–15th siecle): historiographie et perspectives," *Revue des études byzantines*, vol. 61 (2003): 5–48.

CHAPTER 9

# *The "Faithful Memory" from the Annals of Magdebourg to the Paths of Russian Theology by Georges Florovsky*

IN HIS *PENSÉES,* THE MATHEMATICIAN AND PHILOSOPHER Blaise Pascal (1623–1662) affirmed that "the history of the Church should be more properly called the history of truth."[1] He considered Christianity as the true religion insofar as it rests on the fulfillment of prophecies and predictions.[2] "Then came Jesus Christ who is called the Messiah . . . and that clearly shows the truth of the prophecies."[3] In this way Pascal retrieved the regime of truth brought to light by Peter at Pentecost. Christ has fulfilled the Scriptures and this, proclaimed the leader of the apostles, is the strongest proof of his identity as the Son of God. According to this logic, thought is true when it frees itself from "natural reason," from the *cogito* as the unique source of truth, when it makes faithful and confident progress. Pascal writes:

1 Pascal, *Pensées*, Paris, ed. Brunschvig, no. 858, p. 207. Prior to this statement, Pascal had written: "There would be too much obscurity if the truth did not have visible signs. One admirable sign is that of being always (preserved) in a visible Church and a visible assembly of people. There would be too much clarity if there were only an opinion in this Church; what there has always been in the Church is truth for the true has always been there and nothing false has ever been there" (no. 857).

2 "I see several contrary religions, founded on false premises except one. Every religion wants to be believed on its own authority and threatens the unbelievers. On these terms, I don't believe them. Anybody can say that, anybody can call himself a prophet. But I see the Christian religion where I find the prophecies and that is something not anyone can do." Ibid., no. 693, p. 160.

3 Ibid., no. 738, p. 181.

> I admit that one of these Christians that believes without proof will perhaps not have what it takes to convince an infidel who says the same about himself. But those who have the proof of religion will prove without difficulty that this faithful one is truly inspired by God, although he cannot prove it himself. Since God having said in his prophets [prophecies] that in the reign of Jesus Christ he would pour his Spirit upon the nations, and that the sons, the daughters and the children of the Church would prophesy, it is without a doubt that the Spirit of God is upon them, and that it is not on the others. Instead of complaining that God remains hidden, you should give thanks for all that He has revealed; and you will be more faithful to him for not making himself known to the proud sages, unworthy of knowing such a holy God. Two sorts of people know Him: those who have a humble heart and who love lowliness, whatever their degree of intellect, high or low; or those who have enough intellect to see the truth, whatever opposition they encounter . . .[4]

This philosophical attitude, based on a memory of the word of truth, was not pure irrationalism. In the face of an enigma or a dispute among the faithful, Pascal recommended trusting "the Fathers and Tradition" (no. 775). This regime of faithful memory, radically opposed to the new rationality centered on the *cogito* of René Descartes (1596–1650), became paradigmatic in the Christian consciousness of modern times. It goes without saying that this break between faith and reason had lamentable consequences for both the East and the West. The breach also had political consequences. The only properly theological text promulgated by the Holy See during the whole course of the French Revolution was the Bull *Auctorem Fidei* of August 28, 1794.[5] This text, which was not directly concerned with the Declaration of the Rights of Man and of the Citizen but rather with the Jansenist heresy, constitutes a visible trace of the pervasiveness of the memorial paradigm in Catholic consciousness. By questioning the *Acts* of the Synod of Pistoia (18–26 September 1786)—presided over by the reformist and Jansenist bishop

4 Ibid., nn. 287–88, pp. 68–69.

5 Philippe Boutry, "Tradition et autorité dans la théologie catholique au tournant des XVIIIe et XIXe siècles," in *Histoire et Théologie*, under the direction of J.-D. Durand, Paris, Beauchesne (1994): 59–82.

Scipione de Ricci and by the authority of the Grand Duke of Tuscany, the future Emperor Leopold II (who at the time protected the Jansenists)—Pope Pius VI (1717–1799) set out first and foremost to contradict the heretical argument relating to "the obscuration of truth" in the Church. According to Philippe Boutry, this argument was one of the *topoi* of the 18th century Italian and European-Jansenist polemic. Relying on an incarnational theology, and thus the idea of the visibility of truth, the pope defended the authority of the powers of the Roman pontiff on the basis of Tradition and the argument of a "sacred deposit which Christ has confided to the Church."[6]

## ORTHODOXY AS FAITHFUL MEMORY

The identity dimension of orthodox thought has always been one of the essential components of Christian consciousness, as mentioned previously on several occasions. During the first three centuries of the Christian era, the act of *anamnesis*, intricately linked to the Eucharistic celebration, contributed to the formation of an essentially doxological, eschatological and messianic identity. During the following era it reappeared as the constitutive foundation of the orthodoxy of faith. Thus, after the victory of the iconodules over the iconoclasts, the celebration of the triumph of orthodoxy became, in large part, fidelity of the Church to the Council of Nicaea, insofar as the Fathers of the Second Council of Nicaea pointed out that in 325 the 318 Fathers had venerated the holy images. We have also seen that, after the 5th century, historiography progressively lost its originality both in the East and in the West. It primarily sought to adhere to a tradition of fidelity to a historic patron saint as instituted by Eusebius. It is customary to bring the patristic period to a close with St. John Damascene. His exposition of the orthodox faith is so eloquent because it so clearly affirms the memorial foundation of orthodoxy. He wrote: "He who does not believe according to the tradition of the Catholic Church . . . is an infidel."[7] Yet we have seen that during this second period of the evolution of orthodox ecclesial consciousness, the identity dimension of orthodox Christians was always in a situation of dependence upon political power. It was the Empress Irene who affirmed the cult of icons. During the era of Christendom, infidelity had an essentially political

6 According to the expression of Cardinal Hyacinth Gerdil, one of the principle protagonists of the Bull.

7 St. John Damascene, *Exposé de la foi orthodoxe*, IV, chapter 10, PG 94:1128.

significance. The crusades against the Albigensians or the Saracens are undeniable proof. From its beginnings, the Church had set up very different rules for questioning, excluding or reintegrating the Christian who did not share the traditional narrative of origins. We have also seen that in the 13th to 15th centuries, both in the East (with the theology of uncreated energies) and in the West (with scholastic thought) medieval theology sought to emancipate itself from a repetitive and unenlightening use of tradition.

In modern times, things will change to such a point that the term believer will be used to refer to the orthodox Christian.[8] An identity is established between the faith and the bearer of faith. The faithful person is the one who professes what is considered the true religion. According to St. Paul, fidelity is to adorn the doctrine of "God our Savior" (Titus 2:10). Moreover, at the dawn of modernity, there appears a growing awareness that it was not only Peter, Andrew and their successors who were responsible for the deposit of faith and its transmission but the whole Church. This spiritual renewal was the fruit of a fresh fervor born of a renewed desire for conversion. In its beginnings, this corresponded to the Greek notion of *metanoia*, a radical change of life inspired by an awareness of God's personal love and one's sinfulness. John Calvin (1509–1564), Ignatius of Loyola (1491–1556), Maximus the Greek (†1556) and Teresa of Avila (1515–1582) are examples of typical 16th century "converts." It was only gradually that the term conversion came to designate the membership of a new confession, notably because of the expression of a doctrine of election developed by Calvin.[9] The French term "Protestantism," derived from the Latin *protestans,* only appeared in 1542 and designated the followers of Luther at the Diet of Speyer in 1529. But the term Protestantism as a synonym for an established doctrine only appeared in 1623 and was hardly ever used before the repeal of the Edict of Nantes in 1685. Similarly, the term Anglican, with its meaning of *via media* between Catholicism and Protestantism, between High Church and Low Church, only came about during the Tractarian era of the 1830s.

Marie-Thérèse Nadeau writes that it is the ecclesial community "as a community of believers created by the power of the Word and animated by the Spirit which is ultimately called to witness to the divine truth, to

8 "The faithful have no pretext for following these relaxations which are only offered by the alien hands of these casuists in the place of the sound doctrine which is presented to them through the fraternal hands of their own pastors," Pascal, *Pensées*, op. cit., 212.

9 Yves Krumenacker, *Calvin au-delà des légendes*, Paris, Bayard, 2009.

faithfully transmit it to all in its integrity, with consideration given to the diversity of situations and the evolution of cultures. After all, is it not the Body of Christ in its completeness which has received from Christ Himself the following assurance that 'And behold I am with you always, to the end of the age'?"[10] But in the context of a separation among Christians, there is a danger for orthodox consciousness to compartmentalize matters of faith and matters of reason. When the poles of worship, memory, knowledge, and justice are dissociated, thought seeks to give itself the content of its faith or of its convictions. Hence the reaction shared by all confessions, thinking more and more as Churches, is to attach themselves to the anchor of faithful memory. For some, this would be the inobjectivable and unprovable primacy of Peter,[11] for others it would be the incommensurable and unsurpassable authority of the Holy Scriptures,[12] for still others it would be the indispensable and indisputable authority of the seven ecumenical councils.[13] During modern times, all the confessions seek to defend the orthodox tradition before defending the doctrine itself since the latter has been judged incomprehensible by others. All claim to defend the "sound doctrine," that is to say, the orthodoxy of faith, but each does so by defending its own interpretation of tradition. The confessions, synods and councils of Augsburg (1530), Trent (1545–1563), Brest (1596) or Jerusalem (1672) are perfectly clear in this respect. At its 4th session in 1546, the Council of Trent condemned the interpretation of Scriptures *contra unanimem consensum Patrum*. Calvin challenged

10 Marie-Thérèse Nadeau, *Foi de l'Eglise, évolution et sens d'une formule*, Paris, Beauchesne, 1988, 340.

11 The effort to clarify this doctrine, initiated by Johann Eck around 1525 in his *De primatu Petri*, led to the declaration of papal infallibility at the First Vatican Council on July 18, 1870 in the Constitution *Pastor Aeternus*.

12 In 1516 Erasmus published the original Greek text with the Latin translation of the New Testament. Lorenzo Valla had criticized Jerome's translation of the Vulgate and questioned its fidelity to the original text. The following year, on October 31, 1517, Luther posted his 95 theses on the door of the church of Wittenberg. Theses 65 and 66 are a clear demonstration of the opposition between two interpretations of Church tradition: "65. The treasures of the Gospel are the nets once used to preach to people given over to riches. 66. The treasures of indulgences are the nets now used to ensnare the riches of people."

13 In reply to an appeal of Pius IX (*In suprema Petri Apostoli Sede*) all of the Oriental patriarchs, together with 29 bishops, published a solemn encyclical on May 6, 1848 beseeching the pope, in the name of the tradition of "the seven ecumenical councils," not to promulgate the dogma of infallibility and insisting that the truth is guaranteed by the whole body of the Church.

the Acts of the Council of Trent, claiming them to be based on Tradition and not on Scripture.[14] Calvin stated that he respected the Fathers of the Church but that he read them according to St. Paul. Indeed, Article VII of the Augsburg Confession of 1530 identified the Church with "the congregation of saints, in which the Gospel is rightly taught and the Sacraments are rightly administered." In 1613, Lancelot Andrewes (1555–1626), a lord and bishop of Chichester, presented the sources of Anglican faith to King James I: "*One* canon reduced to writing by God himself, *two* testaments, *three* creeds, *four* general councils, *five* centuries, and the series of Fathers in that period—the centuries that is, before Constantine, and two after, determine the boundary of our faith."[15] Through this memorial renewal the West came to know a true renewal of the patristic tradition.[16]

The drama consisted in the inability of the Churches to comprehend the mutual legitimacy of their specific interpretations of tradition.[17] Gradually, each Church began to regard its own memory as sacred, thereby losing sight of the original logic of orthodoxy as a rediscovery of sound doctrine.[18] As early as the 18th century, the French Calvinist Isaac Casaubon lamented that theology now wanted to adapt the Fathers to the thought of Luther and

14 J. Calvin, *Actes du concile de Trente avec le remède contre le poison*, Geneva 1547, French edition 1548.

15 "Concio latine habita, coram Regie Majestate XIIIe Aprilis, A.D. 1613" in Aula Grenvici, in *Opuscula quaedam posthuma Lanceloti Andrewes episcope Wintoniensis,* Oxford, 1852, 91; trans. Andrewes Hall Theological College and Seminary.

16 Cf. specifically Dominique Bertrand "The Society of Jesus and the Church Fathers in the 16th and 17th century," I. Backus, op. cit., who demonstrates that in the 16th and 17th centuries the Jesuits published more works of the Greek Fathers than of the Latin Fathers because of the affinities of the spirituality of Ignatius of Loyola with the Fathers of the Desert and their art of spiritual discernment. In his *Histoire littéraire du sentiment religieux*, 11 vol., Paris, Jérôme Millon (1916–1933), vol. 5, Henri Brémond writes that the summit of French spirituality was attained in the 17th century and was the result of this influx of Eastern patristic culture.

17 R. Keen has this to say concerning the Catholic theologians of the Counter-Reformation: "The use of the Fathers attests to an auxiliary rather than normative role in the life of the Church. . . . The Christian community, under the guidance of the Holy Spirit, is the source of traditions and the Fathers are its witnesses. The sacraments that were being defended were viewed as traditions, not as doctrines, and the controversialists who appealed to the Fathers' insistence upon the authority of the custom of the Church reflected this understanding of what was at stake." Ralph Keen, *The Fathers in Counter-Reformation Theology in the Pre-Tridentine Period*, I. Backus, op. cit., 735.

18 Théodore de Bèze (1519–1605), *Histoire ecclésiastique des Eglises réformées au Royaume de France* (1580). In this major collective opus, the Protestant historian and biographer of Calvin has the Holy Spirit intervening in the institutional history of the Reformation.

Calvin rather than the other way around.[19] In the 12th century, in Constantinople, the Byzantine canonist Theodore Balsamon, who was the Patriarch of Antioch, accepted the principle of translating the liturgies from Greek to the local languages basing himself on the passage of St. Paul (Rom 3:29) where the apostle states that God is not just the God of the Jews but also the God of the Gentiles. Yet in the 19th century it is the principle of loyalty to national tradition that prevails over the principle of understanding in the eastern world. In Russia as in Greece, any authorization to translate the liturgy of St. John Chrysostom into modern Greek, modern Russian or any of the languages of the Orthodox diaspora is out of the question. For Father Congar, the evolution of the rite after the Council of Florence also testifies to the loss of understanding that faith can have diverse expressions: "The rite has become an abstract reality, a thing in itself; it has become reified, an independent entity. . . . The question of the rite has been identified with the very question of the Church."[20] The quarrel over uniatism can easily be understood within this context of tension, both in the East and in the West, between memory over identity and identity over rite.[21] But, as Congar writes, in order to understand the position of Rome, leaving aside real efforts at proselytism which may have taken place here and there, one must adopt an eschatological attitude, an attitude that returns memory to history. For example, it was not the Jesuits who converted Galicia all by themselves but rather the orthodox Galicia that sought to remain faithful to the Council of Florence and maintained its attachment to Rome. For Rome, the Uniate Eastern Churches are, as Congar says, "a sort of promise, somewhat as the presence of Benjamin alongside Judah during the schism of the ten tribes was a promise of a future reunion." It is true, however, that it was not until the early 20th century that a liturgical movement based on the question of the meaning of glorification appeared in the Catholic Church. Dom Lambert Beauduin, one of the leaders of this movement, wanted to put an end to "low" Masses, to celebrations without the participation of

19 Jean-Louis Quantin, "The Fathers in XVII Century Anglican Theology," I. Backus, op. cit., 987.

20 Yves Congar, "Neuf Cents Ans Après. Notes sur le 'Schisme oriental,'" in *1054–1954, L'Eglise et les Eglises*, Chevetogne, editions de Chevetogne, 1954, 40.

21 In this respect, it is interesting to note that certain Ukrainian Greek Catholics who find themselves in conflict with the Orthodox Church have chosen to designate themselves as "pravovernye" rather than "pravoslavnye" — thereby emphasizing the virtue of fidelity (*vernost*) over the concept of glorification (*slava*) which is predominant in modern times.

the faithful, to representations of the liturgy as "a series of painstaking and arbitrary prescriptions imposed, one might believe, to exercise the patience of those who study and fulfill them."[22]

The three principal reasons for this general evolution can be found at its origins. First, the failure of the reception of the Council of Florence in both the East and the West led to Christians being deprived of space for a synodality capable of establishing a common consensus of faith-guided intelligence. The modern era was marked, above all, by this split between faith and reason. The heliocentric revolution (*De Revolutionibus Orbium Coelestium,* 1530) introduced by the canon, canonist and astronomer Nicholas Copernicus (1473–1543) is significant in this respect. During his lifetime Copernicus was not worried about the Church. But in the following century with Galileo, condemned in 1633 by the ecclesiastical court, the context was different. The Reformation and Counter-Reformation, the Thirty Years' War and the formation of international law sanctioning the power of the new nation-states led the Holy See to adopt a defensive and conservative position. This attitude resulted in a distancing of the Church from the scientific world and other humiliations for ecclesial orthodoxy. The Church defended her thesis according to which man and the earth that supports him are at the center of divine thought and therefore at the center of the universe, but it did so using a static and self-enclosed logic. The split with the intellectual elites continued to deepen over the course of the centuries. Certainly, there are notable exceptions. In 1525 Erasmus was translating John Chrysostom's *De Orando Deum*, when he noted that the Archbishop of Constantinople mixed "pleasure with usefulness." Jan den Boeft writes that the Fathers helped Erasmus in his program for the renewal of the Church and of theology towards more purity and simplicity.[23] We know that Luther was violently critical of the humanist of Rotterdam and Louvain, reproaching him for being too interested in heresies, an indication that the reformer also lived in another paradigm, another configuration of orthodoxy. Likewise, the Christian Kabbalah of the universal and cosmopolitan humanist William Postel (1510–1581) could not find its place in the new orthodox thought. Professor at the Collège de France, he was familiar with Greek, Arabic and Syrian. In his utopia *De orbis terrae concordia* written in 1544, he imagined that the political and religious unification of the world was to be realized on

22 Dom Lambert Beauduin, *La Vie liturgique,* no. 2 (1909): 3.

23 Jan den Boeft, "Erasmus and the Church Fathers," I. Backus, vol. 2, op. cit., 567.

the basis of the rational character of religious and moral truths. Suspected of heresy by the Inquisition, he took refuge in Venice where he translated the *Zohar* (twice: 1547–1553; 1562–1569). His mental health deteriorated and he was declared insane. In 1562 he was interned at the Cloister of St. Martin des Champs in Paris. This lack of dialogue between Christian men of science and the religious authorities continued throughout the modern period. Mikhail Lomonossov (1711–1765) was a great Russian encyclopedist, a mathematician, chemist, astronomer, historian, poet, and the founder of the University of Moscow, who wrote *A Morning Reflection Upon God's Grandeur* (*Réflexions matinales sur la grandeur de Dieu*). Yet the Synod of the Russian Church condemned him in 1757 because of his comments on clerical obscurantism.

Secondly, the effective loss of power of the Pope of Rome over the new nation-states (the imprisonment of Pope Boniface VIII by Philip the Fair in 1302) and the collapse of the Byzantine Empire in 1453 will lead in the ensuing period, to a general movement of reconfiguration of the relations between the political power and ecclesial power, although differently implemented according to the time and place. The Council of Trent was indicative of a period of separation between the temporal and the spiritual. It went from an imperial period (1545–1552) to a pontifical period (1562–1563) where the pope succeeded the emperor as the source for ecclesiastic unity.[24] The movement of verticalization within the Roman Church, which began in the 12th century, took another step by reinforcing its authority through the councils. With Vatican I and the definition of the doctrine of papal infallibility, "the appeal to the authority of the Church is now made part of the very definition of divine truth."[25] Even though political and religious identity remained indissolubly linked in Western Europe, at least until the French Revolution, the evolution of orthodoxy now depended much more on confessional memory rather than the identification, consciously accepted by both sides, between the Church and the Vicar of Christ. According to Patrice Veit: "A confessionalization is concretely defined by a confession of faith, a demarcation with respect to other confessions, a new ecclesial and scholastic organization, a system of control and a strong link with the State."[26] Henceforth new questions

24 A. Dupont, "Le concile de Trente" in *Le concile et les conciles*, Paris, Cerf, 1960, 195–243, cited by B. Sesboüé, *Le magistère*, op. cit., 168.

25 B. Sesboüé, *Le magistère*, 175.

26 P. Veit, intervention made at the round table during the study sessions on confessionalization, November 2001, *Etudes germaniques* 3 (2002), cited by Y. Krumenacker, op. cit., 240.

began to arise, that of the delimitation of territories according to the faith of the prince or that of the faithful, that of the sharing of a common temporality (due to the reform of the calendar by Pope Gregory XII in 1582), that of the sources of legitimacy, that of the boundaries between civil law and canon law, etc. As of 1648, international law recognized the inviolable sovereignty of nation-states which had the same power as the lieutenants of God in medieval political theology. The new international geography was the consequence of political divisions resulting from the splintering of the ecclesial body. When the Holy Alliance was formed on September 26, 1815 in Paris, the three victorious European monarchies—the Russian Orthodox Empire, the Austrian Catholic Empire and Protestant Prussia—wanted to restore the unity of the ecclesial body and to thus protect themselves against revolutionary ferment. At the insistence of Metternich, however, the Alliance rejected national aspirations which would be contrary to maintaining the order defined by the Congress of Vienna (November 1, 1814–June 9, 1815). After the death of Alexander I, the mystic tsar (1777–1825), the Holy Alliance broke loose to give free rein to the fatal strategy of alliances among sovereign States.

Thirdly, the challenge of the Reformation with regard to the ecclesial institution once again put the question of remembrance at the center of the problem of truth. This was the fruit of new anxieties about salvation experienced by men and women of modern times. The torments that Calvin and Luther suffered regarding their destiny after death are characteristic of this period. In the East, the icons of the last judgment, which flourished from Moscow to Mount Athos during the 16th century, depicted the flames of hell with increasing realism. Confronted with a medieval eschatology, Christian thinkers, who had been unable to reach a consensus during the Council of Florence, are going to be obliged to face up to the theme of justification in a different manner and, consequently, to a number of related points of doctrine. Salvation by faith in effect implied the negation of purgatory. Before opposing the popes, Luther began by fighting against the Pelagianism of his times as personified by Gregory of Rimini (†1358), the Paris Master of the Augustinians who exaggerated the power of free will to assure salvation. Luther also sought to be loyal to the battle of Athanasius of Alexandria against Arius. He based himself on "the words of Holy Scripture and the Council of Nicaea" in his 11th thesis, which he proclaimed at Leipzig in 1519 against the excessive power which the Roman Church had arrogated to itself since the 12th century.[27] Whereas Erasmus still read the New Testament through the eyes of the Fathers, Luther and Melanchthon wanted to read and judge the Fathers through the eyes of the Bible.[28] John Calvin had suffered from anxiety since childhood. Science was for him nothing more than a bottomless pit, while the Catholic Church seemed to give false illusions through its indulgences. For him, the souls of the righteous were at rest until judgment, while those of the sinners were enchained in hell. Yves Krumenacker writes: "Calvin is in need of internal security if he is to escape the 'abyss' of sin. But the type of piety preached by the Catholic Church did not succeed in appeasing him. He had long since found the solution in evangelism: it is the Word of God, given in Scripture and made intelligible by the Holy Spirit, that saves. . . . Calvin cannot tolerate confusion, jumble, or disorder. He needs clear distinctions, precise boundaries. Since Rome is unable to dedicate itself entirely to the divine truth, one must disassociate oneself from Rome."[29] In the following centuries, the unresolved question of eschatology became a rebellion. Mozart (1756–1773), who was baptized with the name of Joannes Chrysostomus Wolfgangus Theophilus, nevertheless rejected the adage "outside of the Church there is no salvation."[30] He turned to Freemasonry, as did Goethe (1749–1832) and Voltaire (1694–1778). In the opinion of the French historian Pierre Chaunu, Voltaire was orthodox in his belief that the Master of the Universe, the Supreme Being, could hardly, from the Alpha to the Omega, "be solely preoccupied with the state of souls according to the 91st proposition of the papal Bull *Unigenitus*."[31]

In modern times, it is no longer dogmatic theology and canon law that organize knowledge but rather history and philosophy. As Bruno Neveu has shown, the Republic of Letters, an invisible college of European scholars in

27 Luther liked to point out that it was Eusthatius, the bishop of Antioch, who presided at the Council of Nicaea and not the bishop of Rome. Manfred Schulze, "Martin Luther and the Church Fathers," Irena Backus, op. cit., 573.

28 Meijering, *Melanchton and Patristic Thought*, Leiden, 1983, 85.

29 Yves Krumenacker, *Calvin au-delà des légendes*, Bayard, 2009, 146–47.

30 This dictum is taken from the letters of Saint Cyprian of Carthage: "there is no salvation outside the Church" (*salus extra ecclesiam non est*) (letter 73). In the 20th century there was an effort to put this adage into context and explain that the Father of the Church was essentially thinking of Christians who were deserting the Church of Carthage which at the time was rejecting baptisms practiced by dissident sects. Pope Stephan of Rome did not have the same point of view. Bernard Sesboüé, *"Hors de l'Eglise pas de salut": Histoire d'une formule et problèmes d'interprétation*, Paris, Desclée, 2004.

31 Pierre Chaunu, "La connaissance et la foi," *L'historien et la foi*, Paris, Fayard, 1996, 44.

the 16th and 17th centuries, critical of medieval scholastic learning, became a vector for Jansenism, first in France, then in Italy. Marc Fumaroli asserts that, in the battle between the Jansenists and the Jesuits, the Republic of Letters, with its Gallican and Protestant elements, favored "the followers of St. Augustine" who appeared to the college as victims of imperialism attributed to the Jesuits, and of the abusive authority attributed to the papacy. "This solidarity set the stage for the all-out attack of the Enlightenment on the Society of Jesus and even for the total war proclaimed by Voltaire, the new Erasmus, against 'The Infamous.'"[32] This return of the elite of the Republic of Letters to a radical Augustinianism, and in particular to a fatalistic interpretation of original sin, which has no basis in the early apostolic tradition and had never been adopted by the Eastern patristic tradition, also posed an obstacle to any fruitful encounter between Christians of the East and West. As Michel Stavrou points out, the synergism of the Greek Fathers, defended in Provence by John Cassian and Vincent of Lérins, and rejected by the Council of Orange (529), "was accused of semi-Pelagianism from the 16th century onwards by a Roman Church obsessed with the Pelagius-Augustine conflict."[33]

The study of ecclesial historiography between the mid-16th century and the mid-20th century bears witness to these inflections of ecclesial consciousness. This alters the status of the historian. Far from being an investigator at the service of the Church, the historian became a judge of its actions. If indeed the Church passed through the same historical developments as other institutions of this world, both doctrinally and morally, this would mean that the historian could place himself above the Church itself. This critical transformation spread among both Protestant and Catholic historians around the 16th century. It was only in the 19th century that Russian Orthodox historians invited themselves into the debate of German-Latin Christianity. Alexis Lebedev (1845–1908), professor of Church history at the Moscow Theological Academy and one of the principal Orthodox historians of our times, in his study on ecclesial historiography, considered that since the Reformation, "ecclesial history has become a critical science."[34]

32 Marc Fumaroli, "Préface," *Erudition et Religion aux XVIIe et XVIIIe siècles*, Paris, Albin Michel, 1994, VI.

33 Michel Stavrou, "Le péché des origines dans l'orthodoxie et à Port Royal," *Contacts*, no. 230 (April–June 2010): 162.

34 A. P. Lebedev, *Tserkovnaja Istoriografia v glavnikh ieia predstaviteliakhs IV v. do XX veka*, Sob., 257.

## THE 16TH CENTURY: THE CLASH OF MEMORIES

A Dalmatian by the name of Mathias Francowitz (1520–1575), who became Lutheran and latinized his name to Flacius Illyricus, can be considered as one of the first proponents of the new ecclesial historiography. This friend of Luther was impressed by the new representation of the Church as the kingdom of the Antichrist. In 1556, ten years after the death of Luther, he published the following work in Basel: *Catalogus testium veritatis, qui ante nostram aetatem pontifici romano ejusque erroribus reclamarunt*. H. Leclercq has summed up the position of Flacius: "The aim pursued in this *Catalogus* was to show that, notwithstanding the darkness that seemingly obscured the truth, faithful witnesses had at all times defended orthodoxy up until the day when the Reformation had restored to men the light that the Catholic Church had darkened and the truth she had distorted."[35] From the outset, the link between fidelity and orthodoxy is maintained by the reformist. Flacius continued his polemical undertaking of deconstructing Roman historiography by putting together a team of historians willing to uphold his project: Wigand, Judex, Faber, Corvinus, etc.[36] The original title of their collective project, which began to be published at Magdebourg in 1559, was *Ecclesiastica historia, integram Ecclesiae ideam quantum ad locum, propogationem, persecutionem, tranquillitatem, doctrinam, haereses, ceremonias, gubernationem, schismata, synodos, personas, miracula, martyria, religiones extra Ecclesiam et statutum imperii politicum attinet, secundam singulas centurias*.[37] In the 18th century the title was modified according to the plan of the text to read *Centuriae Magdeburgenses, seu historia ecclesiastica Novi Testamenti, cum variorum theologorum continuationibus ad haec nostra tempora, quas excipient supplementa emendationum, defensionum, illustationumque ad priores centurias XIII*.[38] These are studies that narrate the history

35 H. Leclercq, op. cit., 2613.

36 There was a concurrent project of a new orthodox historiography by Sebastien Franck de Woerd, *Chronique Annales et Bible historique*, published in Strasbourg on September 5, 1531. Erasmus, who was treated as a heretic in the opus, condemned it violently. In his thesis, Jean-Claude Colbus suggests that this term was, in fact, a title of nobility that Franck reserved for the martyrs of truth who had struggled with the Roman Church. J. C. Colbus, *La Chronique de Sébastien Franck (1499–1542)*, Bern, Peter Lang, 2005.

37 Per aliquot studiosos et pios viros in urbe Magdeburgicae. Accesit . . . rerum in singulis centuriis . . . , index in folio, Basileae, 1559–1574.

38 Quorum curam suscipiet qui praefationes etiam singulis voluminibus addet S. J. Baumgarten [et J. S. Selmer, ed. J. J. Kauckius], 4 vol in 40, Norimbergae, 1757.

of the Church century by century. Each century is divided into 16 chapters. The first three chapters cover the general history of the century in question and the political situation of the Church; the fourth chapter deals with the development of doctrine; the fifth with heresies; the sixth with rites; the seventh with institutional organization; the eighth with schisms; the ninth with the councils; the tenth with the lives of bishops and the main ecclesial actors; the eleventh with heretics; the twelfth with martyrs; the thirteenth with miracles; the fourteenth with relations with Jews; and the fifteenth and sixteenth with other religions and the political evolution of peoples. The authors were aware of their audacity: "It could be said that to write an ecclesial history after Eusebius is like pretending to write the *Iliad* after Homer."[39]

Blinded as they were by their anger towards the Roman pontiffs, these authors did not know how to rise to the height of their illustrious predecessor. Their history has the merit of denouncing some of the popes' notable untruths. They shed light on the false Pseudo-Isidorian Decretals, written near Amiens around 840, which were one of the most important sources of medieval canon law. Among other things, these decrees sought to protect the orthodox faith and the bishops who defended it, but they ultimately led to legitimizing the submission of the bishops to the centralizing Roman power. The authors of the *Catalogus* question the legitimacy of the attribution, in 606, of the title "head of all churches" to Pope Boniface III by the Byzantine Emperor Flavius Phocas (547–610). But they come to describe the history of the popes in the 2nd century according to the model of the 11th century. The reforming Pope Gregory VII (c. 1015–1085) is referred to as the "monstrum omnium, quae haec terra portavit, monstrosissimum." Moreover, by restricting the Christian doctrine of salvation to the sole perspective of justification by faith, they ended up accusing of heresy a not insignificant number of those considered Fathers of the Church. This Manichean and often unjust representation of history testifies to a deep separation between faith and reason. The originality of their approach is that, given the absence of any dialogue between the revealed Word and its intelligibility,[40] one must use the Scriptures and dogmatic tradition to counterbalance the evolution of the papacy in the West. The second chapter of Paul's second *Letter to the*

39 *Centuriae Magdeburgenses*, Tome 1, Prefatio, p. 1, Norimbergae, 1757.

40 Luther rejected the theory of the four levels of Scriptural truth and only retained the literal meaning. Any obscurity can be overcome by a better knowledge of the language. This axiom led Matthias Flacius Illyricus to compose his *Clavis scripturae sacrae* in 1567.

*Thessalonians* in particular is frequently cited as a reminder of the "mystery of iniquity" represented by the vision of "the son of perdition" who seats himself in person in the "Temple of God" and proclaims himself to be God (2 Thess 2:4). The association of the papacy with this vision of the apostle led to such a polemic that it devalued, for a long time, the critical turning point in ecclesial historiography. Very quickly confessional posturing took precedence over orthodoxy as the search for true knowledge.

Actually, these *Centuries* of Magdebourg provoked Catholics and impelled them to study history. As early as 1561, a Canon of Augsburg, Conrad Brun, published a refutation. But the most reasoned retort came from Italy. St. Philip Neri was the first to realize what was at stake and encouraged Cesare Baronius (1538–1607) to prepare the refutation. The founder of the Congregation of the Oratory required members of his community to read the Fathers every day. After Neri's death, Baronius succeeded him, became the confessor of Pope Clement VIII and was elevated to the cardinalate. Cardinal Baronius, with the help of his secretaries and his profound erudition, wrote and took sole responsibility for the *Annales ecclesiastici*.[41] He succeeded in composing twelve volumes in folio starting from the birth of Christ up to 1198. His work was reedited and revised several times. John Dominic Mansi published a new edition between 1738 and 1759 at Lucca consisting of 38 volumes. Antoine Pagi (1624–1699) continued the work of Baronius and published four more volumes in 1705.

Even though Baronius, in the preface to his work, calls the centuries of Magdebourg the "centuries of Satan," he prefers the models of the *Annales* of the historians of old. In respect of present-day polemic carried through history, he prefers to elevate his narrative to the peaceful and objective temporality of events of the past. He frankly presents the object of his project:

> My task is to show how, down through the ages, the visible head of the Catholic Church, established by Christ our Lord, founded upon Peter and his just and legitimate successors, the first Roman hierarchs, was recognized and preserved, protected by grace and never corrupted, to show that the unique visible head of this Mystical Body of Christ before whom the other members bowed was always acknowledged and protected.[42]

41 C. Baronius, *Annales ecclesiastici*, vol. 1, Antverpiae, 1597.
42 Ibid., praefatio.

This did not prevent Baronius from being critical. Along with the humanist Lorenza Valla, he acknowledges that the *Donation of Constantine*, according to which Pope Sylvester would have received from Constantine imperial rights over the Western Empire, was an 8th century fabrication. But he perfidiously adds that it is the work of the Greeks who were trying to discredit the Romans. On the other hand, he denies that Pope Honorius had been condemned for heresy by the 6th Ecumenical Council of 680–681.

In Magdebourg as in Rome, historical consciousness was still marked by the medieval logic of the sequence of events and dates, some insisting on the errors of the popes, while others set out to demonstrate the glory of the papacy. However, as A. Lebedev points out, according to the historians of Magdebourg, the Church should be "understanding to the letter and transmitting faithfully"[43] that which had been proposed at the time of Christ and the apostles. All thought simply centered on the faithfulness of transmission. The question of the debates among the different theological schools and the concept of theological creativity within the heart of orthodox tradition had still not been raised.

The founding of the Jesuit Order in 1540 by Ignatius Loyola contributed to the development of a new intellectual orthodoxy in the second half of the sixteenth century. This orthodoxy was defined in an internal document to the order entitled *Ratio studiorum*. This text, written between 1580 and 1599, testifies to the new relationship between the quest for orthodoxy and the formation of norms, a report essentially dictated by the vow of obedience of the members of the order to the Roman pontiff. The duty of intelligence is defined first of all by the architects of the *Ratio studiorum*, General Acquaviva and Robert Bellarmine, as a duty of fidelity. Hence the desire to "follow the most secure and approved doctrine," namely Thomism in theology and Aristotelianism in philosophy.[44] From 1565, this necessary obedience favored self-censorship within the Order. Despite all this, the Holy Office forbade the publication of the text in 1590, which speaks volumes about the internal tension between Jesuit orthodoxy and Catholic orthodoxy that existed from the beginning of the order.

43 A. Lebedev, op. cit., 275.

44 Antonella Romano, "Orthodoxie intellectuelle en milieu jésuite," *Orthodoxie*, op. cit., 244.

## THE 17TH, 18TH AND 19TH CENTURIES: CONFRONTATION BETWEEN REMEMBRANCES AND HISTORY

Pietism was a reaction to the polemical and intolerant dogmatism of the Lutheran authors of the *Magdeburg Centuries*. Philip Jacob Spener (1635–1705) inaugurated a movement emphasizing the spiritual over the intellectual, so that the truth was to be found not in dogma, but in an open and repentant heart. Piety consisted in fulfilling one's religious duties and seeking peace through the individual union of the heart with the divinity. This movement of mistrust towards theologians encouraged the self-interpreting of Scripture by the faithful. This logically led to a questioning of the paradigm of orthodoxy as right truth. Gottfried Arnold (1666–1714), a disciple of Spener, published in Frankfort in 1699 an *Impartial History of the Church and Heresies* in which he found more affinity with the heretical movements of history than with the structures of power incarnated in the institutional Church and theological academies. His project was therefore to develop a nonpolitical conception of orthodoxy before it fell under the guardianship of the Emperor Constantine. This had a profound influence on all 19th century Protestant historiography as well as on nonconformist thinkers such as the Russian writer Leo Tolstoy. Arnold's project was taken up by Christian Weismann (†1747), who wrote an eloquent history entitled *Introductio memorabilia ecclesiastica historiae sacrae*, which was published at Stuttgart in 1719. This history claims to be objective. Even though he accepts the action of Providence in the world, Weismann is extremely circumspect of the historical validity of miracles. This is a trait he has in common with Johann Lorenz von Mosheim (1694–1755), the chancellor of the University of Göttingen, who was considered in Germany as the father of this new ecclesial historiography following the publications of his *Institutiones*. The historian refers to the Bible purely to consider the validity of an event. He claims that he does not try to justify any particular confession. For him, as for J. S. Semler (1725–1791), the Church is a society among others. He seeks to explain the sequence of events through the motivations of its personages. It is understandable from this perspective that secularized history, that is, history where Christian salvation is no longer on the horizon, becomes increasingly important outside this sacred history deprived of its purpose.[45]

45 K. Löwith, *Histoire et salut. Les présupposés théologiques de la philosophie de l'histoire*, Gallimard, 2002.

In the 17th century, French Protestant historiography was represented by several currents.[46] S. Goulart tries to prove that, after the apostolic period, true Christianity was always professed by a minority opposed to the Roman pontiffs. Philippe de Mornay, Lord of Duplessis-Marly (1549–1623), governor of the city of Montauban in 1581, opposed to the union of the political and religious powers, was one of the theorists of the Edict of Nantes in 1598. In 1611, after he became governor of Saumur, he sought a historical justification of his convictions with his book *The Mystery of Iniquity* (*Le mystère d'iniquité*), which denounced the pope as the Antichrist. For his part, J. Daillé (1594–1670) attempted to reconcile Protestant doctrine with patristic orthodoxy. These works of historical research set the stage for the emergence of a critical and secular history. Pierre Bayle (1647–1706), the author of the *Historical and Critical Dictionary* (*Dictionnaire historique et critique*) and of *News from the Republic of Letters* (*Nouvelles de la République des Lettres*) is the most eminent representative of this evolution.[47] Bayle was one of the first advocates in France for civil tolerance towards all Christian confessions and also towards Jews, Muslims and atheists. Jacques Solé notes that Bayle "first called upon his coreligionists to consider their origins, with fidelity, certainly, but also with all the disrespect that comes with lucidity."[48] This is why, even if Bayle defended the Reformation's "orthodoxy," he also refused a hagiographic vision of the origins of the Reformation and sought to "carefully distinguish the end pursued and the means employed." According to Élisabeth Labrousse, the common connection between all these reformers is their rationalist optimism, their faith that religious truth can be demonstrated by correct deductions from the postulates they all share. In 1585, Du Plessis Mornay wrote to Henry III:

> Religious dissension was at work in the ancient Church: a number of heresies swarmed among the people and even infected the emperors. What did the Church do? What did the good emperors, the guardians of the Church do? History is the witness. They realized that heresy is an opinion, that every opinion is in one's head, that heresy is a false image of reason which could only be

46 Jean-Yves Lacoste, dir., *Dictionnaire critique de théologie*, Paris, PUF, 1998; English translation *Encyclopedia of Christian Theology*, New York, Routledge, 2005.

47 Philippe Joutard dir., colloquium of Aix (September 22–24, 1972), Paris, Delachaux et Niestle, 1977.

48 J. Solé, "Pierre Bayle, historien de la Réforme," *Historiographie*, op. cit., 79.

> effaced by the presence of reason itself. So they assembled councils, and brought together enough people from all over. Each one peacefully put forward what he knew. Opinion in the end gave way to science, shadows to light, appearances to truth, sophism to reason. . . . The same reason that solves legal difficulties can also solve theological difficulties.[49]

French Catholic historiography experienced a profound renewal in the 17th century. Thanks to the translations of Henry of Valois, the *Ecclesiastical History* of Eusebius (1659) and several other works of Sozomen (1668) and Theodoret (1673) were published. From 1615, the Flemish Jesuit Jean Bolland and his community of Bollandists began publishing a monumental collection of the lives of saints together with the original Greek and Latin texts. In 1672, Philippe Labbé published the Acts of the Church Councils. Dom Hugues Ménard (1585–1644) and Dom Luc d'Achery (1609–1685), the directors of the library of the Abbey of St.-Germain-des-Prés, dedicated themselves to the editing and publication of patristic texts. The Benedictine Congregation of St. Maur, prior to its suppression by the National Assembly in 1790, published more than 700 works by 220 authors including St. Athanasius, St. Basil, St. John Chrysostom and St. Gregory of Nazianzus. Thanks to outstanding scholars such as Jean Mabillon (1632–1707), this community also developed the auxiliary sciences of history such as diplomatics.[50] The Maurists not only published but also established plans for the study of the writings of the Fathers for monks and clergy.

In spite of this the polemic continued, especially after the revocation of the Edict of Nantes by Louis XIV in 1685. Jacques-Bénigne Bossuet (1627–1704), Preceptor to the Dauphin and Bishop of Meaux who, in 1682, drew up a declaration on the freedoms of the Gallican Church, published a first essay which would qualify today as mytho-urgic because of its assumed absence of a critical spirit. The work was a historical justification of the Catholic Church in the face of the novelty of Protestantism. It was published in 1688 under the title *History of the Variations of the Protestant Churches* and provoked a bitter controversy.[51] "The theological watchdog of the 17th century"

49 Opinion of M. Dompnier during a discussion on the occasion of the publication of "The Rapport of Mme Élisabeth Labrousse," *Historiographie*, op. cit., 114.

50 Dom Denis, *Dom Mabillon et sa méthode historique*, Paris, 1910.

51 When the Protestant minister Pierre Jurieu replied to this essay, Bossuet responded with *Avertissements aux protestants sur les lettres du ministre Jurieu contre l'Histoire des*

(as Duchesne calls him) pronounced also the condemnation of Richard Simon (1638–1712), one of the "fathers" of biblical criticism in the French language and one of the promoters before its formulation of the movement of reconciliation among the Churches. After his ordination in 1670 and the publication of a pamphlet defending the Jews of Metz who were unjustly threatened with expulsion, Simon first wrote a book entitled *Fides Ecclesiae Orientalis* (Paris, 1671) that showed the unity in belief on the subject of the Eucharist in the Greek and Latin Churches. His *Critical History of the Old Testament*, published in Rotterdam in 1685, was forbidden in France due to the opposition of both Jacques Bossuet and Antoine Arnauld. With the publication in 1693 of his *Critical History of the Principal Commentators of the New Testament from the Beginning of Christianity until the Present Time*, the critical understanding of orthodoxy presented itself as the logical consequence of the remembrance renewal of ecclesial consciousness. But after his condemnation by his own colleagues at the Oratory and his exile, nobody paid any attention to the little priest of Bolleville.

All the same, French Catholic ecclesial historiography gained recognition in the 17th century, elaborating a new representation of orthodoxy as faithful memory and drawing a certain number of consequences from historical criticism. Sébastien Le Nain de Tillemont (1637–1698) and Abbé Claude Fleury (1640–1723) were aware that dissidence during the reign of the "Roi-Soleil" was futile. Nevertheless, they were able to make a real contribution to historical orthodoxy. The Jansenist Tillemont was a student of Godefroy Hermant who had published a life of St. Basil and St. Gregory of Nazianzus in 1674. In the logic of faithful memory, Hermant was principally interested in the quality of the witness. Tillemont wanted to initiate a more critical approach. Close to the spirituality of the Abbey of Port Royal and Antoine Arnauld, Tillemont once confided to Marguerite Périer, the niece of Pascal, that the reading of Baronius did not leave him satisfied but that he sought "the foundations of the faith in its very sources, that is, in the study of Holy Scriptures and the Fathers."[52] Later, Father Laderci, the successor of Baronius, tried to have him condemned, but the Popes Clement XI and then Benedict XIV spoke highly of the French historian. The ressourcement remembrance theme of the new historiography appears clearly in the title of his 16-volume work which he began in 1693:

*variations*, a clumsy document where he winds up defending slavery.

52 H. Leclercq, op. cit., 2625.

*Memoirs for the ecclesiastical history of the first six centuries, justified by the quotations of original authors, with a chronology where an epitome of ecclesiastical and profane history and notes are made to clarify the difficulties of facts and chronology.* The search for "the truth in facts," therefore, against all skeptical Pyrrhonism of which modern authors are accused by the classic authors, requires an act of remembrance.[53] Tillemont, knowing the power of rational logic which can easily carry so many myths without even being aware of it, is committed to facts and testimonies. If there is no reliable testimony that a donkey and an ox were in the cave when Jesus was born, Tillemont will remain silent. In 1679, when the peace of the Church came to an end, Tillemont left his residence in the Abbey of Port Royal in order to avoid all political and ecclesiastical pressure. He settled in a place near Montreuil, secluded from the world. His critique of the *Golden Legend* of the saints, a work widely diffused during the Middle Ages, was based on St. Paul himself who, as Tillemont pointed out, asks us to "test everything and hold fast what is good" (I Thes 5:21).[54] Even if Tillemont was a great scholar, capable of questioning the myth of the apostolic origins of Gallic Christianity, B. Neveu does not consider him a prophetic historian. He admired Christian antiquity, considering it a golden age worth returning to. According to B. Neveu, "the idea of a certain evolution, of theological progress, was slowly emerging: Christian thought had great difficulty freeing itself from a conception that was systematically unfavorable to time."[55] The faithful remembrance of Claude Fleury was tinged with Gallican orthodoxy. He published a twenty volume *Ecclesiastical History* between 1691 and 1720, which began with the birth of Christ and prudently stopped before the Reformation. This monumental opus was republished several times and contributed to the formation of French Catholic memory of the history of the Church. In this *Histoire ecclésiastique*, the abbot of Fleury did not hesitate to write that the popes had exaggerated their authority by relying on false decretals and that it was necessary to return to the Patristic period.[56] In France, Italy and Spain there were other historians during this era: Bérault-Bercastel (1722–1794), Muratori (1672–1750), Mansi (1692–1769)

53 Paul Hazard, *La crise de la conscience européenne*, Paris, Gallimard, 1968, ch. 2, 48–77.

54 B. Neveu, *Un historien à l'Ecole de Port Royal. Sebastien le Nain de Tillemont, 1637–1698,* La Haye, M. Nijhoff, 1966; Hazard, *La crise,* 48–77.

55 Neveu, *Un historien,* 288.

56 Jean-Louis Quantin, "The Fathers in Seventeenth-Century Roman Catholic Theology," I. Backus, op. cit., 1005.

and Florez (1701–1773). There were also scholars in England who defended orthodoxy, notably George Bull, a member of the High Church (1634–1710), with his publication in 1685 of the *Defensio fidei nicanae*.[57]

The French Revolution altered the political and intellectual landscape of Europe. The monarchies gradually gave way to republican regimes. Deism became the official religion of many European States. Voltaire was the author of the work *Abridged History of World Religions (Histoire abrégée des religions du monde)* (Geneva, Cranmer, 1770). His use of the concept of progress testifies to his intellectual affinity with several Protestant historians such as P. Bayle. But in the opinion of the opponent of Pangloss, the Leibnizian professor of metaphysico-theologico-cosmolo-nigology, this progress is not due to the assistance of the Holy Spirit in the Church. For the author of *Candide* (1759), in disagreement with Rousseau who continued to justify the role of Divine Providence in history, the lives of men can be improved despite the evil in the world by understanding that it has been generated by men alone. The sage of Ferney advocated, for example, that convents become public property.[58] For a new generation of historians, the meaning of history was no longer transcendent, orientated towards the Kingdom of God, based on a transcendent past, but rather immanent, determined by an imaginary perfect future, dominated by the idea of progress. In the philosophy of Hegel (1770–1831) history becomes the dialectical self-realization of the Absolute Idea. Leopold van Ranke (1795–1886), of Lutheran descent, author of *The History of the Popes in the Sixteenth and Seventeenth Centuries* (*Histoire de la Papauté pendant les XVIe et XVIIe siècles*), maintains a distinction between an increasingly objectified God and the history of humanity. His real religion is, however, positivism. The Father of modern historiography, ready to reject whole segments of the history of mankind in the name of humanity, no longer "believed" anything but direct testimony and the most authentic sources. This raises the question of the relationship between the Reformation and the revolutionary movement. For Charles de Villers, a Catholic disciple of Kant who wrote, in 1804, an *Essay on the Spirit and Influence of the Reformation of Luther* (*Essai sur l'esprit et l'influence de la Réformation de Luther*), the Revolution was not a catastrophe but rather an achievement of the Reformation. Conversely, due to the Revolution,

57 Jean-Louis Quantin, "The Fathers in Seventeenth-Century Anglican Theology," I. Backus, op. cit., 171.

58 Louis Trenard, "Voltaire, historien de la Réforme," *Historiographie,* op. cit., 165.

the Reformation found its political and socio-cultural dimensions. It was the source of new insights on history, metaphysics and political science. According to Villers, by virtue of their critique of medieval chronicles, Melanchthon, Grotius, Pufendorf and Bayle invented history. Through their successors — Hume, Gibbon, Robertson — Protestants made it "one of the most important branches of human science." Villers believed that if Francis I had accepted the Reformation, the religious and revolutionary wars could have been avoided. His advocacy formed the basis for liberal thought, from Madame de Staël to Benjamin Constant and Victor Cousin.[59] On the other hand, Balzac, who condemned both the Reformation and the Revolution, established a direct link between the one "spirit of free inquiry in religious matters" and the other "spirit of free inquiry in political matters" in his 1842 essay *About Catherine de Medici* (*Sur Catherine de Médicis*). *La Revue historique* of Gabriel Monod sought to defend both the Reformation and the Revolution.[60] Right up until the First World War, in France, French Catholic and French Protestant historians fought hard over this theme.

New Catholic historians appeared in France such as R. F. Rohrbacher (1789–1856), the author of a 29-volume *General History of the Catholic Church* (*Histoire universelle de l'Eglise catholique*). These historians countered the assaults on the Catholic religion by committing themselves to the defense of the papacy. A minority of Catholic intellectuals, however, such as Frederic Ozanam (1813–1853) and Henri Lacordaire (1802–1861), sided with the Republic. Among these thinkers, Felicité Robert de Lamennais (1782–1854) turned to the Holy See, opposed Gallicanism and pleaded for freedom of conscience and the separation of Church and State. But after the review *L'Avenir* was condemned by Pope Gregory XVI in 1832, Lamennais became the champion of social Christianity. He came to conceive of a Christianity without a Church. H. Leclercq believes that these two tendencies of French Catholic thought have their source in the disagreement between Rohrbacher and Lamennais and in "the recognition of the authority of the *sensus fidelium*."[61] While the former relied on "the first principles of natural reason" for the understanding of right Christian *doxa*, the latter identified this sense of the faithful with an "early Christian Church." For Lamennais

59 Yvonne Knibielher, "Réforme et révolution d'après Charles de Villers," *Historiographie*, op. cit., 171.

60 Intervention of M. Carbonell during the debate following the "Rapport de M. Daniel Robert," *Historiographie*, op. cit., 288.

61 H. Leclercq, op. cit., 2641.

the *sensus fidei* was the driving force of history. For Rohrbacher, however, this vision led to the myth of an early Church "antecedent and superior to the Jewish Church and the Christian Church."[62] In Rohrbacher's view it was reason, without any support of grace, that was moving history. For Lamennais, this meant that reason could only blindly bow down before the authority of the Roman See. Through this debate we can see the source of the non-dialogue between faith and reason, and to remedy the situation, the development of the paradigm of orthodoxy as faithful memory.

The religious historiography of the 19th century will widen this difference even more with, on the one hand, the positivist writings of Ernest Renan (1823–1892) and, on the other hand, the ultramontanist works of Msgr. Louis-Marie Duchesne (1843–1922). Ernest Renan, professor of Hebrew at the Collège de France, a eulogist of anti-Semitism and an enthusiast of the theories of Darwin, published a seven-volume *History of the Origins of Christianity* (*Histoire des origines du christianisme*), which appeared between 1863 and 1881. In 1863 his *The Life of Jesus* (*Vie de Jésus*) was published and became one of most successful editions of 19th century French literature. Renan wrote about God and the Church but denied the existence of the supernatural and even of a God distinct from the world. From his point of view, what has been called the multiplication of the loaves was nothing other than an exaggeration of the frugal life that Jesus and his disciples led in the desert. Louis Duchesne did not hesitate to unmask Renan's prejudices presented under the guise of erudition: He "who speaks so willingly and flippantly of the dogmatism of others has his own dogmatism. . . . [For him] the scientific spirit is the negation of the supernatural."[63] Renan preferred the wisdom of Marcus Aurelius, the emperor-philosopher, to that of the God-man Jesus Christ. Some of his success, however, came from the fact that he demonstrated the spirit of the Christian religion and especially the impetus of solidarity it aroused in people and the new role it gave to women. But for him, compared to modernity, the Church was nothing more than "a counter current of stagnant and putrid water."[64]

Msgr. Duchesne significantly focused his research on the very foundation of Catholic identity remembrance, the *Liber Pontificalis*, an archival

62 Ibid., 2643.

63 L. Duchesne, "Les Evangiles de M. Renan," *Revue du monde catholique*, 1877, vol LI, 314–15.

64 E. Renan, *Marc Aurèle et la fin du monde antique*, Paris, 1882, 537.

collection, initiated in the 6th century, of the lives of the popes from the origins to the present day. As a young ultramontane priest, Duchesne supported the Council of 1870 and the proclamation of pontifical infallibility. He did not pay attention to the fact that the Holy See "was embarking on a progressive dogmatization of the foundations of the faith," as put by Christopher Theobald.[65] Vatican I did, in fact, subscribe to a denial of history. Even though the conciliar Fathers introduced a new truth into the Christian catechism by proclaiming the infallibility of Peter and his successors, they were reluctant to admit the historicity of dogma. The historian A. Gunther was blacklisted because Rome feared "a rationalist conception of dogmatic development in the history of human knowledge." Duchesne's rejection of the modern world related to the encyclical *Quanta Cura* and the *Syllabus* of 1864, his hostility towards Protestantism and his ignorance of the Eastern Church all confirmed him in his confessional identity. His visit to Mount Athos in 1874 only reinforced his contempt for "the schismatic Churches of the East." Quite logically he settled in Rome, a move which earned him much rebuke from his superiors in France. He defended his thesis to the Faculty of Letters at the Sorbonne in 1877, was given the Chair of Church History at the Catholic Institute of Paris and published his thesis, in two volumes, in 1886 and 1892. In 1880, he founded the *Bulletin critique* whose original objective was to unite the "orthodoxy" of doctrine with the "inexorably scientific" nature of research. Msgr. Duchesne was convinced by his thesis that the distinctive foundations of the Catholic faith were not in danger and that this allowed for a new attitude of dialogue with rational logic. He had the support of the rector of the Catholic Institute who assured Cardinal Franzelin that Msgr. Duchesne was developing "orthodox views" on "the development of dogma and the role of the Roman pontiffs."[66] This new attitude was still not to the taste of the majority of Catholics who were little inclined to admit the notion of development in the history of the Church. The last issue of the *Bulletin* is dated November 10, 1908, barely a year after the antimodernist encyclical *Pascendi dominici gregis* of September 8, 1907.

But Msgr. Duchesne had sparked an intellectual renewal which also served those who, like Alfred Loisy, questioned the "absolute right of ecclesiastical authority over the mind and conscience of believers." In fact, Alfred Loisy

65 C. Theobald, *La parole de salut, histoire des dogmes*, vol. IV, Paris, Desclée, 1996, 227. Cited by B. Sesboüé, *Le magistère*, op. cit., 166.

66 H. Leclercq, op. cit., 2692.

(1857–1940) was among the first contributors to the twenty-one volume *Bulletin Critique*. This theologian and French Catholic priest became a professor at the Ecole Pratique des Hautes Etudes in 1900 after his resignation from the Catholic Institute of Paris in 1893. Loisy himself describes how he was forced to leave his post:

> In October 1892, the Superior of Saint-Sulpice, Mr. Icard, forbade his students to attend my classes on Holy Scripture because I had contested the historical character of the first chapters of Genesis. The Rector of the Catholic Institute, Msgr. d'Hulst, thought it would be good to turn the debate towards its least real and most dangerous aspect, the question of inspiration. The result was a violent and confused controversy which led the Council of Bishops, protectors of the Catholic University, to relieve me first from the teaching of Holy Scripture and then from teaching languages.[67]

In spite of his refutation in 1902, in *L'Evangile et l'Eglise,* of the work of the Protestant theologian Adolf von Harnack (1851–1930), *L'essence du christianisme* (1900), Loisy's theses were condemned in the encyclical *Pascendi* and he was excommunicated on March 7, 1908. The following year he became professor and occupied the chair of history of religions at the Collège de France. In his journal, he notes that from this moment on he dedicated himself to the study of the religious rites of Antiquity "apart from all theological orthodoxies and all scientific dogmatism." It was Augustin Fliche (1884–1951) who took up the torch of Duchesne's project. This professor at the University of Montpellier formed a collective of historians who, in 1934, began publishing a weighty twenty-four volume *Histoire de l'Eglise des origines jusqu'à nos jours*. The erudition of this undertaking was indisputable. It had the merit of not being restricted to the external history of the Church (relations with States). It was consistent with the direction of the review *Annales*, which also looked beyond the political to consider questions of economy, society and civilization. But it remained within the paradigm of faithful remembrance insofar as it centered the history of the Church on the personality of the popes of Rome. The *Bulletin critique* was replaced by the *Revue de l' histoire de l'Eglise de France* thanks to the incentive

67 A. Loisy, "Le chemin vers l'excommunication," in *Mémoires pour servir à l'histoire religieuse de notre temps (1857–1927)*, Paris, E. Nourry, 1930–1931.

of Msgr. Baudrillart, Rector of the Catholic Institute; of the publisher and bookseller Leon Letouzey; and of Abbot Albert Vogt, author of a thesis on "The Byzantine Emperor Basil I and the Civilization at the End of the 9th Century" ("Basile Ier empereur de Byzance [867–886] et la civilisation byzantine à la fin du IXe siècle"). As writes Bernard Barbiche, President of the Society of Religious History of France, "the *Revue* was created in order to incorporate and maintain the erudite clergy within Roman orthodoxy."[68]

In Protestant lands, the "father of the new ecclesial history" was Auguste Neander (1789–1850). He was born in Göttingen in the year of the French Revolution into a family of the Jewish religion, and converted to Lutheranism in 1860 after reading Jakob Boehme and Schleiermacher (1768–1834). He became professor of theology at Heidelberg and published between 1825 and 1845 his *Histoire générale de la religion chrétienne et de l'Eglise* in five volumes, which starts with Christ and ends with the Council of Basel. This German historian, faithful to his pietistic predecessors, and reader of Hegel's *The Life of Jesus*, considered that the Church had become decadent from the 4th century onwards. He paid particular attention to all Christian heresies, but refused to judge the orthodoxy of doctrines and limited his narrative to the great personages of the past. Neander saw Christianity as a religion of the Spirit which was neither visibly nor continuously incarnate. It emerged in history through the acts of the baptized. His works had considerable influence in Germany and Russia.

Neander's spiritualism provoked a rationalist reaction from Ferdinand Christian Bauer (1792–1860) and the School of Tübingen (to which belonged David Friedrich Strauss, the author of *The Life of Jesus* whose translation in 1853 by Émile Littré inspired Renan). Between 1852 and 1862 Bauer, characterized by the pantheistic gnosis of Hegel, published *Das Christentum und die christliche Kirche der drei ersten Jahrhunderte* (*Christianity and the Christian Church in the First Three Centuries*). The preface was entitled "The Epochs of Ecclesial Historiography." This text can be considered as one of the first instances when the historians of the modern era became aware of the essential meaning of the historicity of ecclesial science for collective memory. The history of dogmas became the guiding principle of ecclesial orthodoxy. Its dialectical logic, however, led him to elaborate structural antagonisms, most often imaginary, for example between Petrinism and Paulinism, to give an account of the progression of truth. Johann

68 B. Barbiche, "La RHEF a cent ans" in *Revue de l'histoire de l'Eglise de France*, no. 237 (July–December, 2010): 257.

Karl Ludwig Gieseler (1793–1854), professor at Göttingen and author of a six-volume Church history published between 1824 and 1855, stands halfway between the spiritual and rationalist viewpoints. For him it is precisely the criterion of the fidelity of the historical protagonists to the truth of the Gospel that enabled the historian to pass judgment on a given situation. The macro-history of the Church was explained according to the representations of the Kingdom of God held by the protagonists of a particular era.

In the 20th century, following the earthquake of Schopenhauer's and Nietzsche's critique of Kantian morality and the associated notion of abstract truth, the intellectual landscape changed radically. The Protestant theologians Karl Barth, Rudolf Bultmann and Paul Tillich criticized in the 20th century the Jesuanism of their predecessors, but in their concern for distinguishing divine temporality from historic temporality, they minimized the "intrusions" of God in history.[69]

## *German Catholic Historiography*

German Catholic historiography was stimulated by the renewal of Protestant historiography. After studying philosophy and theology, Johann Adam Möhler (1796–1838) was ordained a priest in 1819. He spent two years in Berlin in 1822–23 where he met the principal Protestant historians, philosophers and theologians of that period. He began to teach Church history in 1825 at the University of Tübingen, moving to the University of Munich in 1835. His first work, published in 1825, is entitled *Unity in the Church or the Principle of Catholicism*. Two years later his second book appeared: *Athanasius the Great and the Church of his Time in her Struggle with Arianism*. It was translated into French in 1840. In 1832 Möhler published his masterwork, *Symbolism: Exposition of the Doctrinal Differences Between Catholics and Protestants as Evidenced by Their Symbolical Writings* (translated into French and published in 1859).[70] He tried to avoid polemics and attempted to assure the reader that "the Greek Church is in no way opposed to the Catholics on any article of faith." He is aware that the task is more arduous when it comes to the Protestant world. But on the one hand he makes the task easier by declaring

69 Ernst Breisach, "Historiography: An Overview," in Lindsay Jones, ed., *The Encyclopedia of Religion*, 2nd ed., Detroit, Thomson Gale, 2005, 4034.

70 Johann Adam Moehler, *La symbolique, ou exposition des contrariétés dogmatiques entre les catholiques et les protestants d'après leurs confessions de foi publiques*, Besançon, Outhenin-Chalandre, 1836.

that the papal bulls have no symbolic character; on the other hand he looks to find allies by pointing to a common enemy: "Since Rationalism does not admit symbols, it has no place in *The Symbolic*." Above all, he sought to elaborate a methodology to present sound doctrine in the most consensual manner from the rediscovery of the symbols of faith of the first four centuries. Möhler writes: "By *Symbolic* we mean the reasoned exposition of the dogmatic contrarieties among the Christian Churches as a result of the 16th century religious revolution, a statement of their confessions of faith, their symbols." His task consists in the careful study of the symbolic books of Protestantism not only in order to detect the points of divergence but also to point out the sources they share with Catholicism. This German theologian was able to find favor with the Protestant theologian Giesler who was willing to dialogue with him. In this way he was at the origin of a profound renewal of the definition of orthodoxy. But he also belonged to his time and was unable to renounce the symbolism of the Council of Trent. As the title of his first book indicates, Möhler understood that it was urgent to rediscover the meaning of Catholic identity. In his view, only a retrieval of the apostolic tradition would enable a rediscovery of the power of certitude offered by orthodoxy. The following citation shows the breadth of his ecumenical vision while revealing the belligerence of his proposal towards Protestants of his time. Möhler writes:

> Since the Church and its various members could not prove the identity of their faith, our own faith might appear doubtful, even ours would seem doubtful to us; we would have no certainty that this was the Christian faith; we would find ourselves isolated, and our situation would be untenable. For this very reason there would be no Church; because, as much as the very unity of the interior life, the continuity of the consciousness of this unity is indispensable in all variations of its existence, and this is something that the Church, as a moral person, *should demonstrate by its remembrance*[71] (it is in this sense that we speak of embodied tradition). But as it can be proven through tradition how the spirit of Christianity has always manifested itself and always *in the same way*, one can always positively know the real way of understanding the Christian doctrine, that which has always existed. If one cannot trust

71 The italics are mine.

> tradition, then Christians would rightly despair of ever learning what Christianity really is; they would rightly despair that there is a Holy Spirit which fills the Church, that there exists a common spirit and sure knowledge of Christianity. As we will later see, this is the state in which those who reject tradition find themselves, and for them there can be no such thing as an objective Christianity.[72]

Among the great figures of the Tübingen School, mention must equally be made of Karl Joseph Hefele (1809–1893), appointed professor of Church history there in 1836. Following closely in the footsteps of Johann Adam Möhler, in 1839 he published a complete edition of the Apostolic Fathers. His greatest work was the publication of a seven volume *History of the Councils of the Church* between 1855 and 1874. He was elected bishop in 1869 and invited to participate in the 1870 Vatican Council. He spoke against the declaration of papal infallibility but found himself in the minority.

At more or less the same time as this brilliant generation of Protestant and Catholic historians was emerging within the Germanic Confederation, the Oxford movement was taking shape in the United Kingdom with, among others, J. H. Newman, E. Pusey, J. Keble, H. J. Rose and R. Froude. It represented the most creative current in Anglican ecclesial historiography and was probably the most typical movement of the remembrance period of orthodoxy. The movement was characterized by its support for the doctrine of apostolic succession of the Anglican Church, the use of *The Book of Common Prayer* in its entirety and the disengagement of the Church from the British crown. Its most famous representative was John Henry Newman (1801–1890), an Anglican priest, who began by publishing, in 1833 and anonymously, his *Tracts for the Times*. Newman's preoccupation, based on his own historical research (in 1833 he published his study *Arians of the Fourth Century*) was to attribute a specific identity to the Church of England. Newman was conscious of the fact that his Church was a middle way or *via media* between Protestantism and Catholicism and affirmed it was through its fidelity to apostolic and dogmatic tradition that Anglicanism would realize its full legitimacy. The Scriptures could not be understood without the mediation of the episcopal tradition and the prophetic tradition. For this reason, he immersed himself in the study of the Fathers

72 Jean Adam Moehler, *De l'unité de l'Eglise, ou du principe du catholicisme, d'apres l'esprit des Pères de l'Eglise des trois premiers siècles*, Bruxelles, H. Remy, 1839, 47–48.

of the Church and of the dogmas which were merely "symbols of divine realities."[73] In 1836 his defense of dogma led him to oppose the Unitarian theses professed by Renn Dickson Hampden, a professor of theology at Oxford who based ecclesial identity on the remembrance of the Scriptures but without this implying any faith in the Trinity or the Incarnation. This gave Newman the opportunity to fight against a religious liberalism which gave each individual the right to believe whatever he wanted to believe and to defend the truth of revealed religion. This polemic was decisive for subsequent religious historiography and for the evolution of orthodoxy within the universities of Harvard (which opted for the liberal path of Unitarianism) and that of Oxford (which maintained its Anglican identity).

But Newman's vision of the Church of England as a *via media* between Rome and Geneva, between institutional memory and eschatological memory, fell apart with his rediscovery of the concept of apostolic tradition. The distinction between Christocentric and pneumocentric tradition was dangerous. Orthodoxy is, indeed, a permanent and faithful return, in Christ in the Spirit, to the apostolic tradition. Newman was impressed by St. Augustine's words at the end of the Donatist crisis: "*securus judicat orbis terrarium*,"[74] "the world's verdict is secure." For him, they meant that the truth was in the universal Church, the same everywhere and at all times. Modernity, as a system that juxtaposes the magisterium of doctors with those of the popes, was therefore a historical error.

In 1838, Newman published his *Lectures on Justification* in which he inaugurated a new semantic and ecumenical historiography. In this book he reconciled Lutheranism and Catholicism by encouraging both to rediscover the meaning of the words used in the polemics of justification. For him, faith alone justifies, but only if one understands by faith a movement of the soul, guided by grace, which enables the inner conversion of the

73 Roderick Strange, *John Henry Newman, A Mind Alive,* Darton, Longman and Todd, 2008, 38.

74 Donatism was a heresy which originated among the bishops of Numidia in North Africa who refused to recognize the validity of those bishops consecrated by "traitor bishops" who had consented to burn the holy books during the persecution of Diocletian in the years 295–299. The Numidian bishops also refused to accept the authority of the bishop of Rome who had condemned them and appealed to the emperor Constantine. On August 1, 314, the Council of Arles decided against them. This led, for the first time in the history of the Church, to a police intervention against Christian communities in the name of orthodoxy. The properties of the schismatic bishops were confiscated and their communities were dissolved.

sinner. A return to the Fathers of the Church led, therefore, to a semantic reconciliation between faith and reason, between words and facts:

> The words of Scripture are robbed of their hidden treasures, and frittered away among a multitude of meanings as uncertain, meagre, and discordant, as the one true sense, like a great luminary, is clear and gracious. . . . Our duty is to be intent on things, not on names and terms; to associate words with their objects, instead of measuring them by their definitions. . . . Here is the especial use of the Fathers as expositors of Scripture; they do what no examination of the particular context can do satisfactorily, acquaint us with the *things* Scripture speaks of. They tell us not what words mean in their etymological, or philosophical, or classical, or scholastic sense, but what they do mean actually, what they do mean in the Christian Church and in theology.[75]

As Newman himself relates in his *Apologia pro vita sua*, the decisive moment occurred in 1839. While working on the history of Monophytism, he suddenly realized that the Monophysites had at first sought a middle way between the Eutychians and the theologians of Alexandria. Newman concludes: "I looked at myself in the mirror and saw that I was a Monophysite."[76] Two years later he wrote his *Essay on the Development of Christian Doctrine* in which he proposed "seven criteria of discernment" for the verification of orthodoxy, making it possible for one to distinguish between true and false developments of the faith.[77] The criterion of faithful memory thus began to be replaced by that of true and fair knowledge.[78] It was for the Anglican theologian to rediscover the ontological dimension of the truth while at the same time allowing its questioning by the enlightened rationality of "a body of probabilities with the value of certainty." The notion of conscience was the conceptual tool that enabled Newman to consider the orthodoxy of the faith from the perspective of justice and orthopraxy. He envisaged

75 John. H. Newman, *Lectures on Justification*, 2nd ed., Rivington, 1840, 132–37.

76 John H. Newman, *Apologia pro vita sua*, London, Dent and Sons, 2006, 114.

77 Permanence of the model; continuity of principles; the assimilative power of an idea; the logical sequence of the concepts; the presence of original intuitions; anticipation of the future; the active preservation of the past (by a continuity of the concept throughout its development); the degree of temporal durability.

78 Jean Honoré, *Newman*, Paris, Desclee, 1988, 61.

conscience as "the divine voice that speaks in us." Newman wrote: "conscience is not a judgment upon any speculative truth, any abstract doctrine, but bears immediately on conduct, on something to be done or not done. It is a practical rule."[79] For Newman, therefore, religious truth was eminently practical. Truth is given as something to be acted upon that is to conform to the moral exigency that truth reveals and to acquire this spiritual wisdom which is an intellectual virtue. But at the moment in time, there was no one in the Anglican Church with whom Newman could discuss it. On October 9, 1845 he was received into the Catholic Church and became a cardinal in 1879. All the same, Newman remained a new sort of Christian. His biographer, Jean Honoré, wryly notes that, when the cardinal offered a toast at the end of a meal, he asked that it be drunk first to conscience and only afterwards to the pope.

### *Historiography in the Eastern Church*

In the 17th century, the debates of Catholic and Protestant historiography reached the Orthodox theological academies. The historiographical tradition of the Eastern Church also sought to find its identity through a faithful memory. This historiography, however, was openly polemic and reactionary regarding the new historical representations of the history of the Western Church. The fidelity of the Eastern historians essentially centered on the preservation of the memory of the councils and the apostolic sees. Dositheos of Jerusalem (1641–1707) was born in Greece and ordained a deacon at the age of eleven in 1652. He was the Patriarch of Jerusalem from 1669 to 1707. He opposed the Calvinist influence on the *Confession of Faith* (1629) of the patriarch Cyril Loukaris, which he had condemned by the Synod of Jerusalem in 1672. Urged by Nointel, the ambassador of Louis XIV to the Ottoman Court, and inspired by the *Confession of Faith* of Peter Moghila, Metropolitan of Kiev (1640), Dositheos redacted his own *Confession*, which was approved by the Council of Jerusalem and which had an important influence on Orthodox theology, especially on Metropolitan Philaret of Moscow. Dositheos also criticized Peter the Great, the Tsar of Russia, for having abolished the patriarchate of Moscow. He published a twelve volume *History of the Patriarchate of Jerusalem*, which covered all the histories of the Eastern Churches and defended a conciliar vision of

79 Ibid.

orthodoxy. Dositheos likewise combated the new Counter-Reformation mission of the Congregation for the Propagation of the Faith in Palestine. This led him to denounce the Latin papacy. He used the work of S. Syropoulos as his principal source for the Council of Florence, and severely condemned the 1439 decree of unity. Dositheos called for the union of all Christians within the Orthodox Church which, in his mind, was the only one that was catholic and apostolic. In 1692 he published, at Jassy, an anthology of 14th and 15th century anti-Latin treatises.[80]

Apart from the writings of Dositheos, there are few important historical works in the Orthodox world during the 17th and 18th centuries. There is a debate among contemporary historians as to the reasons for this silence of the ecclesial historiography of the Eastern Church. Some, such as Georges Florovsky (1893–1979), who were convinced by the thesis of the German Nietzschean philosopher Oswald Spengler (1880–1936) concerning the pseudomorphosis of ideas from one culture to another, consider that Russian theology was the victim of a Catholic and Protestant invasion; this would explain the lack of productivity between the fall of Constantinople and the collapse of the Russian Empire in 1917.[81] Others, along with Georges Fedotov (1886–1951), believe that the history of Russian theology, even though it was exposed to exterior influences, was the agent of its own destiny and responsible for the censure it received when it stagnated under the Ottoman yoke or during the tsarist era.[82] Rather than enter into this theoretical debate, we will limit ourselves to the presentation of three major figures of 19th century Orthodox historiography who represent, each in his own way, the current of ecclesial historiography which at that time defined itself as catholic-orthodox.

Eugene Boulgaris (1716–1806) was the bridge between Greek and Russian historiography, and also between the historiography of the Age of Enlightenment and traditional Christian historiography. Born on the Greek island of Corfu, which at that time was a dependency of Venice, he became a monk in 1737. After studying at the University of Padua, he became director of the

80 In this work he included the Acts of a synod supposedly held at Constantinople in 1450 which rejected and anathemized the Union. Even though Allatius, a Greek favorable to the union, considers the document a forgery (there are several incongruities in the text—such as the participation of Mark of Ephesus who died, at the latest, in 1445), the Greek Church recognizes it as right. Cf. Marie Hélène Blanchet, op. cit., 22.

81 G. Florovsky, *Les voies de la théologie russe*, Paris, YMCA Press, 1936, ch. 2, 10.

82 Cf. the introduction to the book by Georges Fedotov, *'Sviatie drievniej Rusi*, Paris, YMCA Press, 1931.

Athonite academy at the monastery of Vatopedi from 1753 to 1759 where he taught philosophy and mathematics. He was expelled by the hierarchy of Mount Athos because they found his ideas too influenced by the Enlightenment. He then directed the theological academy of the patriarchate of Istanbul. He wanted to introduce "enlightened" instruction but was once again forced to retire, in 1761.

The Congregation for the Propagation of the Faith was created in Rome in 1622 in the shadow of the Counter-Reformation. It endeavored to reintegrate pagan, Protestant and Orthodox populations into the fold of the Catholic Church without distinction.[83] In reaction to the Congregation's proselytizing activities, a synod of the Orthodox Churches convened in Constantinople in 1755 in the presence of the Patriarch Cyril V, and with the participation of the patriarchs of Alexandria and Jerusalem. They decided to modify the decision of the synod of 1484 concerning the admission of Latins to the Eastern Church without rebaptizing them. The patriarchs declared that the Latin baptism was invalid, and that a baptism by immersion was necessary before allowing them to participate in the sacramental life of the Orthodox Church. Boulgaris was very hostile to Catholic proselytism, and maintained a correspondence with the French Jansenist Pierre Leclercq on the subject, but this correspondence did not lead to any movement of solidarity towards the Greek Church on the part of the French Church. In 1771 Boulgaris was summoned to the court of Catherine II at St. Petersburg to manage the imperial library. He used the occasion to write an anonymous tract against papal activity in Poland. Confronted with Catholic historians who assimilated all past unions to a single Unio or Ounia, Boulgaris insisted on the differences which opposed them. While remaining coherent with the paradigm of his era, but in another manner, he considered that the *henosis*, or right unity, such as that of 879 which put an end to the schism between Pope Nicholas and Patriarch Photius, had to be doctrinal and could not be founded on a static body of beliefs fixed for all eternity. Boulgaris became archbishop of the new diocese of Kherson but resided at Poltava. He administrated this vast diocese which had been under the jurisdiction of Constantinople prior to the Russian conquest of the territory. He translated Voltaire and

83 It was only in 1917 that Rome recognized the Eastern Orthodox Churches as true Churches through the erection, by Benedict XV, of a Congregation for the Eastern Church within the structure of the Congregation for the Propagation of the Faith. That same year, due to the initiative of Louis Petit, rector of the Uniate seminary of Kadikoy on the outskirts of Istanbul, the Pontifical Oriental Institute was founded in Rome.

John Locke, and published an essay in 1838 entitled "On the Tolerance of Those Who Do Not Share Our Religion."[84] This text is revelatory of a new confessional representation of the Eastern Church which now essentially defines itself in opposition to Catholicism and Protestantism. Boulgaris warns the faithful about dialoguing with the heterodox. "The heterodox Christian is decidedly outside of our faith, be this because he never entered through infidelity, like the pagan or the Jew, or because he left, went astray and followed his own path, like the schismatic or heretic." The Orthodox Christian "should not join the battle for the faith except when it is necessary."[85] On such an occasion he should have at his disposal the texts which the Fathers of the Church have written against the heterodox. In this case he should not hesitate to "reduce error to silence" and to break off contacts with the heretic according to the apostolic commandment (Titus 3:10) and the patristic admonition (Basil of Caesarea, *Sermo*, 12,1).

In the following century, with Greece recovering its independence in 1830, a new generation of historians would not be satisfied with simply condemning Western proselyte historiography. Along with Constantine Paparrigopoulos, the author of a *History of the Greek Nation* published in Athens in 1877, this generation affirmed a Pan-Hellenistic vision of Orthodoxy, "essence of the Greek tradition," based on the 15th century Peloponnesian civilization and the work of George Gemistus Plethon. The latter, founder of the Platonic Academy of Florence, was a neo-Platonic and neopagan philosopher who, after having participated in the Council of Florence, rejected the unification of the Churches.

Vassili Vasilievitch Bolotov (1853–1900) is considered by many 20th century intellectuals (Bulgakov, Fedotov, Kartachov, et al.) as one of the greatest historians of the Church. He was born in the village of Kravotyn in the province of Tver. The son of a deacon, he studied theology at the Tver seminary, then at the Academy of St. Petersburg. He was extremely brilliant and knew more than twenty languages including Coptic, Armenian, Georgian, Hebrew, Syriac and Arab. In 1863, the State universities introduced the study of Church history. Six years later, at the suggestion of Msgr. Makari, Church history became one of the four compulsory specializations taught during the four year course in theology academies. The time was

84 The text has been translated by V. Conticcello and can be found online at www.ephe.academia.edu/VassaKontouma/.

85 Ibid., 7.

ready for a school of ecclesial history within the Eastern Church. Bolotov stepped in and filled the gap. In 1879 he defended his thesis on *Origen's Trinitarian Doctrine*. At the age of 24 he became a professor of the history of the Ancient Church. He published numerous specialized studies notably on fiercely debated questions, such as the year and day of the death of the Evangelist Mark in Egypt (April 3, 63). In 1896 he was appointed to the new chair of Church History founded by the tsar. He died the same year as his friend the philosopher Vladimir Soloviev. His last words before dying were: "Christ is coming." He wrote a four volume *Introduction to Church History* which was only published between 1907 and 1918, after its censure had been lifted. The first volume is a vast methodological introduction to the history of the Church in which he presents his sources, analyzes Greek and Latin historiography as well as contemporary historiography, and justifies his own periodization. Bolotov had a great spiritual openness while identifying himself as a son of his Church. The Church he defines as the People of God. His vision of Orthodoxy went far beyond the narrow confines of the institutional boundaries of the mystical body of the Church. Bolotov warns the reader that his confessional approach is the price he had to pay to have the censure lifted:

> Sometimes it is requested that history be not only universal, but relate to a particular confession. Stated in these terms, such a requirement is inadmissible, for history would thus be a total negation of historical knowledge. But within the limits of the law, the confessionalism of the historian is quite a natural phenomenon and is compatible with scientific objectivity.[86]

Bolotov is neither a spiritual nor a confessionalist. He defends the Orthodox Church in its historical incarnation. But if this Church, which Bolotov expressly designates as *kath'holic* (taking care to use the Greek orthography except when he is designating the post-Tridentine Roman Catholic Church) is holy, its members can be sinners. For this reason, he thus summarizes the paradigm of Eastern orthodox historiography: "Objectivity demands a faithful description of the historic Church. One cannot see only light

86 Vassilli V. Bolotov, "Vvedenie v Tserkovnoujou Istoriou," *Prilojenie k Khristians-komou Tchteniou*, Spb, 1913–1918, vol. 1, 30.

in one's own Church, and shadow in that of others."[87] For Bolotov, this fidelity will be restricted by conciliar decisions.

This explains why his history is punctuated in the following manner: from the end of the first century (apostolic history, according to Metropolitan Philaret, belongs to Biblical history and cannot be the object of historical criticism) to the Council of Chalcedon in 451 (which represents the first break with the Monophysite world, source of the major breach under Islam); from Chalcedon to 1054 (which corresponds to the schism with Rome) and from 1054 to the present (but Bolotov shows little interest in this period). Within this doctrinal tradition where the concept of orthodoxy as right truth was preserved, Bolotov first considers a triadological cycle of theology which extends until 381, followed by a Christological cycle which lasts until 681. He does not question the ecumenical quality of the 6th council but notes that the Churches of Jerusalem and Alexandria are no longer represented. He also finds that the Council in Trullo of 691 adopted numerous canons in contradiction with both Roman and Armenian practices. After this date, the advent and spread of Islam represented, in Bolotov's opinion, a serious failure of orthodox thought, a failure which he believes orthodox theology had not sufficiently reflected upon.

Although he denies any confessional bias, Bolotov is not entirely free from prejudices. He compares the confessions to psychological models and uses the example of a professor giving an unexpected exam to his students: "This produces different reactions," explains Bolotov. Some students base their responses on all sorts of authority, "for example, on that of the last one to speak." Bolotov, who is targeting Catholics here, states that in this there is a danger of falsifying history in the name of celebrating infallible reason. Those who rely on their own strength to respond are the Protestants. Such a vision is also dangerous, he notes, as can be seen by the wandering of free thought in the Protestant world. If freedom of conscience has the merit of fighting against authoritarianism, it can become a rejection of all authority. "Whoever pronounces the absolute freedom of his personal reasoning finishes by questioning the Holy Scriptures which ultimately leads to their rejection." The student who does not rush to give an answer, who reasons in a dialogic way, who does not skip over things in his argumentation, is characteristic of the Orthodox according to Bolotov. "The consciousness of oneself as a part and not the whole of the *kath'holic* Church gives rise to a just judgment

87 Ibid., 31.

of other voices. Even the testimonies of societies which do not belong to the catholic Church today are important, especially the ancient testimonies, for these reveal the voice of the universal Church."[88] Bolotov thus defined himself as an Orthodox historian with all the contextual limitations of the term. He was, however, conscious of the challenge which Islam posed to orthodox theology and of the disastrous consequences resulting from the mingling of the political and doctrinal in the precedent paradigm of orthodoxy. He devoted the last years of his life to scholarly research that aimed to faithfully recover the remembrance of the Nestorian communities. He was also the author of a report on the *filioque* for the commission of the Holy Synod that was concerned with an eventual rapprochement with the Old Catholics who broke with Rome after the Vatican Council. In this document, Bolotov demonstrated that the procession of the Holy Spirit from the Father through the Son could be considered by the Orthodox Church as a *theologoumenon,* that is to say, a legitimate opinion in the Church.

The Russian theologian and historian Alexei Petrovitch Lebedev (1845–1908) was born in the village of Otchakovo, near Kolomna, in the region of Moscow. His father was a priest whose alcoholism led to problems with Metropolitan Philaret. Nonetheless he sent his son to the seminary and then to the Moscow Academy of Theology. In 1870 he became titular of the chair of the History of the Early Church and taught there for 25 years. He was very popular, trained many seminarians, and formed a school of disciples that included N. Gloubokovsky and A. Spassky. He published several books on the history of the Byzantine Church before and after the fall of Constantinople in 1453,[89] and on the history of the councils,[90] which represented for him, as it did for Bolotov, the heart of the memorial identity of Orthodoxy. In 1895, following the tsar's decision that Church history be taught in state universities, he was appointed to the new chair of Church History at the University of Moscow. In 1903 he published a scholarly jewel, *Ecclesial Historiography as Presented by its Principal Representatives.*[91] He had to pay constant attention to the censure exercised by Constantine Pobedonostev, the procurator of the Holy Synod. For this reason, after the revolution of 1905, he called for the reinstatement of the institution of the patriarchate in the Russian Church.

88 Ibid., 36.

89 A. Lebedev, *Istoria Greko Vostotchnoi tserkvi pod vlastiou Tourok*, Spb, Touzov, 1903.

90 A. Lebedev, *Istoria vselenskikh soborov,* Serguiev Possad, Typ. Sneguirevoi, 1896–1897.

91 A. P. Lebedev, *Tserkovnaja Istoriografia v glavnikh ieia predstaviteliakh s IVv. do XX veka*, Spb, izd I.L., Touzova, 1903.

Lebedev's complete works take up more than eleven volumes. Despite all this impressive literature, the Russian immigrant historian Georges Florovsky (1893–1979) considers Lebedev a simple "popularizer." Florovsky asserted that "Lebedev was not an independent thinker" because the latter considered that it was essential to know the literature of Western historiography.[92] Yet an attentive reading of his history of religious historiography reveals that Lebedev was very free with regard to the principal historians of his time. He was well acquainted with Hegelian philosophy and was able to distance himself from the theories of Hegelian historians of the Church such as Friedrich Hasse. Although he was aware of the weight of censure in the Catholic universities, he was sufficiently in command of his subject to appreciate the progress made in the history of the Church by Claude Fleury and Sebastien de Tillemont. A tireless reader, Lebedev also took an interest in the *Histoire de l'Eglise de France* by Wladimir Guettée (1816–1892), a French Catholic priest who converted to the Orthodox Church after his writings were banned by the Holy See. He knew how to guide his students by presenting the originality of German historical science while, at the same time, noting its decadence and its growing submission to the Prussian State. He cited Harnack as an example of "What should not be done!" Although Florovsky did not mention it in his history of Russian theology, Lebedev was the first one to write a history of Russian theology through his study of Russian ecclesial historiography which forms the third part of his master work. Lebedev, citing his sources, mentions in particular Professor Dobrotvorski, professor of Church history at the University of Kazan, and author of a methodology of the Russian Church, published in 1868, which he took as a model.

These historians distinguished between an "orthodox-pravoslavnij" and an "orthodox-orthodoxalnij" point of view. If they rejected the second, confessional, approach, they defined the first approach as the "preservation of principles." They went on to say that the second approach was the one used by the best "liberal" historians of the different confessions. Lebedev added, however, that the key to objectivity was to be found in a sort of "orthodox instinct," namely "respect for ecclesial tradition."[93]

In the *History of Religions*, published in Moscow in 1909 (that is to say, during the most enlightening period of the Silver Age), Alexander Eltchaninoff, Vladimir Ern and Paul Florensky benefited from this historiographical,

92 G. Florovsky, *Les voies de la théologie russe*, Paris, L'Age d'homme, 2001, 347.

93 A. Lebedev, *Tserkovnaja*, op. cit., 566.

ecclesial and intellectual renewal. Following Soloviev and Dostoevsky, these authors and critical readers of both Kant and Marx belonged to the symbolist renewal and the rediscovery of the spiritual and patristic tradition of Christianity. In order to emerge from confessionalism, these authors close to the Academy and to the St. Sergius Lavra, who could therefore not be suspected of heterodoxy, emphasized the crucial notion of "degrees of religious consciousness." Thanks to this concept the new discipline of hagiology, or the study of holiness, appeared. Its emergence was contemporary with the canonization of St. Seraphim of Sarov (1759–1833) on July 19, 1903, by the Holy Synod of the Russian Church. The Russian Church had, in fact, practically no longer glorified any saints during its Synodal period. This intellectual and ecclesial renewal continued to be deepened and developed in France during the 1930s. The Russian Orthodox historian Georges Fedotov published two major books at the YMCA Press directed in Paris by N. Berdyaev. In 1929 *Saint Phillippe métropolite de Moscou*[94] appeared, a hymn to freedom of conscience exemplified by the face to face encounter between the Tsar Ivan the Terrible and Metropolitan Philip (1507–1569), the head of the Moscow Church. Two years later Fedotov's major work *The Saints of Ancient Rus'* appeared. This book, prefaced later by Father Alexander Men (1935–1990), was reissued in hundreds of thousands of copies during the 1990s in post-Communist Russia during the period of mass canonizations in the Russian Church.[95] This new discipline married the fidelity of the ecclesial consciousness with a critical mind turned not towards the limits of the conceptual identity but towards the reality surpassing it. It was therefore possible to begin to take account of both the unity of the Church and the diversity of the historical paths taken by Eastern and Western Christianity. In the chapter on Orthodoxy, Eltchaninoff and Florensky write:

> If one acknowledges religious life as a unique reality of salvation, then one must turn to the experience of those people who have reached the highest levels of religious life, namely those who cannot not be recognized as saints.

In addition, they do not hesitate to include saints such as Francis of Assisi in their history of Orthodoxy. They failed to write a fully ecumenical and

94 In 2009, Pavel Lounguine made this book into a movie entitled *Tsar*.
95 G. Fedetov, *Sviatye dryevniei Russi*, Paris, YMCA Press, 1931.

orthodox history of Christianity. Yet the foundations for a common history of the "Christianity of John, Peter and Paul" had been laid by the master of this generation of intellectuals, Vladimir Soloviev (1853–1900). In his book *The Dogmatic Development of the Church (Le développement dogmatique de l'Eglise)* (1885), Soloviev vigorously affirms that "If, according to the testimony of the Apostle Paul, the life of the Church develops harmoniously, going from strength to strength to become a perfect man and attain the full stature of Christ, correlatively it must also develop in the mind of the believer, rising from light to light, from truth to truth."[96] Just like Newman, the Russian philosopher and poet chose to commune with the whole Church. He even considered that the Russian vision, the vocation proper to the Russian nation, was to realize universal Christianity through a synthesis of its Germano-Latin and Slavo-Byzantine traditions. On February 18, 1896, he entered the Catholic Church during a liturgy celebrated by the Greek Catholic priest Nicholas Tolstoi, while continuing to feel Orthodox.[97] He wrote at the end of his life, in 1899–1900, *Three Conversations*, an eschatological narrative of the unification of the Churches. At the end of the story, which presents the heirs of the Apostles Peter, Paul, and John participating in an imaginary Council of Jerusalem, it is a German Protestant, Doctor Pauli, who saves the Church from the Antichrist and the Great (Sage) Mage. Doctor Pauli's recognition of the primacy of Peter, as a servant and not as a binding authority, leads to a mutual recognition of the Churches and the end of history.

The Russian theologian Georges Florovsky (1893–1979), considered one of the principal 20th century historians of Orthodoxy, belonged to another generation. He radically opposed the new ecumenical and eschatological historiography of his predecessors. And yet he belonged to this same School of Paris which questioned the paradigm of orthodoxy as faithful memory and prepared its shift towards that of true and fair knowledge. In order to better understand this complex and self-evolving reversal, it is necessary to briefly present the life of G. Florovsky. He began teaching at the University of Odessa in 1919. But the following year he and his family had to leave Russia. His academic career was cut short by the Russian Revolution. In France, his

96 V. Soloviev, *Le développement dogmatique de l'Eglise*, Paris, Desclée, 1991, 74.

97 Father N. Tolstoi heard the philosopher's confession and only asked that, before receiving communion, he recite, in Slavonic, the symbol of faith of the Council of Trent, i.e., including the *filioque*. Http://krotov.info/library/18_s/solovyov/okolo.html.

new home country since 1924, no university offered him a position. In 1925, he resigned himself to teach Patristics at the Orthodox St. Sergius Institute and was ordained a priest in 1932. It was at this time that he affirmed that the crisis of Byzantinism in the 16th century was due to the abandonment of the Patristic tradition. In reaction this required a return to the Fathers. This expression was in fact a leitmotiv in the Russian Orthodox academic world for at least a century and had already borne much fruit in the academies of Kazan, Moscow and St. Petersburg. This is why Florovsky's colleagues at the St. Sergius Institute first tried to temper his youthful impulse. But in 1935–37 he severely opposed Sergius Bulgakov on the subject of the doctrine of the Wisdom of God and found himself at odds with the other professors at St. Sergius who supported their dean,[98] and also with Nicholas Berdyaev. In spite of all this, in 1936 Berdyaev published Florovsky's book *Ways of Russian Theology* but then wrote a harsh review of it in the magazine *Put' (The Way)*. There was a total lack of communication between Florovsky and the past generation that went from Marxism to Idealism and, finally, to Christianity. Florovsky deliberately identified the generation of Berdyaev and Bulgakov with the prerevolutionary stage of their thinking to better disqualify it and to make heard the voice of a generation twenty years younger. While the heroes of the Silver Age were too quickly assimilating the desire to anchor Florovsky's patristic theology to the nostalgia for a Golden Age described by Berdyaev as Maurassian, Berdyaev believed that Georges Florovsky, along with Vladimir Lossky, one of the members of the Brotherhood of St. Photius hostile to the dean of the St. Sergius Institute, were victims of the violence of history that had torn them from their mother-country. Therefore, in response, they sought to recover the stability of Byzantine Christianity or the warmth of the Mother-Church.

In reality, beyond this controversy—fueled, what is more, by the political tensions of the time—Florovsky often embraced the analyses of his predecessors. As the conclusion of his book *Ways of Russian Theology* shows, the author recognizes, as did his predecessors, Russian theology's need for "a free encounter with the West"; to reflect upon the spiritual foundations of the "new man" that the civilization of his day sought to build without any reference to God; to raise again the question of theology as a matter of public order. Even though in this work he presents a panegyric of Russian theology in opposition to decadent Western theology, G. Florovsky

98 L. Zander, "Notice biographique de S. Bulgakov," *Irenikon*, no. 2 (1946): 168–85.

cannot ignore the stinging failure that Communism represented for Russian Orthodoxy. Florovsky is one of the first historians of the Orthodox Church to have realized the limitations and sins of his historical Church. From this point on, Orthodox consciousness can no longer afford to be simply remembrance; it must also be creative. Thus, despite the sometimes traditionalist appearances of his writings, Florovsky confirms a new orientation of orthodox thought within the Eastern Church. In his conclusion of the *Way of Russian Theology* (*Les voies de la théologie russe*), Florovsky writes:

> The harsh verdict of history must be transformed into a creative calling to complete what remains unfinished. It is in times of great afflictions that we turn back to the Kingdom of God. Orthodoxy is not merely a tradition, it is also a task; it is not an unknown but a parameter. It is, at the same time, a mission, a leaven, a seed that ferments; it is also our duty and our vocation. . . . It is only in such spiritual toil that a past with premonitions and anticipations can be justified, but also weaknesses and errors of all kinds. Genuine historical synthesis is not to be found in the interpretation of the past but in the creative fulfillment of the future.[99]

After the Second World War when he narrowly avoided capture by the Communist troops of General Tito, Florovsky returned to Paris and, after the death of Bulgakov, taught moral and dogmatic theology at the St. Sergius Institute. In the journal *Dieu vivant*, where he collaborated with Fathers de Lubac and Daniélou, the initiators of the collection *Sources chrétiennes*, Florovsky resumed in French the conclusion of his 1936 book and hammered out his main idea: "A return to the Fathers in any event means progress and not retreat. It is a question of fidelity to the spirit rather than following the Fathers to the letter, of being fired with enthusiasm at coming into contact with their igneous inspiration and not of building a herbarium."[100] Against those who thought that Christian truth cannot be proved from history and can only be affirmed by "faith," Florovsky asserted that the Church recognized "dogmatic events as historical facts." For this reason, he concludes that "the theologian should discover and experience history as a

99 G. Florovsky, *Les voies de la théologie russe*, Paris, YMCA Press, 1936; French translation by Jean Louis Palierne, Paris, L'Age d'Homme, 2001, 452–53.

100 G. Florovsky, "Les voies de la théologie russe," *Dieu vivant*, Paris, 48.

*theanthropic process*, a passage from time to an eternity of grace, to become and build up the Body of Christ."[101] His reflection on the political evolution of the world encouraged him to become more involved in the ecumenical movement while seeking to maintain his identity as a "faithful Orthodox." His path that one could describe as "proselyte openness" was paradigmatic for many other Greek and Russian intellectuals who subsequently followed his footsteps.[102]

101 Ibid., 49.

102 Florovsky composed two texts in preparation for the Amsterdam assembly of the World Council of Churches: "The Nature and Mission of the Church" and "The Body of the Living Christ: An Orthodox Interpretation of the Church." In August, 1948, he participated in the first assembly of the World Council of Churches where he was elected to the executive committee — a post he held up to the third assembly of the Council at New Delhi in 1961 (he remained a member of the Faith and Order commission until the fifth assembly at Louvain in 1971). Given his turbulent relations with the Parisian Orthodox institutions, he looked for another home base. In 1948 he left for the United States and taught dogmatic theology at the Saint Vladimir Seminary in New York where he found himself with Georges Fedotov, Nicolas Arsenev and Nicolas Lossky. He then had the privilege of being invited to teach history at Columbia University and Harvard where he met up with Roman Jakobson, Dmitro Tschijevski and Paul Tillich. In 1950, at Toronto, he succeeded in having the Council clarify that membership did not impose on each member-Church the obligation to recognize the other member-Churches as being Churches in the strict sense of the word. He became dean of the seminary in 1951, founded the *Saint Vladimir's Seminary Quarterly* in 1953 and decided that the classes would be in English. He also taught at Columbia — where he founded an Orthodox Christian Fraternity — and at the Union Theological Seminary where he had P. Tillich and R. Niebuhr as colleagues. During this period he became an American citizen. In 1954 he was obliged to leave Saint Vladimir Seminary due to pressure from the conservative members of the local Russian hierarchy. He returned to the jurisdiction of Constantinople and, in 1955, went to teach at the Greek theological seminary, Holy Cross. Between 1956 and 1964, he taught the history of the Eastern Church at Harvard and organized a seminar on Russian civilization which was the occasion of encounters with A. Blane, M. Raeff and J. Billington. Until the end of his life, he published theological works in English — such as *Bible, Church, Tradition* (1972) — and participated in many conferences.

## CHAPTER 10

# *The "True and Just Knowledge" from Ruth Rouse and Stephen Charles Neill to Guy Bédouelle and Olivier Clément*

### THREE PATHS TOWARDS A FAIR KNOWLEDGE

The 20th century was marked by many violent conflicts mostly stemming from totalitarian ideologies. The doctrines of National Socialism in Germany and Communism in the USSR, both virulently claiming to be anti-Christian, succeeded in mobilizing important sectors of the population with promises of national cohesion and social justice. The Russian philosopher Nicholas Berdyaev was renowned for his knowledge of the philosophy of Emmanuel Kant (1724–1804) and the anthropological change that Kantianism brought to European philosophy. But like Vladimir Soloviev, he criticized the disconnection that the philosopher of Königsberg introduced between the thing in itself and the world of phenomena. Berdyaev was one of the first to detect the specifically religious nostalgia of the theanthropic link that the new ideologies aroused among people. In an article entitled "Philosophical Truth (*istina*) and the Moral Truth (*pravda*) of the Intelligentsia" published at Moscow in 1909 in the famous collection *Signposts* (*Vekhi*),[1] the Russian

1 *Vekhi, sbornik statiej o russkoj intelligentsii,* M., 1909; repr. Frankfurt, Germany, Possev, 1967; English translation: *Landmarks: A Collection of Essays on the Russian Intelligentsia*, New York, Karz Howard, 1977, trans. Marian Schwartz; Introduction Boris Shragin; French trans. by Claire Vajou: Nicholas Berdyaev, Sergius Bulgakov, Mikhaïl Guerchenzon, Alexandre Izgoev, Bohdan Kistiakovski, Piotr Struve, Simon Frank, *Jalons*, introduction by Françoise Thom, afterword by Stéphane Courtois, Paris, Cerf, 2011; "A Vekhi Bibliography. Alphabetical Index of books, articles and notices on *Vekhi*. From 23 March 1909 through 15 February 1910 (217 references in the 5th vol. of *Vekhi*, M. 1910),

philosopher showed that the Russian people, because of the religious education received through the liturgy of St. John Chrysostom, has always sought to identify knowledge of the truth with conciliarity (*sobornost'*) and consequently, with social justice. The term *pravda*, often considered untranslatable in many languages, thus signifies in the Russian consciousness the truth insofar as it is inseparable from justice (*spravedlivost'*) and what is right (*pravo*). This theanthropic approach to truth can be justified from the point of view of Orthodox thought. The worthy glorification, or *pravo-slavia*, was understood from the time of Yaroslav the Wise (978–1054), the son of Vladimir I, as attentiveness to social justice. Vladimir drafted the first part of the Russian Law, or "*Russkaja Pravda,*" which provided strong convictions for any theft, injury or murder.[2] If, however, this link between truth and justice deviates from its Christological axis, it can lead, in Berdyaev's opinion, to extremes. He especially castigates the contempt of the elite for truth in itself as *istina*, or as an autonomous metaphysical reality and not just as *pravda*. At the beginning of the 20th century, the Russian intelligentsia—separated from the clerical circles of the Church at least since the schism of the Old Believers in the 17th century—was ready, according to Berdyaev, "to give credence to any philosophy, on the sole condition that it validates its social ideas."[3] As accurate as his observation might have been, Berdyaev's reaction in 1909 was not, as he later admitted in his memoirs, a suitable one. He was at that time a Symbolist philosopher belonging to the literary currents of the Silver Age. He did not realize that an appeal to a pure and detached philosophy could not have any resonance at a time when the demands of the people for social justice were so important. Yet Berdyaev, a reader of Soloviev and Nesmelov, the main critics of Kantian anthropology, did not resign himself to fatalism. He understood the truth of his time, the profound desire for national unity and social justice. Hence, the editorial success and major controversy that the collection and, in particular, Berdyaev's article evoked.[4] In his contribution he proposed as intellectual alternative to the intelligentsia the concrete idealism of Khomiakov and the ontological realism of Dostoevsky.

---

and from 1918 to 1963," *Canadian Slavic Studies*, Montreal vol. 5, no. 3 (Fall 1971): 355–61.

2 http://ru.wikipedia.org/wiki/.

3 N. Berdyaev, "Verité de la philosophie et vérité-justice de l'intelligentsia," *Les Jalons*, Spb, 1909, French trans., Paris, Cerf, 2011, 23.

4 Antoine Arjakovsky, ed., *Les Jalons Cent Ans Après,* Paris, Lviv, IES/F.X. de Guibert, 2009.

> There are in Russian philosophy traits which are likened to the Russian intelligentsia: the aspiration for a unified vision of the world, for a fusion of the truth and the good, for knowledge and faith. There can even be found, in Russian philosophers with academic tendencies, a certain hostility towards abstract rationalism. And I think that concrete idealism, linked to a realistic approach to Being, could become the foundation of our national philosophical creation and could give birth to the national philosophical tradition that we need so badly.[5]

Further on he adds:

> All historical and psychological data bear witness to the fact that the Russian intelligentsia can only pass to another consciousness on the basis of a synthesis between knowledge and faith; a synthesis satisfying the need (very praiseworthy in itself) of the intelligentsia to link theory and practice, its need of "practical truth," of "truth-justice."[6]

Berdyaev was aware of the urgency of the situation. He sought to continue his reflection on the link between *sobornost* and truth. He immersed himself in research on the work of Alexis Khomiakov, the father of neo-slavophilism, and his reflections on conciliar and just truth. His book appeared in 1912, but it was already too late. The momentum of the revolution described by Boris Pasternak (1890–1960) in *Doctor Zhivago* (1957) and by Alexander Solzhenitsyn (1918–2008) in *The Red Wheel* (1971) was already underway. Just three years after the publication of *The Signpost (Vekhi)*, the Bolshevik press agency of St. Petersburg took the name of *Pravda*. Berdyaev was expelled from the Soviet Union by Lenin in 1922. He emigrated to Paris where he re-created his Academy of spiritual philosophy. It was there that he became involved in the ecumenical movement. Among his Anglican friends of the Fellowship of St. Alban and St. Sergius he rediscovered this awareness, this sign of the emergence of a new paradigm of truth, which John Henry Newman had formulated almost a century earlier: "Reason is made for truth and certainty, just as the conscience is for good and virtue." [7]

5 Ibid., 37.
6 Ibid., 40.
7 Honoré, *Newman*, op. cit., 74.

St. Pedro Poveda Castroverde (1874–1936) was born in the same year as Berdyaev at Linares, in Andalusia, into a Spanish Catholic family of modest means. He also represents, at the other side of Europe and of the spiritual spectrum of Christian consciousness, a figure characteristic of the evolution of the meaning of orthodoxy towards true and just knowledge at the beginning of the 20th century.[8] As a young seminarian at Guadix, Poveda felt himself called to work for the human and social advancement of the most downtrodden. He became a priest in 1897. Convinced that the first truth of Christianity was the commitment of all to a more just world, he founded numerous centers of Christian formation for lay teachers in Spain. One of his objectives at that time was to promote the role of women in society. He created a movement of Catholic students and young women university students. In Madrid, where he had been appointed chaplain of the Royal Palace, he became a member of the Central Board for the struggle against illiteracy. He also participated in the Succor Fraternity of Madrid which concerned itself with the destitute and with abandoned children. The Academy which he founded at Oviedo in 1911 was dedicated to the memory of St. Teresa of Avila. The Academy would later become the Teresian Association. It reflects the desire to anchor oneself in the faithful memory of the Spanish Catholic tradition while interpreting it in a new way. For Poveda, a true and just knowledge is not to be found in the hieraticism and pomp of the then very conservative spirituality of the Spanish Church, but rather in the celebration of all demonstrations of humanity, in putting the Gospel message of love into practice. In a 1916 issue of the *Boletin de la Academia Santa Teresa*, Poveda articulates his theanthropic logic:

> Teresa of Avila was a very human woman. Her works testify to this, the reading of her writings is the proof. I hope that the Teresian Association has this same quality. The name that it bears is a demonstration of this desire.... I claim that those who seek to lead a fully fulfilled life have first to open themselves to the overflowing gift of God. Will there then follow a superabundance of generosity? Of course. Will we attract others? There can be no doubt about that. Seek to destroy what is human? Never! That is a pipe dream. Strive for the fulfillment of the human in other ways? A derisory endeavor. Do without God to accomplish one's

8 *Pedro Poveda, quelques pages,* Bruxelles, Institution Theresienne, 2004.

> work? A stupid illusion. Do you not think that this synthesis is very simple, this process logical and its result infallible? God stretched out to mankind and mankind tends towards God. His Son, who is also God, came to assume our humanity and never abandon it in order to bring it to its fulfillment and to divinize it. Humanity has been fulfilled and divinized because of God's indwelling.[9]

Poveda's foundations have more than 4000 members in 32 countries and include numerous schools, university residences, centers of formation, youth organizations, publishing houses and programs of international cooperation. During the Spanish Civil War, during the religious persecutions of 1936, he was stopped for questioning by the Republican militia who asked for his identity. He replied: "*I am a priest of Christ.*" He was arrested, summarily judged and shot the same day, July 28, 1936. He was beatified by John Paul II in 1993 and canonized on May 4, 2003. In the advice he gave to the teachers and students of the first Academy from 1911–1912, Pedro Poveda insisted on the practical wisdom of the type of just action required in modern times:

> Ask God for light, be prudent, act without haste, consider the merits of what you demand of others, in case of doubt or difficulty, take time to take advice; whatever might be the situation act with righteousness.[10]

Dietrich Bonhoeffer, born in Breslau (today's Wroclaw) on February 4, 1906, was an evangelical Lutheran pastor, theologian, writer and anti-Nazi dissident. He was seminary director of the Confessing Church at Finkenwalde and undertook secret missions on the part of his Church during the Second World War. During one of these missions to Stockholm, he met the Anglican bishop of Chichester, George Bell, through whom he transmitted evidence of the extermination of the Jews by the Nazis to the British; he also asked him for help to eliminate Hitler. But on April 5, 1943, after his engagement, he was arrested and sent to a prison in Berlin.

Among the works he wrote in prison, published after his death under the title *Resistance and Submission (Résistance et soumission)*, is a collection of letters and reflections. During Christmas 1943, he wrote a morning prayer

9 Ibid., 29–30.
10 Ibid., 96.

that allows us to penetrate the most intimate depths of his faith in a God who is both Judge and Savior, subject and object of all knowledge:

> Holy, Merciful God,
> My Creator and my Savior,
> My Judge and my Deliverer,
> You know me and all that I do.
> You hate and punish evil in this world
> And in the next with no respect of persons;
> You forgive sins for the one who asks sincerely;
> You love goodness and reward it on this Earth with a good conscience
> And in the world to come with the crown of righteousness.[11]

Bonhoeffer was aware of his duty to fight with all his energy against the absolute evil of the Nazi anti-Christ regime. The collaboration of his Church with this Nazi regime consequently led the Lutheran pastor to a profound questioning of the conceptual foundations of truth. He understood that the values of fidelity, obedience and submission should be balanced by the values of freedom, critical thinking and, above all, responsibility. He writes:

> Civil courage however can only grow out of the free responsibility of free men. Only now are we Germans beginning to discover the meaning of free responsibility. It depends upon a God who demands bold action as the free response of faith, and who promises forgiveness and consolation to the man who becomes a sinner in the process.[12]

The German theologian participated in the failed assassination attempt against the Führer on July 20, 1944. On October 8, 1944, Bonhoeffer was transferred to the Buchenwald concentration camp. He was hanged on April 9, 1945 at the Flossenbürg concentration camp in Bavaria, near the current German-Czech border. Today, many Christians, beyond the confessional borders, consider Bonhoeffer as a modern day martyr for justice.

11 D. Bonhoeffer, *Résistance et soumission,* Paris/Geneva, Libraire protestante, Labor et Fides, 66.

12 Bonhoeffer, op. cit., 5; Eng. trans. in Dietrich Bonhoeffer, *Letters and Papers from Prison,* accessed at https://archive.org.

## THE CONTEMPORARY MEANING OF ORTHODOXY

According to the Jesuit Catholic theologian Bernard Sesboüé, we have moved from the modern era to the contemporary period, from a univocal concept of truth to a conception of the analogy of truth, from a theocentric representation of justice to its anthropocentric conception.

> In the first instance, the truth is one and indivisible, something is or is not, the truth is either total or non-existent. No distinction is made between different levels of truth. . . . In the second instance, each form or level of truth has a specific status and niche of relevance. They are not the same . . . certainly the human spirit cannot possibly give up the movement that drives it to discover the inner unity of all truths. But this is a prolonged labor of confrontation which will be, depending on the case, with regard to a scientific theory, a conception of history or of a doctrine of a truth of faith. . . .[13]

Sesboüé distinguishes three types of truth within the very heart of orthodox ecclesiology: revealed truth which is intrinsically irreformable, ecclesial truth, that of dogmatic facts, and juridical truth, the authority of what is being judged. These different orders of truth do not mean that the truth is fragmented but their distinction allows a better grasp of the dynamics, and thus the meaning, of truth. This distinction also allows a just consciousness to part with the incidental and non-essential and thus to rekindle the smoldering embers. As Guy Bédouelle writes, for Cardinal Journet, there are certain laws (the law of conforming to Christ, the law of the eschatological tension between death and resurrection) that structure theological wisdom from history. Among them is the law of clarification "according to which, with time, the Church disengages herself from that which surrounds her, from that which is not her, but which is mistaken for her. The Church, by the prompting of the Holy Spirit, arrives at an experiential consciousness of its true nature."[14] Contemporary consciousness is coming to understand that the truth can be both faithfulness to a divine word and the result of a human construct. This is at the very heart

13 B. Sesboüé, *Le magistère à l'épreuve,* Paris, DDB, 2001, 152.

14 Cardinal Journet, *L'Eglise du Verbe incarné,* vol. III, *Essai de théologie de l'histoire,* Paris, DDB, 1969, 691.

of orthodox thought on the theanthropy which has been upheld in the 20th and 21st centuries by personalities such as S. Bulgakov and R. Williams.

This evolution of the meaning of orthodoxy is especially evident in the writings of Léonide Chrol (1902–1982), disciple of Father Sergius Bulgakov. Born in St. Petersburg, the young Leonid received a solid education in music. From 1914 and the age of twelve, he gave piano concerts for wounded soldiers. His musical talent already astounded those who surrounded him. The revolution, however, interrupted his studies. In 1920 after the Russian Revolution, he emigrated first to Prague where he received the first prize for piano at the Conservatory, then to Paris. He continued his studies at the St. Sergius Institute where, influenced by Father Sergius Bulgakov, he became a priest. He and his wife Olga began to associate within the sphere of the Orthodox Action. Close to Mother Maria Skobstoff and Dimitri Klepinin, he remained faithful to Msgr. Euloge Guiorguievsky, Metropolitan of the Russian archbishopric within the ecumenical patriarchate. Founder in 1934 and rector of the Orthodox parish of Montauban,[15] he distinguished himself on Saturday, August 19, 1944, by saving the city from destruction by the 4th SS Regiment "Der Führer," which was confined to it thanks to his linguistic and diplomatic skills. The Waffen-SS division commander was a Mongol who a few days earlier had razed the village of Oradour-sur-Glane.[16] Besides being a pianist and artist, Chrol created two-sided polychrome puzzles which fitted together and were then fixed between two plates of glass.[17] His most famous work is *Le christianisme intégral* (*Integral Christianity*), written during the 1930s and published in 1967 in Montauban. He was among the first to recognize the emerging new paradigm of orthodoxy as true and just knowledge with all the implications that this implied: synthetical intelligence, ecumenical openness and the call for orthopraxis.

> Integral Christianity only asks aspirants to change their "heterodoxy" (*heteran doxan* — a different, more narrow way of thinking than catholic thought) into orthodoxy (*orthen doxan* — correct

15 In the 2002 documentary by Vladimir Kozlov, "Musique et couleurs du père Léonide," Father Chrol can be seen on his bicycle, covering more than 100 kilometers a day to celebrate a baptism or a funeral service. He later bought a 2 CV which was driven by Prince Alexis Kropotkine. On saint Dimitri Klepinin: *Dimitri's Cross: The Life and Letters of St. Dimitri Klepinin, Martyred during the Holocaust* by Helen Klepinin Arjakovsky (2008).

16 An avenue of Montauban is named after him in recognition of this accomplishment.

17 His works can be seen at the Ingres Museum of Montauban and in the collection of Aracine at Villeneuve d'Ascq.

> thinking, straight and divinely broad). For this change, as difficult as it might be, is thereafter perfectly justified: catholic orthodoxy is able to satisfy all the aspirations of every human soul seeking God and eternal truth; it can give a just solution to all problems in all spheres, to every question presented. It is the masterpiece of all cognitive and creative human activity without exaggerating, distorting, or simplifying anything. It is the development of all the talents God has bestowed on us. (Matt 25:14–30, Lk 19: 12–27)[18]

However, warns Bernard Sesboüé, having in mind perhaps that the reaction of Pius X to modernism only dates back to 1907, "the problem of restoring an equilibrium between the necessary recognition of the plurality of truths and the respect of the absolute of truth, especially divine truth, still lies before us."[19] For his part, the French Catholic philosopher Claude Tresmontant (1925–1997) worked to persuade the philosophers of his time, especially the neo-idealist philosophers whom he considered modern gnostics, to learn to distinguish "the Hebrew tradition, orthodox Judaism and orthodox Christianity" among the different metaphysics connecting the Being to the Physical Universe.[20] Moreover, the paradigm of faithful memory has the advantage of seducing many people in search of security in a world marked by constant challenges to intellectual modes. Gilbert Keith Chesterton (1874–1936) converted to Catholicism in 1922, 14 years after he wrote his famous essay *Orthodoxy*, a classic of Christian apologetics.[21] It is acknowledged that there is an important renewal of traditionalist currents within the Churches and of religions more generally at this time of accelerating globalization. Addressing the members of the Third Pan-Orthodox Preconciliary Conference in 1986, Metropolitan Emmanuel Adamakis shares his understanding of orthodoxy as true and just knowledge. He cites the Declaration of the 15 Orthodox Churches:

> We Orthodox Christians, having access to the meaning of salvation, must struggle to alleviate sickness, misfortune and anguish. Having

18 Léonide Chrol, *Alpha et Omega, Essai sur le christianisme œcuménique intégral*, Montauban, 1967, second edition, 18.

19 Ibid., 182.

20 Claude Tresmontant, *Les métaphysiques principales,* Paris, Gallimard, 1984; F.X. de Guibert, 1995, 308.

21 G. K. Chesterton, *Orthodoxy,* London, 1908; Paris, Gallimard, 1984. He had already published a book entitled *Heretics* in 1905.

> access to the experience of peace, we cannot remain indifferent to its absence in our contemporary society. As recipients of God's justice, we strive for a more authentic justice in this world and for the elimination of all forms of oppression. Experiencing divine mercy daily, we fight against fanaticism and intolerance among people and nations. Continuing to proclaim the incarnation of God and the deification of man, we defend human rights for all men and all nations. (...) Waiting for a new earth and a new heaven where absolute justice reigns, we fight here and now, for the rebirth and renewal of man and society.[22]

But the President of the Assembly of Orthodox Bishops in France is also aware that, in spite of the condemnation of phyletism by the Orthodox Church at the Council of Constantinople in 1872, this "heretical deviation" still exists within the Orthodox Churches.[23] This is why, strictly speaking, we cannot speak of a paradigm of true and just knowledge in the present time but only of a new configuration of orthodox epistemology.

Nonetheless, this new doxic system already has tangible signs on the level of international law. The reaction of states to the murderous ideologies of the 20th century in the aftermath of the Second World War led to the invention of a new international law. After the First World War, at the Treaty of Versailles in 1919, at the initiative of Woodrow Wilson, the League of Nations was formed on a purely secular basis. Michel Zyzykine, a Russian Orthodox historian, considered in 1936 that this organization was not viable for theological reasons: "Far from admitting to original sin, as did the more realistic signatories of the Holy Alliance, it implied the natural goodness of man."[24] The League did not stand up to the totalitarian ideologies of the interwar period and was replaced on October 24, 1945, by the United Nations, itself based on the United Nations Charter of June 26, 1945. The notion of States submitting to a transcendent spiritual power was not always accepted. On the other hand, the signatory States undertook to preserve future generations from "the scourge of war" and proclaimed their "faith in the fundamental rights of mankind, in the dignity and worth of the human person, in equal

22 Emmanuel Adamakis, "Heureux les doux, ils obtiendront la terre promise," *Qui nous fera voir le bonheur?* Paris, Presses de la Renaissance, 2004, 57–58.

23 Ibid., 48.

24 M. Zyzykine, "L'Eglise Orthodoxe et le droit international," *Actes du premier congrès de théologie orthodoxe, Athènes 29.11–6, 1936*, Hamilcar Alivisatos, Athens, Prysos, 1939, 417.

rights for men and women as well as for nations large and small." These States also undertook "to create the conditions necessary for the safeguarding of justice and the respect of obligations arising from treaties and other sources of international law, to promote social progress and bring about better living conditions in greater freedom." The General Assembly of the United Nations adopted in Paris on December 10, 1948, a Universal Declaration of Human Rights, which proclaimed the following in its first article: "All human beings are born free and equal in dignity. They are endowed with reason and a conscience and must act towards one another in a spirit of fraternity." The Declaration was written by persons with predominantly Christian and monotheist beliefs while embracing the values of other religions: Eleanor Roosevelt (Protestant), John Peter Humphreys (Catholic), René Cassin (Jewish), Charles Malik (Orthodox), Peng Chun Chang (Confucianist), Hansa Mehta (Hindu). In these texts one discovers a desire to root international law in a universal truth with justice as one of its characteristics. The theocentric vision of the Holy Alliance has been replaced by an anthropocentric representation of international law, in which practical reason was based on the demand for justice. This was further reinforced by successive amendments aimed to strengthen the protection of minorities (international treaties of December 16, 1966, World Conference of Vienna 1993, Durban 2001, etc.).[25]

The time was not yet favorable to the theanthropic vision defended by many orthodox Christians during the 20th century. On the other hand, many personalist ideas, stemming from the debates of the 1930s among Maritain, Berdyaev, and Mounier, found their first expressions on the level of international law. And new ideas, such as the right of interference, capable of questioning, under certain conditions, the sovereignty of a State that persecutes its own people, testifies to this new representation of justice.

On a strictly ecclesial plane, the reactions of Christians in favor of a just truth took the form of conversion and interconfessional reconciliation. For a Christian conscience, only a reconciled Church is able to offer a sense of belonging to a corporeal community and not just a contractual one. This is experienced through a solidarity founded on spiritual bonds and not those of class or race. As Hans Urs von Balthasar wrote in 1944, "the medieval castle, where one danced and banqueted in the Great Hall, above the dungeons and the torture chambers, has crumbled and will not be rebuilt." The

25 Joseph Yacoub, "Les droits de l'Homme: une oeuvre collective de l'humanité," *Aspects* (special edition, 2008): 31–43.

German theologian proposed reconstructing a new vision of the world, a vision not based on the absolutism of truth (which was the temptation of the medieval Church), nor on relativism (the temptation of the modern Enlightenment), but from a theology "which describes Christian existence from the point of view of service, mission and participation in the radiance with which the Church is consumed."[26]

This was also the vision of John Mott who, at the end of the Second World War, received the first Nobel Peace Prize at Stockholm. In 1948, under his presidency, the World Council of Churches was formed with the participation of the Orthodox Church (the Ecumenical Patriarchate), the Anglican Church and most of the Reformed Churches.

Later on, in 1964, the Second Vatican Council created a Pontifical Council for Christian Unity. Subsequently, in 1986, the body of the Orthodox Churches, in the course of a plenary preconciliar assembly at Chambésy, approved a text justifying their participation in the ecumenical movement. This movement of reunion among the Churches, in spite of its highs and lows, gave birth to many common declarations attesting to the rediscovery of a shared faith. Numerous initiatives of common prayer, witness and solidarity have emerged around the world, such as the community of Taizé, founded in France in 1940 by Brother Roger Schütz, or the reunification of the Protestant and Anglican Churches within the Church of South India in 1947. Since 2013 and the Reuilly Statement, there is now an agreement on Eucharistic hospitality between the Anglican Communion and the main Protestant Churches.[27] This movement, which was accompanied by a rediscovery of the patristic tradition, brought about a tangible rapprochement of the Christian faith with human rationality. It has also favored numerous political and social advances as demonstrated by the unity of European Christians in support of the fall of the Berlin Wall (at the Assembly of the CEC and the CCEE at Basel in May 1989 where the theme was "Justice, Peace and the Integrity of Creation") and the unity of Palestinian Christians advocating a peaceful resolution to the conflict between Israelis and Palestinians, as expressed in the December 2009 document *Kairos*.[28]

26 H. U. von Balthasar, "Raser les bastions," *Dieu vivant*, no. 25, Paris, Le Seuil (1953): 32.

27 https://www.la-croix.com/Urbi-et-Orbi/Archives/Documentation-catholique-n-2256/L-Accord-de-Reuilly-2013-04-10-938590; see also: http://anglicanfrance.fr/wp-content/uploads/2017/02/Report-Reuilly_Synode-Archdeaconry.pdf.

28 http://www.oikoumene.org/gr/resources/documents/other-ecumenical-bodies/kairos-palestine-document.html.

The new *doxa* or moral ethos of the liberal democratic world since the 1960s is certainly the requirement of authenticity, as convincingly demonstrated by Charles Taylor. But this paradigm still belongs to the confessional and individualistic era of human history. Contemporary orthodoxy, after the fall of Communism and the repeated crises of liberal capitalism, consists in reuniting the need for authenticity and the belonging to a tradition-community of truth. In his 1995 text *Fides et Ratio*, John Paul II highlighted this basic shift in Christian thinking initiated in the 19th century by a few great figures such as Alexis Khomiakov, Johann Adam Möhler and John Henry Newman. Benedict XVI and Bartholomew I drew the political, economic, ecological and social consequences in their encyclicals, especially in the text of the first, *Caritas in Veritate* [29] published in 2009, and in the letter addressed by Bartholomew to the International Ecumenical Peace Convocation in 2011. In this latter text, published on the eve of the Kingston Ecumenical Gathering on May 22, 2011, the Patriarch of Constantinople writes:

> Many of our efforts for peace are futile because we are unwilling to forgo established ways of wasting and wanting. We refuse to relinquish wasteful consumerism and prideful nationalism. In peacemaking, then, it is critical that we perceive the impact of our practices on other people (especially the poor) as well as on

29 "'Love in truth' (*caritas in veritate*) to which Jesus bore witness during his earthly life and, above all, by his death and resurrection, is the essential dynamic force of the true development of each person and of humanity as a whole. Love—*caritas*—is an extraordinary force that impels persons to commit themselves in the domain of justice and peace with courage and generosity. It is a force that has its source in God, Eternal Love and Absolute Truth. Each one finds his own good by adhering to the project that God has for him in order to accomplish it fully: it is, indeed, in this project that the person finds his own truth and it is by adhering to this truth that he becomes free (cf. John 8:32). To defend the truth, to propose it with humility and conviction and to bear witness to it in one's life are, consequently, exigent and irreplaceable forms of charity. Charity 'rejoices in what is true' (1 Cor 13:6). Everyone experiences in charity a spark which leads to love in an authentic manner: love and truth never totally abandon him because it is a question of a vocation planted by God in the heart and in the spirit of each person. Jesus Christ purifies and liberates our human weaknesses in our quest of love and truth and reveals to us, in plentitude, his initiative of love as well as the project of the true life that God has prepared for us. In Christ, *love in the truth* becomes the visage of his Person. Our vocation is to love our brothers according to the truth of his intention. He Himself is the Truth (John 14:6)." Official translation from the Vatican website.

> the environment. This is precisely why there cannot be peace without justice.[30]

Rowan Williams, the former Archbishop of Canterbury, also mentioned the pathways for rediscovering this link between moral authenticity and membership of a now global body, namely the retrieval of symbolic understanding, the pedagogy of patience, the rediscovery of the "Other who exists beyond violence: the look of love that cannot be eluded nor deflected and that does not possess or seek any advantage."[31] Such a level of consciousness still only concerns the spiritual elite. Few secular media giants or intellectuals most often considered today as "opinion formers" rise to this level. All the same, after the collapse of the great ideologies of the 20th century, this *doxic* perspective is the object of renewed interest. Secularized societies, especially in Europe, are rediscovering profound religious impulses within themselves and are seeking to redefine the role of religions in State institutions. In authors such as Metropolitan Kallistos Ware and Cardinal William Levada, the orthodoxy of the faith is considered less and less as a fixed semantic field.[32] It is seen, rather, as a quality of discernment, a dynamic perception constantly attesting the same

30 http://www.oikoumene.org/fr/nouvelles/news-management/a/fr/article/1634/pour-bartholomee-ier-la.html.

31 R. Williams, *Icones perdues, réflexions sur une culture en deuil,* Paris, Cerf, 2005.

32 Cf. especially this text of Cardinal Levada, dated July 10, 2011, announcing the forthcoming reunion of Assisi and responding to Benedict XVI: "The title chosen for the upcoming meeting at Assisi — Pilgrims of truth, pilgrims of peace — offers us a second indication: to be able to have a reasonable hope of working together for peace, we must have as a criterion this simple truth: 'Ethos cannot exist without logos' (J. Ratzinger, *Je vous ai appelé mes amis. La compagnie sur le chemin de la foi,* 71). Because of the grievously painful experiences of totalitarian ideologies, the pope has a horror of any form of subordination of reason to practice. But there is much more. The original link between ethos and logos, between religion and reason, is definitively rooted in Christ, the Divine Logos. For precisely this reason, Christianity is capable of restoring this link to the world, by participating, as a truthful and efficacious sign of Jesus Christ, in his unique mission of salvation (cf. *Lumen gentium,* 9). So we must firmly reject 'this relativism which affects, more or less clearly, the doctrine of faith and the profession of faith' (*Je vous ai appelé mes amis,* 71). But far from disparaging the diverse religious expressions or the ethical dimension, this valorizes them: 'We should seek to find a new patience — without indifference — with one another and for the others; a new capacity to let the other be other and another person; a new readiness to differentiate the levels of unity and thus realize those elements of unity which are possible today' (ibid.). Peace is not possible without truth and vice versa: the aptitude for peace is an 'authentic criterion of truth' (J. Ratzinger *Europe. Ses fondements aujourd'hui et demain,* 79)."

scriptural truths, capable of manifesting itself in the different cultural and social environments of a globalized world, ceaselessly finding new formulas for understanding and articulating the world's complexity in its deepest truth.[33] Orthodox thought is no longer solely understood as the proper celebration of the mystery of Light incarnate, or as the authentic recognition of truth's ontological dimension, or as a gesture of faithful obedience to the tradition of one's church. Too many post-Nietzschean Christians, from Nikos Kazantzakis (1883–1957) to Philippe Sollers (1936), have undermined the foundations of an orthodoxy which would define itself uncritically. The contemporary semantics of orthodoxy are first and foremost the ability of each person and each community to rightly accomplish the evangelical kerygma, that is to say, in a contextual, hermeneutic and interpersonal way. In 1932, Bulgakov was one of the first modern theologians to become aware of this reversal in ecclesial consciousness. According to him: "Orthodoxy is the Church of Christ on earth. The Church of Christ is not an institution, it is a new life with Christ and in Christ, led by the Holy Spirit."[34] B. Sesboüé describes this new paradigm which is being formed:

> The new face of the faith is that of a reasonable and reasoning faith, a faith inevitably critical. . . . Today's faith is becoming a voluntary faith (not simply handed down in the family), the fruit of a decision of personal freedom, a faith which is informed, a faith which is communitarian and participative (co-responsibility), a faith often remarkable for its generosity and commitment . . . this faith awaits a discourse where the theme of invitation clearly prevails over that of obligation and it intends to live according to the model of communication. This faith wants its deepest desire to be addressed and to be made to understand what is the greatest good of man. . . . This new face of the faith wants to live the "ritual" in living communion with the "existential". . . . This faith also means a return to the Gospel. It seeks to imitate the way of Christ and the apostles; it manifests itself in a certain Christian life style. The solidarity between word and deed, essential to the message of Jesus, is evoked in a sometimes very critical way. Preaching should reflect a way of life.[35]

33 R. Williams, *Icônes perdues*, op. cit.

34 S. Bulgakov, *L'Orthodoxie,* Paris, Alcan, 1932, 1.

35 B. Sesboüé, *Le Magistère*, op. cit., 291–92.

Such a representation obviously has important social and political consequences. The work of Paul Ricoeur (1913–2005), French Protestant philosopher, member of the Pontifical Academy of Science and an avid student of Bulgakov's disciple Paul Evdokimov, lies at the junction between these two epochs of orthodox awareness. In continuity with the post-Kantian tradition, Ricoeur's thought carefully separates the realm of philosophy from the realm of religion. But he also worked on an ethic characteristic of these new times. For him, the ethical aim is that "of a good life with and for others in just institutions."[36] Ricoeur recognized the primacy of ethics over morality, which he understood as a system of rules that constrain the individual living in society, while being aware of the need for the ethical aim to be tested against the norm. But he helped to show the importance of a third sphere of justice in action, "the legitimacy of a recourse of the norm to the aim, when the norm leads to practical impasses."[37] This practical wisdom consists, according to him, in inventing "the behaviors which will best satisfy the exception required by solicitude without betraying the rule."[38] It is the role of the tribunals to be "the public bodies that have the authority to build the new coherence required in exceptional cases."[39]

In this perspective the separation between Church and State is no longer understood according to Plato's model of the separation between body and soul. This is a major realization of the new paradigm of orthodoxy. It is rather notions such as "reasonable compromise in a multicultural society" or "practical wisdom" that govern the new political theologies which are emerging in modern ultrasecularized States. The truth, in fact, in the logic of Sergius Bulgakov (1871–1944), Rowan Williams (born in 1950) or Benedict XVI (born in 1927) is the same for all and must apply at all levels. Simply stated, it must be adapted precisely according to the context, the level of awareness and the degrees of corporality. In terms of worship, Sergius Bulgakov proposed in 1933 that joint liturgies could be celebrated between Anglicans and Orthodox on an occasional and local basis, since, in his opinion, the people concerned with the Fellowship of St. Alban had progressed far and deep enough together to discover that what united them was more important than what separated them.

36 Paul Ricoeur, *Soi-même comme un autre,* Paris, Seuil, 1990, 202.

37 Ibid., 201.

38 Ibid., 312.

39 Ibid., 323.

Pope Benedict XVI also admitted that the decisions of the Second Vatican Council concerning the liturgy could not be applied in a monolithic manner. Since the liturgy of the Council of Trent had been celebrated for centuries by the Catholic Church, it could continue to be legitimately celebrated by those Christians who so desired. On July 7, 2007, he published, accompanied by a letter to the bishops, the motu proprio *Summorum Pontificum* allowing the celebration of the Mass of St. Pius V (as revised by John XXIII) by all priests on request of their parishioners.

On legal grounds, the Archbishop of Canterbury suggested in 2008 that "certain parts of the Islamic *sharia*" could be applied in England. He defended this proposal in the following manner: Citizens must in certain cases have the right to freely choose between two types of jurisdiction. The idea of the Enlightenment that a single law should be applied to all had a religious foundation (the unique paternity of the Creator towards all human beings) but had to be refined so as to allow a real equality between citizens. The starting point is the recognition of the diversity of the communities within a nation. Since Muslims do not recognize themselves as being in the British legal system, for Rowan Williams, certain questions such as matrimonial law could be entrusted to sharia courts for Muslim citizens as soon as inhumane and misogynous punishments are removed from this code.

It goes without saying that this orthodox or neo-humanist, critical, differentiated perspective or lifestyle disrupts the confessional boundaries of truth and carries with it many elements borrowed from cultures and religions outside of Christianity. It accompanies a fundamental movement of global awareness. It sheds light on the scope of the interreligious gatherings of Assisi (four between 1986 and 2011) or the increasingly regular meetings of representatives of the world's major religions at both the global and local levels. It also explains the many tensions, often hastily qualified as fanatical, on the part of those not prepared to embrace this rapid or even brutal broadening of religious consciousness. For this reason, certain Christian intellectuals favorable to this paradigm shift, such as C. Theobald or C. Yannaras, also call for the protection and defense of Christian identities against the excesses of syncretism and globalization.[40] Likewise, it enables us to understand the important success on all continents of 20th-century authors such as Khalil Gibran (1883–1931), Antoine de St. Exupéry (1900–1944) or Paolo Coelho

40 C. Theobald, *Le christianisme comme style, une manière de faire de la théologie en post modernité,* Paris, Cerf, 2007.

(b. 1947).[41] With these authors, orthodoxy is not an authoritarian discourse rooted in the past. It is more an awakening, a healing power, a sapiential opening. Thomas Merton (1915–1968), an American writer who became a Benedictine priest in 1949, is one of the major figures of this literary and spiritual renewal. A supporter of interfaith dialogue, he met with the Dalai Lama and Thich Nhat Hanh and vigorously fought racism. *Seven Story Mountain*, his autobiography published in 1948, has been translated into many languages.[42] In a drawing that illustrates the poem he dedicated to "Hagia Sophia," Thomas Merton represents Wisdom, which he associates with the Virgin Mary, crowning Christ. He writes: "Sophia is God sharing of Himself with creatures. . . . She is in all things as the air receiving the sunlight. . . . She is life as communion, life as thanksgiving, life as praise, life as a festival, life as glory."[43]

It is still premature to consider this new representation of orthodoxy as paradigmatic given the still confessional organization of the Churches and the still highly agnostic constitutions of most modern States. All the same, the movement of historiography testifies yet again to this ecumenical and sapiential evolution of contemporary ecclesial consciousness.

## POST-MEMORIAL HISTORIOGRAPHY

From the point of view of general historiography, it is indisputable that, during the 20th century, there was an objectification of memorial history. As revealed in *Les lieux de mémoire*, a recent history of France produced by a brilliant group of historians under the direction of Pierre Nora, contemporary historiography has tried to become aware of its memorial and communitarian

41 *The Prophet* by K. Gibran was first published in 1922. It was translated into more than 20 languages and was one of the best-selling books of the 20th century in the United States. *The Little Prince*, a poetic and philosophical fairy tale by A. Saint Exupéry, was first published in the United States in April 1943, then in France the following year. This is the most read and best known work of French literature in the world. *L'Alchimiste*, Paris, Anne Carriere, 1988, by P. Coelho, sold more than 100 million copies and was translated into 66 languages.

42 *The National Review* ranks this book among the 100 most sold non-fiction books of the 20th century.

43 T. Merton, "Hagia Sophia," in Christopher Pramuk, *Sophia, The Hidden Christ of Thomas Merton,* Collegeville, Order of Saint Benedict, 2009, 304. I would like to thank Father Michael Plekon for indicating this text to me.

preconceptions.[44] Memory has even become a specialized field of study with contributions by numerous intellectuals (e.g., H. Rousso, F. Hartog, P. Ricoeur, G. Nivat) and institutions (e.g., Institute for the History of the Present Times, the Shoah memorial, the memorial of Caen).[45] This renewal of lay historiography may sometimes have appeared as an "exploded view" of history, to the point of it being characterized as a board game, "*jeu de l'oie*,"[46] of French identity.[47] Nonetheless, it had important consequences on the formation, the development and the crisis of orthodoxy and historical science.

It is no longer the French nation, nor the French Republic, which is the object of study for historians. It is the symbol of France that is being researched. It is no longer the identity of citizens that must be confirmed, but the existential relation of men to their chronotopes which must be questioned. This evolution of historiography relates to nonreligious sources, even though both Pierre Nora and Georges Nivat recognize their Jewish roots. Pierre Nora quotes, alongside his own historiographic research on Lavisse and Michelet, Marcel Proust and his work *In Search of Lost Time* as one of his inspirations. Georges Nivat mentions both Alexander Solzhenitsyn and Sarah Kofman (1934–1994) as the cornerstones for his work *The Sites of the Russian Memory* (*Sites de la mémoire russe*).

This turning point in historiography can nonetheless be aligned with the work of John Henry Newman, Vladimir Soloviev and Yves Congar, the three main critics at the turn of the century of the remembrance definition of orthodoxy. All three were attentive readers of the Church historians of the 19th century. Cardinal John Henry Newman was well versed in the writings of the historians of the School of Tübingen. The philosopher Vladimir Soloviev (1853–1900), son of the historian of the Russian state Sergey Solovyov, knew Bolotov personally and appreciated him greatly.[48] Father Yves Congar (1904–1995) had Möhler and Khomiakov published by Cerf in his collection *Unam Sanctam*.[49] All three aspired to a deeper

44 *Les lieux de mémoire*, Paris, Gallimard, Bibliothèque illustrée des histoires, 3 vols., vol. 1, *La République* (1 vol., 1984), t. 2, *La Nation* (2 vol., 1986), t. 3 *Les Frances* (3 vol., 1992).

45 G. Nivat, *Les sites de la memoire russe,* v. 1, *Géographie de la memoire russe,* Paris, Fayard, 2007.

46 Snakes and Ladders. French game.

47 Henry Rousso, "Un jeu de l'oie de l'identité francaise," in *Vingtième Siècle. Revue de l'Histoire*, no. 15 (1987): 151–54.

48 V. Soloviev, "Vassili Vassilievitch Bolotov, Nécrologue," *Vesnyk Evropy* (July 1900): 416.

49 J. A. Moehler, *L'unité dans l'Eglise ou le principe du catholicisme,* Paris, Cerf, 1938.

definition of orthodoxy. Their theories, however, were not heeded at the time by their respective Churches. Newman (1801–1890) decided to convert to Catholicism in 1845, without fear of losing his Anglican identity, but he was rejected by the Oxford movement he had helped to create. In 1896, Soloviev chose to receive communion from a Catholic priest of the Byzantine rite while continuing to define himself as Orthodox, but the Orthodox Church denied him the sacraments. In 1937, Father Yves Congar laid out the principles of a Catholic ecumenism, but he was the object of a harsh censure until the Second Vatican Council, in which he actively participated.

In modern times, the history of Christian orthodoxy has long been confused in the "Catholic" world with that of the papacy (Fliche and Martin),[50] in the "Protestant world" with that of the national churches (Cotton Mather, *Magnalia Christi America*, 1702, for the American Church) or doctrine (Jaroslav Pelikan), and in the "Orthodox" world with that of the nation (Anton Kartachev) or the conciliary tradition (Kallistos Ware). This historiography has been vigorously questioned over the last forty years by historians from different faith traditions. We will limit ourselves here to mentioning the article by Émile Poulat, "Anamnèse" (in *A History of Christianity*, a 14-volume work published by DDB editions under the direction of Marc Venard, André Vauchez, Charles Pietri and Jean-Marie Mayeur[51]); the work of Diana Butler Bass, *A People's History of Christianity*; and the article by Olivier Clément, "Avenir et signification de la diaspora orthodoxe en Europe occidentale" ("The Future and Significance of the Orthodox Diaspora in Western Europe").[52] At the end of the 20th century, with this criticism of a certain type of Christian historiography intending to be orthodox, a new transdisciplinary synthesis of the notion of orthodoxy as just knowledge was formed. In this new transconfessional approach, the history of the Church is reconciled with her plural and multisecular memory and progressively rediscovers world history. On the one hand, she integrates her aspirations for peace, justice and the dignity of man, and respect for creation; on the other she indicates to this history the *kairos*, her moments of light.

50 A. Fliche and V. Martin, *Histoire de l'Eglise depuis les origines jusqu'à nos jours*, Belgique, Bloud et Gay, 1935–1964, 24 vols.

51 Jean-Marie Mayeur, Charles and Luce Pietri, André Vauchez, Marc Venard, *Histoire du Christianisme*, 1990–2001, 14 vols.

52 Olivier Clément: "Avenir et signification de la Diaspora orthodoxe en Europe occidentale," *Contacts* (Paris, n. 103, 3rd trimester, 1978): 259–83.

## HISTORIOGRAPHY IN THE CATHOLIC TRADITION

It took the shock of the Second World War, the encyclical *Divino Afflante Spiritu* of September 30, 1943 (notable for the discoveries of new conceptions of history), and the holding of Vatican II, with its emphasis on the Church as the people of God rather than a completed pyramidical society, to form a new generation of French historians grouped around Alphonse Dupront (1905–1990),[53] Jean Daniélou (1905–1974), Henri-Irénée Marrou (1904–1977)[54] and Michel de Certeau (1925–1986).[55] Marrou cooperated with Jean Daniélou in the publication (by Seuil) of the first volume of the *Nouvelle Histoire de l'Eglise* which appeared in 1963, a five-volume history, completed in 1966, which sought to be resolutely academic and international.[56] In the face of the claims of positivist history, this work rehabilitates the apophatic dimension of Church history. For Marrou, this dimension, in all its truth, is known only to God. He wrote: "How many saints among us are known to God alone!"[57] The friend of Mounier and the author of a thesis on St. Augustine favored a theandric conception of the history of the Church which would take the human limits of the institution into account. In his preface to the first volume, Roger Aubert, based on the work of Father Congar, pointed out the evolution of the orthodox paradigm among historians of the Church:

> There cannot be two kinds of Church history, one inspired by theology, the other not; there is only one history of the Church, the true history, but it is the same for all: it is theological, confessional and permeated with an ecumenical dimension.[58]

53 Lecturer at the University of Montpellier, he presented his doctorate thesis on *Le Mythe de croisade. Etude de sociologie religieuse,* in 1957. This text remained unpublished during his lifetime and only appeared posthumously in 1997 (Gallimard).

54 Yves-Marie Hilaire, ed., *De Renan à Marrou, L'histoire du christianisme et le progrès de la méthode historique (1863–1968),* Paris, Septentrion, 1999.

55 Beginning in 1958, de Certeau participated in the Groupe de la Bussière (a circle of historians studying religious questions).

56 For obvious reasons, our bibliography is primarily francophone. But one could cite Paul VI: "France bakes the intellectual bread of Christianity." Cf. Gerard Cholvy, *L'historien,* op. cit., 65.

57 Ottorino Pasquato, "Les caractères originaux de l'historiographie religieuse de Marrou," *De Renan à Marrou, l'histoire du christianisme et les progrès de la méthode historique (1863–1968),* op. cit., 19–20.

58 R. Aubert, "Introduction," in J. Daniélou, H.-I. Marrou, *Nouvelle Histoire de l'Eglise,* Paris, Seuil, 1963, 19–20.

As Marc Venard has written, Aubert, while still identifying the "Church" as the Roman Catholic Church, desired that Church history no longer be studied according to the institutional definition of the Body of Christ but as the Temple of the Holy Spirit. In response, this inspired *L'histoire de la France religieuse* (Paris, Seuil, 1988–1992) led by two Catholic historians, Jacques le Goff and René Rémond. This history, open to Christian, Jewish and agnostic historians, "respects its purpose," "takes what it says of itself into account," "but does not sanctify it."[59]

The criticism of the pride of place given to the bishop of Rome in Catholic ecclesiology was a prerequisite of contemporary Catholic historiography in this new configuration of Christian epistemology. Jean Delumeau, born in 1923, significantly named his inaugural conference at the Collège de France "The Prescribed and the Lived." This lecture is a presentation of the religious historiography of his time. By choosing to focus his course on the dialectic between that which is prescribed and that which is lived, Jean Delumeau helped a large number of his listeners to measure the distance separating the truth imposed on the faithful from the truth of consciences in the quest for justice. For him, "Christian acculturation took place through a sense of guilt," and the confessional, mentioned for the first time in 1516, "became the symbol of the new evangelization." Chateaubriand, in his *Memoirs from Beyond the Grave*, tells of the terrors he experienced as a child upon reading a book entitled *Bad Confessions*. "Ghosts dragging chains and vomiting flames announced to me the eternal torment for one concealed sin."[60] Delumeau thus discovered along with Georges Duby that Christianity in the Middle Ages was only fully lived by a rare elite and only comprised the "appearances of Christianity."

In subsequent publications, Jean Delumeau denounced the pastoral fear promoted by the popes of the Counter-Reformation.[61] This insistence on sin, death and judgment was, according to him, a way of blackmailing people and subjugating them. He calls to mind the resumption of torture by Pope Innocent IV in 1252 and gives figures on the extent of the Inquisition. He is careful, however, to put things in perspective by comparing them to the secular tragedies of the 20th century: "From 1480 to 1834 (date of its abolition),

59 Marc Venard, "Dieu conduit l'histoire," *L'historien et la foi*, under the direction of Jean Delumeau, Paris, Fayard, 1996, 331.

60 Chateaubriand, *Mémoires d'outre-tombe*, Paris, Hachette, 2005 (1977), 423.

61 J. Delumeau, *Le péché et la peur. La culpabilisation en Occident (XIIIe–XVIIIe siècle)*, Paris, Fayard, 1983.

the Spanish Inquisition burned around 100,000 people. 100,000 too many, of course! In our time, the Nazi concentration camps exterminated twelve million human beings in less than five years. How many tens of millions were killed by Stalin?"[62] Jean Delumeau also gives a meticulous description of the "unnatural marriage of the Church with money"[63] down through the centuries. For him the ecclesial tax system, in its innumerable forms, could be counted among the major causes of anticlericalism. He castigates "the hatred of the Jew which became a trait of Western civilization by the end of the Middle Ages," the Spanish *conquista* that reduced to enslavement those deemed idolaters and the silence of the Church on the slave trade. Certainly, Delumeau considers that both the Counter-Reformation and the Reformation itself contributed to the emergence of Western modernity. It was during the 18th century, when the Counter-Reformation lost its dynamism, that it enclosed itself in a sealed clerical universe. For Delumeau "contemporary dechristianization is to a large extent the price to pay for this tremendous aberration that lasted for a millennium and a half."[64] The French historian and professor at the Collège de France strongly supported a redefinition of pontifical power as proposed by John Paul II in his 1995 encyclical *Ut Unum Sint* which had itself been initiated by Cardinal John Quinn, Archbishop of San Francisco and president of the United States Conference of Catholic Bishops. Along with Bruno Chenu and Jean-Marie Tillard, he pleaded for the recognition of local Churches in the face of the excessive centralization of Rome. Tillard saw the Bishop of Rome in a reunited Church as a servant of communion, an arbiter, presiding in charity, and in this way joined the voice of Orthodox theologians such as N. Afanasiev, A. Schmemann and O. Clément. Jean Delumeau welcomed the request for pardon made by John Paul II at the Jubilee of the year 2000.

Bernard Sesboüé, in his book *Le magistère à l'epreuve*, has a similarly radical criticism of the teaching role of the papacy, and not just the political and sacramental role. This criticism enables us to understand what is involved in the transformation from a paradigm of orthodoxy as faithful memory to one of true and just knowledge. In the Gospel, according to the French Jesuit Father, the Magisterium consists of a twofold function attributed to the Church: "The pastoral proclamation of the Word in the

62 Ibid., 273.

63 J. Delumeau, *Un christianisme pour demain,* Paris, Hachette, 2005 (1977), 268.

64 Ibid., 302.

name of Christ and the regulation of this proclamation, i.e., the verification of its authenticity with regard to the founding event and the original proclamation or, in contemporary terms, of its orthodoxy."[65] In patristic times, the concept of chair signified the unity between the bishop and the people of God. An affirmation of faith could not be legitimized by the authority that uttered it, but rather because it belonged to the faith of always. It is only in the Latin Middle Ages, with the appearance of schools of theology and later universities that the Magisterium, which until then belonged only to Christ by virtue of Mt 23:10 ("You have only one Master, the Christ") began to be devolved to doctors and pastors.[66]

In 1870, Vatican I linked the magisterial function to jurisdiction and the nature of infallibility to the primacy of jurisdiction. However, in 1965 with the Constitution *Dei Verbum*, the Second Vatican Council brought to mind that the teaching of the Magisterium is relative to what constitutes its norm. The notion of fidelity has therefore been framed between three risks in the modern era: the "Orthodox" risk of imagining that stagnation is the best way to avoid being dogmatizing and thus risking heresy, the "Protestant" risk of believing that doctrinal authority only deserves obedience when it is faithful to Scripture (which presupposes another body capable of judging this conformity... but which?) and the "Catholic" risk of being led to believe that a magisterial teaching is itself sufficient because it comes from a legitimate authority. To solve this limitation of teaching, liturgical application and authority of modern Orthodoxy, Bernard Sesboüé puts forward the hypothesis that the phenomena of "reception of

65 B. Sesboüé, *Le magistère à l'épreuve*, Paris, DDB, 2001, 20.

66 The Eastern Orthodox Church never had universities which included all branches of knowledge precisely for this reason. In Russia, the Tsarine Elisabeth enabled Lomonossov to found the University of Moscow by a decree issued on January 12, 1755. Moreover, the Orthodox Church did not have a Congregation for the Doctrine of the Faith and continued to regulate the control of orthodoxy in a conciliary context beginning with the lowest and most local difference of opinion. This was the case in the 20th century on the occasion of the dispute regarding Sophia in 1935–1937 when Metropolitan Eulogius convoked a commission to examine the orthodoxy of the doctrine of Father Sergius Bulgakov. The commission concluded that the *theologoumena* of the Dean of Saint Sergius were in conformity with orthodoxy. But nearly 70 years later there is still no consensus in the Orthodox Church regarding the doctrine of the wisdom of God such as it was articulated within the School of Paris in the interval between the two World Wars. This is the indication of a weakness that traditional Western teaching authority sought to avoid. A. Arjakovsky, *Le père Serge Bulgakov, philosophe et théologien chrétien*, Paris, Parole et Silence, 2007.

the councils"[67] and the "sensus fidelium"[68] (that is, of non-institutional recognition) are appreciated—that is to say, precisely recognized with their right importance by the Church as a body that is self-aware. It is not a question of the Eastern inclination to "let the Spirit act" to justify one's own inaction. The work of reception requires an active effort of awareness of the acts and symbolic gestures of the ecclesial hierarchy on the part of the faithful, while the *sensus fidelium* should be listened to and taken into consideration honestly and with discernment by the ecclesial bodies. Sesboüé also suggests introducing into modern Orthodox reasoning, oriented as we have seen towards the expectation of the eternal dimension of truth, a new appreciation of the historical and thus imperfect and contingent value of an ecclesial decision. Both theologians and faithful should learn to distinguish between an infallible decision (which has a meaning always and everywhere) and an indefectible decision (which gives meaning regardless of space-time). On an institutional level, he recommends the establishment of an ecumenical college of doctors, based on the corpus of interconfessional agreements signed for half a century and ensuring a real consensual Magisterium. Finally, in dialogue and in conjunction with the Orthodox and Protestants churches, he proposes to subdivide the present Western Patriarchate of the Roman Church, which has become global, into several patriarchates at a continental level.

Recent addresses by Benedict XVI indicate that the pope himself is aware that certain deviations have occurred in the doctrine of the Churches, including in the Catholic Church. He attributes the cause to the division of the churches. Certainly, as written by Marie-Joseph Le Guillou, the rediscovery of Byzantine theology does not necessarily mean a total rejection of Western scholasticism. Alongside the strictly Augustinian tradition of medieval thought, there is also a Trinitarian theology represented by Boethius, Gilbert of Poitiers, Alexander of Hales, and Thomas Aquinas which respected the personalism of the Greek Fathers.[69] Nonetheless, Benedict

67 It took 16 centuries for the council of Chalcedon (451) to be received by the Christianities of Egypt and Syria.

68 B. Sesboüé takes the example of a loan with interest to demonstrate the clear-sightedness of the faithful compared with papal teaching which only recognized the legitimacy of such a loan in 1983.

69 "For Saint Thomas as for this author [Vladimir Lossky], Trinitarian theology finds its expression at the level of the values of consciousness, of love and of liberty and is the foundation of the communion of the Church." M. J. Le Guillou, *L'esprit de l'orthodoxie grecque et russe*, Parole et Silence, 2006, 182.

XVI, in his speech of September 17, 2006, at the University of Regensburg, affirmed, in perfect agreement with John Milbank, that it was the separation of Latin theology from Greek thought that was the cause of these distortions:

> In all honesty, one must observe that in the late Middle Ages we find trends in theology which would sunder this synthesis between the Greek spirit and the Christian spirit. In contrast with the so-called intellectualism of Augustine and Thomas, there arose with Duns Scotus a voluntarism which, in its later developments, led to the claim that we can only know God's *voluntas ordinata*. Beyond this is the realm of God's freedom, in virtue of which he could have done the opposite of everything he has actually done. This gives rise to positions which clearly approach those of Ibn Hazm and might even lead to the image of a capricious God, who is not even bound to truth and goodness. God's transcendence and otherness are so exalted that our reason, our sense of the true and good, are no longer an authentic mirror of God, whose deepest possibilities remain eternally unattainable and hidden behind his actual decisions.[70]

François Laplanche gives the account of the evolution of the history of Christianity in France over the last century. In our times, it is no longer a question for historians to present the history of the Catholic Church from the perspective of its Roman center,[71] an ecclesiocentric phenomenon correlative to the concomitant positivist laicization of secular history, but to describe the life of the Christian people down through the ages in the diversity of its forms.[72] This turnaround opened the history of Christianity to the diver-

70 Official translation from the Vatican website.

71 In defense of Augustin Fliche (1884–1951) and Msgr. Victor Martin, who wanted to do for Church history what Lavisse had done for the history of France, it should be noted that they were careful about consulting groups of specialists and about treating the internal life of the Church and not just its relationships with the State. Cf. Jean-Remy Palanque, "Notice sur la vie et les travaux de M. Augustin Fliche," *Compte rendu des séances de l'Académie des Inscriptions et Belles Lettres*, vol. 118 (1974): 238–49. The academic orientation of their history had been prepared in France by Msgr. Duchesne and his *Histoire ancienne de l'Eglise*—which was put on the Index for a while.

72 F. Laplanche, "De l'Histoire de l'Eglise de Fliche et Martin à l'Histoire du Christianisme," colloquium "Un siècle d'histoire du christianisme en France," Rennes, 1999, *Revue de l'histoire de l'Eglise en France*, vol. 86 (2000): 685–90.

sity of Churches with long chapters on the Eastern Orthodox Churches and the Protestant world. This evolution was further reinforced in the new *Histoire générale du Christianisme* published at PUF in 2010 under the direction of Jean-Robert Armogathe, Yves-Marie Hilaire, Pascal Montaubin and Michel-Yves Perrin. These authors chose to "often treat in common the evolutions of the different Christian Churches" and to "favor the impact of Christianity on cultures."[73] The new Church historians are convinced that "the demands of scientificity require the specialization of fields of knowledge."[74]

However, this is to forget that the criteria of modern scientificity do not always rhyme with those of the truth. This evolution of historiography, marked by the ascendance of the University over ecclesial remembrance, has its limits. In an unpublished presentation text for *L'histoire du Christianisme* published by Desclée (14 volumes, 1990–2001), Charles Pietri explains that the intention of the authors is to relate, among other events, the history of dogmas and of theological constructions but without "seeking to distinguish amongst them in the name of some orthodoxy. . . . Moreover, the purpose of this collection is to recognize Christianity in its ecumenicity, in the original sense of a term gradually extended from the beginning to all continents, in all its diverse expressions of churches and sects as the multiple branches from an originally unique rooting."[75] Émile Poulat attempted to summarize *The History of Christianity* (*L'histoire du Christianisme*) in an article entitled "Anamnesis" (*Anamnèse*), which is also the title of the last volume of the collection.[76]

The historian sadly notes that the "new history," even though it has important advantages over those that preceded it, is a kind of heterodox history, "a Pelagian history" as opposed to a historical Augustinianism that considered all things in the divine light. This history pretends to be self-sufficient and cannot accept the notion of a supernatural fact. It takes only the belief in supernatural facts into account, which is an initial negationist methodological position. According to Poulat:

73 *Histoire générale du Christianisme*, at PUF under the direction of Jean-Robert Armogathe, Yves-Marie Hilaire, Pascal Montaubin and Michel-Yves Perrin, 2 volumes, Paris, PUF, 2010.

74 C. Langlois, "Faire l'histoire du christianisme," *Histoire du christianisme*, XIV, op. cit., 19.

75 M. Venard, "Dieu conduit l'histoire," *L'historien et la foi*, op. cit., 334.

76 E. Poulat had also participated in the survey taken by the review *Concilium* on "the history of the Church as self-understanding of the Church," which was published in his book *Modernistica*, Paris, editions Latines, 1982.

> [Christianity] is inseparable from the transcendence it claims and which our history, methodically confined in its immanence, has no means of attaining. Everyone is entitled to think whatever they want about the Christian faith but it is unthinkable without this "beyond history," without a metahistory that is consubstantial.[77]

Poulat condemns in particular "the loss of the full meaning of the Scriptures" which are submitted to a systematic dismantling, the obligation of neutrality of judgment on the part of the historian, as if this were a guarantee of truth and "a sort of natural history of the Church beginning at Pentecost" which contrasts with medieval and classical histories which, as in Eusebius and Bossuet, originated with the creation of the world and had no difficulty with angelic interventions. In fact, the critical attitude of contemporary historians is more and more out of step with the orthodox tradition of the Churches. Thus, Albert Baumgarten, the author of the first article of the new *Histoire générale du christianisme* which centers on the figure of Jesus Christ, affirms, without batting an eyelid and for him in a completely "non-arbitrary" way, that he does not recognize the Gospel of John as a historical source.[78] It strangely leads to the "certainty" that the "Jesus of history" made his disciples a "third race" of humanity alongside the Jews and the Greeks.[79] Poulat admits that there cannot be two histories of the Church, the one inspired by theology, the other not. For this reason, along with Canon Roger Aubert in his *Nouvelle Histoire de l'Eglise*, he makes the case for a strictly orthodox, "veritative history" of the Church. In his opinion, there are different "levels," temporal and spiritual, but one truth. This was also the opinion of Msgr. Hubert Jedin (1900–1980), historian of the Council of Trent and one-time colleague of Hans Küng, who understood the science of faith as " knowledge based on faith that provides it with purpose, which exists only in faith."[80] For Émile Poulat, this means that, in order to write an orthodox history of the Christian Church, it is not enough to establish what really happened.

77 E. Poulat, "Anamnèse," in *Histoire du christianisme*, vol. 14, Paris, Desclée, 2001, 261.

78 Albert I. Baumgarten, "Jésus de Nazareth," in *Histoire générale du christianisme*, under the direction of J.-R. Armogathe, vol. 1, Paris, PUF, 2010, 22.

79 Ibid., 31.

80 Poulat, op. cit., 268.

> [It is still necessary] to bring out the unperceived, the lost, the unknown, the suppressed, the forgotten, the marginalized, the misunderstood: in short a hidden history under the obvious historic appearances, a history to be sought not beyond history but within its silent depths.[81]

This has affinities with both the epistemology of Foucault and the hesychast spirituality. Poulat goes a step further in his redefinition of orthodox ecclesial historiography by suggesting that for Church historians, to narrate an authentically true history (that is, theanthropic and living) they should interest themselves in the practices of the Churches as well as their common foundations—that is, their faith in the resurrection of Christ, their hope and their charity.[82] This event of the resurrection is indeed at the origin of a new "notion of truth, unknown to ancient civilizations and repudiated by modern culture, but also of the heresy opposed to orthodoxy whose defense legitimates the repression of error."[83] There are many similarities here with the historiography of Pierre Hadot (1922–2010) and Sergius Bulgakov.[84]

There are also echoes of the philosophical considerations of E. Poulat in *History of the Church* (*Histoire de l'Eglise*) published by the Dominican historian Guy Bédouelle in 1997. The French historian devised his manual of the history of the Church according to an original plan in which the Church discovers a consciousness and thus a corporeality as she is subjected to aggression or enters into crisis (that Bédouelle calls the visible summits of her history), which leads her in return to define an orthodoxy which is evolving politically, culturally and spiritually. Bédouelle himself sums up his historical

81 Ibid., 271.

82 Cf. the interesting analysis on this topic by Hyacinthe Destivelle in "L'oecuménisme entre histoire et mémoire dans l'enseignement catholique récent"—a conference given at Kiev in 2008. For the editor of the review *Istina*, the second half of the 20th century has contributed to the rediscovery of the theological status of Church history. Vatican II dedicated history as a theological source. History has become less ecclesiastic and ecclesiology has become more historical. This ecumenical orientation has been enriched by Jewish thought, tragically marked by the Shoah, and has provoked a reflection on the eclipse of God in history. E. Fackenheim, *La Présence de Dieu dans l'histoire. Affirmations juives et réflexions philosophiques après Auschwitz*, forword by B. Dupuy, Lagrasse, Verdier, 2. http://clement.kiev.ua/ru/node/2998.

83 Ibid., 278.

84 Pierre Hadot, "La philosophie comme hérésie trinitaire," *Revue d'histoire et de philosophie religieuses* (1957): 236–51. P. Hadot considered Bulgakov as a "first-class theologian and an extremely pure spiritual light" (239).

research in the quest for orthodoxy: "A history on the summits, therefore, but whose events, from one challenge to another, from distress to recovery, by conversions and successive integrations, give a sort of rhythm to the narrative where the believer would want to continually discern the good grain from the tares, discover the finger of God writing on the sands of time."[85]

The rector of the Catholic University of the West resumes in his conclusion all the recent reflection on the theology of history of G. Fessard (1897–1978),[86] a critic of Hegel; Cardinal Journet, who had read S. Bulgakov; F. Dostoevsky through Jacques Maritain;[87] and Hans Urs von Balthasar, who also continued Bulgakov's rediscovery of the personhood of the Church.[88] Father Guy Bédouelle draws the important conclusion that the pilgrim Church follows Christ who is the Head, in an asymptotic manner. It is this conformity of life and action "never attained" which defines its orthodoxy and which makes it always hear, in a new way, the word of Christ to the rich young man: "If you would be perfect, go, sell what you possess and give to the poor, and you will have treasure in heaven; and come, follow me" (Mt 19:21). It is this loving, eschatological tension between the body and the Head which both unifies and destabilizes the Church because it always surpasses it. The fact that the Church is "without sin but not without sinners," as Journet puts it, makes possible a history of Christianity which is postconfessional and theanthropic. The chapters that G. Bédouelle dedicates to the Reformation and to the Eastern Churches in this respect show great foresight. Following the recommendations of Poulat and the Jesuit historian Bernard Sesboüé, author of a history of dogmas,[89] Guy Bédouelle concludes his history with a prayer, a call to the search for truth in the Spirit.

It is probably when it dared to address head-on the wounds of the past that Catholic historiography was most in line with the emerging paradigm of true and just knowledge. The literature is abundant.[90] The book by Frantishek Dvornik (1893–1975) entitled *The Photian Schism, History and*

85 Guy Bédouelle, *Histoire de l'Eglise*, Paris, Cerf, and Luxembourg, Saint Paul, 1997, 4.

86 G. Fessard, *De l'actualité historique*, 2 volumes, Paris, Desclée, 1959, 1960.

87 Cardinal Journet, *L'Eglise du Verbe incarné*, v. III, Paris, 1969.

88 H. U. von Balthasar, *De l'intégration. Aspects d'une théologie de l'Histoire*, in Revue belge de philologie et d'histoire, tome 49, 1971.

89 *Histoire des dogmes*, under the direction of B. Sesboüé, 4 volumes, Paris, Desclée, 1994–1996.

90 Mention can be made simply of the important book on the subject of conciliar historiography by G. Alberigo, *Christian Unity, The Council of Ferrara-Florence, 1438–39*, Leuven, Peeters, 1991.

*Legend* (*Le schisme de Photius. Histoire et légende*) was published in 1950 in the collection *Unam Sanctam* created and directed by the Dominican Yves Congar. Dvornik, a Czech Catholic priest, was one of the leading specialists of the 20th century in the history of the Slavic world. He taught at the St. Charles University in Prague, at the Collège de France and at Harvard. In his work he reconciles the figure of the Byzantine patriarch Photius with the Catholic world and leads the way to the rediscovery of the council of reconciliation of 879 as well as the Eighth Ecumenical Council of the Christian Church. This council had been forgotten both in the East and the West because of the excesses of the dispute that opposed Rome and Constantinople after the 11th century, the false documents against Photius written under Pope Formosus in the 9th century and the internal struggles opposing zealots and liberals in the Byzantine Empire. This council of reconciliation was replaced in Catholic memory, through Gratian, by the council of 869 of Constantinople, the council which condemned Photius. Francis Dvornik showed that the Council of Constantinople of 879, in which the legates of Pope John VIII participated, officially recognized the Second Council of Nicea as the Seventh Ecumenical Council. In the tradition of ecumenical councils this 8th council adopted a symbol of faith. It is still not officially recognized by the Churches as such. However, John Meyendorff, convinced by the thesis of F. Dvornik, proposed that a joint Catholic-Orthodox commission again recognize this council as the Eighth Ecumenical Council (in opposition to the thesis of Baronius, misled by Gratian, but in continuity with the tradition of Nicholas Cabasilas, Mark of Ephesus, Dositheus of Jerusalem, and others).

This ecumenical historiography also concerns the history of the Russian Church. Two examples only will be given. Pierre Pascal (1890–1983), one of the most eminent Slavic specialists of 20th century France, author of a thesis on Raskol of Avvakum in the 17th century, gave a lecture in 1978 at Strasbourg entitled "Two Catholic-Orthodox Similarities: Religious Tears; Fools in Christ." In his presentation, the Sorbonne professor breaks the clichés concerning the symbols of East and West. Pascal states: "There was a legalism in Byzantium, Roman Churches in the West, paintings of Giotto and Fra Angelico in Italy." The former attaché to the French military mission to Russia during the First World War goes a step further.[91] He considers

91 P. Pascal, *Avvakkum et les débuts du Raskol, la crise religieuse au XVIIe siècle en Russie*, Paris, 1938.

that prayer with tears should not be thought of as a monopoly of Orthodox spirituality in the denominational sense of the word. Alain de Lille saw in the tears a second baptism. It is the same with the holiness known as the Fools in Christ—that is to say, people who abandon their material goods and live a life of transgression of social conventions for religious reasons and simulate folly in order to hide their relationship to God. If Procopius of Ustyug and Xenia of St. Petersburg were venerated as saints in Russia after their death, one cannot ignore, says Pascal, the importance of St. Francis of Assisi and St. Philip Neri in the spiritual tradition of the West. P. Pascal concludes his talk with these remarks:

> I am struck that in the 17th century two treatises by Eastern mystical authors were very much appreciated both by the more religious French Catholics and by the Russian Orthodox: *The Instructions* by Father Dorotheus, published in Slavonic in Kiev in 1628 and in Moscow in 1652 and in the French translation of Rancé in Paris in 1686; *The Ladder of Divine Ascent* by St. John Climacus, published in Moscow in 1647 and several times thereafter, and in Paris in 1652 in the translation of Arnaud d'Andilly. These two weighty books from the Far East in space and in time simultaneously delighted the faithful of Port Royal and those of the Archpriest of Avvakum. Today they are ignored in both the East and the West. The great difference in piety is not in the churches but in the times.[92]

In the same spirit of research of the just truth in history—that is, of the ecumenical truth—Father Antoine Lambrechts, the librarian of the biritual Catholic monastery of the Holy Cross of Chevetogne, gave a conference in Moscow on May 26, 2010 entitled "A Spiritual Reading of Russian Monks: *The Imitation of Christ*."[93] Lambrechts has demonstrated that the work of Thomas à Kempis, in spite of the bad reputation it has acquired in the 20th century in the Soviet Union and in post-Soviet Russia, was very favorably received by the Russian Church from the 17th to the 19th centuries. One of the first translations in 1623 of the main text of the

92 P. Pascal, "Deux similitudes catholiques-orthodoxes: Religieuses larmes; Fols en Christ," in *Aspects de l'Orthodoxie*, Paris, PUF, 1981, 167.

93 A. Lambrechts, "Une lecture spirituelle de moines russes: *L'Imitation du Christ*," Moscow, 2010, manuscript text. My thanks to Father Antoine for having sent me this document.

*Devotio Moderna* has been attributed to Archimandrite Pierre Mohyla of the monastery of the Caves of Kiev. Several new editions were published in the 17th century. St. Dimitri of Rostov, in a sermon preached in 1705 at the Romanov residence in Izmajlovo, praised Thomas à Kempis for his humility. The monastery of Sarov was reputed for its copyists of spiritual and monastic works. Although it is difficult to prove an influence, Father Antoine Lambrechts sees a patristic convergence between certain points in *The Imitation of Christ* ("First, keep yourself in peace, and then you will be able to pacify others") and aspects of the teachings of St. Seraphim of Sarov (1759–1833) ("Acquire the Spirit of peace and thousands around you will be saved"). In the 18th century the *Imitation* found its way out of the monastery walls and attracted the cultural elite, from Pushkin who commended it, to Gogol who recommended its reading. The new translation by Mikhail Speransky in 1816 underwent twelve editions, the last being in 1913. The High Procurator of the Holy Synod, Constantine Pobedonostev, endorsed the text by publishing a preface. Certainly, he explains that this text written by a Western author cannot be received with the same authority as a dogmatic text, but he recommends it as a good work of piety. For A. Lambrechts, the fact that the book was so appreciated by the Russian elite at the time of Alexander I, an elite marked by its interest in esotericism and Free Masonry, discredited the work in certain ecclesiastical circles. The publication of the *Philokalia* in Russian was considered by St. Ignatius Brianchaninov as an exclusive alternative. However, for C. Pobedonostev the two works complemented one another. A. Lambrechts concludes:

> Is the *Imitation* an "unorthodox" book? It goes without saying that it contains typically Western elements, even medieval. It is a work that was conceived in a very special historical context. It does not encompass all the spiritual life of a Christian. Moreover, even in the West, not everyone likes this book. But does every concrete spirituality not have at the same time something universal? Does its spontaneous popularity in Russia (and elsewhere) not demonstrate that it responded to a need, that it touched an "Orthodox chord" or a common chord between East and West? Is not the *Imitation* precisely one of those books that, without wanting it or without knowing it, goes beyond boundaries and divisions?[94]

94 Ibid., 7.

## HISTORIOGRAPHY IN THE PROTESTANT TRADITION

In the Protestant academic world the Lutheran-American teacher and pastor of Slovak and Serbian origin Jaroslav Pelikan (1923–2006), professor of history at Yale University, president of the American Academy of Arts and Sciences, doctor *honoris causa* of 42 universities in the world, played an important role, at least until he converted to Orthodox Christianity on March 25, 1998.[95] His major work, *Christian Tradition: A History of the Development of Doctrine*, was written and published in five volumes between 1971 and 1989,[96] that is to say, before his conversion to Orthodoxy. As he himself wrote, his entire work fluctuates between the two giants of the history of Christianity, Harnack and Newman. He wanted to inject the dynamism of Christian truth into the work of Harnack (who held the orthodoxy he identified with the Eastern Church in deep contempt and considered it ritualistic) and to inscribe in that of Newman (who cared little about the historical meanderings of truth) the meticulous account of dogmatic controversies. Christian historiography will probably be grateful to Pelikan for having shown the many parallelisms in the evolution of doctrines over the centuries within the different Christian Churches. Yet his initial methodological perspective, which can be summarized as a disconnection of the life of the Churches from that of doctrines, was still very theoretical. Although his intention is to relate "the history of the doctrine of the Church in its development" according to a postconfessional viewpoint, he pretends not to notice the necessary historical alignment between the ecclesial formulation and the content of the doctrine, as if a supernatural doctrine of truth had floated above the churches while they disputed its ownership.[97] On several occasions he

95 The German historian Karl Christian Felmy is another example of a contemporary Protestant historian who followed the same intellectual and spiritual evolution towards the Orthodox Church.

96 J. Pelikan, *Christian Tradition: A History of the Development of Doctrine*, 1973, vol. 1; *The Emergence of the Catholic Tradition 100–600*, 1971, vol. 2; *The Spirit of Eastern Christendom 600–1700*, 1974, vol. 3; *The Growth of Medieval Theology 600–1300*, 1974, vol. 4; *The Reformation of the Church and Dogma 1300–1700*, 1984, vol. 5; *Christian Doctrine and Modern Culture Since 1700*, 1989. Published in the U.S. by the University of Chicago and in France by PUF.

97 The only forms that Ernst Troeltsch (1866–1923) recognized were those of the institutional Church, of the sects and mystics, but such an exclusively meta-confessional approach led him to make totally ahistorical judgments. Of the 1,000 pages of his book *The Social Teaching of the Christian Churches*, Troeltsch only dedicated a single page to Eastern Christianity and that explains that the Eastern Church was absorbed by

speaks of different but equivalent versions of orthodoxy in Europe at the end of the 16th century.[98] Moreover, his approach leads him to exclude from his history of orthodoxy many aspects of human history such as the history of philosophy and political theology. The viewpoint retained by Orthodox Churches and notably by Georges Florovsky in the 20th century, which consists in associating the Christian doctrine of incarnation with the very act of Incarnation of the Son of God, and thus in identifying the history of Christian doctrine with the visible institution, prevailed over his original project.[99] This may explain, among other reasons, his decision to convert to the Orthodox Church at the age of 75 with his wife, Sylvia.[100] This does not mean that a history of orthodoxy can only be confessional, a concept Pelikan rightly opposed. It will be seen later on that a postconfessional history of Christian doctrine is possible once orthodoxy is understood as a theanthropic notion in itself. His mistake ultimately was to identify the invariability of divine truth with the concept of orthodoxy. The Russian Orthodox priest, Alexander Men, proposed a different version of orthodoxy:

> Christianity is not an ideology, an abstract doctrine or an established system of rites. The Good News entered the world as a dynamic force, embracing all aspects of life, open to all things created by God in nature and in human beings. It is not just a religion which has existed for the last twenty centuries, but it is the Way towards the future.[101]

---

the State and that its only recourse for reform was through the individual asceticism proposed by Dostoevsky and Tolstoy.

98 "The fact of repeating the definitions of the time of the Reformation which were the result of a competition between different versions of 'orthodoxy' took on another tone now that there was a fundamental 'distinction between Church and religion' and also because, more and more, the competition was between, on the one hand, all these versions and, on the other, their radical rejection." J. Pelikan, op. cit., vol. V, Paris, 1994, 13. It is worth noting that when Pelikan is not comfortable with the concept of orthodoxy, he puts it in quotation marks. He thus writes of the crises traversed by "all forms of 'orthodoxy,'" op. cit., 23.

99 George Florovsky, *Aspects of Church History*, in *Collected Works*, vol. 4, Nordland, 1975.

100 This conversion was followed more recently by that of another expert in the history of the Eastern Church, Father Gabriel Bunge: http://orthodoxologie.blogspot.com2010/09/pere-gabriel-bunge-devient-orthodoxe.html.

101 Elizabeth Roberts and Ann Shukman, eds., *Christianity for the Twenty First Century: The Prophetic Writings of Alexander Men*, New York, Continuum, 1996, 68. Cited by Michael Plekon, "An Eastern Church Perspective from the 'Paris School' and Living Tradition," in P. Berger, *Relativism*, op. cit., 202.

Diana Butler Bass (born 1959) is an American Episcopalian historian whose historiographical project is situated in the line of this idea of journeying in the Way as presented by Alexander Men, not only as the foundation of the first Christian community, but also as the source of an orthodox approach to the history of Christianity. It is therefore in total breach with the approach of J. Pelikan which she deems too intellectual, even too masculine. But she also challenges the catechetical version of Christian history disseminated in the Protestant schools in the United States, which she considers excessively mythologized. She seeks an alternative to the aporias of European academic historiography lost in the hyperspecialized erudition of religious phenomena. Her book, *A People's History of Christianity*, published in New York in 2009, is a landmark among the Church histories written across the Atlantic[102]—not only because it was acclaimed by such eminent figures of American Protestantism as Justo Gonzalez and Jim Wallis, but especially because it put an end to the traditional mythical narrative of the Church widely received in American popular consciousness. Butler Bass names this narrative the "Big C," that is, "Christianity – Christ, Constantine, Christendom, Calvin and Christian America." Considering that this simplistic, linear, and institutional account—quietly leading the history of Jesus Christ in Galilee to the Senate in Washington—was indicative of a pathological "spiritual amnesia," she deliberately wrote a popular alternative history of Christianity which she hoped would be "engendering," that is, going beyond the classical opposition in the politico-religious landscape between conservatives and liberals. She writes: "It is not about victory; it is about following Christ in order to seed human community with grace."[103] Without being aware of it, Butler Bass is responding to Émile Poulat's invitation to historians to once again center themselves on the fundamentals of Christianity when they write its history. For her, the historical incarnation of the two great commandments of Christ, "You shall love the Lord your God with all your heart, and with all your soul, and with all your strength, and with all your mind; and your neighbor as yourself" (Lk 10:25–27) represent the basis of her narrative. Thus there are no "meta-narratives," but rather "campfire stories." There is no tense defense of the past, but memories of hope. There are no long developments on the majority of history, rather a sustained attention to all the "outsiders" of the past. There is no systematic analysis of continuities, rather a mosaic of events.

102 *A People's History of Christianity*, New York, Harper One, 2009.
103 Ibid., 11.

There is no attempt to justify the present, rather its understanding in the strangeness of the past. There is no nostalgic quest for a lost paradise, but wonderment before all the unexpected manifestations of truth, justice and beauty. Her popular history of Christianity is resolutely ecumenical. She points out that it was Erasmus' knowledge of Greek which enabled Christians to rediscover, in contrast to the translation of Jerome ("Do penance!"), the expression "*metanoiete!*" ("Repent!") of John the Baptist. She takes seriously the notion of *sensus fidelium* which she borrows from Catholic theology. But she prefers to avoid "issues of orthodoxy" to concentrate on "the moments when Christian people really acted like Christians."[104] It is not a question of rejecting orthodoxy as an intellectual and experiential system of the truth. It is simply that orthodoxy understood as doctrinal fidelity no longer appeals to the present generation of American Christians.

One of the most popular pastors at present in the United States, Rick Warren, recently affirmed that the first Reformation was concerned with beliefs (creeds) whereas the one he sees emerging today is about actions (deeds). In keeping with Bushnell, a 19th century American theologian, Butler Bass also prefers a history of Christianity as "a correct harmony — not a correct opinion." This new historiography leaves certain evolutions of Christian doctrine unexplained. She understands that a new reform should bring together words and deeds in a more visible way, but by avoiding doctrinal questions she cannot provide an in-depth account of phenomena such as the Nominalism of the 16th-century reformers. She thus renders herself incapable of clarifying the divergence between faith and acts, the permanent "revivals" in the history of Protestantism or the quest — never satisfied and constantly threatened — for a return to the authenticity of the primitive Christian community.

Therefore, to deepen this ecumenical rereading of the history of Christianity, we turn to both the foundational historiographical work of the World Council of Churches and to the new generation of Protestant intellectuals in France and in the United States. The WCC's *A History of the Ecumenical Movement (1517–1948)*, published in 1954,[105] has since been reissued several times and has

104 Ibid., 15.

105 Ruth Rouse and Stephen Charles Neill, eds., *A History of the Ecumenical Movement (1517–1948)*, vol. 1, Geneva, WCC, 1954. Ruth Rouse (1872–1956) was a pioneer of the ecumenical movement. She accompanied John Mott in the Universal Federation of the Associations of Students and was president of the Young Women's Christian Association from 1938 to 1946. Stephen Charles Neill (1900–1984) was an Anglican bishop, the founder of the Church of South India.

been enriched by two additional volumes covering the continuation of the history of the ecumenical movement up to the present day, a history of more than 2000 pages.[106] This history has been enhanced by a whole series of books published by the WCC, which give added depth to the three volumes. Particular mention should be made of the publication in 1991 of the *Dictionary of the Ecumenical Movement*, a volume which also has an ecumenical editorial board (V. Borovoy, M. Conway, L. Vischer, et al.), this time with Catholic thinkers (A. Houtepen, R. Beaupère, T. Berger), and covering many historical articles ("apostolic tradition," "capitalism," "Church calendars," etc.).[107]

One of the first tasks of the new World Council of Churches in 1948 was to get down to the writing of a new ecumenical history of the Church. In 1946, Professor Adolph of the University of Zurich had already proposed an overall plan for the work. Ruth Rouse (1872–1956), a British Anglican, a graduate of Girton College in Cambridge, a former missionary in India and an active member of the World Student Christian Federation became the editorial secretary of the project in 1948. She also wrote two chapters for the first volume of *A History of the Ecumenical Movement*, which was published in 1954. This account was still very much marked by the Protestant view of Church history. Moreover, since it was written just after the Second World War, it still consists of a juxtaposition of remembrance narratives and does not constitute a true historical synthesis. All the same, this history has the advantage of initiating a movement of encounter between historians from different confessions and different continents whose common objective was to seek to understand together their shared history. Contributions were invited from authors of the Orthodox faith such as Georges Florovsky ("The Orthodox Churches and the Ecumenical Movement Prior to 1910") and Nicholas Zernov ("The Eastern Churches and the Ecumenical Movement in the 20th Century").[108] An impressive bibliography at the conclusion of the book enables the reader to further examine delicate questions. Besides, if it is true that the first volume of this history is limited to the period from 1517 to 1948,

106 Volume 2 covers the period between 1948 and 1968 (with the collaboration of historians such as Leslie Newbigin, Vasil Istavridis, Eugene Carson Blake) and volume 3 covers the period between 1968 and 2000 (with contributions from Michael Kinnamon, K. M. George, Emilio Castro, et al.).

107 N. Lossky, J. M. Bonino, J. Pobee, T. Stransky, G. Wainwright, P. Webb, *A Dictionary of the Ecumenical Movement*, Geneva, WCC, 2002 (1991).

108 Ruth Rouse and Stephen Charles Neill, eds., *A History of the Ecumenical Movement*, v. 1, *1517–1948*, Geneva, WCC, 1954 (2004).

there is an important introduction by Stephen Charles Neill (1900–1984), 26 pages long, covering the period from the origins of Christianity to the Reformation. Neill was the former Scottish Anglican bishop of Tinnevelly in India (1939–1944) and later became assistant bishop to the Archbishop of Canterbury. He was a Fellow at Trinity College, Cambridge, and missionary at heart. In 1962 he became professor at the University of Hamburg and from 1973, professor at the University of Nairobi. In his section on the origins, Neill explains that the schism of 1054 is more a memorial reconstruction based on the wounds suffered during the 4th Crusade than an outright historical breach of Christian consciousness. He points out, in particular, that the first crusaders who arrived at Constantinople in 1096 were received as brothers in Christ by the emperor Alexius Comnenus. According to him, the real breach was the sack of Constantinople in 1204. Therefore, for Neill, the history of the ecumenical movement can only be a purification of memories through acts of repentance on the part of all the churches, including those of the Reformation "which like all human history, is a mixture of good and evil."[109]

In general, the historians who collaborated in this endeavor sought to rewrite Church history by recounting the attempts at confessional reconciliation that the great confessional histories of the remembrance period of orthodoxy have tended not to retain in their manuals. Take, for example, the permission granted in 1707 by the city of Geneva to a Lutheran community to establish itself in the city of Calvin. This was then considered a remarkable concession to the ecumenical spirit of the time. This new spirit owes much to the movement of "reasonable orthodoxy," introduced in Switzerland in the 17th century by theologians such as Jean Alphonse Turettini (1671–1737), Samuel Werenfels (1657–1740) and Jean Frederic Osdtervald (1663–1747).[110] This movement sought to form a Republic of Letters, intra and extra confessional, based on the values of peace, fairness, moderation and "gentleness." Descartes, Bayle, Leibniz and Locke were counted among its members.

On a more theoretical level we retain the semantic analysis of the word "ecumenical" offered by Willem Visser 't Hooft, the first general secretary of the WCC. This shows the renewal of the notion of orthodoxy in ecclesial circles during the contemporary period, moving from the all too often

109 S. C. Neill "Division and the Search for Unity Prior to the Reformation," *A History of the Ecumenical Movement*, v. 1, *1517–1948*, op. cit., 24.

110 M. Schmidt, "Ecumenical Activity on the Continent of Europe during the Seventeenth and Eighteenth Centuries," *History*, v. 1, op. cit., 105–109.

associated doctrinal or confessional meaning toward one of ecumenism, belonging without exception to the history of all the churches. In "The Word 'Ecumenical,' Its History and Use," the Dutch pastor shows all the historiographical importance of this term, from the Gospels of Luke (2:1) and Matthew (24:14) and the polemics between patriarchs and popes over its usage by the bishops of the Second Rome, to its new application in the Protestant world at the Evangelical Alliance in London in 1846, the YMCA Paris Conference in 1855, the Ecumenical Methodist Conference in 1881, the New York Ecumenical Missionary Conference in 1900, etc. Visser 't Hooft reminds us that Henri Dunant was not only the founder of the Red Cross, but also one of the founders of the YMCA and secretary of the Evangelical Alliance in Geneva. His correspondence reveals that he was one of the promoters of the ecumenical character of the YMCA. For Dunant, the word ecumenism was no longer reserved for its geographical meaning of inhabited world (as in the first four centuries) or for the legal sense of ecclesial validity of manifestations of the universal Church as for a seat, a doctor, or a Council (as between the 4th and 15th centuries) or for an institutional ecclesiastical sense, when each confession used this term to signify the boundaries of its own memory (as between the 15th and 19th centuries). It now referred to a "common consciousness of the universal Church" reuniting Christians beyond confessional boundaries.[111] The "ecumenical" (without the participation of the Catholic Church) Oxford Conference in 1937 gave a new consensual definition to the term. This definition has been taken up by all Christian confessions and defines the new paradigm of orthodoxy in formation:

> The term ecumenical refers to the historic expression of unity given by the Church. The thoughts and acts of the Church are ecumenical, insofar as they tend to bring about the *Una Sancta*, the fellowship of Christians who acknowledge the one Lord.[112]

In his general conclusion to the first volume of *The History of the Ecumenical Movement*, Neill tries to draw lessons from the different juxtaposed narratives. He is conscious of the limits of the undertaking (notably the fact

111 W. Visser 't Hooft, "The Word 'Ecumenical,' Its History and Use," *History*, op. cit., 738. Cf. also W. Visser 't Hooft, *The Meaning of Ecumenical,* The Burge Memorial Lecture, London, 1953.

112 Ibid., 740.

that the effective work of reconciliation is still largely reserved to the leadership of the Churches) and above all the limitations of his time, marked by the Cold War between the Capitalist and Communist blocs. But he notes that in the long term, ecclesial consciousness has always sought to go beyond the different political, linguistic, cultural and intellectual barriers among peoples. According to him, there were three types of attempts to reunite the Churches in the past: that based on the detailed doctrinal agreement prior to any sacramental union; on a return to what is considered the essential truth of the Gospel; and on the deepening of the existing unity among Christians through prayer and work in common.[113] Here one finds the structural types of orthodox mentality shared by zealots, the spiritual and proselytes. What is perhaps new in the historiography of S. C. Neill is his critical assessment of these three currents and his affirmation that these three orthodox streams, and thus these three types of historical remembrance, are by no means mutually exclusive. Neill writes:

> The most ardent enthusiast for doctrinal purity should recognize that Christianity is as much life as intellectual belief; the advocate for unity through experience cannot become indifferent to truth, otherwise his endeavor is in danger of ending in sentimentalism. In fact, most ecumenical projects have been marked by a combination of two or more of these three types. Never has one of the three approaches ever succeeded in completely dominating the ecumenical movement.[114]

This ecumenical and international evolution did not fail to provoke a renewal of Protestant historiography. In France, Marc Lienhard published in 2007 a summary of recent historical research and ecumenical dialogues in a book entitled *Identité confessionnelle et quête de l'unité*.[115] The professor of the University of Strasbourg presided over the Lutheran Church of the Confession of Augsburg of Alsace and Lorraine between 1997 and 2003. He knows how to appreciate the work of historians of all confessions who contributed, on the question of indulgences for example,[116] to find a right,

113 S. C. Neill, "Epilogue," *History*, op. cit., 726.

114 Ibid., 726.

115 Marc Lienhard, *Identité confessionnelle et quête de l'unité*, Lyon, Olivetan, 2007.

116 According to Bernard Poschmann, the indulgences were based on an implicit revelation (Mt 16:19) but do not have a juridical connotation in the Roman sense of the word. According to Poschmann, the authority to grant an indulgence concerning

faithful and glorifying knowledge of the ecclesial Tradition. He concludes that the Churches should not deny their respective confessional identities which give to each its spiritual significance. In his opinion, it is possible to avoid relativizing the truth while recognizing "the historicity of the expressions of truth," especially since the types of Pauline, Petrine and Johannine faith can find their biblical correspondence in Abraham, Moses or Ezekiel. That is why, in Germany, Oscar Cullman pleaded in 1966 for a real community of totally autonomous Churches, which would remain Catholic, Protestant and Orthodox and where a conciliar structure would enable each one to maintain its charisms, "not to define themselves in relation to others but to form a communion with all those who invoke the name of Christ." This was echoed by the German Lutheran theologian Ernst Jüngel who stated in 2002 that churches should form "an ecclesial community of reciprocal recognition."[117]

The fundamental paradigm of recognition, cherished by Paul Ricoeur, can be recognized here. Lienhard demonstrates the limits of doctrinal ecumenism as practiced in a very formal way by the Churches and with which, he believes, the populations are very far apart. He suggests an ecumenism of friendship that does not aim at the systematic harmonization of positions, but would facilitate the living together of Christians wherever possible according to the levels of consciousness. Where there is profound disagreement, both sides could raise their objections. It would not therefore be a question of indifference or relativism but of a return to the Gospel that asks Christians to mutually correct one another or even publicly in the case of failure. "An approach of this sort rightly underlines the continuing need for self-reform of the particular Churches, including the Catholic Church, and to this end this highlights the necessary and legitimate service rendered by one Church to another by the objections which it presents."[118] Lienhard believes that such objections can only be based on what constitutes a common heritage.

Carl Braaten, Robert Jenson and David Yeago are American Protestant historians brought together by the journal *Pro Ecclesia*. In 1996, these authors

---

life after death cannot derive from the power of the keys. Moreover, the efficacy of the indulgences is uncertain. The pope and the Church do not have any authority over the merits of Christ or of the saints. An indulgence can only be considered as a prayer. In 1999, Pope John Paul II admitted that indulgences "far from being a sort of 'putting off' of the obligation of conversion, are rather an aid to a more urgent, generous and radical commitment." Lienhard, *Identité*, op. cit., 267.

117 E. Jungel, *Il Regno*, March 15, 2002, 145–50.

118 Ibid., 290.

published a book under an explicitly ecumenical title: *The Catholicity of the Reformation.*[119] In this book they show that the Reformation could have been integrated into Catholic ecclesiology and into the Orthodox tradition if the need of the reformers to find a new scriptural basis for the sacramental life had been listened to and justly evaluated. Notably, Luther, in front of Cardinal Cajetan in Augsburg in 1518, was prepared to recognize Confession as a sacrament (on the basis of Mt 16:19), that is to say, as a visible means of justification within the Church.[120] The absence of dialogue between Luther and the pope, treated moreover as an Antichrist by the Augustinian monk, prevented a whole portion of Christian people from rediscovering the link between the truth of doctrine and justification, and the guarantee of salvation offered by this same doctrine. As David S. Yeago writes: "Schism was not the necessary consequence of Luther's theological vision."[121] Robert Wilken, in his contribution entitled "Lutheran Pietism and Catholic Piety," drew convincing parallels between the spirituality of Philip Jakob Spener and Catholic medieval spirituality inspired by Johann Tauler and Ephrem the Syrian. This American historian invites us to understand orthodoxy as a dynamic reality, a capacity of popular reaction based on the *sensus fidei* in contrast to the excesses of theologians and clerics. The most striking example of his thesis, he believes, is the work of Johann Sebastian Bach and his musical understanding of the Passion according to Matthew. Bach was in fact inspired not only by pietism but also by his medieval and patristic sources. In the work of St. Gregory of Nyssa, the "passions" of the soul, such as desire or fear, are not only negatives. They were created by God and therefore have their place in the economy of salvation. For the Cappadocian Father, desire is a sign of what is lacking. It is therefore appropriate to direct one's passions toward the good, to become an instrument of virtue, hence the importance of love and beauty. One finds in the work of Bach, Wilken concludes, "the same movement as in the work of Maximus the Confessor (*Quaestiones ad Thalassium*) and Gregory of Nyssa (*De Anima et Resurrectione*) according to which the knowledge of God without 'passion' does not set the intellect in motion, knowledge should be accompanied by holy love."[122]

119 Carl Braaten and Robert Jenson eds., *The Catholicity of the Reformation*, Grand Rapids, Eerdmans, 1996.

120 "I will give you the keys to the Kingdom of heaven; what you bind on earth will be bound in heaven, what you loosen on earth will be loosened in heaven."

121 *The Catholicity*, op. cit., 34.

122 Ibid., 90.

## HISTORIOGRAPHY IN THE ORTHODOX TRADITION

In the Orthodox Church, in the memorial sense of the term, there are numerous contemporary reference works on Christian history which are recognized as authoritative. Here we will limit ourselves to those that have the following two points in common: first, they identify orthodoxy with the Church whose doctrine consists in the recognition of the seven ecumenical councils, and second, they want to liberate the Eastern Christian Churches from their purely geographic and national definition.[123]

The essay on *The Mystical Theology of the Eastern Church* (*L'essai sur la théologie mystique de l'Eglise d'Orient*) by Vladimir Lossky is not, strictly speaking, a historical study. However, its introduction, entitled "Theology and Mysticism in the Tradition of the Eastern Church" ("Theologie et mystique de l'Eglise d'Orient"), has historical considerations. Moreover, the author had a considerable influence over a generation of Orthodox historians, including J. Meyendorff, A. Schmemann, O. Clément, K. Ware, and others. V. Lossky characteristically presents himself as an Orthodox theologian who cannot accept that what happens in the world might influence what happens in the Church due to the Church's divine and eternal nature. He writes:

> For the "historian of the Church" the religious factor disappears and finds itself displaced by others; such, for instance, as the play of political or social interests, the part played by racial or social conditions, considered as determining factors in the life of the Church. We think ourselves shrewder, more up to date, in invoking these factors as the true guiding forces of ecclesiastical history. While recognizing their importance, a Christian historian can scarcely resign himself to regarding them otherwise than as accidental to the essential nature of the Church. He cannot cease to see in the

123 A. Eltchaninoff, V. Ern, P. Florensky, *Istoria religuii*, Moscow, 1909; Sergius Bulgakov, *Orthodoxie*, Paris, Alcan, 1932; Jean Meyendorff, *L'Eglise orthodoxe hier et aujourd'hui*, Paris, Seuil, 1960; T. Ware, *Orthodoxie, l'Eglise des sept conciles*, Paris, DDB, 1997; A. Schmemann, *Le chemin historique de l'orthodoxie*, Paris, YMCA Press, 1995; John Meyendorff, Aristeides Papadakis, *L'Eglise dans l'histoire*, vol. 1, *Unité de l'Empire et division des chrétiens*, Paris, Cerf, 1993; vol. 2, *L'Orient chrétien et l'essor de la papauté*, Paris, Cerf, 2001; M. A. Costa de Beauregard, Ion Bria, Théologue de Foucauld, *L'Orthodoxie*, Paris, Buchet Chastel, 1979; Olivier Clément, *Byzance et le christianisme*, Paris, PUF, 1964; Olivier Clément, *L'Essor du christianisme oriental*, Paris, PUF, 1964.

> Church an autonomous body, subject to a different law than that of the determinism of this world. If we consider the dogmatic question of the procession of the Holy Spirit, which divided East and West, we cannot treat it as a fortuitous phenomenon in the history of the Church. From the religious point of view it is the sole issue of importance in the chain of events which terminated in the separation. Conditioned, as it may have been, by various factors, this dogmatic choice was for the one party as for the other a spiritual commitment, a conscious taking of sides in a matter of faith.[124]

This position was contested in 1954 by Yves Marie Congar in his political, cultural and ecclesial history of the "Eastern Schism."[125] For this Dominican theologian, "the Eastern schism came about through a progressive estrangement and was consolidated by the acceptance of this distancing."[126] Nevertheless, this work by V. Lossky, published in Paris in 1944, was a turning point in the history of the historical consciousness of the Church of the East. By showing that all genuine theology is mystical, the author invited the historiography of Western Christianity to an in-depth dialogue. In continuity with the work undertaken by S. Bulgakov, M. Lot Borodine and G. Florovsky, he helped to promote a renewed interest in the West for patristic theology. This renewal led to the creation of the collection *Sources Chrétiennes* in 1942 and the emergence of a brilliant generation of intellectuals, with Jean Daniélou, Henri de Lubac, Claude Mondésert, and Victor Fontoynont being some of the most eminent. Vladimir Lossky, who worked closely with the authors who contributed to the journal *Dieu Vivant*, finished by significantly reevaluating Western Christian orthodoxy above and beyond the Merovingian period. In his final book, *The Vision of God* (*La Vision de Dieu*) published by Delachaux and Niestlé in 1962, V.

124 V. Lossky, *Essai sur la théologie mystique de l'Eglise d'Orient,* Paris, Cerf, 1990 (1944), 11.

125 Yves Congar, "Neuf Cents Ans Après. Notes sur le 'Schisme Oriental'" in *1054–1954, l'Eglise et les Eglises,* Chevetogne, éditions de Chevetogne, 1954. These theses were greeted with widespread approval in the academic world. On the other hand, some Orthodox intellectuals continued to defend V. Lossky's concept of a dogmatic explanation of Church history. Claude Laporte, *Tous les saints de l'Orthodoxie*, preface by Msgr. Luka, bishop of Western Europe, Patriarch of Serbia, Xenia, 2008. The author is also a specialist in the "securitization of assets in Switzerland."

126 Yves Congar, "Neuf Cents Ans Après. Notes sur le 'Schisme Oriental,'" in *1054–1954, l'Eglise et les Eglises*, Chevetogne, Editions de Chevetogne, 1954, 8.

Lossky attempts to reconcile the work of the Byzantine Orthodox theologian Gregory Palamas (1296–1359) of the 14th century with that of the 17th century Jesuit theologian Denis Pétau (1583–1652), a scholar and professor of Church history.[127] Lossky understood that the opposition between Byzantine and Latin theology, although real, was ultimately superficial. It is true that the librarian of King Louis XIII and the editor of the work of John Chrysostom qualified as "nonsense" the assertion by Palamas that human beings could not see the Divine Essence. Palamas could have simply reread the Beatitudes to realize that it had been promised to the pure of heart that they would see God. After examining the whole Patristic tradition before judging the contradiction between Pétau and Palamas, Lossky concludes by affirming that one must distinguish between the erotic and neo-Platonic perspective which the Eastern Fathers opposed because of its egoistical tendency, and the agapeic and evangelical approach shared by the Fathers of the East and West. In this latter representation of God, man sees divinity in the measure in which one gives oneself to God. But for this reason, as Lossky welcomes, Pétau is severely critical of the scholastic doctrine of the intuitive vision of the Divine Essence propagated by the 16th-century Jesuits such as Gabriel Vasquez; and this is why, according to the Russian theologian, Western theology should no longer be considered a monolithic block. Lossky concludes his work with these bitter and reconciling words:

> [Pétau] did not see—and this is the great paradox—that all of Palamas's theological work constitutes a defense of the immediate vision of God, and that the distinction between essence and energy, far from being a separation or division of God into two parts, communicable and incommunicable, is an inevitable theological postulate if we wish to maintain the real and not just the metaphorical character of deification, without suppressing created being within the divine essence.[128]

This breach opened in the understanding of Catholic theology in the modern age by Vladimir Lossky justifies a rereading of the history of Western thought in a nonconfessional, post-Manichean dynamic, that is, according to

127 Pétau boasts of having uncovered no less than 8,000 mistakes in the *Annales* of Baronius.

128 V. Lossky, *Vision de Dieu,* Neuchatel, Delachaux et Niestlé, 138.

a properly orthodox perspective.[129] In fact, according to Jean-Louis Quantin, the *Theologica dogmata* of Denis Pétau, which appeared from 1644 to 1650, was very different from scholastic theology. It sought to interpret Scripture through the Councils and Fathers. The same can be said of the *Dogmata Theologica* of the Oratorian Louis Thomassin (1619–1695), which appeared between 1680 and 1689.[130]

Certainly, this orthodox reinterpretation of the history of Christianity obviously cannot be assimilated to the acceptance of all the evolutions of Western Christianity. Panayotis Trembelas (1886–1977) was criticized by K. Ware for his "Westernism." Nonetheless, it would be useful to briefly take note of his major work, *Dogmatic Theology of the Orthodox Catholic Church* (*Dogmatique de l'Eglise orthodoxe catholique*), insofar as it contributes to the rethinking of the history of Christianity in a less memorial sense and more critical manner. This Greek theologian, titular of the chair of liturgy, was strongly influenced by the academic and scholastic thought of C. Androutsos. During the 1950s, P. Trembelas was one of the principal animators of the Zoe Brotherhood, founded in 1911 by Fr Eusebius Matthopoulos, and then, after an internal schism in the Brotherhood in 1959, he became the leader of the movement's conservative right wing, which led to the creation of the Sotir movement in June of 1960. Trembelas participated in the 1954 Assembly of the World Council of Churches at Evanston. In 1976, he presided over the Second Congress of Orthodox Theologians at Athens. His *Dogmatic Theology of the Orthodox Catholic Church*, published in Athens in 1959–61, was translated into French and published in 1966–68. For thirty years, this book was the official manual used by students in Greek theological faculties. It is not lacking in sweeping generalities about Catholics "who have made the pope and bishops the sole instruments of the divine law of Tradition" and about Protestants "who have gotten rid of the authority of Tradition."[131] But Trembelas admits that the situation he observes was not always the case over the course of history. Thus Luther, who accepted the three symbols of faith (the Apostolic Creed, the Nicaean

129 Cf. the works of Henri de Lubac, Yves Marie Congar, Louis Bouyer, H. U. von Balthasar, et al. Cf. especially Pierre Gouraud, *La gloire et la glorification de l'univers chez Saint Jean de la Croix*, Paris, Beauchesne, 1998.

130 Jean-Louis Quantin, "The Fathers in Seventeenth Century Roman Catholic Theology," I. Backus, op. cit., 963.

131 P. Trembelas, *Dogmatique de l'Eglise orthodoxe catholique*, by Archimandrite Pierre Dumont, Chevetogne, DDB, 1966; cf. introduction.

Creed and the *Quicumque* attributed to Athanasius) as ecumenical, thought that tradition had a note of catholicity and was not the exclusive mark of the Western Church. Along the same lines, he recognized that "the exercise of ecclesiastical authority imposes itself in questions of faith because of the reciprocal relationships within a body and their natural interdependence within the community of the universal Church."[132] Trembelas saw no problem in underlining how the reaction of mystics such as Bernard of Clairvaux was beneficial for scholasticism. He particularly appreciated the Italian scholastic Giovanni de Fidenza or Bonaventure (1221–1274), the Cardinal Bishop of Albano, whom he considered a saint and "the most subtle theologian of his times." Above all, Trembelas had a very great esteem for the Dutch Calvinist theologian Jan Jacob van Oosterzee (1817–1882) and his Christ-centered theology. The Utrecht professor did not hesitate to describe himself as "an Evangelical or an orthodox Christian." Trembelas had a very original criticism of the work of St. John of Damascus. On the one hand, he rejoices that the West had recognized him as a Doctor of the Church. But, on the other, he finds that this patristic synthesis is not satisfactory for contemporary orthodox theology. In fact, John of Damascus deals only with two sacraments (Baptism and the Eucharist), neglects ecclesiology, and concerns himself essentially with "light, fire, the stars and the wind!"[133] For this reason, Trembelas, along with Gregory Palamas, believes that Orthodox tradition is not based on just the seven ecumenical councils. He adds the 14th century councils of the Ecumenical Patriarchate as well as the 17th century symbolic books by metropolitans P. Moghila and Dositheus of Jerusalem ("worthy auxiliaries of the Orthodox dogmatist"), the acts of the synods of Constantinople (1638), Jassy (1643) and Jerusalem (1672) and even the works of C. Androutsos (*Dogmatique de l'Eglise orthodoxe catholique,* 1907).

Such a representation of the history of orthodox tradition is not acceptable to Timothy Ware (b. 1934), a British theologian who converted from the Anglican Church to Orthodoxy in 1958. His book, *The Orthodox Church* (1963), revised several times at each of its reeditions and translations, currently enjoys great prestige in the Orthodox world. Kallistos Ware became a priest and monk in 1966, bishop of Dioclea under the aegis of the ecumenical patriarchate in 1982 and metropolitan bishop in 2007. He was a

132 Ibid., 54.
133 Ibid., 72.

professor at the University of Oxford for 35 years and published numerous works — among them an English translation of the *Philokalia*. This is a work of great erudition, and reveals a certain openness to the spirit of ecumenism. Ware has contributed to breaking down the barriers in the Orthodox world and enabled it to rediscover a conciliar identity after centuries of internal divisions and external persecutions.

He has not been able, however, to respond to all the questions of the contemporary historian. On the one hand, he separates the history of the Eastern Churches, which appears painful and tragic, from their faith and rituals, which are presented as immutable and inflexible. This primary methodological position leads K. Ware to take disconcerting positions in terms of both the unfolding of events and the level of the definition of doctrinal and spiritual truth. We will only take three examples. K. Ware limits the history of Orthodoxy to that of the territories under the jurisdiction of the leaders of the Orthodox churches, which leads him to reject the history of Western Orthodox Christianity from the medieval period onward. For the English theologian, when the pope broke relations with Byzantium in 1054, the entire Latin Church suddenly lost its link with Orthodoxy.[134] Of course, this position, widely accepted in the manuals used in seminaries of the Orthodox Church, is generally presented with more nuances.[135] John Meyendorff, in particular, insists that the Crusades were the source of the "real and definitive rupture."[136] Whatever might be the case, as K. Ware writes, "the unity of the Mediterranean world would gradually disappear

134 "Such is the incident which conventionally marks the beginning of the great schism between the Orthodox East and the Latin West." K. Ware, *L'orthodoxie*, op. cit., 60.

135 "But this separation, as most historians now recognize, is not an event whose date can be precisely determined," op. cit., 60.

136 John Meyendorff, *L'Eglise orthodoxe, hier et aujourd'hui,* Paris Seuil, 1960, 50. This author also uses the dichotomy between history and doctrine and spirituality. This same plan can be found in *L'Eglise orthodoxe* by Olivier Clément, written during the same period. V. Lossky does not take history into consideration in his *Essai sur la théologie mystique de l'Eglise d'Orient*, while A. Schmemann, in his *Le chemin historique de l'Orthodoxie,* does not treat questions of doctrine and spirituality. In this generation of neo-patristic synthesis, it was only the opus of John Zizioulas, *L'être ecclesial*, which finally denounced a dichotomy between history and eschatology which led some to positivism and others to millenniarism. Because for the Church Fathers (and for Ignatius in particular), truth becomes historical without ceasing to be ontological, Zizioulas proposes a synthesis between the historical and eschatological perspectives in an article published in the review *Istina* in 1974, entitled "La continuité avec les origines apostoliques dans la conscience théologique des Eglises orthodoxes."

during the following centuries, beginning with the demise of political unity."[137] In short, no regrets for Kallistos Ware if the account of the history of Christianity has to do without the Cathedral of Chartres, the University of Bologna, or the Cistercian order.

This position has been challenged by the Orthodox historian Olivier Clément, who, in his two 1964 books on medieval Byzantine Christianity, considered the history of Western Christianity an integral part of orthodox Christianity. The proof is for him to be found in the fact that the Eastern patriarchs agreed, without any condition of prior repentance, to participate in the ecumenical councils of Lyon and Florence where they signed the acts of reunification. It is difficult to imagine that the history of Western culture suddenly became orthodox again on the morning of July 6, 1439, when the formula of agreement was signed, the Bull *Laetentur Coeli*, between the Latin theologians (the pope himself participated in the deliberations of the council, a fact unprecedented in the history of ecumenical councils) and the Byzantine theologians (the text was signed not only by the Patriarch and the Emperor but also by the future Patriarch of Constantinople, Georges Scholarios, the humanist Msgr. Bessarion, the bishop of Nicaea, Msgr. Isidore, the metropolitan of Kiev, etc.).

On a larger scale, the disconnect most Orthodox historians make between Eastern and Western orthodoxy from the 11th century onwards, poses the problem of the recognition by Eastern Orthodox of the principal fruits of this Western culture, from Gothic architecture to spatial technology, from the holiness of Francis of Assisi to that of Martin Luther King. For this reason, Father Thomas Hopko, the former dean of the Orthodox Institute of St. Vladimir and the author of correspondence courses on Church history, made a point to set aside, at the end of each century studied in his courses, brief notes on the evolution of Western Christianity. He usually only relates events, but after mentioning the First Vatican Council and its declaration of papal infallibility, he briefly adds, as if in anticipation of the future age of the reconciliation of memories: "The *Curé of Ars* and the Carmelite Theresa of Lisieux lived during this period."[138]

There is a second methodological problem posed by the separation of history and doctrine and the unequivocal identification of the doctrine of the seven councils with the Eastern Church. K. Ware affirms that "as long as there is

137 K. Ware, op. cit., 61.

138 T. Hopko, *Cours d'histoire de l'Eglise,* Paris, Saint Sergius Institute, 1984, 70.

not unity in the faith, there cannot be sacramental communion."[139] Such an affirmation, which not only rules out sacramental communion but also the reconciliation of memories, has not always been historically prevalent in the Orthodox Churches. It is common knowledge that, during the Middle Ages, sees which were not in communion with Rome, such as that of Constantinople, were, however, in mediate communion with the Chair of Peter through their communion with the see of Antioch. As Father Robert Taft has pointed out, many regions on the border between the Byzantine and Latin Empires, such as Calabria in Italy and Kiev in Russia, practiced intercommunion at least until the end of the 18th century. Mention can also be made of the intercommunion among "Orthodox" and "Catholics" authorized from 1969 to 1986 by the synod of the Russian Church.[140] More generally, many cases in the Church's history of the recognition of the baptism of repentant heretics silently witness that the boundaries of the visible Church do not fully coincide with those of the mystical Church. It was in any case, as indicated by Father André Borrély, the position of the Second Ecumenical Council of Constantinople (381) whose 6th canon forbade the rebaptism of repentant Arians.

Thirdly and lastly, the Orthodox identification of a church with a territory prevents reconciliation with other historical Christian Churches. As long as the reality of the diaspora of the Eastern Churches is considered only from the unique perspective of mission, as is the case in chapter nine of the book by K. Ware, the Orthodox Church finds herself confronted with the phenomenon of proselytism and lack of respect for her "canonical territory." The historical reality of the ecclesial organization of Christianity, however, is that Orthodox ecclesiology has always been pastoral and synodal before becoming territorial and vertical. A. Schmemann has shown that it was the emperor Constantine who, after having legalized the Christian faith, decided to intervene in the affairs of the Church to resolve the Donatist schism (whereas the Church had previously been used to resolving its tensions by confiding in the Holy Spirit in a synodal process) and on the other hand territorialized the relationship of the bishop to his community (whereas at the beginning the Church was formed through the relation of the apostles to the local communities).[141] This is apparent from the mere reading of the Letters of St. Paul to the churches he helped found.

139 K. Ware, *L'orthodoxie*, op. cit., 401.
140 Cf. Antoine Arjakovsky, *En attendant le concile*, op. cit., 311.
141 A. Schmemann, *Le cheminement*, op. cit., 23 and 90.

A less conceptual approach to the history of orthodox Christianity can be found in an address entitled "The Future and Significance of the Orthodox Diaspora in Western Europe" given by Olivier Clément to the Congress of the Orthodox Fraternity of Western Europe which took place at Amiens in 1977. This conference questions the whole traditional historiography of the Orthodox Church. Olivier Clément sees the trace of the undivided Church and, consequently, of orthodox doctrine in the history of a "Latin West" which he avoids interpreting as a hermetical concept (if only by the initial recognition that "Latinity" is not its only characteristic, just as Byzantine is not the only tradition in the East). For him, Roman art and 12th century Cistercian theology are indisputable signs of the inspiration of the undivided Spirit. Clément affirms that the growing apart of the East and West, so well described by Father Yves Congar, was not an obstacle for the continued expression of orthodox doctrine in both Eastern and Western Europe, even after the failed reception of the Council of Florence. In the 1977 conference at Amiens, O. Clément had this to say:

> The ferment of the undivided Church has not ceased to be active in this country. The 17th century French School of Spirituality and Pascal, the manifestations of holiness in the 19th and 20th centuries, from the Curé of Ars to St. Theresa of Lisieux, from Father de Foucauld to Madeleine Delbrel and Massignon, a powerful literature of Christian inspiration, from Leon Bloy to Bernanos, the biblical and patristic renewal during the 1950s, all witness to the richness of the Tradition, however awkward, however shattered this witness might be; we could develop a whole Christian concept of the wiles of the Holy Spirit!

The Orthodox theologian goes on to say:

> We cannot be blind to the fact that the influence of the Gospels, of the Eucharist and of at least the first four Ecumenical Councils never ceased in the West and brought forth a holiness perhaps all the more impressive and all the more heroic in that it lacks theological breathing room.[142]

142 O. Clément, "Avenir et signification de la diaspora orthodoxe en Europe occidentale," *Contacts*, no. 103 (1978). Republished by M. J. Guillou, "Les chances du dialogue

Such a perspective, even if it is still a minority opinion, is far from being considered marginal. Msgr. Stephanos, the Orthodox Metropolitan of Estonia, has stated that Olivier Clément "gave the best of himself"[143] in his address to the conference. The Greek archbishop also notes that Olivier Clément's remarks concerning Orthodox phyletism are still very much *à propos*. He cites the text of the professor at the St. Sergius Institute:

> Among other things, it could first be asked if the link which has been established in the Orthodox Church between nationality and ecclesiastical jurisdiction has not changed its meaning in the Diaspora: originally it meant a transfiguration of the ethnic community by the Church, but it often became a specifically Orthodox form of secularization of the Church by the ethnic community. In such a perspective, Orthodoxy seemed to be only an aspect of national culture. The descendants of the immigrants, in the measure in which they became assimilated, quite naturally abandoned an Orthodoxy that no longer concerned them. The hemorrhage has been gigantic. It has never been measured. . . .[144]

Moreover, a new generation of Orthodox theologians and historians want to put an end to the apologetic aspect of the history of the Orthodox Church. This movement, which started at the beginning of the 19th century with historians such as A. Lebedev, was continued into the 20th century by theologians and courageous bishops such as Father Alexis Kniazev (1913–1991), Father Alexander Schmemann (1921–1983), Father Nicholas Afanasiev (1893–1966) and Metropolitan Emilianos Timiadis (1916–2008). Alexis Kniazev became the dean of the St. Sergius Institute in 1965. He participated as an observer in the Second Vatican Council and was involved in many ecumenical undertakings, such as the *Ecumenical Translation of the Bible* in 1975. Along with Father Alexander Schmemann, he dared to speak of a profound crisis in the structures of the Orthodox Church "due to historic outgrowths." In 1978, Kniazev wrote: "These outgrowths have reached such a point that the Orthodox Church risks losing its true identity and having its

---

entre l'Eglise catholique et l'Eglise orthodoxe," in *Aspects d'Orthodoxie*, Colloquium of Strasbourg, November, 1978, Paris, PUF, 1981, 113.

143 Msgr. Stephanos, Metropolitan of Tallin and all Estonia, "Olivier Clément et l'unification de l'Orthodoxie en France" (Paris, January 16, 2010), www.orthodoxa.org.

144 Ibid.

catholicity suffocated because its organs have become progressively blocked by purely human interests: political and religious nationalism, provincialism and parochialism, servile submission to the imperialistic goals of the State."[145] Alexander Schmemann considered that these different practical heresies originated in "the historical sin of Orthodoxy," the theocracy of Constantine.[146] Schmemann, who was the confessor of Solzhenitsyn, was critical of both caesaropapism and the romanticism of V. Soloviev, the author of *The History and Future of Theocracy* (*Histoire et avenir de la théocratie*),[147] whose theses were revived by the Russian historian Anton Kartachev.

It is not certain, however, that these two historians of the St. Sergius Institute really understood what the Russian philosopher meant to say. When, in 1887, Soloviev studied the history of theocracy in the Bible, it was not with the intention of steering Tsarism towards a new Constantinian age. His reasoning was based on a strange fact of evangelical history. At his baptism, and during his first burial, Christ justified his action to John the Baptist with the following words: "Let it be so now; for thus it is fitting for us to fulfil all righteousness" (Mt 3:15). In this scene, Soloviev saw the prefiguration of the coming spiritual theocracy:

> Christ, representing the royal house of David, the founder and unique right head of the Kingdom of God in humanity, took upon himself the task of accomplishing all righteousness by an evident act of submission to John, son of the priest Zacharias of the family of Aaron. . . . When it becomes our turn to accomplish an act which corresponds to that of Jesus, when we will reestablish, in all truth, our spiritual bond with the universal Church of the past, when, with a clear conscience, a free moral impetus of national spirit, we will rediscover ourselves in a state of right filiation with respect to a paternity common to the whole world, only then will there be a possibility for this perfect fraternity of all peoples, a fraternity animated by love and lived with a free unanimity. Such is the ideal and future of the universal Church as well as our right national ideal. . . .

145 A. Kniazev, "La crise des structures et le concile pan orthodoxe," in *Aspects de l'Orthodoxie*, Paris, PUF, 1981, 107.

146 A. Schmemann, "La Théocratie byzantine et l'Eglise orthodoxe," *Dieu vivant*, Paris, 33–54.

147 A. Soloviev, *Histoire et avenir de la théocratie*, translation by Mireille Chmelewsky, Paris, Cujas, 2008.

> [The Church] will appear as a conscious being, morally free, acting by itself for its own accomplishment, like a true companion of God, like a creature united to the Divinity in a full and perfect union, absorbing the Divinity entirely within itself, in a word, like *Sophia*, the Supreme Wisdom of God to whom our ancestors, guided by an astonishing prophetic intuition, dedicated altars and temples even though they still did not know who She was.[148]

Contemporary Orthodox political theology was, therefore, not just a neo-Slavophile criticism of parliamentary democracy (Kartachev) or of the Byzantine caeseropapist past (Schmemann). In 1896 Soloviev wrote to Eugene Tavernier that his plan was to take seriously, to consider as an anticipation of a future development for the State as well as the Church, the return in glory of Jesus to Jerusalem.

> We have to abandon, once and for all, the idea that the power and the exterior grandeur of theocracy is a direct and immediate goal of Christian politics. The goal is justice, and glory is but a consequence that will come about on its own.[149]

The School of Paris benefited from this growing consciousness of the central role of justice in Orthodox theology. Nicholas Afanasiev, a colleague of Schmemann and Kartachev at the St. Sergius Institute, founded the Liturgical Weeks in 1953 with Father Cyprian Kern and Dom Olivier Rousseau. He devoted himself to the study of the doctrine of the primacy in the light of ecclesiology, by way of a conference he delivered at Saulchoir in 1953 (published in *Istina* in 1957) and of two articles "The Apostle Peter and the Roman Bishop" (*L'apôtre Pierre et l'évêque romain*) and "The Catholic Church" (*L'Eglise catholique*) published in *Pravoslavnaha Mysl'* in 1955 and 1957. His research culminated in the major article "The Church which Presides in Love" (*L'Eglise qui préside dans l'Amour*) written in 1957 and published in the collection *The Primacy of Peter in the Orthodox Church* (*La primauté de Pierre dans l'Eglise orthodoxe*) (Neuchatel, 1960). This article, recommended to the Council Fathers in 1964, earned him an invitation to participate as an observer at the final session of the Second Vatican Council (as a guest of

148 Ibid., 32–33.
149 Ibid., 270.

the Secretariat for Christian Unity). One can find, according to Dom Olivier Rousseau, in chapter III of the definitive constitution *De Ecclesia* (no. 26), a doctrine related to his own which would lead one to suspect his influence. In 1962, he published an essay, "Una Sancta," written "to the memory of John XXIII, the Pope of Love" and published in 1963 in *Irenikon*. His article "Statio Orbis" also appeared in 1962. On December 8, 1965, he assisted at the lifting of the anathemas between the Catholic and Orthodox Churches. In 1965 he reaffirmed his ecumenical conviction in *Irenikon* that the Eucharist is "the principal link between the Catholics and the Orthodox."

The consequence of the theological renewal of the School of Paris was not just the criticism of the confessional definition of Orthodoxy but also of its juridical rigidity dating from the Byzantine period. In a 1933 article in the journal *The Way* (*Put'*), Nicholas Afanasiev proposed distinguishing between an eternal truth found in a canon from a custom that has become outdated.[150] He points out, in "The Canons and Canonical Consciousness," that the canonists of the era of the emperor Manuel Comnenos (1118–1180) did not consider themselves prisoners of the edict of the Council of Trullo which proclaimed the invariability of the canons. But after the fall of Constantinople, their creativity was forgotten and there was a return to a stagnant representation of orthopraxis. In the opinion of Afanasiev, canonic validity could only be invoked insofar as the canon fulfilled the purpose for which it had been decreed. He gives numerous examples that demonstrate the contradiction between the so-called orthodox application of certain canons and their original intent,[151] the neglect of certain canons in practice by the Orthodox faithful,[152] and finally the belief of certain zealots in the eternal validity of the canons.[153] Afanasiev notes that Christ did not give any canonical norms to his Church (he references Lk 12:14), "Man, who made me a judge or divider over you?" On the other hand, Christ gave life-giving truths and confided the power of the keys to his apostles. For Afanasiev, this power to bind and to loose excludes the concept of divine

150 N. Afanasiev, "Kanony i kanonitcheskoie soznanie," *Put'*, n. 39, prilojenie, 16c, 1933.

151 Apostolic canon 50 envisaged the excommunication of the priest or bishop who baptized using just one immersion. But the intent of the canon was to respect the words of Christ that baptism be in the name of the Father and of Son and of the Holy Spirit.

152 Apostolic canons 8 & 9 envisage the excommunication of any layperson or cleric who does not stay until the end of a liturgical service.

153 The ecclesial organization which Paul gave to the Corinthians only lasted several decades.

right but does authorize the Church to formulate canonical norms, which may differ according to time and circumstances, as long as the life-giving truths of Christ are respected.

The renewal of the paradigm of orthodoxy as true and fair knowledge has also affected other traditions of Orthodox theology, from Greek theology to Romanian or Antiochian theology. Thus the approach of Afanasiev, which tries to marry "tradition and creativity," has been subsequently taken up by Metropolitan Maximus of Sardis.[154] This Metropolitan has no qualms about using Latin terminology; he believes that "the ecclesial consciousness expressed by customs constitutes down through the centuries the worthy testimony of faith of the fidelity of the *traditio continuativa* to the true canonical tradition, the *traditio constitutiva*."[155] Msgr. Emilianos was Permanent Representative of Patriarch Athenagoras to the World Council of Churches in Geneva for 25 years (1959–1984), observer at the Second Vatican Council, Bishop of Meloa from 1960 and Metropolitan of Silvyria from 1977. In 1967 he published an Orthodox theology of penance in which he criticized the loss of both the medicinal significance of the *epitimia* in the Orthodox Church and the appreciation of penal literature, notably in the *Pedalion* of St. Nicodemus the Hagiorite. Msgr. Emilianos regretted that the ministry of penances, indulgences and satisfaction has remained rigidly fixed in most manuals.[156] His approach has been continued in Orthodox theology by eminent personalities. These assembled in Athens for the Second Congress of Orthodox Theologians in 1976. Conscious of the recurring temptation of nationalism in the Orthodox world, Nicholas Lossky called for "see[ing] how one can read in an Orthodox manner certain elements that have often deviated because of the context in which they were expressed."[157] But Msgr. Stylianopoulos went one step further in a critical approach by aiming at the very institution of the historic Orthodox Church. He stigmatizes the pride that threatens to make the Orthodox Church a sinful institution.[158] The theologian Nikos Nissiotis, for his part,

154 Metropolitan Maximus of Sardes, *Le patriarcat oecuménique dans l'Eglise orthodoxe*, Thessalonica, IPEP, 1973; Paris, Beauchesne, 1957.

155 Ibid., 332.

156 The review of the book by E. Timiadis, *Metanoia*, was written by A. de Halleux for the *Revue d'Histoire ecclesiastique*, vol. LXIV, no. 1 (Louvain, 1969).

157 N. Lossky, *Procès verbaux du deuxième congrès de théologie orthodoxe*, Athens, 19–29 August 1976, Savas C. Agouridès, Athens, 1978, 411.

158 T. Stylianopoulos, *Procès verbaux*, op. cit., 196.

thinks that Christian Orthodox thought "too often assists as a spectator of history and ecclesiastical life" and calls for a self-criticism of an Orthodox theology which he considers insufficiently eschatological.[159] John Zizioulas contributed to the discussion at Athens by criticizing a vision of the truth that is too traditionalist and too intellectual and called for a truth lived in a Eucharistic and koinonic way.

> We cannot say: "First you must accept the true faith and then you will enter into a communion of love." Love is something that comes from the life of the community. Communion and community are identical.[160]

To conclude this summary overview of contemporary orthodox historiography, one can therefore consider that there are at present three principal schools among historians belonging to the Orthodox Church. On the one hand, there is the work written in the 1960s by K. Ware, an orthodox historiography orientated towards the defense of the memorial and institutional identity of the Orthodox Church with insistence on its universal significance in time and space. Since the work of G. Florovsky in the 1930s, however, this historiography gradually incorporates the fact that the mystical boundaries of the Church extend beyond its ecumenical borders.

On the other hand, there is a historiographical tradition which, refusing to draw the historical consequences of the spiritual renewal of the School of Paris, opts for an encyclopedic eclecticism. In 1999, Patriarch Alexis II, with the assistance of specialists from 15 autocephalous Orthodox Churches and many other autonomous churches, launched an ambitious historiographical initiative in the context of a vast, more than 25-volume *Orthodox Encyclopedia*. Forty thousand copies of every volume were published, and each volume contained more than 800 illustrated pages. This project now has a website (www.pravenc.ru)[161] that publishes articles concerning not only the Eastern Churches but also those of the West (for example, articles on Gallicanism, Luther, Calvin, Henry IV). These Orthodox luminaries, most of whose writings give proof of serious erudition, are all the same struggling

159 N. Nissiotis, "Introduction," *Procès verbaux du 2e congrès de théologie orthodoxe*, Athens, August 19–29, 1976, Savas C. Agouridès, Athens, 1978, 75.

160 J. Zizioulas, "1st Comment," *Procès verbaux*, op. cit., 143.

161 Last Access: July 2018.

with their mere alphabetical logic to find a unified vision of the history of Christianity and make a redefinition of Orthodoxy all the more necessary.

Finally, there is a third historiographical current represented by Olivier Clément and John Zizioulas which, especially since the 1970s, integrated the paradigm shift represented by the imperative of a fair and just truth and its ecumenical implications. The future of Orthodox historiography and of the ecclesial memory of Orthodox populations will depend, to a great extent, on the critical and fraternal dialogue which will have to take place among these three schools.

# CHAPTER II
# *Orthodoxy Today*

## ECUMENICAL HISTORIOGRAPHY

It is only in the 20th century that the history of ecclesial truth and the doctrine of truth historically maintained by the Church emerged from a confessional and theocentric representation. To begin with, there is the famous anthology entitled *God, History and Historians*, published by Oxford University Press (New York, 1977). Among the contributing authors to this ecumenical collection (with an important bibliography) are some of the most eminent intellectuals of the time, for example: Christopher Dawson, Reinhold Niebuhr, Herbert Butterfield, R. Bultmann, P. Tillich, A. Toynbee, K. Barth, J. Maritain, H.-I. Marrou, C. S. Lewis, G. Florovsky. With these authors, writing after the tragedy of the Second World War, one observes a common desire to part with a naive optimism regarding human nature, to question the secular vision of history as progress, to challenge the Marxist and Liberal interpretations of history and to return to the historiographical depths of writers such as St. Augustine. In spite of the diversity of theological points of view, these authors share a common commitment to ecumenism. Their ecumenical work began in the 1930s, notably at the 1937 Oxford Conference (Niebuhr, Tillich, Barth, Dawson, Latourette, Florovsky, et al.) that had as one of its themes "The Kingdom of God and History," and led in particular to the creation of the World Council of Churches in Amsterdam (the theme being *Man's Disorder and God's Design*) and the publication of an important text entitled *God in Nature and History*, which was published in 1968 on the occasion of the Assembly of Uppsala.[1]

1 *God in Nature and History. Appendix to Workbook for the Assembly Committees*, Fourth Assembly, Uppsala, Sweden, 1968, reprinted from Faith and Order Paper 50, WCC, 1968.

In this same ecumenical spirit, the work of the historical commission of the American branch of Faith and Order (World Council of Churches) represents a further advance of Orthodox Christian historiography. This commission, composed of representatives of 24 Churches (Catholic, Protestant and Orthodox), worked under the direction of professors Lauree Hersch Meyer and O. C. Edwards from 1988 to 1991 on the drafting of 14 principles of ecumenical history published in collaboration with the review *Ecumenical Trends*. Jeffrey Gros, then director of Faith and Order, had been interested in the experience of CEHILA (Comisión para el Estudio de La Historia de las Iglesias en América Latina) and wanted to reproduce it in the United States. Their work was based on the study of a book by Williston Walker, Richard Norris, David Lotz and Robert Handy entitled *A History of the Christian Church* (New York, C. Scribners and Sons, 1985) and the creation of a bibliography of ecumenical historiography of Christianity (Douglas Foster).[2] The text presented by Charles Brockwell and Timothy Wengert is divided into five sections — universality (principles 1–3), context (4–6), points in common (7–8), particularities (9–12) and perspectives (13–14) — and mostly references biblical sources as a form of justification. Principle n. 1 affirms that "an ecumenical history of Christianity understands the history of the Church as the history of those who describe themselves as 'Christian' and pays particular attention to those whose history has been ignored or suppressed."[3] Principle n. 2 states that this history must be global. Principle n. 3 should enable readers to distinguish the catholicity of different Churches and to understand their apostolicity in a variety of contexts. Principles 4 to 6 require the development from different sources (iconography, oral traditions, liturgies, etc.) of the contextual relations between the Gospel and cultures, and the taking into consideration of the doctrinal as well as the spiritual and practical elements of the life of the churches. Principle n. 7 states that every generation and tradition reads the past in light of the present. Principle n. 8 encourages the discovery of parallel situations to contemporary problems in other times in order to reexamine the sources of division. Principle n. 9 requests that the voice of every identity group be respected "in the conversation of the communities of faith." Principle n. 10 explains that every ecumenical history of Christianity confronts each

2 T. Wengert and C. Brockwell Jr., eds., *Telling the Churches' Stories, Ecumenical Perspectives on Writing History*, Grand Rapids, Eerdmans, 1995.

3 Ibid., 4.

particular tradition with the critical analysis of other traditions. Principle n. 11 relies on Matthew 25:35 and Romans 12:13 to encourage a search into the past in a spirit of hospitality. The 12th principle explains that an ecumenical history should not be written in a defensive spirit but in a spirit of repentance and mutual forgiveness. From Matthew 7:1–5 ("Judge not, lest you be judged") principle 13 asks the historian to understand and recognize his own a priori assumptions and to seek to overcome what could be prejudicial in them. The last principle affirms that an ecumenical history recognizes that no narrative can claim complete objectivity and seeks to integrate particular histories.

*Confessing History*, the recent collection of the work of a generation of young historians belonging to different Churches and published by the University of Notre Dame in the United States, is a witness to this renewal.[4] These historians continue the work of their predecessors and in particular that of the "Conference on Faith and History," which, since its inception in 1968 by Protestant Evangelical historians, regularly organizes colloquiums, published in their review *Fides et Historia*, on the question of the relationship between faith and history. As Eric Miller, professor of history at Geneva College writes, this generation has come to question the so-called "academic" history teaching programs in American universities as well as the *cursus honorum* required of young historians in the course of their secular career. To "rightly see the dead," in the words of the Catholic historian Una M. Cadegan, Miller esteems that it is necessary to get out of the system of hyperspecialized research, based on the method aimed at seeking "observable cultural forces" and on a pseudo-epistemic neutrality. According to William Katerberg, a century of historical research and four decades of theoretical debate reveal something: they have not provided "a stable foundation on which the truth claims, moral decisions and political projects can be based."[5] On the contrary, in the opinion of Christopher Shannon, contemporary historical science has only legitimated the secularized modern world whose ultimate goal is "the maximization of individual liberty." This is why Shannon, in opposition to the rationalist and individualist philosophy of John Rawls, recommends the major works of Alasdair McIntyre (*After Virtue*),[6] Robert

4 John Fea, Jay Green, Eric Miller, eds., *Confessing History, Explorations in Christian Faith and the Historian's Vocation*, Notre Dame, Notre Dame University Press, 2010.

5 Ibid., 11.

6 A. McIntyre was born in 1929. He is professor of philosophy emeritus at the University of Notre Dame.

Bellah (*Habits of the Heart*),[7] and Michael Sandel (*Democracy's Discontent*)[8] to rediscover the source of a commitment to justice.

An example of this new historiography aimed at a just truth rather than a conceptual self-affirmation, is probably that of the ecumenical work on the history of the Council of Florence.[9] At first in the West, especially with the work of M. Viller, historians rediscovered the Union of Florence not as a simple interested and calculated event on the part of the protagonists involved, but "rather as the necessary passage of the negotiations between the pope and the emperor, the only formal framework in which at that time the discussion could take place."[10] Re-placed in the extended negotiations between Rome and Constantinople, the motion in favor of the Union on the Byzantine side acquires greater coherence. It reveals an underlying secular fracture within the Churches, just below the surface, between the elite laity in favor of unity and the people attached to the established forms of rites. More recently in the East—that is, in the Russian diaspora that was in contact with the St. Sergius Institute in the 1930s and with the St. Vladimir Institute in the United States in the 1950s—but also in Greece and Russia, there has been a more academic reinterpretation of the events of the council. John Meyendorff and C. Tsirpanlis both defended the thesis that Mark of Ephesus, far from being absolutely opposed to the Union, regretted, above all, that he had not been understood on a theological level.[11] D. J. Geanakoplos reveals the political rather than specifically religious problem of the Unions of Lyon and Florence, namely, the Emperor's inability to enforce them, thus calling into question the limits of the caesaropapist paradigm. The Greek historian P. Gounarides draws the conclusion that a purification of the understanding of "right faith" would have been necessary in order to reexamine the connection between the patriarch Bekkos and the emperor in the 13th century above and beyond any commitment to all things Roman.

7 R. Bellah, born in 1927, was professor of sociology at Berkeley. Cf. http://www.robertbellah.com/lectures_5.htm.

8 Born in 1953, M. Sandel is professor of political philosophy at Harvard (http://www.justiceharvard.org). He published a bestseller entitled *Justice: What's the Right Thing to Do?*, New York, Farrar, Straus, and Giroux, 2009.

9 G. Alberigo, ed., *The Council of Ferrara-Florence (1438/39)*, Leuven, 1991.

10 M. Viller, "La question de l'union des Eglises entre Grecs et Latins depuis le concile de Lyon jusqu'à celui de Florence (1274–1438)," *Revue d'histoire ecclésiastique* 17 (1921): 260–305 and 505–32, and 18 (1922): 20–60.

11 Constantin Tsirpanlis, *Mark Eugenicus and the Council of Florence: A Historical Reevaluation of His Personality*, Thessalonica, 1974.

In effect, contemporary historians note that three legitimate orthodox bodies confronted one another on the occasion of the unions: the Empire, the Papacy and the theologians.[12] For this reason, in his book *Rome autrement* published in 1997, Olivier Clément, responding to the call of John Paul II to reconsider the place of the Bishop of Rome in the universal Church, suggested imagining logic in the tensions among these three bodies. So that each might participate in the common work, so that none of the three has the last word, and so that in a renewed theanthropic vision of the Church, the Spirit can receive the authority that is his.

Yves Congar has observed that Jesus only spoke of his Church on two occasions, in Matthew 16:18 and 18:18. Some personal conclusions could be drawn, beyond the one made by the Dominican himself, on the workings of the orthodox consciousness.[13] The first occasion is when Christ tells Peter that he will "build his Church" on his confession of faith and give him the keys to the Kingdom of Heaven. Henceforth, says Christ, what is bound and loosed on earth — that is to say, whether it is recognized or not on earth — will be bound and loosed in heaven. The second time is Christ's explanation to his disciples of ways to bring peace to the Church in the event of conflict with a brother who has sinned. If one-to-one dialogue is not enough, if two or three witnesses do not succeed in diffusing the situation, then Christ recommends submitting the case "to the Church." And if the sinner "refuses to listen even to the Church, let him be to you as a Gentile and a tax collector," that is, like people who do not deserve an ecclesial recognition. These are two faces of the same Church. In the one case one finds the personal consciousness of the universal Church, which is recognized as the foundation of the apostolic college. Even though the promise has been given on the condition of maintaining the identity of the faith and the one who professes it, Christ first addresses the person of Peter. In the other case, the Church appears in its local reality, according to its degrees of communitarian responsibility, and each one of these degrees, beginning from the lowest, is essential for maintaining peace. In an orthodox epistemology that synthesizes worthy glorification, right truth, faithful memory and true and just knowledge, it seems conceivable to marry the logic of the

12 D. J. Geanakoplos, "Church and State in the Byzantine Empire. A reconsideration of the problem of caesaropapism," *Church History* 34 (1965): 381–403.

13 Yves Congar, "Neuf Cent Ans Apres. Notes sur le 'Schisme oriental,'" in *1054–1954, l'Eglise et les Eglises*, Chevetogne, editions Chevetogne, 1954, 82.

unifying nomination with that of communitarian subsidiarity. Openness to the Creator God is not incompatible with the fulfillment of a personal justice. The key of the conditional recognition goes hand in hand with that of the gradual testimony. The verticality of the theanthropic relation does not contradict the horizontality of the anthropocosmic relationship.

## THE REDEFINITION OF LAICITY BY THE STATES

The renewal of historiography is one of the fruits of the ecumenical movement, concomitant with the formation of the paradigm of orthodoxy as true and just knowledge. Thanks to the movement of ecumenical rapprochement, marked by the advent of numerous dialogue institutions, journals and symposia, the sources of division among the Churches appear more and more political and cultural rather than properly theological.[14] The elimination of the principal lines of confessional tension has many consequences which are being felt today. The political consequence is the most immediate. For the past decade, many political leaders of liberal societies in the Western world have been calling for a redefinition of democracy, of ideological groups, the place of religion in political institutions and of economical values. In France, President N. Sarkozy, in his Lateran speech on December 20, 2007,[15] made an appeal for new initiatives in laicity. On March 3, 2011, at Puy-en-Velay, against the current use of Republican neutrality, the president called to mind, "without any complexes" according to the reports in the media, France's Judeo-Christian heritage.[16] Within the European Union, the new European treaties incorporated into the "Treaty of Lisbon" attest to this new desire of the States to establish a constructive dialogue with representatives of the main religions and ideologies.[17] The

14 The official dialogues among the Churches have manifested the problems of translation and semantic evolution of certain terms such as, for example, *ekporesis* (in the debate between the Eastern and Western Churches over the procession of the Holy Spirit in the Trinity) or *physis* (in the debate between the Chalcedonian and non-Chalcedonian Churches concerning the recognition of divine-humanity of Christ). The dialogue between the Catholic Church and the Lutheran Church arrived at the recognition that past cultural reasons of division on the subject of justification are no longer valid today.

15 http://www.voltairenet.org/article153862.html.

16 http://www.la-croix.com/Actualite/S-informer/Monde/Discours-de-Nicolas-Sarkozy-au-Puy-en-Velay-_NG_-2011-03-03-564431.

17 Cf. article 17 of the Constitutional Pact: "1. The Union respects and does not have any bias regarding the status which Churches and religious associations and communities

election of President Barack Obama in the United States in 2008 also testifies to this evolution of Western democratic societies. In a speech delivered in 2006, he admitted to the failure of politics to recognize the power of faith in peoples' lives and called for a debate to "reconcile faith with our modern and pluralistic democracy."[18]

In the genealogy of the American nation the American president includes the names of Abraham Lincoln, Dorothy Day and Martin Luther King. Friend of the evangelists Rick Warren and Jim Wallis, he criticizes with them the secularists who ask believers to leave their religion at the door before entering into the public square. For Obama, it is a "practical absurdity" to say that men and women should not inject their "personal morality" into public policy debates, because American law is by definition a codification of morality, much of it grounded in the Judeo-Christian tradition. Conversely, he asks believers to "translate" their concerns into universal values, comprehensible to all, "in a way that reconciles the beliefs of each with the good of all."[19] While it may be appropriate for political leaders to show their benevolence towards religion, it is also undeniable that the Hegelian paradigm, so powerful in the 20th century, of the neutrality of the State is today in sharp decline. In South Africa, Brazil, or countries of the former communist bloc there is a desire for rapprochement between political power and religious institutions. Specialists prefer to speak in terms of "thresholds of secularization" to describe the degrees of conscientization of States as regards their own religious foundations. And above all, as Jean Baubérot and Micheline Milot write, they make a clearer distinction between agnosticism, which is an ideology, and impartiality, which is a value of justice:

---

of the member States enjoy in virtue of national laws. 2. The Union also respects the status which philosophical and non-confessional organizations enjoy in virtue of national laws. 3. Recognizing their identity and specific contribution, the Union maintains an open, transparent and regular dialogue with these Churches and organizations." Cf. http://ec.europa.eu/dgs/policy_advisers/activities/dialogues_religions_index_fr.htm. Council of the European Union, Consolidated version of the pact regarding the European Union and the functioning of the European Union, Charter of the fundamental rights of the European Union (JO C 83, 30.32010), http://www.consilium.europa.eu/showPage.aspx?id=1296&lang=fr, 2011.

18 http://www.nytimes.com/2006/06/28/us/politics/2006obambaspeech.html?pagewanted=all.

19 "Democracy demands that the religiously motivated translate their concerns into universal, rather than religion-specific, values."

> Neutrality does not mean that the State is "without values" since state governance is based on fundamental values such as democracy, tolerance, respect for diversity and human rights. There is no absolute neutrality. All the same, political power must show impartiality towards different beliefs.[20]

## ORTHODOX CONSCIOUSNESS AND GLOBAL *EPISTEME*

A half century of debates among Christian and agnostic historians in France has led to a conclusion shared by the majority of historians: "Truth is therefore, in history as in all science, in what allows better understanding and understanding a phenomenon further; it is in what is efficient. The hypothesis of God does not alter in any way the quest of historical science."[21] Conversely, according to Abbé Huvelin, "orthodoxy must come to terms with the truth, it is her business."[22] The very concern for the integrity of the faith forbids the believer to set aside the truths issued from his creed. Certain historians, aware of the additional enlightenment brought by Orthodox thought, have gone further. Nicole Lemaître, a Catholic historian, argues that, against the most refined forms of contemporary scientism, the believing historian also refuses to absolutize in order to better respect the only truth worth knowing, "Christ himself." According to this historian of the Sorbonne, the historian believer must therefore admit that "the rules of the game" between God and men "change at each match," at the risk of offending those theologians who often confuse infallible truths with indefectible truths. To affirm, for example, that only the Mass of Pius V is orthodox, according to the Catholic historian and academic René Rémond (1918–2007), is tantamount to thinking that "the Church has erred for 1600 years in its search for truth in matters of liturgical celebration and forbids the Holy Spirit from intervening in the life of the Church."[23] Pierre Chaunu (1923–2009), a French Protestant historian, was one of the great contemporary figures of the ongoing reconciliation between epistemic and orthodox thought. In a very personal contribution given at the request

20 Jean Baubérot, Micheline Milot, *Laïcités sans frontières,* Paris, Seuil, 2011, 1.

21 N. Lemaître, "Vérité historique et vérité de foi," *L'historien*, op. cit., 116.

22 Phrase cited by A. Loisy in *Mémoires pour servir à l'histoire religieuse de notre temps*, vol. 1, Paris 1930, 286. Cf. Jean-Pierre Massaut, "L'Histoire lieu théologique," *L'historien*, op. cit., 188.

23 R. Rémond, "Ce que la foi apporte à l'historien," *L'historien*, op. cit., 297.

of his friend Jean Delumeau in 1996 to the collection *L'historien et la foi,* he sums up his spiritual and intellectual journey. He concludes with an unbridled hymn to the glory of divine creation:

> The exact sciences, the new cosmologies, relativistic and quantum physics, the historicization of all knowledge (at this point it would be appropriate to speak of natural history), the *rapprochement* around a mystique inspired by the greatness of the fantastic *adaequatio* between the logic of the Universe and that of our brain, of a Universe where everything has a meaning, where each particle carries a destiny, where each term leads to some new beginning, where there is always something beyond the veil to the point that the beyond pierces every moment in the forest of signs that besiege us, where everything bears the mark of the tremendous solicitude of... the great Being, Adonai, who will perhaps ask of you your help, through the hand outstretched toward you of the wounded person at the side of the road, the one whose presence old Simeon had discerned on the face of a very small child.[24]

Let us add a final word to suggest the interreligious and universal consequences of the contemporary redefinition of orthodox thought. The newfound attitude of humility on the part of Christians belonging to different Christian confessions was particularly acute in the aftermath of the two World Wars. This is evidenced in the Malines Conversations between Catholics and Anglicans after the butchery of the 1914–1918 war and the creation of the review *Dieu Vivant* after the destruction of London, Stalingrad and Dresden. The governing committee of the journal *Dieu Vivant* consisted of Louis Massignon, Maurice de Gandillac and Marcel Moré. The review, under the leadership of Pierre Leyris, provided a forum for Vladimir Lossky and Hans Urs von Balthasar, Jean Hypolite and Gabriel Marcel. In their 1944 preface, the editors of *Dieu Vivant* take as their starting point the observation that Christians did indeed "participate in the murder of God" by refusing to search God's mystery with their intelligence and their heart. This is why they affirm that "the battle we have to fight today is first spiritual." To this end one must be aware, they say, that humanity is "in the era described in the Apocalypse." This has the consequence that the

24 Pierre Chaunu, "La connaissance et la foi," *L'historien et la foi*, op. cit., 51.

idea of progress only makes sense in this space-time if it is linked to that of the resurrection. The religious and philosophical perspectives they draw consist primarily in a dialogue among divided Christians. This dialogue is based on an exchange of gifts. About the vision of the Divine Glory of the Orthodox, it is appropriate, they say, "to make it shine on a world that groans in the darkness." The Orthodox, on their part, they continue, could benefit from the concern for the social aspect of the Church so prevalent in the West. Catholics and Orthodox finally need the Protestant reminder of "the constant reawakening that fights the numbness of the heart." While Protestants, in dialogue with other Christians, could reflect on the need for the "complete incarnation of the Church." But more broadly, the authors of this preface believe that this orthodox unity concerns all the descendants of Abraham for whom the earthly Jerusalem is but a prefiguration "of this Church which will rise to meet the Heavenly Jerusalem to be reunited as one." Rejecting beforehand any accusation of syncretism, they go so far as to invoke the spirituality of India by mentioning Jules Monchanin and all the spiritual experiences lived by "the witnesses of the Dead God . . . in search of the Absolute." Ultimately, these men and women of *Dieu Vivant* are themselves in search of a new orthodoxy, based on friendship. "She is flying over the oceans, said Sophocles."[25]

25 "Liminaire," *Dieu Vivant*, no. 1 (1944): 1–13.

## CONCLUSION

# *Looking Back at the Journey Traveled*

OUR INVESTIGATION OF ORTHODOXY BOTH AS A criterion of truth and a quality of faith is an invitation to embrace the history of Christian thought and the history of rationality in a new synthesis. In the first part, the Orthodox Church is presented in a historical, geographical and doctrinal manner. An explanation is offered as to why the confessional definitions led it to a deep identity crisis. The crisis of the pan-Orthodox conciliary process is, in this respect, symptomatic of this confessional definition of self. It is for this reason that our thesis consists of philosophically, theologically and historically revisiting the very notion of orthodoxy. The second part offers a contextual presentation of the contemporary debates on orthodoxy from Michel Foucault to John Milbank, from Jean-Marc Ferry to Charles Taylor, from Jürgen Habermas to Joseph Ratzinger, from Paul Ricoeur to Sergius Bulgakov. The third part presents a possible methodological synthesis of the two paths of reason and faith, both in search of "the assurance of things hoped for" and of "the conviction of things not seen."[1] To respect, however, the logic of each of these two approaches, and to draw some contemporary consequences from the inextricable relationship between truth and history, we focus our interest in the third part on the semantic development of the notion of orthodoxy in the history of Christian civilization. Our research has enabled us to reveal the presence of the four initial meanings of orthodoxy in Christian Scriptures and to show how each of these has assumed a dominant position in relation to the others according to the contexts of the different cultures and eras. Orthodoxy, understood as rationality enlightened by the Christian faith, can be defined according to four fundamental senses which have become, in the course of history, four major paradigms: worthy glorification, right truth, faithful memory and just knowledge.

1 Hebrews 11:1.

Our method consists in relying on the concept of "ecclesial consciousness" in order to historically update its doxic structure and its evolution according to sociopolitical contexts and representations of the truth. It is indeed the moment of awareness, of historiographical objectivity, which is most likely to demonstrate the mechanisms of the formation of the paradigms of orthodox consciousness and the evolution of the meaning of the notion of orthodoxy. This structure of the ecclesial consciousness of the Judeo-Christian tradition is characterized by a double paradoxical tension between, on the one hand, the poles of recognition and memory and, on the other hand, the poles of law and justice. This can be represented by a cross at the extremities of which are the poles of memory identity and celebrated otherness (vertical axis) and the poles of universal nature and personal culture (horizontal axis). This doxic field forms the ecclesial consciousness whose historical limits are determined by the individual and collective rudder of orthodox thought. At its center is Jesus Christ who is, in the Christian tradition according to St. Paul, "Wisdom of God and Power of God." The observation of historiographical consciousness allows one to draw a vertical theanthropic axis that defines the historical relationship between humanity and God in history. This axis is marked by an identity-otherness relationship, or image and likeness, magnetized by memory logic on the one hand and the logic of worship on the other. Similarly, a horizontal or anthropocosmic axis can also be drawn and this would be defined by the poles of universal and personal justice. The updating of this doxic structure of ecclesial consciousness which involves its unity, its holiness, its catholicity and apostolicity is not, in itself, a discovery. It can be found in certain authors such as Jean Borella, Anton Houtepen, Hans Urs von Balthasar and Danièle Hervieu-Léger. The originality of our research consists mainly of its dynamic presentation in the context of historical consciousness. It allows a clarification of the meaning and dynamics of notions or historical realities which have become institutional and confessional in Orthodoxy, Catholicism and Protestantism.

Our historiographical study analyzes the four great historical and archetypical discourses: the evangelists (in particular Luke and John); the medieval historians from Eusebius of Caesarea to Sylvester Syropoulos; the historians of the modern age, Flacius Illyricus, Cesar Baronius, Vassili Bolotov; and contemporary historians such as Stephen Charles Neill, Olivier Clément and Guy Bédouelle. Although it is quite impossible to summarize in a few dozen pages — let alone a few lines! — two millennia of evolution, it seemed nevertheless didactically useful to put together in an extremely schematic, that is to say, in a symbolic way, certain major developments of orthodox thought during this period. At the times of early Christianity, Christian orthodox gnosis defined itself as doxo-logical. This is reflected in the New Testament texts and the writings of the apologists. The orthodoxy of the first centuries should not be understood, as is traditionally the case in the contemporary academic world, according to its subsequent sociological objectifications: namely, as the dominant, self-legitimated and conservative discourse of the majority over the minority. Orthodoxy, in its historical and semantic depth, is a sur-knowledge, a counter-discourse with regard to the logic, whether conceptualist or irrationalist, of its time. At the time of Paul and Origen, it manifested itself as an identification of Jesus Christ with the Logos, affirmed by Scripture, the witness of the ecclesial community and by personal experience. This *syn-hodale* and *kath'holic* or fractal[2] knowledge of the communitarian and conciliary journey was not based exclusively on ideas, on the observance of nature or Holy Scriptures. It was, fundamentally, a symbolic, eschatological and antinomic participation in the life of Jesus Christ resurrected in the Holy Spirit.

The following period of Christian consciousness dates from the legalization of the "Christian religion" by the Roman emperors to the last ecumenical council of Christianity in 1439, the Council of Florence, which was, for the first and last time in the history of Christianity, co-presided by the emperor and the pope. This period saw, through the mediation of eminent figures such as Eusebius of Caesarea and Augustine of Hippo, the political, dogmatic and ultimately nomocanonical consciousness of orthodoxy Christianity. In the age of Christendom, the pole of the moral law organized doxic thought. *Ortho-doxia* then consisted in protecting the true knowledge, that is, the revealed knowledge, transmitted by tradition, against the deviations emanating from its partial knowledge. This dogmatic effort was accompanied by a juridical and politico-military effort to separate the "heretics" from Christians, faithful to the emperor and the pope. In the political theology of the time, when the neo-Platonic conception of the separation between soul and body still prevailed, the place of the divine power was to be assured by a universal mediator.

2 A fractal is an object or quantity that displays self-similarity, in a somewhat technical way, on all scales. The object need not exhibit exactly the same structure at all scales but the same "type" of structure must appear at all scales. The term fractal was first used by Benoit Mandelbrot in 1975 and is derived from the Latin word *fractus,* meaning broken or fractured.

The arrival of the modern era in the 15th and 16th centuries was marked, among other events, by the fall of Byzantium, the affirmation of nation-states, the emergence of the Reformation and the worldwide expansion of Christian powers. The orthodox Christian consciousness has been divided by three major incompatibilities between faith and reason, pitting the notions of authority, synodality and freedom against one another. Moreover, the democratization of knowledge realized during the Middle Ages and the failure of medieval theocratic institutions to maintain peace, was accompanied by a democratic desire of a greater unity between the body and the head within the national and linguistic communities. In view of the historiographical evidence, in the 16th century the Christian orthodox consciousness thus went from a political identity to a remembrance identity according to the three major hermeneutical poles: the "Catholic" orthodox identity reinterpreted its identity on the basis of the specific role, presented in the Scriptures and in the ecclesial tradition, of the Bishop of Rome in the Church; the orthodox "Protestant" identity has privileged the relation between freedom of conscience and Holy Scripture in order to recover the communitarian dimension of the ecclesial body and its capacity to participate in salvation; finally, the Fathers of the Church and the ecumenical councils constituted the hermeneutical axis of the "Orthodox" identity consciousness of those Christians who defined themselves as "orthodox." These three axes of Christian consciousness formed creative sources of identity redefinition, and revealed, in a more or less confessional manner, major differences in political theology (use of religious influence to maintain the keys of power to organize the perfect pyramidal society; separation of Church and State, leading the latter to organize the religious power; maintaining the "symphony" model where civil power and ecclesial power share duties). All three axes, however, are anchored in the same dynamic structure of "faithful memory" in orthodox thought. This structure of the Christian consciousness, blind to itself, was not able to prevent the interconfessional splitting of the ecclesial body. It provoked a reaction which led to the formation of a secularized consciousness characterized in particular by the rejection of providentialism, the emergence of an individualistic rationalism and the defense of human dignity. Modern secular historical science has its origins in several Christian historians of modern times such as P. Bayle, S. Le Nain de Tillemont, L. Ranke and A. Lebedev.

Although it has not strictly speaking become paradigmatic, the meaning of Christian orthodoxy has been evolving since the beginning of the 19th century, but most significantly since 1944, towards "true and just knowledge," capable of reuniting the mode of being to the mode of thought and action. After the Second World War, since V. Soloviev, J.H. Newman and C. Möhler, a certain number of conceptual advances in orthodox thought—notably the rediscovery of the communitarian, involutive and creative dimension of ecclesial tradition—fostered a new understanding of these ecclesial traditions and thereby a reconciliation between faith and reason. The demanding dialogue that took place among Christian confessions, especially from the time of the Edinburgh Conference in 1910, gave birth to the ecumenical movement. It contributed to a new representation of the truth. This is no longer perceived solely from the perspective of the hermeneutical tradition. It is also now considered according to the degrees of consciousness and the communication/communion of the reflexive community. On the other hand, a certain number of sociopolitical developments, such as the growing awareness of blatant social inequalities and racial discrimination, the emergence of violent totalitarian ideologies, or the massive migrations of peoples and cultures, have contributed to the emergence of the realization that states, traditionally considered by Churches at the time of the separation of political and religious powers as transitory and worthless entities, must be based on the ideals of justice, peace, respect for human dignity and creation. This critical new historiography, ecumenical and even theanthropic, teaches us along with Ernst Troeltsch that, more effectively than the confessional approach, the orthodox consciousness must be studied from the point of view of religious mentalities (zealot, proselyte, critic and the spiritual) found in the different confessions in different periods of history.[3]

This study of the historical consciousness of ecclesial orthodoxy, which gives an account of the truth of the confessional identities of the Churches while recognizing their common shared consciousness, thus opens the possibility

3 It would be easy to point out the image of these mentalities in search of truth in the secularized and agnostic universes which became dominant in the 20th century (the militant secularist, the humanist, the person who is "sincere" and the one who is "indignant"). The American equivalent of the revolt of the indignant can be found in the "Occupy Wall Street movement" whose typical representative is "the anonymous one." According to Chris Landers of *The Baltimore City Paper* (April 2, 2008), "'anonymous' is the first form of superconsciousness constructed through the Internet. Anonymous is a group something like a flight of birds. How do you know that it is a group? Because they are traveling in the same direction. Birds can join or leave the group at any time or go off in an entirely different direction than the one before." Chris Landers, "Serious Business: Anonymous Takes on Scientology (and doesn't [sic] afraid of anything)."

for a new ecumenical history of the Church and a new history of philosophy. More widely, by proposing a more precise definition of the nature of orthodoxy, this study allows us to now envisage a universal history of doxic consciousness and highlight the many studies on this subject that are flourishing in the world today. The historical redefinition of orthodoxy allows a new exchange between certain philosophical and postmodern scientific discourses (J. Kristeva, M. Gauchet, J. P. Dupuy) and contemporary theology (Christian, but also Jewish, Islamic or Buddhist). As certain contemporary thinkers (whether they be agnostics such as Michel Foucault or believers like Sergius Bulgakov) have demonstrated, the epistemology of a civilization is in permanent tension with its doxic thought. Furthermore, the updating of the contours of the semantic evolution of ortho-dox Christian thought ushers in a new way of looking at the histories of philosophy and the sciences — not, as has mostly been the case so far in academic discourse, to systematically devalue the *doxa* by assimilating it to the realm of mythology, prejudice, or cliché, but to remember its semantic origin of glory or wisdom. It would reveal the permanence of beliefs in perpetual adaptation to the dominant thought of an era, beliefs that are in themselves sources for the evolution of conceptual thought.[4]

4 "Les Français sont prisonniers d'une *doxa* au sujet de l'islam," Moncer Marzouki, http://www.lejdd.fr/International/Maghreb/Actualite/Moncef-Marzouki-le-nouveau-president-tunisien-fustige-la-condescendance-francaise-envers-son-pays-441047/?from=cover.

# INDEX OF NAMES

CPSIA information can be obtained
at www.ICGtesting.com
Printed in the USA
LVHW042307050922
727615LV00001B/69

9 781621 384205